B 829.5 .P466 1983

Phenomenology in a
 pluralistic context

STOCKTON STATE COLLEGE LIBRARY,
POMONA, NEW JERSEY 08240

Phenomenology in a Pluralistic Context

*Selected Studies in Phenomenology
and Existential Philosophy 9*

Board of Editors

Ronald Bruzina, *University of Kentucky*
David Carr, *University of Ottawa*
Edward Casey, *SUNY—Stony Brook*
James Edie, *Northwestern University*
Don Ihde, *SUNY—Stony Brook*
Hugh Silverman, *SUNY—Stony Brook*
Bruce Wilshire, *Rutgers University*
Richard Zaner, *Vanderbilt University*

Executive Committee

Harold Alderman, *Sonoma State College*
Bernard Dauenhauer, *University of Georgia*
Joseph Kockelmans, *Pennsylvania State University*

Phenomenology in a Pluralistic Context

William L. McBride
and Calvin O. Schrag

Editors

State University of New York Press

ALBANY

Published by State University of New York Press, Albany

© 1983 State University of New York

All rights reserved

Printed in the United States of America

No part of this book may be used or reproduced in any manner whatsoever without written permission except in the case of brief quotations embodied in critical articles and reviews.

For information, address State University of New York Press, State University Plaza, Albany, N.Y., 12246

Library of Congress Cataloging in Publication Data
Main entry under title:

Phenomenology in a pluralistic context.

(Selected studies in phenomenology and existential philosophy; 9)
    1. Phenomenology—Addresses, essays, lectures. I. McBride, William Leon. II. Schrag, Calvin O. III. Series.
B829.5.P466   1983   142′.7   82-19609
ISBN 0-87395-730-X
ISBN 0-87395-731-8 (pbk.)

Contents

Contents

Contents

Introduction

Volume 9 of Selected Studies, *Phenomenology in a Pluralistic Context,* contains papers and symposia contributions selected from the seventeenth, eighteenth, and nineteenth annual meetings of the Society for Phenomenology and Existential Philosophy. These meetings were held at Duquesne University (1978), Purdue University (1979), and the University of Ottawa (1980). In selecting the contributions to this volume, the editors were particularly attentive to fresh approaches in the interpretation of the classical sources of phenomenology and existential philosophy; phenomenological and existential analysis in cognate fields and ventures toward an interface with sister disciplines; and the awareness of contemporary trends and emerging topical interests.

Some of the papers that have been selected deal specifically with the thought of some pivotal figures in the history of recent European philosophy, for example, Sartre, Merleau-Ponty, and Heidegger (Bell, Dauenhauer, Flynn, Hamrick, Schürmann, and Seigfried). Others take as their principal focus the relation of existential motifs and phenomenological procedures to certain other traditions in the history of modern philosophy (Bakan, Grabau, Rockmore, and Schrader). Some of the other selected papers pursue a more specific format of addressing issues in the phenomenology *of* this and that. For example, there are contributions dealing with the phenomenology of medicine (Zaner, Rawlinson, and Dallery); the phenomenology of art and aesthetics (Anderson and Dwiggins); the phenomenology of language (Bruzina, Levin, and Mohanty); the phenomenology of religion (Williams); and the phenomenology of social relations (Carr and Marsh).

The panoply of selected contributions reflects the changing scene and ongoing discussions in American and European phenomenology and existentialism. Discernible throughout are dialogues and disputes with representatives of structuralism, poststructuralism, critical theory, analytical philosophy, Marxism, and process philosophy. This itself stands as a testimony to the cosmopolitan thrust of original phenomenological and existential reflection and its resistance to philosophical closure. In this we see an expression of that genuine spirit of philosophical inquiry as it was proposed and shaped by its founders. Philosophy is seen as a task to be assumed time and again; the philosopher is portrayed as a perpetual beginner.

Ever resisting the solidification of its procedures and insights into a final philosophical program, phenomenology and existentialism in their original inspiration caution us against the temptation to become but another "school of thought," congealed into heavily varnished methodological and metaphysical construction. Given this open-ended spirit of inquiry, there can be no espousal of a purity of doctrine nor vaulted claims for an unimpeachable first philosophy. Indeed, an indigenous feature of phenomenological reflection, in its multiple applications, is the "possibilizing" of the world and human experience. This not only secures an unqualified tolerance of the variety of extant philosophical persuasions but it also provides an explicit invitation to reconsider philosophical traditions.

In its encounter with these different traditions and the intermittent emerging new modes of thought, phenomenology and existentialism must allow for the possibility of new descriptions of the posture of human existence and the texture of experiencing the world, even if these new descriptions require a scuttling of some of the presuppositions, language games, and conceptual constructs that phenomenologists and existentialists have learned to love and cherish. Phenomenology and existentialism remain open to the challenge of the new and the untried. They summon us through their voices of freedom to the ongoing conversation of mankind. Herein resides the radicality of phenomenological and existential reflection. The editors are indeed gratified that the collected essays of this volume have fallen out in such a manner that this radicality, openness, passion for dialogue, freedom, and interest in pluralism are made transparent throughout.

CALVIN O. SCHRAG
Purdue University

It is with a mixture of pride and deep sorrow that we call special attention to the essay "Kant's Proto-Phenomenology" by Richard F. Grabau. Originally presented by him at the Purdue University meeting in a symposium in which his former mentor, George A. Schrader, Jr., was also a participant, it now appears posthumously. Richard Grabau, our erstwhile close colleague and department head, died of cancer after a relatively brief period of illness, in September 1980.

WILLIAM L. MCBRIDE
Purdue University

PART 1

INTERPRETATIONS OF THE
PHENOMENOLOGICAL TRADITION

1. Loser Wins:
The Importance of Play in a
Sartrean Ethics of Authenticity

LINDA A. BELL

Jean-Paul Sartre observes in *Being and Nothingness* that play, "which has freedom for its foundation and its goal, deserves a special study [which] . . . belongs rather to an *Ethics*. . . ."[1] Like various other remarks that Sartre promised to explain someday in his unwritten or at least unpublished book on ethics, this statement haunts anyone who reads *Being and Nothingness*, especially anyone interested in ethics.

Similarly, Sartre's readers are tantalized by his footnote references to authenticity, "a self-recovery of being which was previously corrupted,"[2] and to "an ethics of deliverance and salvation."[3] Many readers, however, have concluded that authenticity and such an ethics of deliverance and salvation are impossible if, as Sartre says, 'man is a useless passion"[4] and ". . . it amounts to the same thing whether one gets drunk alone or is a leader of nations."[5] Still others, not deterred by the latter claims, have no doubt reacted with hopeless dismay when Jean Genet is depicted by Sartre as a "saint" and when Sartre's most heroic characters in his plays, novels, and short stories are presented not only with "dirty hands" but also as playing, even consciously, a rather perverse-sounding game of "loser wins."

In this paper I argue that these several threads can be woven into a coherent ethics that features play and "loser wins" and yet offers a viable account of authenticity and is indeed "an ethics of deliverance

I am grateful to John Beversluis, Joseph S. Catalano, and C. G. Luckhardt for their helpful comments on earlier drafts of this paper.

and salvation." My emphasis is on the theme of futility and on the way in which play and "loser wins" constitutes an authentic deliverance from the problem of futility.

In *Being and Nothingness*, Sartre recognizes the inevitable failure of all human projects. Man is the desire to be in-itself-for-itself, that is, God, an impossible being, and is, therefore, "a useless passion." Inasmuch as all actions sacrifice man to this impossible goal and all are doomed to fail, they are equivalent. "Thus it amounts to the same thing whether one gets drunk alone or is a leader of nations."[6]

Against those who claim that such futility was the result of an extreme form of individualism that Sartre later remedied in his work on Marxism, it is important to emphasize that the idea of futility persists in his *Critique of Dialectical Reason*. In the *Critique*, Sartre traces the various attempts to overcome seriality, the separated and unreciprocal existence of individuals, from the group to the institution. He repeatedly notes the "contradictions" in each of these attempts to create the group as a unity, and he indicates that inevitably there will be a lapse back into seriality.[7] There are, he says, limits to the group's activity: although it is formed in opposition to alienation, its activity always embodies and thereby alienates itself in matter; and this alienation is then the source of the group's undoing.[8] Although notable achievements may be made in the course of this development from the group to the institution, there is nonetheless an ultimate futility with respect to the attempt to achieve a community.

The kind of futility recognized in the *Critique* can be specified more precisely by noting that the group exists between the seriality of the collective and the unity of the organism. The idea of the practical organism becomes for the group an idea in the Kantian sense, "an unrealisable task which becomes regulatory by constantly positing itself as capable of being realized the next day."[9]

The group is thus haunted by an impossible ideal just as in *Being and Nothingness* the individual is haunted by the in-itself and by the impossible desire to be God. For the group as for the individual, the unity sought cannot be attained. There is, however, also an important difference between them inasmuch as the group is not an individual and the adopted inertia of the group prevents common praxis from having the same translucidity as individual praxis. One's right and duty, for example, in so far as one is a member of the group, "appear with a dimension of alterity . . . as . . . [his] free alienation from . . . [his] freedom."[10] Members of a group may, therefore, not be able to experience as intense and lucid an awareness of the group's futility as that experienced by an individual aware of the futility of his own actions.

Sartre's discussion of futility is not restricted to his philosophical works. It occurs quite frequently in his novels and plays, often juxtaposed with the theme of "loser wins." In "The Wall," Pablo Ibbieta experiences the disintegration of his revolutionary's world and all its value as he awaits his death before the firing squad. Freed from the seriousness of his past and its values, which no longer matter to him now that his illusion of immortality has been shattered, Pablo decides to play a trick on his captors who have promised his release in return for information concerning the whereabouts of another anarchist, Ramon Gris. Pablo must choose between his own life and that of Gris; and although he realizes that Gris' life has no more value than his own, he nonetheless chooses with "a droll sort of gaiety" to send his captors on a wild-goose chase through a cemetery rather than to the farmhouse where he believes Gris is hiding.[11]

Still awaiting his death on their return, he enjoys imagining the ludicrousness of the serious but entirely futile search of the cemetery by his captors. When they return and free him, Pablo is bewildered but later learns that Gris was captured in the cemetery. At that point Pablo bursts into hysterical laughter. Loser wins, in a sense, although the last laugh is on himself. Even his playful choice of his own death fails inasmuch as the intended consequences of his action depended upon others over whom he had no control.

In the play *The Devil and the Good Lord*, Sartre is explicitly concerned with good and evil. The central character of the play, Goetz, realizing that it is relatively easy to do evil, resolves to be good. In spite of his resolution and his valiantly persistent effort to accomplish his goal, Goetz has nothing but evil to show for his perserverance when his actions and their consequences are weighed a year later. As he murders the priest to whom he was to prove that it is possible to do good, Goetz declares, "The comedy of Good has ended with a murder."[12] He now realizes that he must begin with crime.

> "I must demand my share of their crimes if I want to have my share of their love and virtue. I wanted pure love: ridiculous nonsense. To love anyone is to hate the same enemy; therefore I will adopt your hates. I wanted to be Good: foolishness. On this earth at present Good and Evil are inseparable. I agree to be bad in order to become good."[13]

Though the play ends here, and we remain ignorant of the ultimate consequences, Goetz is now playing "loser wins." He feels assured of victory if his men are more afraid of him than of the enemy.[14] To bring about "the kingdom of man," Goetz says,

7

"I shall make them hate me, because I know of no other way of loving them. I shall give them orders, since I have no other way of obeying. I shall remain alone with this empty sky over my head, since I have no other way of being among men. There is a war to fight, and I will fight it."[15]

This character, Simone de Beauvoir tells us, is made to do what Sartre himself was unable to do; Goetz becomes "the perfect embodiment of the man of action as Sartre conceived him": he "accepts the discipline of the Peasant War without denying his own subjectivity, within the enterprise he perserves the negative moment."[16] It thus looks as if Goetz's final strategy is one that Sartre saw as at least potentially a way to "win."

With Jean Aguerra in scenario *In the Mesh,* the winning through failure is more evident. Although aware that his deportations and other acts of "tyranny" will result in his overthrow and execution, Jean knows he has avoided war long enough to save the revolution. Even though he will be cursed, he knows he has done what he could to bring about justice.[17]

Like Jean Aguerra, Hoederer, in the play *Dirty Hands*, admits that his hands have been plunged into filth and blood and are dirty. He argues against the idealistic and principled Hugo that for one who loves men and wants to change the world "all means are good when they are effective."[18] Even though Hoederer is killed, he wins in several ways. First, he was right in his analysis of Hugo—that Hugo is an intellectual and that "an intellectual is never a real revolutionary; just good enough to make an assassin."[19] More important, though, Hoederer triumphs even though dead: his policies win out while Hugo finally sees his own act of murdering Hoederer as at best as "farce."[20]

Although these references far from exhaust Sartre's discussions of "loser wins," they suffice to indicate the importance to Sartre of this rather perverse-sounding game. Moreover, they enable me to raise what I think an important, though blunt, question: Just what is the game of "loser wins" and what is its role in Sartre's philosophy? Although play may sound trivial and "loser wins" may even seem perverse, their significance cannot be exaggerated. For they are nothing less than Sartre's way of resolving the problem of futility with which he was concerned in *Being and Nothingness*, in the *Critique of Dialectical Reason*, and in many of his plays, novels, and stories.

The necessity and significance of play has been noted by commentators and critics. William Leon McBride, for example, has observed that if we take seriously the inevitability of the gap between the individual's projects and their accomplishment, which is itself the result of the gap that Sartre has discerned between being-in-itself and being-for-itself, *all* labor must have about it something of the futility, the non-seriousness, that we have described as the essential characteristic of play. And this comes as no surprise whatever if we recall to ourselves the famous Sartrean epigram with which he terminates the main body of the text of *Being and Nothingness*, just prior to the conclusion: Man is a useless passion.[21]

Similarly Douglas Kirsner recognizes the "ontological necessity" of play for Sartrean man, who is eternally absent from himself: "Man is doomed to never cease playing roles for he can never take on an authentic identity: he is condemned to be free."[22]

Sartre himself contrasts play with "the spirit of seriousness" in which "the serious man" gives "to himself the type of existence of the rock, the consistency, the inertia, the opacity of being-in-the-midst-of-the-world."[23] The serious man, Sartre says, is concerned with consequences.

At bottom [he] is hiding from himself the consciousness of his freedom; he is in *bad faith* and his bad faith aims at presenting himself to his own eyes as a consequence; everything is a consequence for him, and there is never any beginning. That is why he is so concerned with the consequences of his acts.[24]

Play too is concerned with the consequences, but in a very different way:

What is play indeed if not an activity of which man is the first origin, for which man himself sets the rules, and which has no consequences except according to the rules posited? As soon as a man apprehends himself as free and wishes to use his freedom, a freedom, by the way, which could just as well be his anguish, then his activity is play. The first principle of play is man himself; through it he escapes his natural nature; he himself sets the value and rules which he has established and defined.[25]

By recognizing the ultimate futility of human action, Sartre places man quite clearly in the frustrating position of Sisyphus. Man is haunted by value, by the desire to be God, by the need to achieve a community; and his efforts to actualize these ends inevitably fail. Whatever Sartre's ethics, it must confront the recognition that in terms of consequences, all human actions are on a par—they all fail.

Immanuel Kant encountered in his ethic a lesser problem with futility. For Kant morality demands a perfection that we cannot achieve. All we can do, according to Kant, is continually strive for it. Convinced that "ought" implies "can" and aware that in so far as it involves action, morality demands a continual striving to achieve perfection, Kant proposed that immortality and the existence of God are necessary postulates of morality. Without postulating an infinite progress and the existence of God who would see this infinite process as complete in an eternal now and who would reward us with happiness in exact correlation with our worthiness of it, we would, according to Kant, find ourselves in a psychologically problematic position with the demands of morality practically impossible and "strained to an unattainable destination."[26]

For Sartre, on the contrary, there is and can be no God. God is a logical impossibility. Moreover, even if there were a God, this would not help to resolve the problem with futility that Sartre faces. No god could offer an escape from Sartre's problem of futility inasmuch as it is at least partially a logical impossibility that this god must overcome. If man is a vain and useless passion to do and be that which is logically impossible, God's eternal vision would be of no more use than man's temporal vision in envisioning this goal as accomplished.

A Sartrean ethics, then, must resolve more than the psychological problem of inevitable failure to accomplish goals that are too high. It must present a viable way of living with the realization that one's actions are ultimately futile precisely because one's ultimate goals are logically impossible. Moreover, it must provide some stance from which, however much ultimately futile actions may be on a par with one another, some acts may nonetheless be distinguished as authentic and moral and opposed to others that are recognized as inauthentic and immoral. Play and "loser wins" enable Sartre to take these steps so vital to an ethics of authenticity.

Denying any preexisting justifications for our actions and recognizing that even God could not bridge the gap between our goals and our accomplishments, Sartre turns to play to resolve the problem of futility. For Sartre man must himself create and sustain in existence his own values as exemplified in his choices and actions. In play, man creates, apart from preexisting values. Children in play create characters, dialogues, situations, and actions, even values that may differ from those taught them by parents. Adults invent games and sustain these in existence by freely following the rules they have created and thus "playing" the game. As Sartre says, "What is play indeed if not an activity of which man is the first origin, for which man himself sets the rules, and which has no consequences except according to the rules posited?"[27]

Sartre's authentic individual must create his own values through his actions and must, moreover, recognize that his choice of these values is not a necessary one and is not supported or justified by anything whatsoever. Furthermore, he must acknowledge that he is free not only with respect to the world and the values of others but also with respect to his own past choices. In other words, he must realize that he and he alone brings the values on which he acts into existence and sustains them in existence into the future.

Moreover, given Sartre's recognition concerning the impossibility of realizing our ultimate aims, Sartre seems well-advised to turn to play. Play enables him to overcome futility, even the futility associated with logically impossible ideals. In a game we participate as if the rules or values of the game have some sort of necessary and objective reality; at the same time, as long as we are *playing* and not so caught up in, for example, winning that we mistake the game for something else, we recognize that these rules and values do not have such necessity or objectivity. Even more important, inescapable futility and even logical impossibilities are not problems for those who play. In play we may exert great effort to balance unbalanceable objects and to fill sieves with water.

In turning to play to resolve the problem of futility, Sartre's answer is reminiscent of Kierkegaard's response to the futility suggested by the clergyman's claim that "a man can do absolutely nothing himself." Although this claim makes all action futile and would seem to justify our doing anything whatever, Kierkegaard argues that this is not the case:

> But if a man proposes to himself every day to bear in mind and existentially to hold fast what the clergyman says on Sunday, understanding this as the earnestness of life, and therewith again understanding all his ability and inability as a jest: does this mean that he will undertake nothing at all, because everything is empty and vain? Ah, no, for then precisely he will have no occasion to appreciate the jest, since the contradiction will not arise which brings it into juxtaposition with the earnestness of life: there is no contradiction involved in that everything is vanity in the eyes of a creature of vanity. Sloth, inactivity, the affectation of superiority over against the finite—this is poor jesting, or rather it is no jest at all. But to shorten one's hours of sleep and to buy up each waking period of the day and not to spare oneself, and then to understand that the whole is a jest: aye, that is earnestness.[28]

For Kierkegaard, humor and the comic cancel the contradiction experienced by one who realizes that "against God we are always in the wrong."[29] The "law of the comical" is, Kierkegaard says, "quite simple: it exists wherever there is a contradiction, and where the contradiction is painless because it is viewed as cancelled."[30] The contradiction experienced by the ethical/religious person can be canceled by a "legitimate comic apprehension."[31]

Where "loser wins" resembles ordinary play is in the fact that in both we accept this lack of coincidence between the apparent and the real. In ordinary play we recognize this and continue nonetheless to play and to enjoy the game. The authentic individual must act in a similar manner. With the latter, however, the emphasis is not on enjoyment but rather on lucidity and on the awareness that he is doing what he can as a free and responsible human being.

However much "loser wins" involves play, it involves something more, and this additional element is clearly of great importance to Sartre. For Sartre not just any game will do. The waiter in the cafe, a well-known example from *Being and Nothingness*, may be playing at being a waiter;[32] but for Sartre this game is unacceptable. The waiter, in his desire to be God, tries to achieve the ultimate identity of freedom and facticity through a game of pretense, of self-deception, which ignores and attempts to deny altogether the ambiguity of his own existence as an uneasy tension between necessity and freedom, the determinateness of the past and the openness of the future, and the inevitably disparate ways he is seen by others and by himself.

In such bad faith, the individual tries to achieve his ultimate goal through magic and incantations very like the fearful individual who, according to Sartre, magically causes by fainting, the "disappearance" of the threat.[33] Through fainting, the individual relinquishes or denies his responsibility for his body and its actions; he retreats into pure subjectivity. Futility enters into his behavior, but in an entirely different way than it did in the foregoing discussion of the problem of futility. There is no *problem* of recognizing one's intention in the consequences of fainting. As we know, fainting does not remove the threat but rather simply leaves the one who faints completely vulnerable, unable to resist or escape from the threat. The consequences here are quite the opposite of the safety and security that was sought. The waiter would seem to be in a similar position inasmuch as his robotlike behavior is and will remain antithetical to what he sought: the more he becomes objectlike the *less* he is the subjectivity-as-object that he sought to become.

Admittedly, the individual who tries to flee from his freedom and responsibility may actually seek this second sort of failure. In these cases it is difficult to see what, if anything, could count for the individual himself against his action and choices. The point is simply that in other cases consequences *may* count *against* the individual's actions and choices. This can be affirmed at the same time that one affirms that, owing to the ultimate futility of human actions, consequences will never justify the value of any particular actions.

What this analysis of consequences means then is that Sartre can affirm a particular way of playing as that appropriate to the authentic individual. This individual accepts and affirms the futility of actualizing his ultimate goal and yet continues to do what he can to actualize it. Men like Pablo Ibbieta, Hoederer, and Genet acknowledge and accept their freedom and the ultimate futility of their actions and yet enter the fray, resolved to control what they can control and to change what they can change. Though they may neither control nor change the course of history, they nonetheless act as men: they realize their finitude and their essential ambiguity and work within it even while striving ultimately toward an impossible ideal. They win to the extent that they do create, in their actions and perhaps outside themselves in the group,[34] syntheses, albeit unstable and fleeting, of subjectivity and objectivity. Though not the undifferentiated unities sought, these syntheses, at least for a moment, are temporal and ambiguous intimations of those ultimate but impossible goals toward which they strive.

2. Merleau-Ponty's Political Thought: Its Nature and Its Challenge

BERNARD P. DAUENHAUER

In the preface to *Signs*, Maurice Merleau-Ponty (1908–1961) explicitly directs us to think history according to the model of *language* (parlance) or of being. We are, he says, "in the field of history as in the field of parlance or of being."[1] That is, we are born into history as we are born into both parlance and perceptual being. These fields are neither chaotic nor fully determinate. Rather they all both manifest previously established structures and at the same time provide the resources and opportunities required for us to make our own distinctive contributions.

Less explicitly but nonetheless clearly Merleau-Ponty also thinks politics according to this same pattern. This is indicated by the regularity with which his remarks on politics are connected with a discussion of history. In this paper I want to show just how this pattern is at play in his political thought.

The politics that emerges from such an approach is properly characterizable as a politics of hope. Such a politics is, to be sure, subject to substantial challenges. But a politics of hope also provides a striking alternative to some prevailing approaches to politics. The last remarks of this paper will try to sketch the major lines of the challenges that a politics of hope both poses and is subject to.

I

Politics is a special case of both history and parlance.[2] Like both, politics is constituted in its actuality by an agency that is always situated. On the one hand, though Merleau-Ponty does not, to my knowledge, say so explicitly, the specific character of concrete political situations consists of the peculiar intertwining of men and things that obtains at some juncture of time and geography. On the other hand, political agency is the endeavor to preserve or modify *directly* the prevailing shape of the intertwining. That is, whereas productive industry works on the intertwining through working on things and thought works on the intertwining through working on men, politics works on both men and through working on their intertwining.

To be more specific about the consequences of thinking politics as a special case of both history and parlance, let me detail how the central elements of Merleau-Ponty's political thought are structurally comparable to the principal features of parlance that Merleau-Ponty appropriated from Saussurean linguistics. These features are: (1) the distinction between *langue* (language) and *parole* (speech), (2) the distinction between the synchronic and the diachronic dimensions of language, and (3) the essentially intersubjective character of all parlance.[3]

Consider first the political counterpart of the distinction between language and speech. Just as no speech can be articulated apart from the background of the language in which it is uttered, so no political accomplishment can be achieved apart from the previously established background of "things" and institutions. The things in question here are not, of course, mere things. They are things recognized as available or unavailable material or cultural resources. That is, they are institutionalized things. Thus, there can be no genuine political enterprises today that ignore the presence or absence of such cultural resources as the prevailing legal, educational, and religious institutions. Nor can the relative availability of material resources such as oil, grain, cobalt, or copper be overlooked. And the same holds good for both the level of technology and industry and the quantity, quality, and distribution of military might. All these elements, and more, enter into the constitution of the political language that both makes possible and constrains the political speech. Any putative political initiative that pretends that the specific background whence it arises is irrelevant is mere babble.

But just as language neither dictates nor necessitates some specific speech, so neither does the political situation decree or necessitate a specific political undertaking. No living politics simply acquiesces in the factual situation as it finds it. Every politics, Merleau-Ponty says, insists upon its right to alter the way in which its tasks and problems are posed.[4] Indeed, this alteration is not merely a right that a politician may exercise at his discretion. The transformation of the situation is constitutive of politics itself.

Precisely what Merleau-Ponty praises in Machiavelli is the latter's recognition that we need never be mere victims of *fortuna*, of some given political situation. Political action consists in a grasp of the concrete possibilities that the situation presents, coupled with a bold effort to actualize them.[5] Thus, genuine politics requires not merely the acknowledgement of the weight of the determinate political situation, the language in which one finds oneself located, but also the risky endeavor to transform that situation, to revivify it by the exercise of *virtù*, the uttering of the new speech.

Nothing, of course, guarantees ahead of time that the new political endeavor will either succeed or be appropriate. Even if, as the Marxists have it, men make their own history, still they often do not and cannot know the history they are making.[6] In Merleau-Ponty's words, "If everything counts in history we can no longer say as Marxists do that in the *last analysis* historical logic always finds its ways, that it alone has a *decisive* role, and that it is the *truth* of history."[7] For one thing there is no last analysis. For another, contingency and not merely logic is ineliminable from human affairs.

Political situation and political initiative, then, like language and speech, belong together. Each has its *sens*, its meaning and direction, only by reason of its reference to the other.

II

The ramifications of thinking politics according to the language-speech model become clearer when one takes note of the counterpart in Merleau-Ponty's political thought to the Saussurean distinction between the synchronic and the diachronic dimensions of language. Here I want to call particular attention to one feature of Merleau-Ponty's political thought that emphasizes the *synchronic dimension* of the political situation and two features that emphasize the *diachronic dimension*.

First, the synchronic feature. For Merleau-Ponty it makes no sense to attempt to divide the elements of the political situation into unqualified blessings and unmitigated curses. As is the case with language, in political situations there are no elements that have full sense apart from the context in which they are located. Every element of the political situation is simply a component of a whole. None is self-subsisting with an independent positive meaning. Any responsible political initiative, like any speech, must acknowledge the irreducible complexity of the context against which it arises. Responsible initiative must avoid what Merleau-Ponty calls, in a somewhat different setting, the cops and con-men conception of history and politics.[8] Thus, for example, capitalism cannot be regarded as unmitigated evil nor does Soviet Communism deserve simplistic, virulent denunciations. Each has its meaning in function of the other.[9]

The diachronic features of Merleau-Ponty's political thought, however, introduce subtle but substantial modifications into this conclusion.

First, however systematically intertwined the elements of the political situation may be, none of them is so definitively fixed in its meaning and bearing that it preserves some identical sense regardless of all temporal considerations.[10] This fact is, of course, a necessary condition for any political initiative. But more to the present point, this fact requires that political initiative not attempt either to reverse history or to annihilate the effective weight of anything brought by history to the present situation. Such attempts would be to plan for an imagined world that can no longer exist.

For example, Western men and Third World peoples have already come into contact with one another. Even though the terms of this context have been nothing for either side to boast about, that is no sufficient reason for either side to try to withdraw and perhaps start afresh. It makes no sense to consider this contact simply evil. And, as Merleau-Ponty puts it, "In any case, it is something settled; there can be no question of recreating archaism; we are all embarked and it is no small matter to have begun this game."[11] But, of course, as Merleau-Ponty makes clear in his essay on Indochina, this does not mean that a failed specific policy must be clung to simply because it has been the policy.[12]

But even the initiative that acknowledges both the synchrony of the elements in the political situation and the uniqueness of the temporal moment that each of the elements inhabits cannot be guaranteed in advance to succeed and thus be presented intact as part of a new situation, a new political language. This is a second diachronic feature. All shifts in the situation are indeed brought about by external influence, here specific initiative. But the outcome of these influences is always not only particular but also accidental. What Merleau-Ponty says of history is likewise applicable to politics. Politics "works on a question that is confusedly posed and is not sheltered from regressions and setbacks."[13] As a consequence neither a science nor an intuition can prescribe an undertaking whose outcome can be guaranteed. This fact disappoints those who believe in a definitive salvation and a single means to that salvation. But this fact does not make initiative absurd. To the contrary, it calls for unending initiative, "*virtù* without resignation of any sort."[14]

At least two other significant aspects of Merleau-Ponty's political thought can be seen to be entailed by the necessity to consider the political situation both synchronically and diachronically. First, Merleau-Ponty recognizes that all political initiative that is efficacious must be timely. Though there is no ideal or perfect moment for initiating some specific action, there are timely and untimely ones. What once could have been a solution to a problem ceases to be one. Or a problem that once had a likely solution no longer does but may in the future again do so. From another standpoint a particular agent's capacities to engender solutions can both wax and wane. And do what one may, neither the appropriateness of the solution nor its timeliness can be guaranteed in advance.[15]

Second, and of major importance for Merleau-Ponty, the consideration of both the diachronic and the synchronic dimensions of the political situation leads to a distinctive view of the institutions that men inhabit. Institutions, he insists, are not inert. With Marx, Merleau-Ponty holds that there is a coming-to-be of meaning in institutions.[16] Sartre notwithstanding, institutions, as social apparatuses, are human and cannot be set over against man as something less than human.[17] Rather, institutions endow our experiences with durable dimensions and allow them to form a history. At the same time, they invite us to further experience and thus make possible a future.[18] Indeed, far from regarding institutions as obstacles to freedom and political creativity, Merleau-Ponty maintains that one of the most crucial political tasks for our era is "to find institutions which implant this practice of freedom in our customs."[19]

III

When one considers parlance in a Saussurean fashion, one realizes that parlance necessarily involves a historical community of speakers. There is no isolated individual speech.[20] All parlance is intersubjective. Genuinely to speak is also to hear.[21]

This feature of parlance, too, has its structural counterpart in politics. All politics, whether domestic or international, is necessarily intersubjective. Political leaders and the people they lead are ordained to one another. They meet and address each other by virtue of the interworld constituted by institutions and the cultural and material resources that the institutions provide. No one, Merleau-Ponty says, either commands or obeys absolutely.[22]

When one attends to the fact that political activity is not only intersubjective but is also embedded in some unique situation that involves institutions, one realizes that politics is essentially dialectical. This dialectic, of course, neither moves toward some preestablished terminus nor does it subsume everything under itself. Contingency is never banished from it.[23] As is true of all history, in politics there is no immunity from error. The rational always remains to be imagined and created. It never gains the power of simply replacing the false with the true.[24]

One consequence of the open dialectic that genuine politics is is that it is always appropriate to consider complicating or altering the terms of the prevailing dialectic precisely to further the dialectic. Thus, it made sense for Merleau-Ponty to promote a new left force that would transform the interchanges between the United States and the Soviet Union by becoming a full participant in the expanded dialectic.[25]

Further, because politics involves an open dialectic, genuine politics requires tolerance. It necessarily takes people as they are, with their prejudices, notions, and so forth.[26] This tolerance is not a matter of strategy. It is required because no agent can be a pure presence either to itself or to some object.[27] No one alone can possess the truth either about him- or herself or about the world.

Dialectical politics thus demands an opposition that is free. Truth and action can never come together, Merleau-Ponty says, "if there are not, along with those who act, those who observe them, who confront them with the truth of their action, and who can aspire to replace them in power."[28] These and similar considerations lead Merleau-Ponty to his well-known endorsement of parliaments. Whatever its limitations, and clearly it has limitations, parliament is the significant institution, a proven element in the political situation, against which fresh, free, and living political initiative, political speech, can stand forth. "Parliament," according to Merleau-Ponty, "is the only known institution that guarantees a minimum of opposition and truth."[29] It likewise preserves the opposition needed to insure an intersubjectivity worthy of the name.

However tolerant and dialectical politics may be, it still involves the amassing and wielding of power. There can be no effective freedom, the freedom necessary for dialectical politics, without power.[30] Those who amass this power do so without the benefit of some unimpeachable prior title to it. Their power can only find its legitimation in their exercise of it.[31] In wielding power one necessarily impinges upon others. But political abstention is no solution. It simply yields the initiative to others. Merleau-Ponty therefore concludes, "I would rather be a part of a country which does something in history than of a country which submits to it."[32] Unless people risk the revitalizing "speech" of political initiative, the institutions from which they have drawn their sustenance will either ossify or grant their opportunities to others, others who will be left without the benefit of appropriate opposition.

What I have said thus far about politics, on the basis of thinking it according to the model of parlance, takes on another dimension when one attends to the fact that there is no universal parlance. There is only a multiplicity of parlance that undergo translation into one another. Similarly there is no universal politics. There are only multiple concrete politics. Different times and lands have different institutions and stocks of cultural and material resources. These differences call for and make possible different initiatives. It is idle to weigh situations against some abstract standard. Situations are to be lived through, not judged from some putatively independent spectator's vantage point.[33]

But even if the appropriate political initiative, the concrete political speech, is always geared to a specific, more or less local, situation, today, Merleau-Ponty holds, all responsible politics must be resolutely international. "The main concern of our time is going to be to reconcile the old world and the new."[34] This intertwining of the local and the global is not the achieving of a teleologically ordained ideal. It is simply a contingent fact of our era. But it is a fact of consummate importance today.

These two considerations, namely that there is no single universal politics but that today responsible politics must be international, are summarized by Merleau-Ponty in this way:

> There is no universal clock, but local histories take form beneath our eyes, and begin to regulate themselves, and haltingly link themselves to one another and demand to live, and confirm the powerful in the wisdom which the immensity of the risks and the consciousness of their own disorder had given them. The world is more present to itself in all its parts than it ever was.[35]

Politics, like parlance, then, is not a seamless, stable whole. Rather it is a vibrating, moving complex.

IV

When politics is thought according to the model of parlance, the character of political judgment must be thought in a distinctive way. Merleau-Ponty has made this explicit. He says:

> Political and historical judgment will perhaps never be objective; it will always be a bastard judgment. But precisely for this reason it escapes morality as well as pure science. It is of the category of action, which makes for continual oscillation between morality and science.[36]

Political judgment, that is, is not to be identified with the sort of moral judgment that would spring from some Kantianesque categorical imperative adopted without regard for material circumstances. Political judgment does not pretend to have the sort of autonomy that moral judgment of this kind must presuppose. On the other hand, political judgment is no mere acknowledgment of some already established state of affairs and the consequences derivable therefrom. Unlike scientific judgments, political judgments are neither mere predictions nor mere retrodictions. They are inventive. They issue in actions that modify the prevailing state of affairs. This distinctive character of political judgments makes sense, Merleau-Ponty maintains, because the world to which they refer is dense and mobile and not, as Sartre would have it, opaque and rigid.[37]

But even if politics is not reducible to morality, it is nonetheless not contrary to morality. In fact, there must be a positive relationship between them.[38] Granted that values and principles are insufficient for genuine politics, they are nonetheless necessary. There must be, Merleau-Ponty recognizes, a guideline to distinguish between political *virtù*, the excellence in acquiring and wielding power to make the most of the opportunities provided by *fortuna*, and political opportunism, the make-shift accommodation to prevailing pressures aiming merely at survival.[39]

For Merleau-Ponty, I think, this guideline consists in making the preservation and extension of the dialectic the overarching objective of all political initiatives. Political judgments, for all their regard for the situation to which they are inextricably linked, must all issue in action that has this as its ultimate objective. This guideline warrants Merleau-Ponty's conclusion that reform, far from being outmoded, "alone is the order of the day."[40] This conclusion in turn provides the basis for Merleau-Ponty's support for parliamentarianism as the best candidate for that form or institution that can keep power in reins without annulling it.

In brief then, political judgment inhabits an interworld. It draws upon and oscillates between imperatives of will and acknowledgment of facts. Thus, on the other hand, it itself has structural features like those of parlance. On the other hand, the specific content of genuine political judgments reveals that they refer to a world that is appropriately though according to the model of parlance.

Before I attempt to assess the results of Merleau-Ponty's thought about politics, it is worth noticing that his approach to both politics and parlance is simply an application of his general philosophical position to these two domains. Or from another standpoint the ways in which Merleau-Ponty handles the topics of politics, history, and parlance are the ways in which he handles all philosophical topics. He says:

> It is true that in the last resort there is no judge, that I do not think according to the true alone, nor according to myself alone, nor according to the others alone, because each of the three has need of the other two

and it would be a non-sense to sacrifice any one. A philosophical life always bases itself on these three cardinal points. The enigma of philosophy (and of expression) is that sometimes life is the same to oneself, to others, and to the true. These are the moments which justify it. The philosopher counts only on them. He will never accept to will himself against men, nor to will men against himself, nor against the true, nor the true against them.[41]

V

Let me turn now to an assessment of the consequences of Merleau-Ponty's thinking politics according to the model of parlance. As a first step, I want to show that this way of thinking politics yields what can appropriately be called a politics of hope. Then I want to raise the issue of whether a politics of hope, as an alternative to other kinds of politics, is an acceptable basis for political conduct.

In calling Merleau-Ponty's politics a politics of hope, I am using the term *hope* in a sense much like that developed by Gabriel Marcel in his essay, "Sketch of a Phenomenology and a Metaphysic of Hope."[42] Hope, Marcel points out, has no antecedently determinate object, no ultimate accomplishment of state of affairs that would terminate it. Hope involves, rather, an abiding union of persons. Its proper formulation is: I hope in you for us.[43] Further, Marcel holds, hope always implies a connection between a return and something completely new. Preservation or restoration, on the one hand, and renewal on the other, are two aspects of one and the same unitary movement. What hope aspires to, according to Marcel, is the paradoxical "as before, but differently and better than before."[44] Merleau-Ponty's politics, I suggest, both rests upon this sort of hope and aims at having as many people as possible embrace this hope. It is a politics whose ultimate aim is to free as many people as possible to take part in a dialectic that has no terminus.[45]

The sense of the hope that inspires Merleau-Ponty's politics takes clearer shape when it is contrasted with attitudes contrary to hope. First, hope is opposed both to fideism and to sheer voluntarism. These are two vices that have shown up rather often in both Communist and capitalist practice. Both of them, at times, have dogmatically believed their own principles and insights to be exhaustive of political wisdom, disregarding in the process available evidence to the contrary. At other times both of them have pursued policies recognizably inconsistent with their own principles simply for the advantage of those amassing and wielding power. The former vice is tantamount to fanaticism, the latter to cynicism.

By contrast a politics of hope preserves and protects opposition to itself. Without such opposition the dialectic that constitutes politics would be truncated, in effect terminating politics. Without such opposition there would be no *you* in whom *I* could hope for *us*. But with opposition both criticism and self-criticism can flourish. And criticism is a sine qua non if errors are to be sloughed off.

Second, a politics of hope avoids the twin pitfalls of presumption and despair. It avoids presumption by keeping constantly in mind that its own policies and principles need defense. The mere communication of its own position is not sufficient to ensure its acceptance. Its opponents do not simply need to be enlightened. They must be coerced into accepting the practitioners of hope as fellow actors on the political scene. Even a politics of hope cannot afford to eschew all violence. A politics of hope, then, avoids the smug presumptuousness of merely enunciating high-sounding sentiments, a pose which lacks all seriousness.

On the other hand, a politics of hope never yields to the temptation to deny freedom. It never despairs. Even if the specific circumstances in which one lives at present do not furnish a basis for initiative, the practitioner of hope waits expectantly for changes in that situation that will allow him room for action. No situation is ever accepted as definitely foreclosing the possibility of exercising *virtù*. Similarly, the practitioner of hope never consigns an opponent to the ranks of the perpetual enemy. Today's opponent may become tomorrow's ally. A politics of hope never presumes to preclude that possibility. A politics of hope, then, rises above both the trivializing of the differences among men and the absolutizing of any specific set of those differences.[46]

In avoiding both presumption and despair, a politics of hope reveals the essential role that forgiveness occupies in its makeup. What Merleau-Ponty says about Claudel is applicable to his own standards for responsible political conduct. Claudel, Merleau-Ponty says, forgives readily after the deed, even though he lays stringent requirements on both the prospective conduct and the actual prosecution of the deed.[47] Because of the contingency and ambiguity of all human enterprises, Merleau-Ponty saw, this forgiveness is extended not only to others but also to oneself. If one is to pursue a politics of hope, one must not exempt oneself from the ranks of those who need pardon for their deeds.

But a central question remains. Is a politics of hope an acceptable basis for political conduct? I will limit my response here to preliminary remarks concerning the application to this sort of politics of two tests.

Merleau-Ponty himself recognized that a defensible political doctrine must satisfy them. First, does Merleau-Ponty's politics of hope, unlike the politics of Machiavelli for example, possess a sufficiently strong guideline for distinguishing between political *virtù* and mere opportunism? Is it enough to say that a politics is justified if it tends to preserve and extend the dialectic, if it tends to promote reform rather than either revolution or the status quo? At first, it might appear that this is too permissive a standard, that it permits too much. But I think that this appearance is deceptive. Given Merleau-Ponty's view of the dialectic in question here, this guideline turns out to be stringent. To satisfy this guideline, the policy or deed in question should in principle be recognizable to everyone as something that each person or state could rationally endorse being carried out by someone, even if not by oneself. If I am correct about this matter, then Merleau-Ponty's guideline is hardly too lax. If anything, it could be challenged as being so rigorous that it cannot in practice be observed. On my reading, Merleau-Ponty's position does not fall victim to the same fault from which Machiavelli's politics suffered. It might, however, fall victim to the opposite fault, the fault of legitimating too little instead of too much.[48]

This possibility leads to a consideration of a second test proposed by Merleau-Ponty. Can a politics of hope successfully compete against other types of politics? Though success is not a sufficient condition for justifying a politics, it is, for Merleau-Ponty, a necessary one.[49] The praxis endorsed by Merleau-Ponty must, if it cannot be true, at least not be false.[50]

Failure can threaten a politics of hope from two directions. From within, political agents who adopt the delicate posture of a politics of hope may lose their footing and collapse into the less demanding positions of complete or attenuated fideism, voluntarism, persumption, or despair. Given the evidence of history, can it be prudently expected that enough people with enough power will risk adopting a politics of hope so that such a politics has a reasonable prospect of success? To defend Merleau-Ponty's position, one would have to hold that the evidence of history, mixed as it is, when coupled with the new possibilities of global interaction does have such a prospect. Indeed it may be, and I am inclined to think that it is the case, that in the novel circumstances that constitute our age, to risk a politics of hope may be far slighter risk than is the risk involved in lapsing into any of the available alternatives.

A politics of hope can also be threatened with failure from without. How will the practitioners of such a politics fare when confronted with practitioners of competing alternatives? To mention only one aspect of this problem, will not the criticism, from both self and others, to which a politics of hope is resolutely and unremittingly committed, so weaken it in the execution of its politics that it cannot withstand assaults from fideists or voluntarists?

No firm rejoinder can be made to this challenge. The available historical evidence that supports the practical wisdom of living a politics of hope is far from conclusive. But it is not trivial. Consider, for example, the widespread and long-standing penchant for federations, leagues, compacts, and so forth. And there is reason to say that both some Marxists and some capitalists, in phases of their political conduct that have won approval from diverse quarters, have been practicing a politics of hope under another title. At the least, this evidence is strong enough to permit one to claim that a politics of hope is not fatuous, that it has not already been refuted by history.

The conclusion, then, to which I am led is that Merleau-Ponty's politics of hope does not satisfy beyond all plausible questioning his own tests for a legitimate politics, a politics that both preserves and extends the dialectic. But the presently available political alternatives can only pass these tests at the expense of abandoning this dialectic. If these tests and this objective are appropriate, and I take it that they are, the failure of its competitors is reason enough for adopting a politics of hope. In fact, one would probably be mistaken if one looked for a stronger conclusion, for politics, like history, has only errors to be avoided. The truth of politics, as Merleau-Ponty pointed out, consists in nothing but the "art of inventing what will later appear to have been required by the times."[51]

3. From "*Socialisme et Liberté*" to "*Pouvoir et Liberté*": The Case of Jean-Paul Sartre

Thomas R. Flynn

Sheldon Wolin defines a political theory rather broadly as "a set of concepts—such as order, peace, justice, power, law, etc.—bound together . . . by a kind of notational principle that assigns accents and modulations."[1] Using this generous definition, can one discern the elements of a coherent and comprehensive political theory in the writings of the French existentialists Sartre and Merleau-Ponty? Given the political differences that came to divide them so sharply, if we limit ourselves to the basics, can we discover any "notational principles" that are common—to continue Wolin's musical metaphor—to the compositions of both of them? In other words, in view of the notoriously amorphous character of existentialism itself, is there any such theory as *political existentialism* at all?

I wish to argue that there are three such "notational" principles, mutually distinct but interrelated, that define political existentialism and that unite the otherwise disparate political postures of Sartre and Merleau-Ponty. These are original and persistent commitments to (1) socialist humanism and (2) individual freedom, as well as (3) the central position accorded by both men to the means-end question.

Because I have chosen to study the case of Jean-Paul Sartre, I shall refer to Merleau-Ponty only briefly and by way of confirmation or contrast. Likewise, I shall not delve deeply into the Marxist inspiration of this political theory except to remark certain conceptual similarities between the two, especially as philosophers of history.

After treating the *nature* of political existentialism as embodied in Sartre's writings, I shall turn to the *challenge* it holds for contemporary political thought, focusing on several questions raised by Sartre's position that invite comparison and contrast with the thought of other political existentialists, namely, (1) Is Sartre's resolution of the means-end issue, that is, proximately by appeal to "dirty hands" and ultimately with a kind of antipolitics, believable or even coherent? (2) What sociopolitical vehicle is most apt for implementing the ideals of political existentialism? (3) What is the relationship between political existentialism and violence? and finally (4) What does political existentialism contribute to the ongoing dialogue that is Western political philosophy?

The Nature of Political Existentialism

Returning to occupied Paris after several months in German military confinement, Sartre joined with Merleau-Ponty to found a resistance group of intellectuals called *"Socialisme et Liberté."*[2] Although the group didn't last a year, its twin values of socialism and freedom anchored the political theories that both men would subsequently develop. Let us examine each concept in some detail.

SOCIALIST HUMANISM

Stuart Hampshire has characterized socialism as "a method of solving social problems according to the aspirations and need of underprivileged classes."[3] Although Merleau-Ponty's view on the matter seems to have changed over the years, this rather accurately describes Sartre's position in assessing socio-historical change, namely, that we "look upon man and society in their truth, that is to say, with the eyes of the least favored."[4] As much as his almost congenital hatred of the bourgeoisie, it is this sensitivity to the lot of the exploited and oppressed that drew the moralist Sartre into politics in the first place.

Although both thinkers eventually moved beyond support of the French Communist Party—Sartre fraternizing with ultraleftist *groupuscules* and Merleau favoring the center-left *L'Express* people for whom he wrote several articles—each retained throughout his career a fundamental commitment to socialism and to the view of man as the supreme value for man. Ironically, their respective readings of socialist humanism were to warrant moves in opposite political directions.

For the existentialist, socialist humanism is a corollary to the basic "ontological" fact that human reality is being-in-situation. In "Materialism and Revolution," Sartre wrote that whatever social philosophy existentialism might develop would be an expression of the concepts "situation" and "being-in-the-world."[5] And in *Anti-Semite and Jew* he charted the basic tactics of political existentialism:

> Thus we do not attack freedom, but bring it about that freedom decides on other bases and in terms of other structures. . . . Political action can never be directed against the freedom of citizens; its very nature forbids it to be concerned with freedom except in a negative fashion, that is, in taking care not to infringe upon it. It only acts on situations.[6]

It is the decisive power of socioeconomic situation, which Merleau-Ponty had long acknowledged, that Sartre gradually came to appreciate. *Possibility* came to mean not only the futural temporal ecstasis, as it did for Kierkegaard and Heidegger, but the *objective possibility* of Marx, Weber, and Lukács. To give people some choice other than submission or death became his goal. But this could be effected only indirectly, that is, by transforming the *bases* and *structures* of choice.

Sartre likewise came to see that "situation" is not the individualist phenomenon he had taken it to be. In *Saint Genet* he confesses: "For a long time we believed in the social atomism bequeathed to us by the eighteenth century. . . . The truth is that 'human reality' 'is-in-society' as it 'is-in-the-world.'"[7] Political action, therefore, must be directed to the *situation* of citizens, and that situation is basically social.

The negative goal of such political action is the end of exploitation and oppression, *exploitation* being primarily an institutional phenomenon (in Merleau-Ponty's sense of that term) and *oppression* denoting some kind of sustaining praxis, whether individual or collective, though ultimately individual. Merleau-Ponty was right on target when he remarked that "with Sartre, as with the anarchists, the idea of oppression always dominates that of exploitation."[8] What he failed to note was that this follows from existentialism's commitment since Kierkegaard to the *ontological* and *moral primacy* of the acting individual. Merleau's remark would seem to imply either that he never acknowledged such a primacy himself or that he was attenuating its purport, allowing greater influence to "situation" than Sartre had done thus far. The latter seems more likely, especially in view of Merleau's development of the concept of an interworld (*l'intermonde*) as the locus of the specifically social, a concept which Sartre himself would adopt in *Search for a Method*.

The positive goal of political action as Sartre makes abundantly clear in the *Critique* and by implication in *L'Idiot* is *full positive reciprocity*: the practical interchange among equals in voluntary relationships. One of his earliest expressions of this ideal occurs in his polemical *Reply to Claude Lefort*, where he writes that "universal reciprocity . . . must create truly human relations."[9] In the *Critique* he insists that *all* human relations are basically reciprocal and that their positive or negative character (cooperation or struggle) depends entirely on what mediates these reciprocities.[10] His sociopolitical ideal, what he terms "the City of ends," overthrowing Kant's monarchy with a word, comprises "a system of the world which does not yet exist and which will exclude all privileges de facto and de jure."[11] All revolution, including the one he advocates, is an attempt "to bring it about by violence that society move from a state where freedoms are alienated to another founded on their mutual recognition."[12] Since this presumes not only a change in sociopolitical structure but the overcoming of material scarcity, Sartre terms this ideal "socialism of abundance."[13]

But if Sartre's political existentialism is socialistic due to the realization that the bases and structures of the current social situation are exploitative, his is a socialist *humanism*, a commitment to the possibility of self-creative choice on the part of each individual. *Le socialisme* must be tempered by *la liberté*. It is to this second arm of the existentialist anchor that we now turn.

INDIVIDUAL FREEDOM

What prohibits existentialists generally from subscribing to "scientific socialism," that is, to DIAMAT (the wooden, so-called "orthodox" version of dialectical materialism) with its dialectic of nature, is commitment to the insuperable freedom of the individual. If taken in an atomistic, Enlightenment sense, *la liberté* is incompatible with socialism. But a critic like Raymond Aron who sees an antinomy here is admittedly arguing from an analytic, as opposed to a dialectical, viewpoint.[14] Understood *dialectically*, in terms of the essential relatedness of persons to each other via social entities, individual freedom balances socioeconomic conditioning to achieve an ongoing interchange whose ideal is full self-realization. In this dialectical sense, individual freedom demands socialist humanism and vice versa. As the Yugoslav Marxist, Gajo Petrović, insists: "The basic principle of socialism . . . [is] that a society is to that extent socialist in which it provides the possibilities for a free creative development of every individual."[15] It is Sartre's discovery of dialectical reason that justified his otherwise hyperbolic claim that no one can be free until *all* are free.[16]

It was necessary for political existentialism to retain the values of individual freedom and responsibility in the midst of the most impersonal social movements. Sartre achieved this by translating consciousness (the *pour-soi* of *Being and Nothingness*) into *praxis* (roughly, human activity in its material environment) and by making individual praxis the sole constitutive component of the social dialectic. I call this Sartre's principle of the primacy of praxis. It has several important consequences for his political philosophy.

I have just mentioned the first and most important, preserving a place for the characteristically "existentialist" values of individual freedom and moral responsibility throughout collective undertakings and social ascriptions. One can always look for responsible praxis at the base of the most "necessary" social effects. This is the ontological source of the priority of oppression over exploitation which Merleau-Ponty remarked.

But this principle grounds a certain pragmatism in Sartrean political theory. The context is one of doing, not reflective knowing, and the very nature of truth is revised.[17] Accordingly, what will appear to others as a double standard will for Sartre be the perfectly justifiable expression of a single goal: whatever furthers the possibility of full reciprocity among all people is good and to be chosen; whatever hinders this value should be opposed. We shall consider the means-end aspect of this consequence in a moment.

Another result of Sartre's use of this principle is the denial of the possibility of a *complete synthesis* of individuals in the state or even in the group. Contrary to some interpreters who see in the later Sartre the dissolution of the individual in some superorganism, he insists that a tension of immanence-transcendence characterizes the social whole even at its peak of integration. As Sartrean consciousness could never become in-itself-for-itself, so "praxes can never achieve full organic unity among themselves." The root of this failure is the same in both instances: the existentialist claim that human reality is ontologically noncoincident with itself. This is the source of ontological freedom: "man is free because he is no self but self-presence,"[18] and it is the reason behind Sartre's historically accurate but politically ominous claim that "fraternity-terror" is the basic relation among members of the pledged group. Because human reality is no self but self-presence, each member remains *potentially a traitor*. This is the ancient dilemma of reconciling freedom and security that has plagued would-be predestinarians in politics as well as theology over the ages. It is particularly intense for the political existentialist.

A final consequence of this principle of the primacy of praxis is that it renders every other political undertaking intelligible. To the extent that they are all praxes comprehending their own situations, each agent has an insight into the work of others that it could not enjoy with regard to natural processes. The only limits to this intelligibility of the social are the contingency of other praxes and that material recalcitrance that Sartre terms the "practico-inert."

Radical individual freedom, therefore, is a nonnegotiable for Sartre. He subsumes it into social categories via his principle of the primacy of praxis. This principle gives a certain libertarian flavor to his most "collectivist" analyses in the *Critique*. And mounted as pivot of the dialectic, it moderately reconciles the two arms of the anchor of political existentialism.

MEANS-END QUESTION

Addressing the opening session of UNESCO at the Sorbonne, November 1, 1946, Sartre delineated the responsibility of the writer in our time: "He must . . . give his thoughts without respite, day in, day out, to the problem of the end and the means; or, alternatively, the problem of the relation between ethics and politics."[19] This issue continued to haunt Sartre for the rest of his life.

If existentialism is above all an ethical theory (or at least an ethical style), we can expect that political existentialism will focus on the moral dimension of political activity—and so it does. It was ethical concerns, as we said, that brought Sartre into the political arena in the first place, and despite a period of what he terms "amoralist realism" during his fellow-traveling years, it is ethical concerns that kept him there.[20] This is particularly clear from his sympathy with *les maos* (the Maoists) after the events of May 1968. Recalling those days Sartre observes: "I found myself with comrades who struggled and who once more posed morality as something which exists in politics."[21] There is a touchingly naive directness in Sartre's remarks to some young Maoist friends when he avows:

> A strong relation between you and me is the idea which you have of ethics (*la morale*); the idea that love of Justice and hatred of Injustice are real forces which move the people to act. Thus you don't ever engage in machiavellian tactics, unlike the Communists, who say: "if you talk Justice to the people, they'll march," but who don't give a damn for justice and first of all want power. You propose truly just causes to people. (*ORR*, p. 76)

If Sartre joined Marxists generally in decrying bourgeois ethics, he never failed to do so in the name of a deep sense of injustice and alienation that everyone should feel. "[The Maoists] demonstrate," he notes, "that in effect when one engages in politics one must not consider that ethics is a simple superstructure, but must consider that it exists at the very level of what is called substructure—which has always been my opinion." Indeed he distinguished the living ethic that obtains at the very level of production from dead ethical theories that inhabit the superstructure. (*ORR*, pp. 118–19) Though he is vague and even somewhat romantic in the few allusions he makes to this living ethic, it clearly has its root in "those rare but important notions which exist among all classes and which, though not completely the same from one class to another, contain common elements." One such notion, we're not surprised to hear Sartre claim, is freedom (*ORR*, pp. 341–42). Indeed, it is implicit appeal to this notion that saves Sartre from the self-defeating relativism that plagues more orthodox Marxists.

Thus, it is freedom, meaning among other things the capacity and the exigency for self-realization, that thrusts the means-end question to the forefront of political existentialist concerns. It calls for liberation from alienating social structures and the advent of "the reign of freedom" on the one hand, while insisting, on the other, that it is immoral to violate another's freedom in bringing this about.

If we pause for a moment to range over the other so-called French existentialists, a similar concern for the ethics-politics relation is evident. In Camus this becomes excruciating in the face of the mutual torture and terror among his fellow Algerians in that civil war. For Merleau-Ponty the issue warranted his break with Sartre, whom he regarded as having callously subordinated ethics to politics in his "realist" years. Finally, Simone de Beauvoir, admitting that "political choice is an ethical choice," counsels that we "not conceal the antinomies between means and end, present and future; they must believe," she warns, "in a permanent tension; one must neither retreat from the outrage of violence nor deny it, or, which amounts to the same thing, assume it lightly."[22] The situation of the political existentialist in this matter, including Sartre himself, could perhaps best be summarized in the judgment Sartre made of the lifelong predicament of Albert Camus: "Ethics (*la morale*) taken by itself both demands revolt and condemns it."[23]

That political existentialists accord pride of place to the means-end question does not, of course, imply that they all resolve it in similar fashion. They differ among themselves especially regarding the morality of violence in the service of ultimate justice. But this is a challenge raised within the basic means-end context just described, and a challenge to political theory in general. As such, it is more properly dealt with in the second portion of our study.

Before launching into the other half of our inquiry, I should deal with a likely objection that the foregoing could raise. Are not these three conditions—socialist humanism, individual freedom, and concern for the means-end question—really characteristic of revisionist Marxism in general and not at all specific to political existentialism? In other words, by these criteria are not the early Lukács, Lucien Goldmann, the Yugoslav praxis school, and Eric Fromm, for that matter, *all* political existentialists? In response I would admit a certain convergence in the thinking of political existentialists and the revisionist Marxists just named. In some instances one can even speak of a mutual influence between members of these groups. But what sets the existentialists apart is their *terminus a quo*: the Kierkegaardian insuperability of the individual, Husserlian intentionality, and Heideggerian *Existenz*. In Sartre's case, these are synthesized and pressed into political service via the principle of the primacy of praxis. If these French thinkers resemble the revisionists to the extent that they are political, they differ precisely in so far as they are still existentialist.

The Challenge of Political Existentialism

Having brought to light the basic features that "assign the accents and modulations" proper to political existentialism, we are now in a position to review this theory's responses to several current questions in political philosophy.

THE MEANS-END PROBLEM, AGAIN

Focusing on Sartre, we find that he offers two "solutions." The first, proximate, is simply to grasp the issue with all its ambiguity, aware that one cannot avoid getting dirty hands once one moves from antiseptic theory to grimy practice. This is not so cynical a counsel as some have claimed. Sartre's thesis is that in an exploitative and oppressive society with its own ethical code developed in large part to defend the status quo, one cannot help transgressing some prohibitions of that system in order to overturn its socioeconomic base—one cannot bring about a revolution without telling a few lies.[24] Others might state the matter thus: once you decide that purity of intention is not enough, Kant's lapidary claim that the only thing good without qualification is the good will, assumes a particularly tragic sense. Nowhere is the ethical ambiguity of the human enterprise more sharply underscored than in the political arena. All the political existentialists seem to have been aware of this.

But if Sartre's proximate counsel is political commitment despite necessary moral ambiguity, his ultimate hope is to overcome this dilemma by the surpassing of politics itself. With a kind of Rousseauian nostalgia, he claims that "the true relationship among men is reciprocity which excludes commands properly speaking."[25] And in his discussion with the young anarchists, mentioned above, he remarks that in the classless society the professional politician will be superfluous: "Each man will become mediator of the ensemble."[26] In this socialism of abundance, the gentle force of persuasion will replace the command-obedience relationship.[27]

Sartre's argument is that *all* authority is of the command-obedience variety. But command-obedience is essentially an alienating relationship. Hence all authority is alienating politically just as is belief ("the Other in us") in the epistemic realm.[28] Sartre thereby joins Rousseau and Marx in promising an *anti*political, that is, an ideal society where power and authority are replaced by eye-level relationships based on reason and persuasion.[29] This aspect of Sartrean political existentialism, at least, fulfills the *utopian* function in political theory.

Political Vehicle

What is the *political vehicle* most apt for realizing these values of socialism, personal freedom, and ethical sensitivity? Should it be a constitutional democracy? The temporary dictatorship of the proletariat? Some kind of libertarian association?

Here too, the existentialists are divided among themselves. If the goal is to dismantle authority—that is, command-obedience relations—altogether, then its proper means would seems to be one that anticipates that egalitarian status while generating the necessary collective force to effect the requisite structural changes. In the early '50s, Sartre thought that this called for a strong party apparatus. Merleau-Ponty castigated that as Sartre's "ultra-Bolshevism." But this "amoral realism" was contrary to his deeper convictions; and besides he came to see that what the Communists wanted was not justice but power. Politically he concluded that the dictatorship of the proletariat is "an absurd idea"[30] on the one hand, but on the other, that Western democracy, with its parliaments and periodic elections, is "a trap for fools."[31]

What remained? Some sort of participatory democracy is what he came to favor in the late '60s and '70s. This too attracted him to *les maos*.[32] if one takes seriously the principle of the primacy of individual praxis as well as the vintage existentialist commitment to personal freedom and moral responsibility, then direct democracy does seem to meet these norms more properly than either totalitarianism or even parliamentarianism. With regard to the latter, the existentialist raises anew the problem of reconciling complete social autonomy with the existence of a set of individuals empowered to "act in your name." To this, Sartre adds remarks about the inevitable "mineralization" of interpersonal relations in the bureaucracy. Indeed, a large portion of the first volume of the *Critique* is devoted to that problem.

It was precisely this radical refusal of all organization coupled with a deep sense of fraternity and spontaneity that burst forth among the students in Paris during the events of May 1968. As we shall see shortly, there was something peculiarly Sartrean about the spirit of these events. As evidence of the convergence I mentioned earlier, Lucien Goldmann interpreted these same happenings as the confused yet real preview of a new society in process of being constructed. Facing our problem of "the forms of organization of a truly socialist movement in contemporary industrial societies," he too saw something prophetic in these students' refusal of hierarchy and of bureaucratic discipline.[33]

THE OUTRAGE OF VIOLENCE

Because of their sensitivity to the means-end question, the existentialists have always been plagued by the problem of political violence, violence in service of the cause of freedom.

Contrary to some critics' opinion, Sartre has never favored violence for its own sake. In fact he has explicitly condemned such senseless violence, a violence, as he puts it, "in love with itself." But violence "born of exploitation and oppression," that is something else.[34] Such violence is really counterviolence; and he recommends it as a last, necessary resort.

Such is the violence prescribed to the native in Sartre's preface to Frantz Fanon's *The Wretched of the Earth*. This essay was a scandal to the liberal establishment because it linked all who benefited from colonial exploitation with the violence inherent in that system: "the settler which is in every one of us."[35] Like the moral prophet and the conscience of the age, which he doubtless was, Sartre aimed to unmask what he took to be our collective bad faith with the challenge: either victim or executioner. Violence is unavoidable, he argues; the question is, in the name of what will it be employed?

If violence is everywhere, will it ever come to an end? To answer this, we must delve into what beyond our common usage Sartre means by *violence*. In the *Critique* he describes it in existentialist terms: "The only conceivable violence is that of freedom against freedom through the mediation of inorganic matter." Like the look in *Being and Nothingness*, violence is a reciprocal negation of freedoms through the intermediary of matter. Material mediation once more makes the difference. Only with the *elimination* of *scarcity*, "should this ever occur"[36], can we hope for a nonviolent society.

In the meantime, violence will continue to be the thread of our social fabric, and this in two directions. Either it will serve to destroy the other's freedom outright or "place it in parentheses" by manipulation, mystification, and the like; or it will be directed against the abuse of freedom within the group whereby one's brother becomes an other.

Sartre calls this latter violence "terror"; the inner life of the pledged group is thus one of fraternity-terror.

Once more, the existentialists differ in the matter of violence just as they differ on the question of dirty hands, and for similar reasons. Yet whether in Merleau-Ponty's *Humanism and Terror*, Sartre's Fanon preface, or Camus' play, *The Just Assassins,* a deep concern for what de Beauvoir calls "the outrage of violence"[37] permeates the thought of political existentialism and stands as a challenge to contemporary thought.

POLITICAL EXISTENTIALISM AND THE WESTERN PHILOSOPHICAL CONVERSATION

The three marks of political existentialism as well as the foregoing challenges suffice to give it entry into that ongoing dialogue that is the Western philosophical tradition. But at what juncture should its voice be heard? This is a matter of *pedigree*, on the one hand, and of *current relevance* on the other.

Concerning pedigree it should be noted first that despite Sartre's excessive remarks in *Search for a Method* about existentialism's being to Marxism as ideology to knowledge, political existentialism is not simply a "Marxification" of its own theses in philosophic anthropology. Indeed, in Sartre's case and even more in that of Merleau-Ponty, it is "Marxism" that stands in adjectival position to "existentialism."

Sartre's antecedents in political philosophy seem to lie among those in France who influenced Marx himself, namely, the libertarian socialists and ultimately Rousseau. Whether it be his concept of the mediating third party judging and action *as if* he or she were part of an organic whole, or his distrust of an alienating bureaucracy whose paradigm is the state, Sartre's political theory resembles most that of the anarchists. Rather than meandering politically, therefore, Sartre was coming home when in his final years, he took up the cause of libertarian *groupuscules* in the struggle against institutional authority.[38]

This raises the question of whether Merleau-Ponty and Camus, to the extent that they favored representative rather than participatory democracy, were not thereby moving away from existentialism itself. The answer depends on how radically we understand our three hallmarks, especially individual freedom.

Turning from pedigree to current relevance, I would offer two considerations: first, that the events of May 1968 in Paris were the most perfect incarnation of political existentialism that we have seen and, secondly, that what these happenings, now more than a dozen years old, continue to tell us is what political existentialism basically has to say.

Briefly, it will be recalled and that for a few days that spring thousands of students and sympathizers took to the streets of the Latin Quarter in an effort initially to effect changes in an outmoded educational system. The move quickly escalated into demands for sweeping reforms, not only in government but in socioeconomic relations generally. What had been called the largest strike in French history ensued. For a short time, it seemed as if the government might fall. Certainly, embarrassing cracks appeared in the monolith of the Fifth Republic. Georges Pompidou admitted that "nothing would ever be the same again."[39] A professor at Nanterre described these events as a "Sartrean" revolution.[40] Its spontaneity, humanistic concern, moral outrage, spirit of comradery (reciprocity), and profoundly antiauthoritarian flavor resembled closely that "sudden resurrection of freedom" by which Sartre characterized the fused group in the *Critique*.[41] As if to ratify their deeds, the students invited Sartre to address them in the main hall of the Sorbonne at the height of this uprising. Significantly, he reaffirmed that he considered socialism and freedom inseparable: "If you don't insist on that first of all" he warned, "you'll lose freedom for several years and then socialism."[42]

And what can we learn from this brief experience and from the political existentialism that, *ex hypothesi*, helped inspire it? I would underscore five lessons in political philosophy that they hold for our times:

1. The overriding value of the human individual as someone whose freedom makes both cooperation and betrayal equally possible.
2. The need to create *human situations* (bases and structures of choice) so that this freedom can be exercised positively.
3. The importance of faith in the power of face-to-face relationships and of the conviction that bureaucracies tend inevitably toward dehumanization.
4. An abiding sense of the *moral* dimension of every human undertaking and of the corresponding respect due the ethics of *means* as well as ends.
5. A new regard for *political imagination* as the necessary vehicle for appreciating the nonnecessity of the present and the possibilities of the future.

None of these lessons is exclusively that of political existentialism, much less the sole property of the events of May 1968. Several of them will figure in the message of any popular revolution. But the entire set as mounted in the historical setting of existentialism itself (the *terminus a quo* mentioned above) and further contextualized by reference to the problems of alienation and bad faith in our high-technology, mass societies, speaks to the conscience of our age. Political existentialism is a voice in the conversation, not the end of the discussion.

Epilogue: *"Pouvoir et Liberté"*

At the time of his death in April 1980, Sartre was at work with Benny Lévy on a *livre à deux* that, he claimed, would require that all of his previous work be seen in a new light. The focus of the study, to be called "Power and Freedom," was an ontology and an ethic of the "We."[43]

Although the volume has not appeared and, if and when it does, will constitute a hermeneutical nightmare, its projected title is significant. For it suggests that the two-armed anchor of political existentialism will not secure the ideal community until the winds of power have permanently subsided. If the realist in Sartre warned of dirty hands in the business of politics, the aging revolutionary who lived through the hope and ultimate failure of 1968 has come to see that the dismantling of political power in the modern state is not the work of a spring afternoon. And yet his final treatment to us is one of hope: "The world seems ugly, evil and without hope. That's the peaceful despair of an old man who will die in it. But the point is that I am resisting and I know that I shall die in hope."[44]

4. Interests, Justice, and Respect for Law in Merleau-Ponty's Phenomenology

WILLIAM S. HAMRICK

What will Merleau-Ponty's phenomenology of the social world permit us to say, if anything, in defense of the ideal of respect for law? Within the limits of this brief essay, I would like to examine one aspect of the complex answer to this question, namely, the relationship of interests, justice, and their legal embodiments and how the latter effectively threaten the possibility of our respect for law and fidelity to it.

I shall first indicate why the problem exists, in Merleau-Ponty's view; and then I shall briefly summarize an early and decisively negative response to the possibility of upholding the values at issue here. (This takes place largely within texts such as *Sens et non-sens* and *Humanisme et terreur*.) Then I shall try to work out the sense of a much later— and, as far as I can tell, rather final—answer (in *Les Aventures de la dialectique*). The latter statement of his views is, by and large, much more conciliatory than its predecessors but I think also much more puzzling.

Within Merleau-Ponty's early works, the reason why the relationship of interests and justice threatens respect for law emerges from the following considerations. In the first place, human existence may be accurately defined by its power to transcend what is actual by conceiving of and/or respecting what it is not. And in this self-defining exercise, we can detect the origins of society, law, and culture: "It suffices to make some men live together and to associate in one and the same task for them to work out of their life in common some rudimentary rules and a beginning of law. In considering things thus, one has the feeling that men have immense resources. . . . There is something to say in favor of the 'natural light.' Men secrete culture in some way without willing it. The human world, as different as it might be from the natural or animal world, is in some way *natural for man*."[1]

But culture is not secreted in a vacuum, nor is any one cultural aspect generated independently of all the others. Rather, the whole culture stands to each of its aspects as a gestalt whole does to its parts: the latter can be brought into focus only against the contextual background of the whole culture, they are related interdependently rather than independently *partes extra partes*, and each of them mirrors the whole. Thus, Merleau-Ponty noted in the *Phénoménologie de la perception* that "the conception of law, morals, religion, and economic structure mutually signify each other in the unity of the social event as the parts of the body imply one another in the unity of a gesture . . . and it is impossible to reduce interhuman life either to economic relations or to juridical and moral relationships thought by men, as it is impossible to reduce individual life either to corporal functions or to the knowledge that we have of that life."[2]

For this reason Max Weber was correct to point out the profound unity in the various aspects of a culture's historical development: there is a "prodigious interlacing of reciprocal influences among the material infrastructures, the forms of social and political organization, and the spiritual content of the cultural age of the Reformation."[3] As a result of "the ambiguity of historic facts, their *Vielseitigkeit*," Merleau-Ponty noted that "religion, law, and economics make up one sole history because each fact of one of the three orders brings out in a sense the two others, and it even belongs to their nature that they all insert themselves in the unique web of human choices" (*AD*, p. 28).

For Weber as for Merleau-Ponty there is a fundamental "solidarity of the economic order with that of the political, the juridical, and the oral or religious, starting from the moment when even an economic fact is treated as a choice of a relationship with men and with the world and takes it place in the logic of choice."[4] This being so, as the major lines of force emerge in a given society that determines its economic and political allegiances, the kind of legal system that will develop is already implicated in those other choices. Thus, for example, "Capitalism for Weber supposes a certain technique of production and through it science in the Western sense, but also a certain type of law, a government founded on formal rules without which the capitalism of adventure or of speculation is possible, but not the bourgeois enterprise." (*AD*, p. 26).

But since law as well as other interrelated aspects of a social system emerge as the expression of concrete interests shared by the majority of participants in the system, justice may be threatened in a variety of different ways. For example, the interwining of politics and principles may, and often does, erode impartial administration of the law. Eugen Ehrlich once said and no less a jurist than Benjamin Cardozo agreed that "there is no guaranty of justice except the personality of the judge."[5] But more fundamentally, partial interests can be and are written into constitutions and/or positive laws in what concerns the distribution of property, civil and criminal rights, and so forth. This is not the same as the cynical and too easy accusation of law as sanctioning the equation of might with right. For it is logically consistent with this view to say that there could be quite enlightened legal systems that make special provisions in various ways to protect minority rights, to neutralize the overlap of politics and the creation of law, and so on. And it is also true that there are many different modes of such intertwining, some of which are far more suspect than others.

But whatever the degree of evil in a particular legal system, this description of the relation of law to other social phenomena shows why at least the threat of injustice is always posed and with it the twilight of the idol of respect for law. As Lon Fuller complained of certain constitutions that came into existence after World War II, they had not uncommonly had built into them

> a host of economic and political measures of the type one would ordinarily associate with a statutory law. It is hardly likely that these measures have been written into the constitution because they represent aims that are generally shared. One suspects that the reason for their inclusion is precisely the opposite, namely, a fear that they would not be able to survive the vicissitudes of an ordinary exercise of parliamentary power. Thus, the divisions of opinion that are a normal accompaniment of lawmaking are written into the document that makes law itself possible. This is obviously a procedure that contains serious dangers for a future realization of the ideal of fidelity to law.[6]

Now there is no evidence that Merleau-Ponty ever read Fuller. But certainly the former's first position on the ideal of respect for law could easily appropriate the latter's observations as grist for his sceptical mill. For, one of the most serious motifs of *Humanisme et terreur* is in effect to prolong and generalize Fuller's critiques to apply to all major Western democracies. Just as the subtitle to *The Twilight of the Idols* is "How One Philosophizes with a Hammer"—how one uses the tuning fork of a more highly developed consciousness to sound out the hollowness of the old idols—so also is this motif in *Humanisme et terreur* pure Nietzsche. Its aim is to expose for its unwitting victims a fundamental hypocrisy in the putative contrast of Communism, lies, propaganda, and political realism on the one hand, with respect for truth, for law, for individual consciences, and for liberal values on the other hand. This contrast is but a "liberal mystification"[7] because all societies are violent—either necessarily or contingently. Obviously, much turns on the interpretation preferred, but Merleau-Ponty is far from clear as to which it is. But in any case, he tells us that in "the liberal State," law is used as a shield for violence and for the protection of special interests (*HT*, p. 122, 139). As a result between Marxist states and liberal democracies, "it is only a question of different modalities of one fundamental situation" (*HT*, p. 122). As he was to say much later in *Signes*, the doctrines of "liberal humanism" and "formal democracy" are in ruins[8] because laws are fundamentally interested, rather than disinterested, phenomena that exist at the intersection of politics, economics, private moralities, and so forth.

Hidden under the liberalism of pure ideas, "the juridical dream" of liberalism of merely formal rules, law as it really exists in Western democracies produces "an aggressive liberalism that is a dogma and already an ideology of war" (*HT*, pp. 66, 18). The Marxist knows that because "each human initiative polarizes interests all of which are not acknowledged" (*HT*, p. 87). Laws that let capitalists be treated as ends in themselves treat workers as mere means to those ends. Thus, "In a world in struggle, no one can flatter himself by having clean hands" (*HT*, p. 87). No one, that is, except children, precisely because they are not yet struggling: "Children alone imagine that their lives are separable from those of others, that their responsibility limits itself to what they have done themselves, and that there is a frontier between good and evil" (*HT*, p. 87).

Now, one way of meeting this well known sort of Marxist objection and trying to maintain respect for law is to disentangle the particular values of a given society from the formal values that make up the moral point of view itself. For example, H.L.A. Hart attempts this by separating the "formal values" and "material values" that are both necessary ingredients "in the practice of any social morality."[9] The material values refer to the content of the morality dominant in the particular society; and laws that crystallized these interests in enforcing a moral conservatism could certainly be vulnerable to Merleau-Ponty's criticisms. But at the same time, an essential fairness in the administration of the law could still instantiate the "formal values" of social morality that preserve the moral point of view in the first place: "In moral relationships with others the individual sees questions of conduct from an impersonal point of view and applies general rules impartially to himself and to others; he is made aware of and takes account of the wants, expectations, and reactions of others; he exerts self-discipline and control in adapting his conduct to a system of reciprocal claims. These are universal virtues and indeed constitute the specifically moral attitude to conduct."[10]

But there is little, if anything, to suggest that the author of *Humanisme et terreur* would accept any such form/matter bifurcation as being able to defend the ideal of respect for law in "formal democracies"—at least for those in which law implements, defends, and consolidates a capitalist system. This is so because in his straightforwardly Marxist criticisms, such a system is already exploitative and therefore unjust. Thus, it is not so much form as it is content that determines the respectability of law. Or, more precisely, content will shape from depending on what social values are being sedimented in the cultural gestalt. And no respect is possible for law that is but an outer shell of an inner core of institutional violence—whether overtly as in the USSR or covertly and hypocritically as in Western democracies.

This much of Merleau-Ponty's views on the respectability of law may be controversial but at least it is clear. Indeed, I find it uncharacteristically clear. But when one looks at its denouement in *Les Aventures de la dialectique*, his arguments become more normally murky. In the "Epilogue" of this text, he considers the possibility of respect for law in the political context of a "new liberalism" (AD, p. 303). He sees this politics of a non-communist left as the best way of coming to grips with a world polarized between those forces that are nostalgic about Communism and those who try to avoid seeing all the problems of the "free world" on the pretext of an anti-Communist defense (*AD*, pp. 301, 302). The *new* liberalism is to be distinguished sharply from its obsolete predecessor that Merleau-Ponty perceives to be an optimistic, superficial philosophy that reduces social history to "speculative conflicts of opinion, political struggle to exchanges of viewpoint on a clearly posed problem, and human coexistence to the relations of cocitizens in an empyrean politics" (*AD*, p. 303).

On the contrary, class struggle exists and must exist because there are classes, and the proletariat has a legal (and moral) right to achieve social representation and to strike. It has a legal (and moral) "right to have itself represented, if it wishes, by a party that refuses the rules of the democratic game, because this game disfavors it. The Communist Part is and must be legal" (*AD*, p. 303). This is not desired because the "new liberalism" secretly wants after all to bring about the revolution that will install a dictatorship of the proletariat, but rather because "Communist action and revolutionary movements are only accepted as a useful danger, as a continual reminder of order" (*AD*, p. 303). The non-Communist left "does not believe in the solution of the social problem by the power of the proletarian class or by its representatives, and . . . one only awaits progress from an action that would be conscientious and confronts the judgment of an opposition. . . . A non-Communist left is for us this double part taken of posing the social problem in terms of struggle and of refusing the dictatorship of the proletariat" (*AD*, pp. 303–304).

Merleau-Ponty's defense of the legal rights of the Communist Party makes it plan that he considers one essential ingredient in making law worthy of respect that it permit freedom of discussion and the experience of opposition that are, in his view, both necessary for discovering the truth. (In this respect the new liberalism is not very different from the old, and one is certainly struck by the almost total absence of references to Mill and Bentham throughout Merleau-Ponty's writings.) But such a position, unelaborated and unqualified, only begins rather than ends serious debates. It does not conclude but rather generates many well known discussions in the philosophy of law about respect for law, the difficulties of democratic, freedom-loving societies tolerating intoler-ance,[11] and First Amendment debates about sedition laws and the limits of free expression.

Even though the non-Communist left does not wish the revolution that will bring about the dictatorship of the proletariat, it proposes to tolerate and sanction the legal rights of the Communist Party because the latter is a "useful danger." But what if its danger is no longer useful because the revolution is, or seems to be, imminent? If the dictatorship of the proletariat became a live option in a society of which the non-Communist left were the dominant party, would the legal rights of the Communist Party be restricted or eliminated? More-over, then or now, would the new liberalism attempt to provide us with a conceptually clear and legally enforceable distinction between advocating revolution and actively fomenting it? As Joel Feinberg indicates, "The focus of the disagreement over sedition laws is the status of *advocacy*. The normal law of words quite clearly outlaws counseling, urging, or demanding (under certain conditions) that others resort to crime or engage in riots, assassinations, or insurrections. But what if a person uses language not directly to counsel or call for violence but rather (where this is different) to *advocate* it?"[12]

As Feinberg goes on to point out, after the Russian Revolution, flamboyant spokesmen for working-class parties in the United States "were commonly charged with violations of the Federal Espionage Act during and after World War I, of state sedition laws in the 1920s, and, after World War II, of the Smith Act," but their trials "for advocacy of revolution tended to be extremely difficult and problematic partly because it was never clear whether revolution in any usual sense was something taught and approved by them, and partly because it was unclear whether the form of reference to revolution in the Marxist ideology amounted to 'advocacy' of it."[13]

Well, it is certain that the Communist Party, the legal rights of which Merleau-Ponty is concerned to defend, wants to say far more than that "there are conceivable circumstances under which revolution would be justified."[14] Rather, the circumstances are actual and pressing. So perhaps in the legal system of a society it dominated—however temporarily, the new liberalism would resort to something like Oliver Wendell Holmes' "clear and present danger" test from his famous opinion in *United States* v. *Schenck*: "the character of every act dependes upon the circumstances in which it is done. . . . The most stringent protection of free speech would not protect a man in falsely shouting fire in a theatre, and causing a panic. . . . The question in every case is whether the words used are used in such circumstances and are of such a nature as to create a clear and present danger that they will bring about the substantive evils that Congress has a right to prevent. It is a question of proximity and degree."[15]

In any event, in the absence of such clarifications, it is impossible to say exactly how liberal the new liberalism would be in terms of tolerating intolerance—particularly with reference to the Communist Party; and it is therefore likewise difficult to say exactly how Merleau-Ponty conceived the limits of freedom of discussion and respect for law that can make it possible. Nor is this problem squarely addressed in what makes up the remainder of his new political commitment, namely, a defense of parliamentary democracy.

This defense is developed as a response to the following objection posed by Communists to the new liberalism. Suppose that it is true that the non-Communist left wants to address the social problem in terms of both struggle and a refusal of the dictatorship of the proletariat (*AD*, p. 304). Nevertheless, struggle can only be for power; and a non-Communist left is either condemned to exercising power in a "parliamentary and bourgeois sense"—which is to say, not at all—or else what power is available to the new liberalism is "only for it a transition toward dictatorship," and in that case, the non-Communist left is "crypto-Communist" after all (*AD*, p. 304).

Merleau-Ponty's reply to this argument has essentially two prongs. First, political action of the members of a non-Communist left can be distinguished from that of the Communists because the former, unlike the latter, enjoy a "liberty of criticism" adequate for clearly posing "the problem of the nature of the Soviet State" (*AD*, p. 304). Clarification of the social problem "appears impossible in principle in a Communist regime but possible in the non-Communist world" (*AD*, p. 306).

The second prong of Merleau-Ponty's reply focuses on "the limits of parliamentary and democratic action" (*AD*, p. 304). As concerns the ideal of fidelity to law, this is clearly the most important part of the new liberalism, and it is here that its author moves substantially beyond his earlier texts described above. Merleau-Ponty's later view is as follows:

> As for the limits of parliamentary and democratic action, there are some that belong to the institution; and they must be accepted because Parliament is the only known institution that guarantees a minimum of opposition and of truth. There are others that pertain to parliamentary customs and to manoeuvres; these have no right to any respect. But they can be denounced in Parliament itself. Parliamentary mystification consists in not posing true problems or in only posing them obliquely or too late. A non-Communist left could do much against it. (*AD*, p. 304)

Before we can raise critical questions about Merleau-Ponty's hopes and expectations of parliamentary democracy, we need briefly to look at the conclusion of his defense of the new liberalism. This consists of a poignant observation that he has advanced no "solution" to the social problem in the sense of a "solution to a crossword puzzle or to an elementary problem of arithmetic. It is rather the resolution to keep in hand the two ends of the chain, the social problem and liberty" (*AD*, p. 305). Geographically as well as ideologically, he finds himself defending a position with no effective base of support, suspended between Communism and capitalism. Both are for him, in the last analysis, examples of what E. E. Cummings derided as ideas that "like Gillette Razor Blades having been used and reused to the mystical moment of dullness emphatically are Not to Be Resharpened."[16]

But even in this conclusion, it is capitalism rather than Communism that receives the harsher criticism. "The only postulate" of his politics, he tells us, is that it not be only or necessarily a defense of capitalism. There can be a dialectic if capitalism ceases to be a "rigid apparatus, with *its* politics, its ideologies, its imperious laws of functioning; and if instead of its contradictions, another politics *than its* could come about" (*AD*, p. 305).

With this conclusion to Merleau-Ponty's politics before us, we may now take up certain critical questions about the way that respect for law is bound up with a respect for parliamentary democracy. Now a fairly obvious set of condictions have to be satisfied so that parliament could serve as "the only known institution that guarantees a minimum of opposition and of truth" (*AD*, p. 304). For example, legislators must adhere to fairly passed and administered procedural rules, the legislature must be constituted and function in such a way that it is really responsive to the needs of the people, and parliamentary debates must be real truth-finding exercises rather than mere window dressing for power politics. It must be possible to disentangle principles from politics, or, in Merleau-Ponty's own idiom, those limits of parliamentary action that pertain to the nature of the institution as distinct from those that are only manoeuvres.

But has anything in Merleau-Ponty's view of law and the political process prepared for this confident assurance that principles and politics can be so neatly unhinged from each other? Indeed, what is now being proposed is very much like what Hart argued in trying to distinguish moral conservatism from the preservation of morality. Or, as Joel Feinberg put it in a legislative context, "We must think of an ideal legislator as somewhat abstracted from the full legislative context, in that he is free to appear directly to the public interest unencumbered by the need to please voters, to make 'deals' with colleagues, or any other merely 'political' considerations."[17] But if some such view really does lie at the core of Merleau-Ponty's respect for parliamentary democracy, this bifurcation of the "form" of parliamentary procedure from the "matter" of political and economic interests remains puzzling to the degree that, as we have already seen, *Adventures of the Dialectic* merely elaborates rather than alters his earlier view of the basic intertwining of law and social interests in the concrete gestalt of the social world.

Moreover, this same difficulty also extends to Merleau-Ponty's conclusion in which he so thoroughly repudiates capitalism: "A non-Communist left is no more bound to free enterprise than to the dictatorship of the proletariat" (*AD*, p. 305). He also makes it plain that his defense of, and respect for, parliamentary democracy, is not reserved for utopias but rather for his actual historical situation. This is so because the social problem is posed in terms of "struggle," and he is admittedly offering no "solutions" to it. But suppose we ask whether we can respect and be faithful to a parliamentary democracy in any given capitalist system, which is almost certainly his intended locus for carrying on the struggle. Given all that Merleau-Ponty has told us, it seems that the answer could be "yes" only if it were grounded on unreasonable expectations or else by capitulating after all to one of the Communist objections noted above, namely, that the new liberalism cannot effectively struggle for power. That is, the essential condition for respecting a parliamentary democracy in a capitalist system would have to be that, in Merleau-Ponty's view, it allow itself to become a forum for presenting real, as opposed to merely theoretical, challenges to the society's economic order. In a very important way, respect for law here would be keyed to the legal system's ability to allow its legislature to work against it. But precisely because of the nature of the social gestalt and because of what Max Weber said about the connection between formal rules and the development of capitalism, one would expect to find ample constitutional protections of free enterprises that would certainly dampen, if not entirely frustrate, Merleau-Ponty's hopes for what parliamentary democracy could accomplish.

It is true that Merleau-Ponty is not placing all his faith in a system of formal rules as such—if they could even exist. As we saw above, he was to say in *Signes* (5 years later) that that sort of doctrine is "in ruins." But, on the other hand, it is not clear either that he is entitled here to much comfort from his commitment to parliamentary democracy. Perhaps he would even agree to this and say that the narrowed scope of his expectations is why he does not view the non-Communist left as a solution. And perhaps he would say that respect for parliamentary democracy can be maintained on the weaker claim that it can serve as the honest forum of serious debate about, say, basic constitutional protections of free enterprises. If this is all the new liberalism comes to, however, despite its attractiveness as a political program and for what it entails as concerns the respect possible for law, I am not sure that Merleau-Ponty avoids the Communist allegation of giving up the struggle for power in favor of ideas, words, and perhaps empyrean politics after all. Something, it would seem, must be given up one way or another. Of course, Marxists have disagreed among themselves about what is necessary to bring about the revolution[18] but the Communists Merleau-Ponty is considering would hardly agree to limit the means of legal change to parliamentary debate and social tactics such as, say, noncoercive lobbying.

So in conclusion, it may be that Merleau-Ponty's own final statement on politics and what it implies for respecting law is not a "solution" for reasons other than those he himself had in mind. We shall never know. Many papers on his theories of perception, art, and ontology—including those by the present author—break off at the point of obscurity in interpretation with a lament about Merleau-Ponty's premature death and the unfinished state of his last papers. That cannot be my refuge here, however, since in writing a social philosophy, he lost not his life, but his interest.

5. "What Must I Do?" at the End of Metaphysics: Ethical Norms and the Hypothesis of a Historical Closure

REINER SCHÜRMANN

The *nomos* is not only the law but more originally the injunction contained in the dispensation of being. Only this injunction is capable of inserting man into being. Only such insertion is capable of supporting and carrying. Otherwise, all law remains merely the artifact of human reason. More essential than instituting laws is that man find the way into the truth of being so as to dwell there.[1]

These lines from Heidegger's *Letter on Humanism* indicate how ethical norms fare in his general project of deconstructing metaphysics. They appear as conditioned by what he calls "dispensations," *Schickungen*. This is clearly a transcendental move: Heidegger, in these lines, steps back from the fact of law to a set of conditions that make such a fact possible. What is the a priori condition of law in general and of ethical norms in particular? "The injunction (*Zuweisung*) contained in the dispensation of being." Stated otherwise: the conditions are provided by the modality according to which at any given time in history, phenomena enter into relation with one another. What makes a law—presumably not only positive, but also natural and divine law— possible is the constellation of phenomenal interconnectedness in which we "dwell" in a given age or into which we are "inserted." It is "more essential," then, to obey that epochal constellation of *aletheia* than to decree and enforce laws. Our primary obligation is, it seems, to the *nomos* as aletheiological; and our secondary obligation to the *nomos* as "rational." The law as "artifact of human reason" reads like a barely veiled allusion to Kant and to the law that reason gives to itself. Are we to understand that the moral *ought* by which pure practical reason binds itself is as secondary as positive law? What is sure is that the lines quoted curiously turn Kant against himself. The distinction between *nomos* as a binding epochal order and *nomos* as an act of reason historically locates Kant's quest for universality and necessity in morality. With Kant we had become confident that what is right and wrong can be discovered by any rational being; but now we hear that such trust in reason is indicative of but one way of finding oneself "inserted" into the history of being—but one way of responding to the "injunction contained in the dispensation of being."

If this is an acceptable account of Heidegger's strategy in the epigraph above, one understands that the question, "When are you going to write an ethics?," posed to him shortly after 1927,[2] arose from a misunderstanding about the radical character of his undertaking. It is radical indeed because it amounts to uprooting a certain rational rootage of morality. And before lamenting a defeat of reason and a return of the irrational, it would be wise to see how such a subversion can legitimate itself.

A first legitimation for historically locating norms and normative ethics can be found in the very content of Heidegger's "turning," *Kehre*, around 1930. What he discovered then was that being-in-the-world has a history; that the existential structures spelled out in *Being and Time* are not as timeless as they seemed there. The "history of being" affects all areas of life, the ones traditionally called theoretical as well as the ones traditionally called practical. The rule of norms has its history and so does the very quest for universal and necessary principles for action.

A second, and more decisive, justification stems from the subject matter that provides the starting point for the phenomenology of the later Heidegger: no longer our daily activities in a world made of things ready-to-hand, but technology. And technology as one era in Western history. Just as for Kant the point of departure is the *fact* of experience and the *question* of a priori conditions, so for the later Heidegger the point of departure is the *fact* of technology and the *question* of "being." These two foci allow him to speak of technology as the end of metaphysics. And if it should turn out that this end may be described by a withering away of norms, in a sense to be specified, then the two foci compel us in turn to ask: What happens to the question, "What must I do?" at the end of metaphysics? And furthermore: What must I do at the end of metaphysics?

"What Must I Do" at the End of Metaphysics

Epochal Principles and the Hypothesis of Closure

It used to be the awesome task of philosophers to secure an organizing first principle to which theoreticians of ethics, politics, law, and so forth could look so as rationally to anchor their own discourse. These points of ultimate moorage provide legitimacy to the *principia*, the propositions held to be self-evident in the order of intelligibility. They also provide legitimacy to the *princeps*, the ruler or the institution retaining ultimate power in the order of authority. They lay out the paths that the course of exploitations and the discourse of explications follow, and they are observed without question in a given epoch. When questions are raised about them, the network of exchange that they have opened becomes confused, and the order that they have founded declines. A principle—the sensible substance for Aristotle, the Christian God for the Medievals, the cogito for the moderns—has its ascent, its period of reign, and its ruin. We can trace the rise, the sway, and the decline of a mode of presence so instituted by a First, that is, we can trace the *archē*, the origin as the founding act of an era. We can also unearth the theoretical and practical foundations on which that era rested, its origin in the sense of both *principium* and *princeps*. But the question is whether we can speak of an origin from which has issued that very lineage of representations held to be authoritative, measure giving. Can we speak of a beginning and an end of the various guises that the awesome task of construing a "first philosophy" or "general metaphysics" has assumed? Is the disintegration felt in the human and social sciences an indicator that these principles have a pedigree, their genealogy and necrology? I should like to suggest that we may have more to gain from hastening the withering away of what I will call epochal principles than from attempts at their resuscitation.

The first to draw a genealogy of those figures esteemed highest for an age was Nietzsche. In one single page he spelled out what has become the model for today's deconstructionists and archeologists of knowledge. In that one page, entitled "How the 'True World' Finally Became a Fable,"[3] Nietzsche enumerates six stages of the metaphysical First. In each state the First served to regulate and sanction all things knowable and doable for a time, and through these stages it progressively exhausts itself in that function. These stages are: Plato's "virtuous man," Christian salvation, Kantian duty, positivism, the "free spirit" of scepticism, and finally Nietzsche's own joyful nihilism, at which stage the "true world" has become a fable. What Nietzsche sees fading away is not just any one representation of an ideal, but the sequence itself of ultimate standards for thinking and acting. His "gay science" consists in saluting the "high point of humanity" when the old quest for an unshakable and indubitable ground has come to an end and when "innocence is restored to becoming."

This genealogy of metaphysics in Nietzsche allows us to determine a little further the concept of epochal principles. They rest entirely on the representation of a relation that Aristotle called the *pros hen* (relation to the one). They are an entity to which knowing and doing—theory and practice—are referred as to a yardstick. I may add that in Aristotle the *pros hen* relation properly obtains only in the context of fabrication, in which all steps of manufacturing are oriented towards the object to be produced and in which the "idea" to be realized in wood or marble serves as the working measure. From the *Physics* to the *Metaphysics* occurs that *metabasis eis allo genos*, that undue transposition, by which the *pros hen* relationship becomes the heart of any first philosophy and this first philosophy, a doctrine of an ultimate ground.

Nietzsche's genealogy also allows us to introduce another technical term that will serve to designate the locus to which our ignorance concerning morality in the social sciences points. This term is "hypothesis of closure." Nietzsche's genealogy of the "ideal world" operates under the hypothesis that the centuries in which theory and practice could be measured by some one ideal yardstick have come to a close. Hence the subtitle given by him to that page: "History of an Error."

Epochal principles and the hypothesis of closure constitute the two coordinates of Heidegger's "deconstruction of metaphysics." As is well known, at the end of the Introduction to *Being and Time*, he announced a "phenomenological destruction of the history of ontology."[4] Later he spoke of the "deconstruction [*Abbau*] of representations that have become current and empty [so as] to win back metaphysics's originative experiences of being."[5] On the general project, he does not deny his partial indebtedness to "Nietzsche, in whose light and shadow everyone today thinks and poetizes with his 'for him' or 'against him'."[6] The indebtedness is patent when Heidegger enumerates the epochal principles that in his view have concretely ruled over Western history: "the ideas, God, the Moral Law, the authority of Reason, Progress, the Happiness of the greatest number, Culture, Civilization." But his indebtedness is patent also when he places this sequence under the hypothesis of closure. Metaphysics is that historical space, he writes, wherein it becomes our destiny that these figures "lose their constructive force and become nothing."[7] Thus, the deconstruction is the method of laying bare the sequence of epochal principles under the presupposition of the hypothesis of closure. On this hypothesis, Heidegger is very cautious. His thinking prefers to move "about" the line that encircles the closed field of metaphysics rather than "across" that line ("*über die Linie*" in the sense of "*de linea*" rather than of "*trans lineam*").[8] Elsewhere, however, he clearly states that to raise the question "What is Metaphysics?" already amounts, "in a certain way, to having left metaphysics behind."[9] What counts is that the method of deconstruction is a topological one: it assigns us our place, namely on the borderline where "special metaphysics" is uprooted from "general metaphysics," the body of human and social sciences from "first philosophy," or still more generally, cultural discourse from philosophical discourse.

It should be noted that the deconstruction remains phenomenological. The principles are not construed speculatively, but described as epochal forms of the a priori. This phenomenology is thus transcendental not in that phenomena are examined according to their subjective conditions but in that the principles provide the synchronically universal and necessary conditions according to which all that appears can show itself. This phenomenological method can be transcendental and yet at the same time antihumanistic for the simple reason that its starting point consists in a move away from man as constitutive of presence. Its starting point is, as I said, the discovery that being-in-the-world (or the "life world") has a history. The point of departure of this entire enterprise thus is nothing very innovative. It is the very traditional wonderment before the epochs and their slippages: How is it possible to account for the fact that in the heart of an epochal enclosure (those enclosures called "polis," "Roman Empire," "Middle Ages," etc., or, according to a scarcely more discriminating division, "seventeenth," "eighteenth," "nineteenth" centuries), certain practices are possible and even necessary, which are not possible in others? How does it happen that a Revolution was impossible in the Middle Ages, just as an International was during the French Revolution, and a Cultural Revolution was at the moment of the First International? Or, according to a perspective that is less alien to the question of the "principles" than it may seem: How does it happen that a Duns Scotus, although surnamed *Doctor subtilis*, could no more write a critique of pure reason than Kant a genealogy of morals? How does it happen, in other words, that a domain of the possible and necessary is instituted, endures for a time, and then cedes under the effect of a mutation? "How does it happen?": a descriptive question asking for conditions of possibility and not to be confounded with the etiological question: "Why is it that . . . ?" The causal solutions brought to bear on these phenomena of mutation, be they 'speculative," "economist," or whatever, leave us unsatisfied for the very reason of the causal presupposition that they cannot question—which they cannot *situate*, for this presupposition is only an epochal incidence of the *pros hen* schema.

With the "turning" in Heidegger's thinking, what comes to be first in the order of phenomenal constitution is no longer man's "project," but the modalities of presence, the ever new aletheiological constellations, that is, the "history of being." Within the closed field of metaphysics, these constellations are governed by the representation of a most real ground. "The *principia* are such as stand in the first place, in the most advanced rank. The *principia* refer to rank and order . . . . We follow them without meditation."[10] This is not to say that they have any efficacy of their own—an idealist construction for which Karl Marx already derided Proudhon.

> Each principle has had its own century in which to manifest itself. The principles of authority, for example, had the eleventh century, just as the principle of individualism had the eighteenth century. Consequently, it was the century that belonged to the principle, and not the principle that belonged to the century. In other words, it was the principle that made the history.[11]

No hypostatization of this kind can occur in the deconstruction because it remains confined to describing modalities of presence. These modalities have nothing noumenal. Nor are they empirical facts: the deconstruction is not an historicist enterprise either. Between the Scylla of noumenal history and the Charybdis of mere historicism, it follows the middle road of the categorial. Basic categorial features of presence that remain the same throughout the "history of being" are, for instance, in Heidegger's vocabulary, "concealedness and unconcealedness." But a historical deduction of categories would reveal more "pervasive traits"[12] than these two.

The word *deconstruction* has been popularized more recently by Jacques Derrida.[13] Although he is more triumphant than Heidegger about the hypothesis of closure,[14] and although he adds to this method a few useful concepts—logocentrism, différence/différance, and so forth—I fail to see how, on the issue of deconstruction itself, Derrida goes beyond Heidegger as he claims he does.[15]

The hypothesis of closure rests entirely on a phenomenology of technology that, for Heidegger, is essentially ambiguous. In the global reach of technology, principal thinking comes to its fullest deployment. At the same time, this climax may signify its consummation. To Heidegger the ambiguity of technology is suggested by Hölderlin's lines: "But where danger is, grows / The saving power also."[16] Technology is essentially Janus-faced, looking backwards with the most rigidly principial gaze ever and forwards with what can be described as anarchy.

The *"Principle of Anarchy"*

We are now in a position to look anew at the question What must I do? and at the way it is tied to the fate of metaphysics. If it is true that the question of norms depends essentially on a first philosophy— or a critique of practical reason, on a critique of pure reason—and if on the other hand, technology "closes" the era of such derivations, then technology places us in a peculiar state of ignorance. With the withering of ultimate principles, be they substantive as for the medievals or formal as for Kant, it seems that there is only one answer left to the question, What must I do?, namely: I do not know. Let us examine this ignorance. Perhaps it is not accidental or due to the lack of some specific power of insight. In any case, it can be paralleled with a few "confessions" of ignorance in Heidegger's writings that will place it in context:

> The greater the work of a thinker—that is in no way measured by the extent and number of his writings—all the richer is what remains un-thought in that work, that is, what emerges for the first time thanks to it, as having not yet been thought.[17]

> The fact that the real has been showing itself in the light of Ideas ever since Plato, is not a fact brought about by Plato.. The thinker only responded to that which addressed itself to him.[18]

> The pluralistic character of the essence of reality at the beginning of modern metaphysics is the sign of an authentic [epochal] transition.[19]

> What Kant, beyond his express formulation, brought to light in the course of his laying the foundations . . . Kant himself was no longer able to say anything about. Generally, whatever is to become decisive in any philosophical knowledge is not found in the propositions enunciated, but in that which, although unstated as such, is brought before our gaze through these propositions.[20]

Like the works of Plato, Descartes, and Kant, *Being and Time* itself is traversed by something unthought or unsaid that is not due to chance: "Do not our own efforts, if we dare compare them with those of our predecessors, ultimately evidence a hidden avoidance of some-thing that we—and certainly not by accident—no longer see?"[21]

A very distinct ignorance, then, seems to prevail at the moments of transition betwen epochs, at the "decisive" moments (*decidere*, in Latin, means *to cut off, to set apart*). What if the avowal of ignorance were integral to the constellation of presence in postmodernity? What if this ignorance were so necessary to the contemporary order of discourse that without such a confession today's social sciences would no longer quite constitute a text, a fabric governed by internal laws? The deconstruction cannot dispense with the assumption that an epochal discourse constitutes an "autonomous entity of internal dependencies" (Hjelmslev's definition of structure). Can it be said, then, that—beyond the empirically observable "loss of standards"—today's discourse about man and his doings is structured according to rules that are few in number, one of which directly concerns this ignorance? That this ignorance is closely inwoven with the texture of today's theorizing *because* on the level of discourse it echoes a break, a rupture, a *Kehre* (turning) in the way things, words, and actions enter into mutual exchange today? In Heidegger's own itinerary, the turning in his thinking is merely experienced as the reverberation of a turning in the order of things. As is well known, he describes technology as the *Gestell*, (enframing). Referring to Hölderlin he can say: "The essence of "enframing" is the danger. . . . In the essence of this danger there conceals itself the possibility of a turning such that . . . with *this* turning, the truth of the coming to presence of being may expressly enter into whatever is.[22] As we shall see, "the truth of the coming to presence of being" designates nothing more and nothing less than the withering away of the epochal principles; a modality of presence such that the "fable" of the ideal world—Heidegger's notion of epochē—is no longer necessary to give it coherence and cohesion. The "truth," *aletheia*, of being designates the utterly contingent flux of interchange among things, without the governance of a metaphysical First.

As the ground recedes on which to rest a theory of action, the postmodern turning in the way things are present to each other must appear as the moment of the greatest danger. Ever since Socrates philosophers have consistently repeated that "virtue is knowledge"; that practical reason receives its architecture from pure reason; and that *theoria*, because it is what is most noble within our reach, prescribes the routes to *praxis*. But the method of deconstruction no longer allows one to claim that *agere sequitur esse* (action follows being). Even worse, it not only disrupts the unity between the moral or "practical" and the scientific or "theoretical" discourse, but by depriving thinking and acting of their model or canon, it renders them both literally an-archic.

The method of deconstruction thus not only dissociates "being and acting." It leads to the pulverization of a speculative base upon which life is to find its steadiness, its legitimation, and its peace. Deconstructing metaphysics amounts to dismantling what Kant called the "doctrines" of first philosophy. The deconstruction interrupts, throws out of gear, the derivations between first philosophy and practical philosophy. It does more than disjoin the ancient unity between theory and practice. It is the method of raising the question of presence in such a way that questions of action and morality already find their solution—their dissolution, rather, because the ground is lost on which they can at all become a question. To ask What ought I to do? is to speak in the vacuum of the place deserted by the successive representations of an unshakable ground. The epochal constellations of presence have always prescribed already, not only the terms in which the question of morality can and must be raised (ousiological, theological, transcendental, linguistic terms), but also the ground from which it can and must be answered (substance, God, cogito, discursive community) as well as the types of answers that can and must be adduced (hierarchy of virtues; hierarchy of laws—divine, natural, and human; hierarchy of imperatives; and hierarchy of discursive interests, that is, cognitive or emancipatory). The deconstruction of the historical constellations of presence thus shows that one can speak of the closed unity of the metaphysical epoch at least in one respect: the concern with *deriving* a practical or moral philosophy from a first philosophy. "Metaphysics" is then the title for that ensemble of speculative efforts with a view to an archē for both the theoretical and the practical discourse. In the light of the deconstruction, that ensemble appears as a closed field. The hypothesis of closure—or, as we can now say, of transition towards anarchic presence—functions doubly (even though the opposition between system and history needs to be revised): it is a *systematic* closure, inasmuch as the norms of action formally "proceed from" the corresponding first philosophies, and it is an *historical* closure, because the deconstructionist discourse can arise only from the boundary of the era over which it is exercised. The hypothesis of closure confers its ambiguity on much of contemporary philosophizing: still enclosed in the problematic of presence, but already outside the fief where presence functions as constant presence, as identity of self with self, as unshakable ground.

The hypothesis of closure also confers its radicality on the deconstructionist move: action bereft of *archē* is thinkable only at the moment when the problematic of "being"—inherited from the closed field of metaphysics but subjected on its threshold to a transmutation, to a passover—emerges from ontologies and dismisses them. If in the epoch of postmodernity (in short, since Nietzsche), the question of presence no longer seems capable of articulating itself as a first philosophy and if the withering away of epochal principles annihilates the quest for a complete possession of self by self, then in the epochal constellation of the twentieth century, the possible discourse about society, as well as possible action in society, proves to be essentially an-archic.

"Anarchy" is only the complement of the two premises I have advanced, namely, (1) traditional doctrines of *praxis* refer this concept to an unsurpassable first science from which proceed the schemata applicable to a rigorous reasoning about action, that is, to moral doctrine; (2) in the age of metaphysics's closure, this procession from, or legitimation by, a first science proves to be *epochal*—regional, dated, finite, and finished in both senses of the word: complete as well as terminated. Correlatively, here anarchy means: (1) The prime schema that practical or moral philosophy has traditionally borrowed from first philosophy is the reference to an *archē*, the *pros hen* relation. This attributive-participative schema, when translated into the doctrines of praxis, results in the ordering of acts to one measure-giving focal point. None of the continual displacements or transferences through history of this focal point destroys the attributive, participative, and therefore normative, pattern itseslf. The *archē* always functions in relation to action as substance functions in relation to its accidents, imparting sense and *telos* to them. (2) In the epoch of closure, on the other hand, the regularity of the principles that have reigned over action can be laid over. The schema of reference to an *archē* the reveals itself to be the product of a certain type of thinking, of an ensemble of philosophic rules that have their genesis, their period of glory, and their decline. Anarchy in this sense does not become operative as a concept until the moment when the great sheet of constellations that fix presence in constant presence folds up, closes on itself. The body of social and human sciences appears without a common discourse—and action, without principle—in the age of the turning, when presence as ultimate identity turns into presence as irreducible difference (or reducible only categorially). If these are the contours of the program of deconstruction, the necessity of an avowal of ignorance begins to be glimpsed; the very question of a norm-giving standard for behavior pertains to principial constructions.

The most adequate expression to cover the whole of these premises would be *the principle of anarchy*. The word *anarchy*, though, clearly lends itself to misunderstanding. The paradox of this expression is nonetheless instructive, dazzling. Is not the backbone of metaphysics—whatever the ulterior determinations by which this concept would have to be specified—the rule always to seek a First from which the world becomes intelligible and masterable, the rule of *scire per causas*, of establishing "principles" for thinking and doing? *Anarchy*, on the other hand, now designates the withering away of such a rule, the relaxing of its hold. This paradox is dazzling because in two words it points within and beyond the closure of metaphysics, thus exhibiting the boundary line of that closure itself. The paradox that the expression *principle of anarchy* articulates locates the deconstructionist enterprise, it indicates the place where it is situated: still implanted in the problematic of *ti to on* (What is being?), but already uprooting it from the schema of the *pros hen* that was connate to that problematic; retaining presence, but dislocating it from the attributive schema; still a principle, but a principle of anarchy. It is necessary to think this contradiction. The principal reference then appears to be counteracted, both in its history and in its essence, by a force of dislocation, of plurification. The referential *logos* becomes "archipelagic speech," "pulverized poem" ("parole en archipel," "poème pulvérisé").[23] The deconstruction is a discourse of transition. By putting the two words *principle* and *anarchy* side by side, what is intended is to prepare oneself for this epochal transition.

The anarchy that is at issue here is the name of a history affecting the ground or foundation of action, a history where the bedrock yields and where it becomes obvious that the principle of cohesion, be it authoritarian or rational, is no longer anything more than a blank space deprived of legislative, normative, power. Anarchy expresses a destiny of decline, the decay of the principles to which Westerners since Plato have related their acts and deeds in order to anchor them there and to withdraw them from change and doubt. Indeed, "in principle" all men do the same thing . . .

The avowal of ignorance concerning the moral criterion for action in the technological age now appears more coherent, better inscribed, at least, in the general unity of the epochal texture exhibited by the deconstructionist method. If the question of moral criteria can become an issue only within principial modalities of presence; and if, on the other hand, the lineage of epochal principles comes to an end in the age of closure, then weighing the different methods of gaining objective practical knowledge about how we should live is a rather untimely way of looking at our possibilities and limitations. From Heidegger's writings the inevitability of ignorance can be shown in several ways.

First, and this is the best-known factor, it can be shown by the opposition between thinking and knowing. In Heidegger no dialectic links thought and knowledge, no synthesis makes it possible to pass from one to the other: "Science does not think." This opposition, inherited from Kant, establishes two territories, two continents, between which there is neither analogy nor even resemblance. "There is no bridge that leads from science to thought."[24] We "think being" and its epochs, but we "know beings" and their aspects. There is a generalized ignorance, then, that strikes thought in all its advances. Heidegger so ostensibly invokes this necessary poverty of philosophy only because it is the lieu-tenant of a necessity within the "history of presence" (*Seinsgeschichte*).

Furthermore, for Heidegger the matter of thinking is, on the boundary line that encircles a long history, to "repeat" or retrieve presence itself, to "win back the originative experiences of metaphysics through a deconstruction of representations that have become current and empty."[25] If this long history actually reaches its end, then in the crisis, the structure of this field gets out of order; its principles of cohesion lose their efficacy; the *nomos* of our *oikos,* the economy that encloses us, produces fewer and fewer certainties. The moment when an epochal threshold is crossed is inescapably one of ignorance.

Finally, the necessary ignorance concerning moral criteria and their respective merits results from the constellation of presence whose dawn is described to us: cessation of principles, dethroning of the very principle of epochal principles, and the beginning of an economy of passage, of anarchy. In the epoch of transition, then, words, things and actions would come to presence in such a way that their public inter-action is irreducible to any systematicity.

This said and understood, nonetheless it must be added that the avowal of ignorance on the part of the deconstructionist is of course a feint. And one that is more than strategic—unless the word *strategy* is understood not in relation to human actions and the art of coor-dinating them but in relation to the economies of presence. Then we see that there are strong reasons for feigning. Indeed, after having outlined the withering away of principles, it is difficult to avoid questions of the following type: How, then, is one to evaluate action at all? What is your theory of the state? And of property? And of law in general? What will become of defense? And of our highways? Heidegger, to stay with him, makes himself scarce. After one of the most direct devel-opments of what could be called ontological anarchy—expressed at this juncture by the concept of "life without why," borrowed from Meister Eckhart (via Angelus Silesius)—Heidegger concludes: "In the most hidden ground of his being, man truly is only if in his way he is like the rose—without why." The "without why" points beyond the closure; therefore it cannot be pursued. The brusque halt of the development— "We cannot pursue this thought any further here"[26]—as well as the feigned ignorance, is inevitable when "another thought" is attempted. To strengthen this point a little further: a life "without why" certainly means a life without a goal, without *telos*; also it is said that "in the most hidden ground of his being"—hence, totally—man must be de-prived of *telos*. For man to be "in his way like the rose" would be to abolish practical teleology. It is clear that the objections rebound: But without *telos* action would no longer be action . . . Indeed. Whence the necessity of the feint.

"What Must I Do" at the End of Metaphysics

Anarchic Presence as Measure for Thinking and Acting

The phenomenology of the technological "turning," as it reveals the cessation of modalities of presence governed by epochal principles, entails a few consequences concerning the question, What must I do at the end of metaphysics? It is yet another aspect of technology's Janus-faced character that we still cannot but ask, What must I do? and that at the same time we find ourselves unable to point to any ultimate measure for action. Technology, I said, is still a principle, but already a principle of anarchy.

1. The consequence that is easiest to see—and perhaps easiest to tolerate—is a certain breakdown in the received divisions of the sciences of man. The reason for this breakdown is however not the one that is frequently invoked when scientists complain about the impermeability of partitions between disciplines, namely that man or human nature is one and that therefore the inherited division into fields of research is artificial. On the contrary, there is no unitary dream that moves the phenomenological deconstruction the way I have tried to outline it. The figure of "man" as *one* is precisely the chief epochal principle instituted with the Socratic turn, the turn due to which "the specific feature of all metaphysics consists in its being 'humanistic'."[27] The properly principal role of man dates back still more recently, to the beginning of modernity: "modern man is barely three hundred years old."[28] With the turn out of the epochal, principial, metaphysical, and that is to say humanistic, history, man as one can no longer serve as the measure for discourse in the sciences called *social* and *human*. It is therefore not the unitary figure of man that leads to the observation that with the technological age, life is reified according to economical, sociological, anthropological, and other perspectives. The partitions are artificial not because this subject matter is ultimately simple but because, once the *epochē* is overcome, it appears on the contrary as irreducibly multiple.

2. A subject matter so irreducibly multiple requires multiple modes of discourse. "Only a manifold thinking will succeed in entering the discourse that corresponds to the 'matter' of that subject matter."[29] A "plurivocity in discourse" is required to respond to "the all-playing structure of never resting transmutation"[30] in a modality of presencing no longer obfuscated by the "fiction" of an "ideal world," that is, a presencing no longer "withholding" (*epechein*) itself. The ceaseless transmutation in the constellation of presence and therefore in discourse beyond the technological closure is what Heidegger opposes to the "reification" that he deplores in the social and human sciences. There

exist not too many types of discourse about "man and his society" but rather too few.

3. The plurification in thinking and speaking as it results from the hypothesis of closure involves a subversion—an overturn (*vertere*) from the foundations (*sub-*)—that does not stop with the mere wish for discursive proliferation. The domain most thoroughly and decisively structured by the *pros hen* relation is grammar. Metaphysical thinking has to be seen as the universalization of the relation by which a predicate is attributed to a subject. This primary attributive relation is what would have to be unlearned if the borderline of the metaphysical field were at all to be transgressed (that is to say, if metaphysics were to be "worked through" as one surmounts (*verwindet*) grief or pain).[31] At the end of his last public lecture, Heidegger complained about the chief obstacle: "This lecture has spoken merely in propositional statements."[32] He suggests that all we can do is "to prepare somewhat the transmutation in our relation to language."[33]

> The difficulty lies in language. Our Western languages are, each in its own way, languages of metaphysical thinking. It must remain an open question whether the essence of Western languages is in itself marked with the exclusive stamp of metaphysics . . . or whether these languages offer other possibilities of utterance.[34]

4. The other domain, besides grammar, in which the *pros hen* relation has held sway without challenge is that of ethics. Aristotle enunciates the methodological teleocracy in the very first lines of the *Nicomachean Ethics*: "Every art and every inquiry, and similarly every action and pursuit, is thought to aim at some good."[35] In all our undertakings, we aim at some *telos*. This reign of the end, couched in the question "What is the good for man?," constitutes the guiding thread of all moral research and doctrine. Without the representation of a measure-giving end, no such doctrine can be conceived. But teleocracy cannot survive the transition towards an order of presence where "innocence is restored to becoming," to the flux, to perpetual transformation. Heidegger proposes ever new concepts and metaphors to suggest this aboliton of teleocracy in action. One of these is the metaphor *woodpaths*, the tracks used for felling and cartage of timber. What is distinctive about such tracks is that they lead nowhere. "In the wood are paths that mostly wind along until they end quite suddenly in an impenetrable thicket. They are called 'woodpaths'."[36] Like these cart tracks, doing—as opposed to making—when freed from the representations of *archē* and *telos*, would follow an itinerary that ends in the impenetrable. Another term in Heidegger to express the same idea is borrowed from

Heraclitus. Human action, Heidegger writes in a commentary, would have to follow the sole movement of coming-to-presence, of *phyein*. Beyond the closure of metaphysics, the measure for all our enterprises can be neither a noumenal First nor the simple pressure of empirical facts. What provides the measure is the ceaselessly changing modality according to which things present emerge, appear, show themselves: "Human production espouses that which emerges by itself and addresses man. His *poiein* takes the *physis* as its measure, it is *kata physin*. . . . Only he is knowledgeable who "produces" in keeping with what comes forth by itself, that is, with what discloses itself."[37] Human action *kata physin*, following the way things enter into mutual relations, would be irreducible to the representation of an "end for man" that sanctions the morality of his ventures.

In yet another attempt at conceptualizing the overcoming of teleocracy, Heidegger quotes from Nietzsche a declaration of faith that directly contradicts the Aristotelian declaration of faith in teleology: "'The absence of an end in itself' is our principle of faith."[38] In all of these attempts at subverting teleocracy, what is at stake is to confine the rule of end to the domain where it initially and genuinely obtains, namely to fabrication. Aristotle's *Physics*, Heidegger charges, is the "foundational book of Western philosophy"[39] precisely because of the rule of end established in it—the rule of end that Aristotle translates into his key concepts of *entelecheia* and *energeia*.

5. To answer the question "What ought I to do?" thinking—understood as pure response to *phyein*, to "coming-to-presence," "presencing," "appearing"—has nowhere else to turn than to itself. Indeed, after Parmenides and to a certain extent against the modern opposition between subject and object, Heidegger holds that the basic traits of thinking and those of presencing are the same. As Hannah Arendt puts it: "If there is anything in thinking that can prevent men from doing evil, it must be some property inherent in the activity itself." Moral evil does not stem from the election of some wrong end or maxim or principle. Hannah Arendt speaks of the "interconnectedness of non-thought and evil."[40] The measure for good and evil that thinking finds in itself is *physis*, the emergence out of concealedness. A measure, to be sure, that has nothing permanent. But a demanding measure nevertheless: "Thoughtlessness is an uncanny visitor who comes and goes everywhere in today's world."[41] The contrary of "thinking," then, is not feeling or willing. Nor is it the body or the animal. The contrary of thinking is *hybris* or *adikia*, "extracting oneself from the transitory while" and "striking the insurrectionary prose of persistence"[42]—which is precisely the chief characteristic of all epochal principles.

What must I do at the end of metaphysics? Combat all remnants of authoritative Firsts. In Nietzsche's terms: after the "true world" has turned out to be a fable—after "God is dead"—the task is to dethrone the many idols with which we still adorn public and private life. Or in the terms of the epigraph above: unlearn the *nomos* as an artifact of reason and follow the sole *nomos* as the "injunction" contained in the ever new "dispensation of being." The closure of principal thinking can actually be seen as implicit already in Kant and as becoming more and more explicit with Nietzsche and Heidegger. Indeed, because the Kantian moral law is constituted or "declared" by the transcendental subject, its transgression lies ready as a possibility in its very legislation—even more, inasmuch as the subject is the "master" of what it enacts, the act of transgression is identical with the act of legislation. In Nietzsche the moral law appears as one of the obstacles that the will to power sets up for its own preservation and enhancement. The establishment of the law is thus quite expressly already its transgression. In Heidegger, finally, the moral law has as its condition of domination the rise of principial thinking in classical Greece. As an immobilization of the flux of *phyein*, the formation of the moral law constitutes, here most evidently, its own transgression: a transgression towards that full sense of *physis* that Aristotle discarded for the sake of a "first philosophy" entirely guided by the representation of ends; a transgression, in other words, towards a mode of acting purely "according to anarchic presence," *kata physin*.[43]

The French poet, René Char, may have sensed this same withering away of any measure-giving First at the end of the epochal economies structured by *pros hen* relations, when he wrote: "Amont éclate" ("upstream bursts").[44] And he may have felt the same urgency of hastening the fall of what remains of them so as to set free a more originary multiplicity: "Cette part jamais fixée, en nous sommeillant, d'où jaillira DEMAIN LE MULTIPLE" ("That part never fixed, asleep in us, from which will surge TOMORROW THE MANIFOLD")[45]

6. Heidegger and the Problem of a Unified Theory of Action

HANS SEIGFRIED

At the beginning of his inaugural lecture on knowledge and human interests, Habermas describes how in the language of Parmenides and Plato, the religious term *theoria* was transferred to the mere contemplation of the immutable structures of the cosmos in the hope that such contemplation would help to provide some stability for the conduct of life by letting men know how to fit their actions into the context of the harmonious motions of nature. "This concept of theory and of life in theory," Habermas claims, "has defined philosophy since its beginning."[1] According to the philosophical tradition, then, the theory of action, any such theory, can and must be derived from the pure, contemplative theory of the structures of the universe, in other words, from ontology. However, it has become obvious by now, Habermas insists, (1) that all attempts so far to derive a unified theory of action from ontology have failed, and (2) that a theory of communicative action can be developed today "only on the ruins of ontology."[2]

The purpose of this paper is to introduce Heideggerian perspectives in order to advance the discussion of Habermas's central claims. For one would expect that such perspectives could be helpful for coming to a decision about these claims one way or another. After all, there should be some lessons to be learned for this discussion from the most radical attempt so far to revive and transform traditional ontology in Heidegger's earlier work on fundamental ontology as well as from his later work on the deconstruction of the history of ontology and from what he has to say about both the epochal nature and destiny-character of the "truth of being" and the play-character of the *Ereignis* (event) through which it emerges.

One might easily get the impression that the lessons to be learned unqualifiedly support Habermas's claims. As a matter of fact, Heidegger's analysis of existence was not followed by an analysis of action. After all, *Being and Time* did not succeed in providing a developed concept of being as such from which one could subsequently derive rules for action.[3] And later Heidegger insisted that the 'more rigorous' thinking of the truth of being can provide no help for the theoretical understanding of action nor for its calculating and explicit planning, not even indirectly.[4] However, despite his confessed inability to develop a theory of action, Heidegger nevertheless frequently acknowledged the urgent need for such a theory.

I will argue in this paper, seemingly against Habermas, that it is possible to derive some basic outlines for a philosophically promising unified theory of action from Heidegger's transformed ontology. This theory of action, I submit, not only makes good sense in itself and of *Being and Time*,[6] but also of Heidegger's remarks on both the responsive thinking of being and the epochal nature of the history of being as well, which allegedly make a unified, hermeneutical theory of action impossible.[7]

I will try to do two things. First, I will discuss some problems that arise for the theoretical understanding of action from Heidegger's deconstruction of the history of being and from his remarks on the *Ereignis*, as well as from his retreat into a complete "*Theoretizismus*," as Prauss calls it, that is, from his alleged appeal to a merely contemplative thinking of being as a "more rigorous" form of thinking, more rigorous in the sense of more promising for our dealing with the problem of action.[8]

Secondly, I will show how these problems can be overcome by interpreting the relationship between theory and practice, thinking and acting, in terms of the detailed analyses of *Being and Time*—and by extension of them. In particular, I will show that Heidegger's later remarks on epoche can be interpreted in terms of his earlier remarks on situation in *Being and Time*, where he explicitly refers to the problem of the relationship between theory and practice and claims that his analyses show how it has to be reinterpreted (*SZ*, p. 300f.).

My conclusion will be that Heideggerian analysis can show (1) that Habermas's claim is justified, after all, in the sense that in order to develop a unified theory of action we have to abandon altogether as idle dialectic the traditional understanding of the relationship between thinking and acting, theory and practice, ontology and ethics (*SZ*, p. 300f.), and (2) that the understanding of this relationship along the Heideggerian lines reconstructed in this paper looks promising enough (a) to invite a renewed interest in the development of a unified theory of action, and (b) to dispel the reservations harbored against it by our epochalist colleagues.

I

Was Heidegger concerned with the problem of a unified theory of action at all, and does he have anything to contribute to its solution? What are the concerns of a unified theory of action, anyway?

In the terminology of *Being and Time*, a unified theory of action is concerned with the tasks, rules, standards, urgency, and extent of all concernful and solicitous being-in-the-world. It wants to know, explicitly and transparently, the origin and limitation of each and how they are decided upon (cf. *SZ*, p. 268). Although "existential analysis cannot, in principle, discuss what Dasein factually resolves in any particular case . . . nevertheless, we must ask whence, *in general*, Dasein can draw those possibilities upon which it factically projects itself" (*SZ*, p. 383, p. 268) and which are circumscribed in the tasks and rules of its concernful dealings and solicitous being-with others. No doubt, *Being and Time* provides at least an outline for an answer to this question and, consequently, for a unified theory of action.

In the terminology of the "Letter on Humanism," devoted thematically to the revision of our thinking about action (cf. *BH*, p. 53/270), a unified theory of action is concerned with (to borrow my phrasing from the text) the assigning of "all the directions [*Weisungen*] from being itself which must become for man law and rule" (*BH*, p. 114/ 300) and which provide the hold and measure for all action (*BH*, p. 115/300). No doubt, again, the reflections in the "Letter on Humanism" try to show how the "more rigorous" thinking of being can provide "directives" (*Anweisungen*) (*BH*, p. 111/298) for all action, by letting itself be "taken into service" by being (*BH*, p. 53/271) in order to spell out the "directions" (*Zuweisungen*) contained in the "dispensation" (*Schickung*) and provided in the truth of being (*BH*, p. 114f./300).

Now, by reflecting on the history of being, thinking is supposed to give itself its own law first, namely, the law of saying what is proper of being (*Schicklichkeit des Sagens*), by binding itself to the law of being, that is, to what is proper (*schicklich*) and in accordance with the fateful dispensation of being (*Geschick des Seins*) at a given moment in the history of being (*BHP*, p. 118/301). Having bound itself in this way, thinking can then tell what is appropriate for action as well, and thus provide the hold, measure, and law for proper behavior.

However, this description seems to suggest that the *Gesetz der Schicklichkeit des seinsgeschichtlichen Denkens* (law of the destiny or historical thought of being) (*BH*, p. 118/302) cannot, in principle, provide the hold and measure for *all* action and proper behavior *throughout* the history of being. Instead, the thinking in terms of the history of being seems to be restricted in regard to action and behavior to the defining of the tasks, rules, standards, and the urgency and extent of action and behavior at a given moment in the history of being; and consequently it seems to be unfit, after all, to contribute anything to the development of a unified theory of action.

But this suggestion seems to be misleading, for reflecting on the history of being and telling the fateful dispensation and truth of being "does not only include our recollecting each time *what* is to be said about being and *how* it is to be said. It remains equally essential to consider whether that which has-to-be-thought may be said, to what extent, at what moment in the history of being, in what dialogue with it, and with what claim" (*BH*, p. 118/301). And these remarks seem to imply that thinking in terms of the history of being cannot rest, at any time, with the epochal truth of being, accepting it as law, because before we can accept the claims and dictates of *any* epochal truth of being we must first ask what, *in general*, constitutes a moment or epoch in the history of being and how we can gain access to what determines "the way in which being takes place [*wie Sein geschieht*]."⁹

Well, we are frequently told (especially in *On Time and Being*) that what determines a moment in the history of being, any such moment, is the interplay, and this alone, between disclosure and concealment, dispensation and withdrawal of being, and that this interplay has the character of an "event" (*Ereignis*) that "destines" everything and brings it into its own (including man—*BH*, p. 84/285f.)¹⁰ such that it can subsequently be perceived, seen, and seized upon as a definite something to be dealt with concernfully or to be brought about in solicitous being-with-others (cf. *SZ*, p. 194). In order to avoid free-floating speculation in its attempt to make this interplay conceptually transparent, the thinking of being must try to gain initial access to it by studying the various ways in which being has already taken place in the history of being. And because these ways have already found their expression in what thinkers, responsive to them, have said in the past (*BH*, p. 117/301) and what has come down to us in their writings, it is through the study of these writings that the thinking of being must find its way to that all-determining, fateful interplay, which is "*the* law" from which the law of being as well as the law of proper behavior in *any* epoch must ultimately be derived.¹¹

Naturally, merely historical research cannot accomplish this task. The study must take form of a dialogue.¹² It must try to recall what it was in each case that opened up, and determined the limits of, the whole aural and visual field of an epoch,[13] and always remind itself that its real goal must remain to spell out what it is that invariably determines the ways in which being takes place *throughout* the history of being and from which *all* thinking, responsive to it, takes its measure and direction (*Geheiss*).[14]

It matters little whether this program of the late Heidegger is radically different from the program of repetition through the destruction of the history of ontology, outlined in Heidegger's early writings (cf. *SZ.*, pp. 19-27).[15] Nor is there any need to rehearse any one of Heidegger's many attempts to recall in what way and from what source being itself received its specific epochal determination, say as "the will to reason"[16] or as the *Ge-stell*.[17] For all we need to know is what the great efforts in the pursuit of this program finally were able to accomplish in Heidegger's later writings—with regard to the problem of a unified theory of action, that is, the attempt to establish the measure and law of all human behavior through thinking, and thinking alone.

Recall that it became necessary for Heidegger to design this program on the following two assumptions (see p. 67, above): (1) The measure and law for all proper behavior must receive its binding force from the first law of thinking, and (2) the first law of thinking, in turn, must receive its force from the law of being. On these two assumptions, to make the binding force of the law for all behavior ultimately transparent must mean to show what constitutes the binding force of being itself and how it is brought about. Does man, for instance, play a part in it such that in "submitting" to the law of proper behavior he is autonomously binding himself; or does he have no hand in it at all so that his "submission" means total surrender to the heteronomy of being?

What the study of the epochal history of being seems to "teach" in this regard, can be briefly summarized as follows. First, the thinking of being is always struggling against the tendency to concern itself only with the things around us and their characteristics, as disclosed to us, and to let the problem of spelling out what originates and "destines" the truth of being itself (which determines that and how things and their characteristics are disclosed to us in the first place)[18] slowly drift into oblivion. And this explains why theories of action nearly always try to derive directives for action from the world of things or from the structures of the cosmos, as Habermas would say.

Second, what determines the way in which the truth of being itself takes place, at *any* moment in the history of being, is the interplay between the disclosure and the concealment or between the dispensation and withdrawal of being.

Third, this interplay has the character of an "event" (*Ereignis*) which, by determining being, "destines" everything into its own and retains it there (cf. *ZS*, p. 21/20), but it is itself not "destined" by any thing. It is not initiated by and it does not take place between things (it is not a *Vorkommnis, Geschehen,* or *Ergebnis*) (*ZS*, p. 21/20).[19] All that remains to be said about it is: The destiny destines.[20] It escapes all explanation.[21] It is without "why." It is pure play.[22]

Fourth, this play can never take place without man,[23] in the sense, so it seems, that it simply could not be understood as the interplay between dispensation and withdrawal without a "constant receiver" (*ZS*, p. 11f./12). In other words, man's part in this play seems to be reduced to mere "responding" [*Fuegung* or *Entsprechung*].[24] Consequently, the thinking of being, so to speak, the defining action of man, according to the "Letter on Humanism," belongs altogether to being such that it is eventuated (*ereignet*) by and responding to being (*BH*, p. 57/272). As in Rilke's *Duino Elegies* the angel snatches up "the husks," so the "destiny" of being seems to be playing its play "over and above us."[25] In other words, man's thinking of being seems to resemble completely the responsive action of a marionette, for both its agency and its "content" are that of the "destiny" of being, and so Heidegger saw fit to qualify (if not retract altogether) in his later writings a major thesis of *Being and Time*, namely, that "being clears itself for man in ecstatical projection," by adding: 'But this projection does not create being. . . What projects in projection is *not man, but being itself* which destines man to the ex-sistence which is the essence of da-sein. This destiny is realized [*ereignet sich*] as the clearing of being, which it is" (*BH*, p. 84/285f.).[26] It is hard to see how such pure responsiveness differs from the purely contemplative character of traditional theory, which it is supposed to overcome, according to the "Letter on Humanism."[27]

Clearly, then, neither the program of the thinking in terms of the epochal history of being nor its basic messages militate, in principle, against the concerns of a unified theory of action, as has been frequently alleged.[28] But are they worth having? And what is, after all, the relationship of the thinking of being to theoretical and practical behavior, more exactly and concretely?[29]

It seems that the messages of the "more rigorous" thinking of being remain so disconcertingly vague and ambiguous, aside from being repulsive, and the grounds for accepting them so wanting, that one cannot help but be tempted to dismiss them as belonging to those "extravagances of genius" that Kant so justly criticizes at the end of his second critique.[30] And also, it seems that these messages cannot be made more accessible, and even less so can they be made more acceptable merely by being put back into the elaborate context of Heidegger's later writings. For in these writings, readers frequently complain, the means employed to make a claim both accessible and acceptable is basically mere evocation. Occasionally, Heidegger gives the impression that he even prides himself for not trying at all, indeed, for not making *claims* at all, to begin with.[31]

Without implying that these impressions are fully justified, I would like to suggest that the messages of the thinking of being for a unified theory of action can be made accessible and acceptable by interpreting them in terms of the detailed analyses of *Being and Time*—and by extension from them. After all, Heidegger himself insisted that "only by way of what Heidegger I has thought does one gain access to what is to-be-thought by Heidegger II."[32] The remainder of this paper provides pieces for a thought experiment to this effect.

II

I would like to show now (1) that these messages can be turned into lessons that are indeed worth learning, and (2) that the relationship of the thinking of being to theoretical and practical behavior can be much more satisfactorily described than the "Letter on Humanism," and other later writings, seem to allow—if these messages and this relationship are revised and interpreted in terms of *Being and Time*. I believe that such a revision can show, for instance, that the pure responsiveness of the thinking of being is radically different from the purely contemplative character of traditional theory because being itself, together with its law, is necessarily dependent on man's action such that without it being cannot take place at all (cf. *SZ*, p. 212). Naturally, if this can be shown, it would follow that all attempts "of saving for thinking an independence in the face of doing and acting" (*BH*, p. 55/ 271) and of basing a unified theory of action on the purely contemplative theory of an independent realty, would be doomed to failure.

I have already indicated above how the concern for the theoretical understanding of action in general and its calculating and explicit planning according to fixed rules, can fit into the program of *Being and Time*. In view of what this program meant to accomplish, even though in fact *Being and Time* did not carry out the whole program, the following things, in general, can be said about the theoretical understanding and planning of action.

First, such theoretical understanding and planning is always already "derivative" from the existentiell understanding, that is, from the understanding in the mode of dasein's assigning itself "to an 'in-order-to' . . . in terms of a potentiality-for-being for the sake of which it itself is" (*SZ*, p. 86). Like all theoretical understanding, it presupposes (1) a break in or an abstention from the assigning, and a suspension of dasein's absorption in its assignments, and (2) a taking up of a new direction towards what is then merely perceived as something that is just there and a placing it within a definite framework in order to let it emerge as a specific something to be described and determined in sets of true propositions. In theoretical understanding then, dasein achieves a new "status of being" (*Seinsstand*) towards the world that has already been discovered and grasped originally in our existentiell understanding and concernful dealings. The new directions and the definite conceptual frameworks and fixed rules methodically introduced are themselves "derivative" in the sense that they are motivated by and grounded in our dealing concernfully with the world. Although by now theoretical understanding has become necessary and a task to be gradually accomplished in ontological and scientific research, we have to keep reminding ourselves of its "derivative" and piecemeal character and persistently qualify the sense in which it can and must take over the "guidance" of our being-in-the-world. For if Heidegger's claim about the "derivative character" of all theoretical understanding is justified, then our theoretical understanding and planning of action cannot be genuinely derived, as in our tradition (with few exceptions, e.g., the works of American pragmatism), from our theoretical understanding of the world from the perspective of a mere spectator. Rather, analysis must derive both, and in conjunction with one another, from our existentiell understanding, that is, from the originating action through which *Dasein* constitutes itself—from dasien's ontical constitution.[33]

Second, the discussion of the possibility and necessity of theoretical understanding and planning, consequently, has to commence with existential analysis, in other words, it demands above all an elaboration of the existential (conceptual, theoretical) constitution of dasein's being, that is, transparency of existentiality (cf. *SZ*, p. 146–148).

Third, the transparency of existentiality, however, can be provided only after the conceptualization, that is, the explicit elaboration and fixation of the concept of being as such. In order to prepare such an elaboration, the concept of the being of a paradigmatic entity has to be "provisionally" elaborated first, the entity chosen being dasein. *Being and Time* proposed ecstatic temporality (*Zeitlichkeit*) as the horizon for the preparatory elaboration of the "provisional" concept of the being of the paradigmatic entity. On the basis of this provisional concept, the question of being as such has then to be thematically (re-)stated and a way found for answering it. Time is proposed as the horizon for the conceptualization of being as such.

Fourth, on the basis of a fixed and definite concept of being as such, the question of the transparency of existentiality has then to be thematically (re-)stated (*SZ*, p. 436), and a final conceptualization of existence be worked out.

Fifth, only on the basis of a "final," that is, fixed, concept of existence, can something like a unified theory of action then be worked out.

Now, *Being and Time* accomplishes neither the conceptualization of being as such nor the final conceptualization of existence. Clearly, then, it does not provide a fully developed basis for a unified theory of action, but the outline of the whole program, together with an appropriate extension of some of the things that have been accomplished, and their coordination with the program and the messages of the thinking in terms of the history of being, should make it possible to come up with at least *some* basics for a unified theory of action à la Heidegger.

Being and Time leaves no doubt that the traditional distinction between thinking and acting must be abandoned (cf. *SZ*, pp. 300, 69, 316), and the "Letter on Humanism," twenty years later, starts out by complaining that there is still far too little reflection on the nature of action (*BH*, p. 53/270). It then introduces, quite axiomatically, new definitions of thinking and acting that are supposed to make it possible (1) to recognize thinking as the most fundamental action, and (2) to see the utterly derivative character of the traditional notions of thinking and acting.

Now, the "Letter on Humanism" defines action as fulfillment (*Vollbringen*) in the sense of carrying out or unfolding something, which already is, in its fullness. If one assumes with Heidegger that "that which, above all, 'is', is being," then one must, of course, define the thinking that unfolds, in language, being in its relationship to man, as a form of action, indeed, as "the simplest and, at the same time, the highest form of action" (*BH*, p. 53/271). Naturally, the action of thinking, in this sense, does not make and generate being in its relationship to man, a relationship in which the human condition itself as well as what is ready-to-hand or just present-at-hand within it, are both fatefully disclosed and concealed. The thinking of being merely helps to unfold this relationship of disclosure and concealment, that is, the truth of being. By unfolding it in language, it merely performs the service of a midwife for the truth of being. It is in this sense "*l'engagement* by and for the truth of being" and its history, a history which "sustains and determines every *condition et situation humaine*" (*BH*, p. 54/271).

But, traditionally, both thinking and acting have been defined differently. Acting was "known only as the bringing about of an effect"

(*BH*, p. 53/270) on what was given within the situation, to be assessed by its usefulness for accomplishing what the situation demanded. And thinking was originally defined, merely "technically," as deliberating and calculating in the service of doing and making. It was understood to be "merely *l'engagement dans l'action* for and by 'what is' actual in a given situation" (*BH*, p. 54/271). Subsequently, in a reactive move to save for thinking some independence in the face of acting, thinking was also "theoretically" defined as the pure contemplation (*BH*, p. 115/ 300) of what is given within the situation (*BH*, p. 54f./271), or, in the language of *Being and Time*, as the encountering of "entities within-the-world purely in the *way they look*" (*SZ*, p. 61).

Clearly, then, thinking and acting in the traditional sense are both derivative from the thinking of being, as defined in the "Letter on Humanism," for they are both possible only on the supposition that a "*condition et situation humaine*" has been opened up, that is, that the thinking of being has already unfolded the truth of being in its history. And this thinking itself is neither theoretical nor practical in the traditional sense. "It occurs [*ereignet sich*] before such a differentiation" (*BH*, p. 111/298), and it is superior to both theoretical and practical behavior (*BH*, p. 115/300).

However, the thinking of the truth of being, as the mere unfolding of something that already is, cannot be man's fundamental action, that is, the primordial transaction (*Geschehen*) (*SZ*, pp. 375, 384) of dasein. It merely surveys, so to speak, the human condition and the truth of being as it has already been epochally staked out from what infinitely escapes us in language (*des grenzenlos Wortlose*), to borrow from Rilke.[34] It merely helps man to settle down[35] by telling him what he could and could not do with what has been cleared and closed off in the transaction in which his homestead has been staked out originally. We are already familiar with the *claim* that this transaction itself has the character of a fateful event, and so forth (see p. 70 above), although we still need to know how it can be demonstrated at all.

Now, the detailed analyses of *Being and Time* can be taken to demonstrate how and under what conditions, exactly, the primordial transaction of dasein can take place in each case. For they show how something like a situation can be opened up and disclosed such that something within it can possibly be encountered, looked at, objectified, or manipulated, and that the question as to what could or needs to be done can arise at all.

When *Being and Time* finally gets down to business, it starts out with the discussion of the conditions under which it is possible to encounter the kind of things that we come across in our ordinary dealings *in* the world and *with* the things in it (*SZ*, p. 66f.).[36] In these dealings we come across equipment (such as equipment for writing, sewing, and measurement), the dasein of the others, and our own dasein (cf. *SZ*, pp. 119, 126).

Being and Time argues that the condition for the possibility of coming across and recognizing a piece of equipment is the prior familiarity with its environment. For "taken strictly, there 'is' no such thing as *one* equipment, in which it can be this equipment that it is. Equipment is essentially 'something in-order-to . . . .'" (*SZ*, p. 68). And this "in-order-to" has the structure of an "*assignment* or *reference* of something to something" (*SZ*, p. 68), that is, of contextuality. The prior familiarity with its context then makes it possible to make out a piece of equipment, and without such familiarity it could not be recognized or used at all. "Before [an 'individual' item shows itself], a totality of equipment has already been discovered" (*SZ*, p. 68f.), however, not through bare perceptual cognition in "just tarrying alongside" (*SZ*, p. 61) but rather through concernful circumspection, that is, through the special kind of vision that propels us when we "concern ourselves with [equipment] in some such way" (*SZ*, p. 67) in our dealings and in "practical" behavior (*SZ*, p. 69).

Thus, in order for it to be possible to make out the things we come across in our dealings, our dealings must "subordinate themselves to" and "accommodate themselves with" what concernful circumspection discloses beforehand, namely, "the manifold assignments of the 'in-order-to'" (*AZ*, p. 69), that is, the assignment context (*Verweisungszusammenhang*) and the totality of involvements (*Bewandtnisganzheit*). This totality is such that it ultimately leads to a possibility of man's being as its ultimate "for-the-sake-of-which [*Worumwillen*]" and ground (*SZ*, p. 84). For instance, a particular piece of equipment, say a hammer, has been assigned to hammering, hammering to make something fast, making something fast to protect against bad weather, "and this protection 'is' for the sake of providing shelter for Dasein— that is to say for a possibility of dasein's being" (*SZ*, p. 84). In short, the assignments are in each case determined beforehand by the totality of such assignments—ultimately, however, by a possibility of dasein's being.

To say, then, that the *being* of equipment has the structure of reference or assignment means that "it has itself the character of *having been assigned or referred [Verweisenheit]*" beforehand (*SZ*, p. 83f.). The being of equipment is this "*having been assigned or referred*," in some specific way, within a context of assignments or references—nothing else besides, that is, the "being-in-itself" of equipment must be defined as "holding-itself-in [*Ansichhalten des Zuhandenen*]" (*SZ*, p. 75), in the context of assignments or references. If it falls out, or if it is taken out of this context, it ceases to *be* an item of equipment.

Thus, the conditions for the possibility of coming across and of using any piece of equipment in our dealings are (1) that the piece of equipment has already been assigned within a context in a specific way, (2) that its "having been assigned" has been disclosed through concernful circumspection, and (3) that in our dealings we submit to and accommodate with that assignment (cf. *SZ*, p. 85).

But under what conditions is such a context of *a priori* assignments possible? We know already that the assignments are in each case determined beforehand by a totality of assignments and, ultimately, by a possibility of dasein's being. And we are told that "*that wherein* [*Worin*] Dasein understands itself" in its dealings, in which it has assigned itself beforehand to some "in-order-to", is exactly "*that for which* [*Woraufhin*] we let entities be encountered beforehand" (*SZ*, p. 86), that is, the context of *a priori* assignments. For it is in the context of our dealings that we ordinarily and originally come across both the dasein of the others and our own dasein (*SZ*, pp. 119, 126). What we want to know now, in addition, is how a mere possibility of dasein's being can ultimately render factual assignments such that a condition and a situation could arise that makes specific demands on us.

Granted, then, that the context of *a priori* assigments is ultimately always determined by a possibility of dasein's being, we must ask now, (1) under what conditions, in general, such possibilities can themselves emerge, or "whence, *in general*," dasein can "draw those possibilities" (*SZ*, p. 383), and (2) under what conditions, in general, such mere possibilities can determine the assignment context of our factual dealings.

Being and Time argues that that wherein dasein understands itself in the mode of assigning itself is cleared and opened up in dasein itself, however, "not through any other entity, but in such a way that it is itself the clearing" (*SZ*, p. 133). In other words, dasein's possibilities to be are opened up by dasein itself. *Being and Time* argues that they are opened up through dasein's state-of-mind (*Befindlichkeit*), understanding, and discourse, such that dasein finds itself, as a matter of fact, always already "thrown" into or "delivered over" to a range of possibilities whose "whence" and "whither" remain an enigma, and that it can project itself towards a final existential goal only in terms of them. In short, the context of assignments is opened up in and through dasein's "thrown" projection.

Clearly, then, one of the conditions under which it is possible that a mere possibility can determine, to some extent, the definite assigment-context of our factual dealings is the facticity of the "thrownness" of dasein's projection. However, dasein finds itself always "delivered over" to a whole range of "factual possibilities" (*SZ*, 383). *Being and Time* occasionally gets carried away and even talks about "the endless multiplicity of possibilities which offer themselves" (*SZ*, p. 384). under what conditions, then, is it possible that dasein can project itself towards a final existential goal in terms of its endless factical possibilities such that a finite context of concrete and definite assignments emerged to which dasein in its factical dealings must submit and with which it must accommodate?

Being and Time argues that this is ultimately possible only under the condition that dasein grasps the finitude of its existence by anticipating its own death, that is, that it resolves to snatch itself "back from the endless multiplicity of possibilities which offer themselves" by projecting itself towards a final existential goal exclusively and "unambiguously in terms of its ownmost distinctive possibility. Only being-free *for* death, gives dasein its goal outright and pushes existence into its finitude . . . and brings Dasein into the simplicity of its *fate* [*Schicksal*]" (*SZ*, p. 384). To the extent to which dasein is essentially being-with-others, its fateful resolve is essentially *interaction* (*Mitgeschehen*) that brings dasein into its *destiny* (*Geschick*) (*SZ*, p. 384).

Consequently, it is this resolute transaction of dasein that makes it ultimately possible that the context of factual assignments can be *determined* by a mere possibility of dasein's being. In other words, "*that wherein* Dasein understands itself in the mode of assigning itself" and "*that for which* we let entities be encountered beforehand" (*SZ*, p. 86) opens up and emerges only through this fateful transaction of dasein. It is then ultimately this fateful transaction of dasein that "destines" and determines the way in which the primordial truth and disclosedness of existence (cf. *SZ*, p. 307) *and* of being is brought about in each case (see p. 70, above). And the condition or situation in which man finds himself faced with an unambiguous task and called upon to effect what is actually given within a factual situation can arise only from this transaction, that is, something like an "*engagement dans l'action* for and by 'what is' actual in a given situation" (see p. 74, above) is only possible as a result of dasein's resolute transaction.

The resolute transaction of dasein itself (although it needs to be schematized by ecstatical temporality—*BT*, section 65ff.) can obviously not be calculated and planned in advance according to the rules for proper behavior in a given situation, nor according to the laws of being, the being that we come across within the assignment-context of our dealings, that is. For such rules and laws are always the results of dasein's transaction in which it projects itself towards a final existential goal. The thinking of being, as "*l'engagement* by and for the truth of being" (see p. 73, above), merely unfolds the assignment-context and explicitly appropriates what can be disclosed and discovered in terms of that final existential goal which dasein has fatefully and in its destiny given itself in its resolute projection. And the contemplation and theoretical inspection of the circumstances of the situation and of what we come across in it merely spells out what dasein must submit to and put up with in order to calculate how what needs to be done can be done most effectively.

Although dasein's authentic goals, the laws of being, and the rules of proper behavior emerge from dasein's resolute transaction, this transaction itself has no goal, obeys no laws, and is governed by no rules imposed upon it from outside. It is tempting to see it as pure, unbridled willing, and to conclude that any theory of action based on the notion of such an action must be voluntaristic. But we should resist this temptation because it is impossible to see dasein's resolute transaction as willing. For, as *Being and Time* argues, willing is possible only under the condition that this transaction has taken place beforehand (*SZ*, p. 194).

However, when we ask under what conditions, in general, those factical possibilities towards which dasein projects itself in its resolute transaction can themselves emerge, then we find in *Being and Time* an answer that creates the impression that dasein's transaction is totally dependent on external, accidental, and circumstantial conditions. For *Being and Time* argues that they do not themselves emerge in and through dasein's transaction (*SZ*, p. 383).[37] Instead, the resolute transaction, "as thrown, *takes over*" and gathers the "factical possibilities of authentic existing" from the "heritage" (*SZ*, p. 383). And *Being and Time* even seems to imply[38] that dasein projects itself *exclusively* in terms of inherited possibilities. Resolute or irresolute, dasein seems to remain under the tyranny of its tradition. A gloomy prospect, indeed, for dasein's resolute, primordial transaction.[39]

Considering this "thrownness" of dasein's projection, one is tempted to be carried away with the later Heidegger into thinking that "what projects in projection is not man, but being itself" (*BH*, p. 84/285). But I think we should resist this temptation. For *Being and Time* demonstrates (especially in sections 53 and 61) that it is possible, after all, to "acquire power over dasein's existence" (*SZ*, p. 310) through dasein's resolute transaction, although never fully because of Dasein's facticity. For "taking over" the factical possibilities from the heritage does not mean that dasein must surrender its power of choosing its authentic existence. This "taking over", or "appropriating" (*SZ*, p. 21) is accomplished through the "repetition" of a possibility of existence that has come down to us" (*SZ*, p. 385). But by "going back into the possibilities of the dasein that has-been-there" (*SZ*, p. 385), dasein hands down *to itself* a possibility that has been as a possibility for *itself* to *choose*, that is, what has come down to us as a blinding commitment is rendered as our ownmost possibility to be decided upon in the freedom of choosing ourselves and taking hold of ourselves, now and again (*SZ*, pp. 188, 385f.). In the appropriation and repetition in which we hand down to ourselves a possibility that has been, "the Dasein that has-been-there is not disclosed in order to be actualized over again. The repeating of that which is possible does not bring again something that is 'past', nor does it bind the 'Present' back to that which has already been 'outstripped'. Arising, as it does, from a resolute projection of oneself, repetition does not let itself be persuaded of something by what is 'past', just in order that this, as something which was formerly actual, may recur. Rather, the repetition makes a *reciproactive rejoinder* to the possibility of that existence which has-been-there. But when such a rejoinder is made to this possibility in a resolution *now* [*als augenblickliche*], it is at the same time the *disavowal* of that which in the 'today,' is working itself out as the 'past'. Repetition does not abandon itself to the past, nor does it aim at progress. Authentic existence in the now [*im Augenblick*] is indifferent to both" (*SZ*, p. 385f.).

Consequently, dasein's "thrown" projection remains a primordial transaction that, in principle, has no goal, obeys no laws, and is governed by no rules imposed upon it from outside. As I have tried to show, it is in every respect the same as the great interplay that Heidegger so mysteriously describes in his later writings as the "event" which "destines" everything into its own and retains it there (see p. 70, above), except one: It does not play "over and above us," but only *in* and *through* us. We must insist against the late Heidegger that it is the play of dasein itself, only that and nothing else besides.

At every moment in the history of being, this interplay can be brought about only by dasein's understanding in the mode of assigning and projecting itself towards a final existential goal "unambiguously in terms of its ownmost distinctive [and factical] possibility" (*SZ*, p. 384). All *"responsive" thinking in terms of the history of being*, as the mere unfolding of the epochal truth of being, necessarily limps along after dasein's primordial transaction, as do, even more so, all *theoretical inspection and objectification* of what is made accessible and given through that transaction, and all *calculated practical action* concerning it.

Consequently in our attempt to make our practical actions conceptually transparent, we cannot halt at the theoretical inspection of what is given, that is, traditional ontology. At any time the fixed laws and rules for the calculation of practical action, provided by the theoretical inspection of what is given, can and must be justly accepted only if they can be recognized in each case as emerging from dasein's primordial transaction, that is, from dasein's fateful and resolute projection of itself, in interaction with the others (see above), towards a final existential goal in terms of its ownmost factical possibility. A unified theory of action seems to be possible, after all, and it seems to be possible only under this condition. As Habermas insisted for reasons of his own, we must renounce the classical tradition of building theories of action on the theoretical inspection of what is given.

PART 2

PHENOMENOLOGY AND

OTHER PHILOSOPHICAL CURRENTS

7. Karel Kosik's
Phenomenological Heritage

MILDRED BAKAN

I

Jan Broeckman, in his book *Structuralism*,[1] cites Karel Kosik as one of the leading contributors to the development of genetic structuralism in Czechoslovakia. He notes the affinity of Kosik's thought to that of Goldmann and also the importance of Husserlian phenomenology in the history of genetic structuralism in Czechoslovakia. But the themes of *Dialectics of the Concrete*, Kosik's major published work, are in many ways closer to Heidegger than to Husserl. Indeed, *Dialectics of the Concrete* may be characterized as a brilliant and suggestive amalgam of Hegelian-Marxist and Heideggerian strands of thought.

In effect, Kosik criticizes reductive Marxism from the perspective of existential phenomenology and phenomenology from the perspective of a Hegelian Marxism. This double-edged critique is suggested in the very title: the theme of the concrete picks up a central phenomenological concern, but Kosik's use of dialectical analysis is methodologically Hegelian Marxist. In the end Kosik's amalgam achieves a deepened reading of Marxism and an interesting critique of Heidegger.

For Kosik as for Husserl, the Being of the thing itself is a focal theme, as a clue to the Being of man. Kosik literally begins and ends *Dialectics of the Concrete* with the question: what is the thing itself? The think itself with which he is concerned is by no means the inaccessible Kantian *Ding-an-sich*; it is similar rather to the Husserlian thing itself (*die Sache selbst*) intentionally constituted in terms of essence and knowable through concrete fulfillment. Kosik retains Husserl's sense of essence as having both static and temporal dimensions but insists that essence in its static aspect is generated temporally as the interrelation of whole and part, operative in both nature and history. In *Ideas* Husserl correlates the static dimension of essence, constituted as a noematic nucleus, to our sense of future and past. In effect it is in terms of the identification of something as the same—its essence—that man is open to a world (of things) and to history. The Idea of the thing itself amounts to a Kantian schema, allowing us to anticipate the future and remember the past, grounding the conception of truth that informs science, indeed Reason, as the very telos of humanity. In his later work, Husserl claims that the sense of the thing, though presupposed by science, is practically and socially constituted in the *Lebenswelt* (life-world). But Husserl's position remains unchanged regarding the founding sense of the thing, as the ground of rationality as well as science.

For Kosik, too, the sense of the thing is practically and socially constituted in the *Lebenswelt* and presupposed by science and Reason as the telos of humanity. But Kosik singles out work as that uniquely human activity that first opens man to the thing as objectively being. By incorporating this Hegelian theme, Kosik opens up issues that are recognizable in Heidegger's own appropriation of Husserl.

Though work opens man to the thing, Kosik insists the thing itself is not immediately given. The think itself—as the disclosure of its essence—is accessible only dialectically. "To grasp it calls not only for a certain effort but also for a detour."[2] Kosik distinguishes the mere representation (*Vorstellung*) of the thing from the concept (*Bergriff*) of the thing. The representation of the thing is our familiar, taken for granted, understanding of the thing, whereas the concept of the thing is its dialectically grasped essence. A familiar understanding reaches only a false concreteness in that the thing itself is concealed as it is revealed. Yet it is only through the false concrete that initial access to the thing itself is gained. The grasp of the thing itself, as the graps of its essence, reaches the full reality of the thing itself: its *being as generated* in contrast to its everyday *appearance*. Thus, essence is not merely *intentionally* constituted. The essence of the thing is also the *real form* governing its genesis. But if form is essence, it is only completed, as we shall see, in dialectical relation with its fulfilling content. Kosik is a Hegelian Marxist who takes dialectics seriously both as a mode of analysis and as ontology.

Kosik insists, however, that the *reality* of the thing itself cannot be given to mere contemplative thought. A grasp of the reality of the thing can be achieved, at least initially, only by *practical* activity. Praxis, says Kosik, is man's opening to Being. Indeed praxis is, following Marx, the *clue* to man's unique being as an objective subject. Praxis amounts to man's self-formation as a socio-historical being. And it is on the ground of this self-formation that man is open to Being.

But man as open to Being is precisely Heidegger's *Dasein*. Not only does Kosik identify man as Heidegger's *Dasein*; he also shares Heidegger's sense of the everyday world as both concealing and revealing. According to Kosik, the very sense of reality is constituted through ordinary practical activity. This practical activity achieves an unmediated showing of the thing itself that is *partial*, and fixates this partial showing as a mere *representation* of the thing *limiting possible reality* and *possible activity*. Practical everyday activity cannot avoid selective focus, and insofar as this focus is not criticized and broadened, it remains frozen in its partial representation of reality, which is mistaken as Being or world.

Kosik describes the world of practical activity as a world of tools, instrumental things, means to the satisfaction of needs. Clearly, this is the everyday world of things, accessible to us, according to Heidegger, only in terms of the "hermeneutic-as." From the standpoint of phenomenology, Kosik seeks to save the Husserlian project of truth as a rational social telos grounded, however, in Heidegger's hermeneutic-as. Kosik retains Husserl's concept of essence as both the aim of knowledge and disclosive of the thing itself; but essence is now a hidden essence that can only be grasped dialectically through a detour, to use Kosik's own expression. Indeed, Heidegger himself, by emphasizing the hidden aspect of Being, introduces a dialectical moment missing in Husserl: the dialectic of light and dark. Kosik retains something of this dialectic, rejecting, however, what he considers its irrational thrust. Kosik draws on the *dialectical disunity* of our everyday lives as the basis of a rational critique of everyday intentionality. This dialectical disunity is *lived* as social conflict—the conflict of master and slave, ruler and ruled, of exploiter and exploited, manipulator and manipulated—and as the split of man and nature—subject and object, freedom and necessity, intent and causality. The very *disunity* has as its telos, *unity*, as a merely implicit or horizonal *totality*. Man open to Being lives in a *world as a horizonal totality*, rather than an environment. Partial disclosure founds a claim to truth that itself demands question and criticism in terms of a larger relevant totality. Whereas both Heidegger and Husserl attribute to Western civilization a unified telos in terms of a disclosure of Being by virtue of which we *are* a community, Kosik takes us to be divided by the hierarchical social organization of our work-mediated relation to nature. It is only through historical dialectical struggle that the essence of being human is developed, transformed, and realized. Man as an objective subject is at once in nature and history by transcending nature through social praxis. But dialectical historical struggle is itself an instance of that dialectical mediation of whole— or totality—and part, which governs the realization of essence in nature as well.

Though Kosik begins with the *methodological* problem of access to essence, it is because essence *is itself dialectically constituted* that, methodologically, access to essence requires a detour. In a sense Kosik accepts Heidegger's conception of a hidden though prevailing historical unity of meaning; that is, of a hidden unity of Being that our everyday lives disclose in a fragmented and partial way. But in contrast to Heidegger, this unity of meaning, as our root conception of reality, has been and is to be *practically worked out*, developed *humanly* in the world as a real resolution of dialectically related splits: between person and person and between person and nature. This unity of meaning, as achieved and to be achieved, is *known* as our conception, rather than representation, of reality, to which we are opened through our work. But it is developed and explicated through art and philosophy (whose major concerns are the relation of man and cosmos), through science (which aims at the spiritual duplication—interpretive decoding—of the genesis of things), and also through a critique of our everyday understanding, precisely by *aiming* at the resolution of lived dialectical splits. Thus, it is as a *true conception of reality* that this unity of meaning demands and achieves fulfillment in the real world.

Generally speaking, the basis of critique of our everyday lives is a dialectic relation of our *conception of reality*, as a cognitive moment, and *reality as lived*, as its existential counterpart. But this dialectical relation is the very stuff of history as well, insofar as history is rational. Our conception of reality is itself a social construct, as our mode of being open to a world we are collectively making. Man collectively makes a world, which can be *conceptualized* as reality. We are not, however, locked in our social being. *By making a world we also develop diverse abilities and sensibilities that effect our opening to the Being of the thing in the manner of Husserlian inentionality.* Precisely because our social being is achieved through praxis—making a world—we are open to the cosmos—nature—itself. But to take what is as *real*, whether as represented or conceptualized, is to go beyond what is present in terms of a *telos*—a direction. Thus our mode of being open to reality is the telos in terms of which we live, opening our future as relevant possibilities for our lives.

The Husserlian sense of truth as more than what is, as a telos relative to an intentionality that goes beyond itself to its fulfillment, is retained. But is is retained as Heidegger's sense of *world* as totalizing and hidden Being. Truth is *aletheia*—uncovering—and as such does not separate the emotive from the cognitive. Moreover, for both Kosik and Heidegger, the everyday world as the context of our mode of work is of decisive importance with respect to the disclosure of Being. But it is just at this point that Kosik breaks with Heidegger's thought. According to Heidegger, our mode of work is informed by an implicit, covered over, disclosure of Being, granted to a people. Fundamentally this disclosure of Being is a *poetic* grasp of totality, disclosing the Being of things *as* it opens a socially shared future for those who hear its message. Kosik rejects this analysis as a bit of contemporary romanticism, reminiscent of Schelling's denigration of work as dirty. In a work world organized along bureaucratic lines, in which social relations are manipulated and dominated by a technology that we for the most part do not understand, we feel incapable of doing anything about our situation. So according to Kosik, Heidegger's analysis of the everyday world as a world in which we live *without initiative* is of a piece with his conception of dasein as the place of the granted self-disclosure of Being. Man is taken as essentially *passive*. Kosik, on the contrary, takes our conception of reality to be relative to a world made by man through work and creatively elucidated and unified as reality or Being through art, philosophy, religion, and so forth, in a way that integrates the conception of reality and reality as lived. The possibility of science itself is grounded in that opening to the Being of things that arises with work. According to Kosik, scientific truth *duplicates* the very genesis of things; it is a project to which man is disposed by virtue of being a *working* or *making* creature. Work is thus given not only the epistemological importance of the hermeneutic-as, but the ontological importance of *separating man from nature*, and originating the dialectical splits whose resolution in the real world is our shared telos— our shared opening to the future—informing history itself.

According to Kosik, work as world-making is already totalizing. Work is not simply informed by a totalizing disclosure of Being, as Heidegger would have it; it is what gives rise to our totalizing grasp of reality as Being. Work itself, as world making, opens man to Being as a totalizing grasp of reality. By splitting man from nature, work grounds that claim to truth in which we live, and which has, as its moments, the thing itself as transcendent power and also our partial knowledge of its being. The totalizing grasp of reality is itself a problematic resolution of the dialectical split from nature that work originates. The resolution of this split requires a creative integration of nature and history, as Being, in terms of which we are transformed and our future opened anew as a shared telos to be realized.

Kosik's claim is that any conception of man and his world which ignores the role of work in *transforming* that world and man himself is a mystification, an inauthentic romanticization. Basically, Kosik claims that Heidegger has failed to recognize praxis as the primordial determination of man, in which *temporality itself is grounded.* Drawing on both Hegel and Marx, Kosik argues that work is the basis for temporality, our sense of future and past, and so the basis of our awaren ss of the possibility of dying, a central theme of Heidegger's *Being and Time.* Thus, what is for Heidegger *authentic* disclosure, is for Kosik *inauthentic.* Work opens history and itself renders the leisure for art possible. Praxis, says Kosik, is the opening of man to Being, but praxis itself is a dialectically *achieved unity* of work and its subjective moments: temporality, anxiety, joy, language. So man makes himself— that is, as a *person*—as he makes his world collectively. And economy is the totalized integration of work, as the region of necessity, with art, as the region of free activity. Work is a making dominated by extraneous purposes, whereas art is a making dominated by purposes intrinsic to the object itself.

In fact, Kosik does little to argue the ontic relation of work to temporality beyond Hegel's analysis of work in the context of the master-slave relation. Kosik points out that labor creates an object as a stable, spatial embodiment of human activity and thus objectively integrates the past and future *as* present. As such, labor achieves a specifically human "identity of time (temporality) and space (exten-sion)."[3] It creates an object as a piece of man's world by incorporating human meanings into nature, transforming nature through *human ob-jectification.* In just this sense, labor is world-making Praxis as an integration of work and subjectivity that forms our very culture, for subjectivity must be integrated with work as collectively world making.

For both Kosik and Heidegger, work generates the sense of envi-ronment as home, a conception that is recognizably Hegelian. In that sense work humanizes the world. Heidegger, however, insists that the earth allows us to humanize it, and it is this that technology has covered over, a relationship to nature that remains in close response to its call. It is the poet who recognizes this relation of work to nature, and who thus *establishes* the relation of work to Being as a tradition we keep. More accurately, for Heidegger, it is not work that is primordially distant from nature (as Kosik claims), but work informed by poetry. We can put it this way: *it is poetry that converts animal nest building into work as world-making.*

Perhaps Kosik says so little about the relation of work to temporality because he simply presupposes the Hegelian analysis of the relation of work to temporality through deferred desire. (According to Hegel, it is deferred desire in the context of labor that is transformed into thought.) What is more serious is that Kosik fails to take due account of the close relation of work to language. The relation of work to language in effect introduces the problem of the relation of praxis to language, which Kosik seems to regard as secondary. Work as the transformation of things is thought informed. The object as the product of work involves a sense of future as the possible object that is not now, but is to be made. The possible object as the object to be made is absent. Reference to an absent object is precisely what language achieves. Though the point of Hegel's own analysis is that work itself is primordial thought (as an activity that opposes itself to an independent and enduring object), surely thought does not develop without language.

Kosik's failure to take due account of language introduces some ambiguity into his analysis of the dialectics of the master-slave relation. Kosik recognizes that on the Hegelian analysis, it is in the context of the master-slave dialectic that the uniquely human sense of future arises. Somewhat confusedly, drawing on a gloss by Engels, he argues that the master and slave project themselves into the immediate future as respectively master and slave! Subjective temporality is thus—quite interestingly—tied to personal self-formation in the social context of labor with the future taken as an *immediate* future.

But it is important to note that dominance does not yet imply that sense of the future that the Hegelian master-slave relation establishes only through work. Submission under threat remains at the level of merely animal (or natural) effort. Language that accomplishes reference to what is absent can itself be taken back to the unique mutuality of intersubjective human address. That *opening* to Being that Kosik and Heidegger both speak of is also the mutual *opening* of person to person in terms of the potentiality for speech. And the context of person to person mutuality—the precise context of dialogue—is also the context of oppression as a violation of recognition.

Though Hegel clearly recognizes that work and thought go together and that thought is inseparable from the human demand for equality, Hegel grounds the bare freedom from nature primordially in the Greek courage to die. But the courage to die is not the same as merely animal dominance and submission. The courage to die is set in the context of a demand for recognition that marks the birth of the ego. The demand for recognition that Hegel grounds in the telos of the absolute idea is itself implicit in speech as the mutuality of personal address, a point to which I will return later.

Nevertheless, the difference between work and speech is crucial. Insofar as we are open to each other dialogically, we let each other be. We understand each other in terms of a mutual development of intentionality. To be open to *things*, however, in terms of *work*, is to be open to their *possible transformation*. The transformation of things opens us to their causal relations. The transformation of nature requires the intelligent use of natural resources, which requires bodily effort and social organization. Furthermore, speech itself is hardly enough to overcome domination. Our modes of working together, as our mode of relating to nature, are embedded in the dual exigencies of natural and socially organized force. By virtue of the *transformation of the thing* man relates to what is, as a power on which he is dependent and knowledge of which is decisive for his survival. Heidegger at best ignores and, at worst, denigrates these aspects of our relation to nature as merely technical. From the standpoint of a Kosikian analysis, what Heidegger terms merely "categorical" thought, limits and opens up the *possible transformation of things*. (So a thing must be some color, some shape, some size, etc.) Work is not only constitutive of the hermeneutic-as; it is also constitutive of the "apophantic-as."

Kosik, by taking work as our primordial opening to the thing itself, is able to bridge the gap between meaning and causality that neither Husserl nor Heidegger can manage. Neither Husserl nor Heidegger has any place for the reality of things as a power on which we are dependent *and* of which we can nevertheless have knowledge. By taking work as grounding perception and language rather than the reverse, Kosik emphasizes our active, bodily relation to the thing in terms of its categorical possibilities.

Kosik, following Hegel's concept of reality as a hierarchy of levels of organization, takes the highest level of totality to be an integration of nature and history, which man as a social being develops. This integration opens up our future as a *meaningful telos* that takes account of our past and our relation to nature, transcending nature as we are opened to nature. Teleological totality, as concrete totality—the very thing itself, as Kosik concludes—is thus nothing less than man's *achieved*—and *achieving*—relation to reality *in* reality, a subject-object unity, which work renders problematic by splitting man from nature. Indeed, Kosik claims it is impossible to live humanly except in terms of some such totalizing telos.

III

A conception of Being that opens our future as a telos to be lived amounts to a mode of humanly living desire that *integrates thought and desire.* Indeed, according to Kosik, social praxis can be more or less rational according as it is informed by objective knowledge of totality. Though teleological totality is always historically effective, history is reasonable only insofar as we are reasonable. Yet ultimate totality is *never* fully known. Ultimate totality is radically horizonal, as a telos in terms of which we live. Moreover, whatever knowledge we may achieve of structures—whether of things or of society—is, insofar as we know, knowledge of *partial* totalities. That ultimate totality is radically horizonal guarantees the ongoing possibility of critique of our totalizing conceptions as partial and the advance of knowledge itself, through the double process of integration and analysis of partial totalities.

This is the conception of rationality—indeed cognition—Kosik repeatedly draws on in his specific analyses, ranging from the brilliant textual interpretation of Marx's writings to the concepts of social and natural science. Though this conception of rationality is by no means adequately developed, it is philosophically one of the most exciting themes of this book. Kosik demands that every integrative totalization be tested in terms of its implications for its relevant parts. In particular, a totalization must be able to account for the genesis of the parts totalized. Vague though this criterion may be, it is highly suggestive.

I want now to dwell especially on the implications of this concept of rationality for the recovery of authenticity. With respect to everyday life, which is for Kosik the special domain of social praxis, a totalizing grasp of relevant structures brings us back to our everyday situation with something like a Kierkegaardian second immediacy to inform our praxis with a *conscious* relation to totality. Through a dereifying grasp of the *genesis* of our everyday life, we gain insight into our world as *humanly made* and therefore possibly otherwise. Despite the mediating role of totality, Kosik, like Husserl, insists that rationality is essentially *individual* insight. So insight into the genesis of our everyday life should recover the *authentic* sense of ourselves as *makers*, much as, for Sartre, the recovery of oneself as the origin of one's project is in some sense the recovery of one's freedom. The recovery of our authentic being as makers transforms us as persons. On the one hand, we gain a sense of ourselves as able to change our situation, and on the other hand, we achieve an informed sensibility opening us to aspects of our situation to which we would otherwise be blind.

Clearly Kosik's concept of totality, as the *form-governed genesis of its parts*, goes far beyond Husserl's concept of totality as a merely *meant* identifiable unity. Kosik takes objective knowledge—science— to be a spiritual reproduction of the genesis of what is real. Just as work is making, so knowledge is *making*, but as the reproduction of the *real* making—or genesis—of things through a process of decoding. Indeed, he appears to interpret objective knowledge as belonging to our *authentic* mode of being open to the universe, with virtually no further exploration of the relation of praxis to knowledge. But Kosik's sense of the relation of science to praxis is considerably clarified if we recognize the focal importance of his concept of nature as *natura naturans* (nature creating—forming—itself). Man himself is a maker who belongs to nature as *naturans*. The recovery of knowledge of the genesis of things relates man *intellectually* to nature as *naturans* and so belongs to a recovery of man's own authentic nature as creative. In effect, man, recovering himself intellectually as *natura naturans*, understands himself as creative and vital, in his own being integrated with nature as making itself. This amounts to a recovery of oneself as the place of disclosure of Being, as *Dasein*, at the point of fusion with *nature as productive in the Greek sense*: a conception of nature Heidegger seeks to undo in the direction of what he takes to be a deeper disclosure of nature in terms of fate and measure. This concept of authenticity is implicit in Kosik's concept of objective knowledge as a recovery of the real form-governed genesis of things and his claim that man loses a revitalizing aspect of his own being without the sense of himself as natural. The nature that is the object of scientific thought is Spinoza's *natura naturans*, knowledge of which revitalizes man's own being by achieving the integration of intellect and nature as the integration of intellect and desire.

Clearly, Kosik retains Husserl's strong sense of the self-determination of man. But for Kosik, man is primordially free as concretely making himself. It is by virtue of making himself collectively by *making his world* (the richest meaning of work) that man is open to Being and knowledge of the thing. It is as though man's conscious shaping of things sensitizes him to nature as shaping itself. Making and rationality, as insight into essence, belong together. The possibility of acting on the basis of objective knowledge is an essential aspect of human freedom, and correlatively human activity—praxis—itself implies the ongoing possibility of the development of rational critique.

We can discern in Kosik's concept of objective knowledge the aim of Husserlian genetic phenomenology, as the recovery of the constitution of essence, projected, however, into the regional idea of the things themselves, as the genesis of their Being. In this deciphering of the nature of things, totality enters as that in terms of which they are deciphered. Everything, that is, is part of a specific whole. But it is part of a whole as an instance of *natura naturans*. Though, to my mind, this is a very interesting development of the Husserlian position, Kosik barely develops its implications in *Dialectics of the Concrete*.

Indeed, Kosik's apparent vision of human being as a maker belonging to *natura naturans* lends itself to an over-simplification of the relationship of teleological totality—and its fulfilling praxis—to objective knowledge.

Ultimate teleological totality is inextricably involved in our Being-in-the-world as a shared telos whose achievement is inseperable from our personal (and social) integrity. Teleological totalization structures possibility as a promise of our future. Our totalizing telos is itself to be achieved as a demand of our own Being-in-the-world. But then it is lived, by informing praxis, at so deep a level that it cannot be separated from our personal identity. Our telos, as a totalizing orientation, is not reducible to the possible being of a specifiable object, though our totalizing orientation may open us to specifiable objects. Furthermore, as Kosik himself recognizes, our mode of being open to specifiable objects is not quite the same as our mode of being open to each other, though our mode of being open to each other has as its facticity our praxis-generated social being. Indeed, our telos as a totalizing orientation demands fulfillment in a real world shared by others, in the context of our *social relations* to each other.

What is the relation between personal identity and our mode of being open to the cosmos, on the one hand, and our mode of being open to each other on the other hand? Kosik insists that freedom is "an historical activity that forms corresponding modes of human coexistence"[4] yet he maintains that all philosophy has as its fundamental problem the conceptualization of the relation of man to the cosmos. Not only is social reality to be understood in terms of man's relation to the cosmos; social reality is *itself shaped* by our understanding of our relation to the cosmos to which we are opened in the social context of our transformation of nature. As for Heidegger, so for Kosik, our mode of being open to the cosmos is inseparable from our mode of being open to each other. Dasein is *Mitsein*, being-with-others. But we have to qualify Kosik's position in the following way: our mode of being open to each other has as its facticity our social existence as structured by the social organization of the productive forces of society. Quite specifically, in our time the social organization of productive forces occludes—covers over—the *subjective* side of what is indeed objective. By restoring its context as concrete totality, what is culturally objective is revealed as made by experiencing actors, who, while fashioning socio-human reality, are, as *subjects*, open to the infinite cosmos. And it is as makers of socio-human reality that our own Being is at issue. Repeatedly Kosik points out the revolutionary potential of the demand for recognition in the context of exploitation. But a demand for recognition can make sense only as the social acknowledgement of individual Being-in-the-world: in short, as objective subjectivity. As a demand for recognition, freedom from exploitation involves a life and death struggle on the plane of the ego: *conscious* opposition or negativity with personal identity at stake.

Kosik's position suggests an ongoing dialectical relation between desire and rationality, essentially mediated by personal identity, which he hardly explores. Man himself belongs to nature as a living creature who is radically originative. He is radically originative as distant from nature and yet in working, transforming relation to nature. Only a creature that is radically originative can speak. (Speech itself opens and closes alternative possibility.) Though scientific theory may thrive in an atmosphere of debate, we cannot maintain any personal integrity— identity—apart from a socially shared integrative synthesis of nature and of our sense of the future and the past. This integrative synthesis specifies and limits an otherwise essentially indeterminate future transcending what is simply objective. So we can acknowledge something like a fundamental poetic disclosure of Being as a hermeneutic, heuristic dimension of thought—even of scientific theory—ineradicable by virtue of our being open to the future in terms of the Being of things as some integrated synthesis. This poetic dimension remains essential because man himself belongs to nature as a living creature who is radically originative. But precisely because human being is radically originative, a rational critique of scientific theorizing and of our mode of being open to the future need not be surrendered.

At just this point, Kosik's concept of a generative part-whole relation as a clue to the Being of things can ground a concept of rationality. The genius of science itself lies in an ongoing process of imaginative synthesis and analysis that respects both technique and, as Kosik points out, detail. Analysis breaks up integration and allows—indeed demands—imaginative reintegration. In the end the ground of the possibility of rationality is that any totalization can be put in question as a totalizing structure. But a totalizing telos as the promise of our future specifies our future as tied to our personal identity. The ground of the possibility of rationality is as we shall see also the ground of the possibility of irrationality.

Desire is nature on the inside, nature as lived body, establishing its integrity as it makes itself, on the Hegelian analysis, which Kosik accepts: a *felt* contradiction between subject and object, negativity as deficiency. Desire, *insofar as it is integrated with personal identity*, is informed by an interpretive context, which amounts to, following Kosik, an integrated synthesis of our understanding of nature and history. But the integration of *desire* and *personal identity* is problematic. Desire can break out, disrupting personal identity; it can be suppressed, re-pressed, or simply entertained and evaluated.

Kosik insists that oppression does not lie in our knowledge of nature but in oppressive relations to each other. In a provocative statement confined to a footnote, Kosik points out that the master-slave dialectic is the very model of praxis. He takes as a crucial aspect of this model that the slave must know himself to be a slave—and indeed a laboring slave—and that the slave's plight is shared by other slaves. (This Kosik calls the existential dimension of praxis.) But to be oppressed and to know that one is oppressed are quite different matters. The rupture of personal identity as an integration of desire and thought must move from *depression, as the loss of future hope, to confrontation, as the readiness to die for a future* if oppression is to be acknowledged so as to open us to the possibility of social change and an altered perspective of the way things are.

When is the readiness to die rational? The courage to die can spend itself in a riot or ongoing rebellion. In the context of oppression, the recovery of vital desire can erupt as a desperate and immediate act of bravado that is not of itself a conscious recovery of oneself as able to change one's situation. And yet, if *shared*, such recovery of desire, however limited, may lead to constructive change. A social problem is at least brought into the open. Relevant discourse and action with others in a similar situation may open up new perspectives on the objective social situation and is *itself* politically and personally trans-formative.

Personal identity is *essentially* constituted through dialogue—more specifically addressive dialogue. Character structure, as an aspect of personal identity, opens up and closes the space of social discourse. But as a personal telos, a character structure is also a mode of being open to the world—especially the everyday world—as an arena for fulfillment in the context of our social relations to each other. At this point we reach the limits of dialogue. Those who share our telos are those with whom we can speak and act collectively. Those who oppose our telos are those against whom we must engage in struggle. Clearly, not everyone can risk a disruption of character structure on rational grounds alone. To complicate the matter further, the development of personal identity is itself dependent—and perhaps more deeply—on nurture by individual persons, more or less in the context of social structures. Dialogue itself is constitutive of personal identity only in terms of what might be called a dimension of nurture. Intimate social ties, as well as character structure, may be threatened by rational insight.

Yet, because we are human, our orientation can be individually suspended, put in question. Precisely because personal identity as an integrative whole is not simply a matter of natural necessity, personal identity can change through rational insight into its informing totality; but personal identity can resist change by irrational self-closure, or endure an intermediate crisis period of deep personal conflict that takes time to resolve itself. On the one hand, what might be called the objective social totality enters into the potentiality for self-reflective awareness in terms of, say, the objective potentiality for personal power and the objective potentiality for communication and access to information. On the other hand, the potentiality for self-reflective awareness depends on courage, ranging from the readiness to die to oneself to the readiness to challenge another.

Despite the shortcomings of his effort, Kosik's conception of Nature as *natura naturans* has a compelling political thrust. In effect, the conception of man as belonging to nature that makes itself is a call to man consciously to make himself, a call to assume responsibility for our socio-historical being, as, in fact, generated by man, and to assume this responsibility not in resigned alienation from nature, as Sartre would have it, but as part of nature itself as, so to speak, entitled to desire by desire.

Man, though he belongs to nature, is not simply determined. Yet human creativity is informed by a split from nature, which renders rational critique possible and relevant but not decisive. Human creativity that does not recognize rational critique can be demonic. At best it remains blind. Blind desire, nature as lived, erupts without relation to knowledge of objective structures. Our split from nature demands an integration of desire and rationality, of nature as lived and as known, which remains, however, tenuous. Praxis involves a dialectical relation of thought and desire mediated by the sense—or meaning—of one's life as a whole.

On the one hand, Kosik is establishing social science as objective science. On the other hand, he is answering the political question: what is to be done? By tying rationality to the demand for recognition of man as subjective-objective, Kosik is developing a vision of a society that respects science and technology but cherishes subjectivity as the very condition of rationality. That he shares with Husserl. He is *also* calling for the recognition of ourselves and others as objective subjects in a way that overcomes the distinction between master and slave and unifies the regions of necessity and free activity. Kosik's work is *itself* a call to rationality as—to use his words—revolutionary praxis. As such, his work is an instance of rationality as personally transformative and potentially historically effective as a call for a society that will live in the truth of what is concretely happening. Marxism acquires a profoundly phenomenological dimension.

8. Marx and the Roots
of Existential Social Thought

TOM ROCKMORE

It is a philosophical truism, which is well known, but not frequently illustrated, and more often ignored, that basic and unbridgeable differences arise between positions in virtue of the differences in their respective starting points or ultimate assumptions. In the following paper, I shall explore one such difference in perspective as it affects the dialogue between Marx, Marxism, and existential phenomenology.

The discussion will proceed in four stages. To begin with, I shall identify, with respect to Descartes's position, a problem of continuing interest in the later philosophical tradition. I shall then suggest that in part the turn of certain representatives of existential phenomenology to Marx and Marxism can be understood in terms of a concern to resolve the problem identified in Descartes's thought. Thirdly, I shall defend existential phenomenology against a specific, but I believe mistaken, criticism leveled against it from a Marxist perspective. Finally, I shall suggest that one constraint in the dialogue between Marx and existential phenomenology can be located in a quasi-Cartesian view of intellectual freedom accepted by representatives of existential phenomenology, but rejected by Marx, which in turn points to differences in their respective views of human being.

In a recent posthumously published book, the suggestion has been made by Lucien Goldmann that Marxism provides the intellectual jumping-off point for existentialism, through the supposed influence of Georg Lukács on Heidegger. Although there may well be some truth to a weaker version of this thesis, it should come as no suprise, in view of the political and intellectual importance of French Marxism, that French existentialism is profoundly marked by the encounter with it. If for present purposes, we limit the discussion merely to Sartre and Merleau-Ponty, two of the main representatives of French existentialism, it can safely be said that the importance of Marxism for their respective views of social thought is considerable. Indeed, it seems to me difficult, and perhaps not possible, to provide an adequate account of the conceptual development of either philosopher over time without reference to Marxism and France and as such.

If we turn now to an account of the dialogue of existentialism with Marxism, we can immediately see that this dialogue can be approached on several planes. One level is that of the impact of Marxism on French cultural life, through the role of the French Community Party. A second level is that which was generated by the enormous and well documented influence of Kojève's lectures on Hegel in French intellectual circles. Third, there is the specific logic of the development of French existentialism in terms of its own internal philosophical problematic. Because in part my aim in this discussion of the existential encounter with Marxism will finally be to address the significance of that dialogue, I shall concentrate here mainly on the intrinsic logic of the existential turn to Marx, mindful however that this procedure tends to eliminate from the discussion an important, but essentially prephilosophical, component of the total situation. Nevertheless, beyond the restrictions imposed by space here, I would defend this approach on the grounds that in the final analysis at least as much, if not more, is to be learned by a simplified account than through a more complex discussion of all possible factors, which would ultimately obscure the points at issue in the attention to detail.

The problem that I believe is central to an understanding of the existentialist dialogue with Marxism can be raised in terms of Descartes. Although his role in the shaping of the modern philosophical tradition has often been exaggerated, it seems clear that he provides a framework that, even if more often rejected than accepted, largely influences the modern tradition and in particular provides a standard to compare the views of existentialism and Marxism. Sartre, to be sure, has often been called the last of the Cartesians; and it has been suggested that Merleau-Ponty is the first post-Cartesian French philosopher. But from another perspective, the situation is rather more complex. For there are numerous, profound similarities between the positions of Sartre and Merleau-Ponty, in virtue of which they can both be fairly labeled existentialist phenomenologists. And although Sartre may well be closer in spirit and doctrine to the Cartesian position, it would be simplistic, I believe, to assert without qualification that he is Cartesian and his colleague is not. On the contrary, in some ways both can be classified as Cartesian—in particular, as I shall show, with respect to their adherence to a quasi-Cartesian view of human freedom, which is one of the constraints upon the dialogue in question.

In turning now to Descartes, I should immediately indicate that I shall focus neither on the intrinsic resources of his position, nor on its full interpretation, but rather on a problem it seemed to raise for later philosophy. There are, I submit, many interesting problems that emerge from Descartes' position but probably none that has been of more enduring importance for subsequent thought than his famous ontological division of reality into two realms of being, thought and extension, different not in degree but in kind. Of immediate interest here is the relation of this ontological distinction to the Cartesian conception of subjectivity. A full account would study the relation of will to intellect in the Cartesian position, but we can be briefer because it is another aspect of the theory that has relevance here. It is well known that on Descartes's view the subject is not an actor but a spectator; and the Cartesian subject is further unconstrained by its surroundings and hence wholly free, presumably in virtue of the distinction between thought and being. But because for Descartes the concepts of ontology and subjectivity are apparently interrelated, it is not wholly unexpected that the later move away from Cartesian ontology is linked to a turn towards another, non-Cartesian, indeed anti-Cartesian, form of subjectivity.

The presence of an anti-Cartesian reaction has often been remarked in studies of the modern tradition, although its significance for the relation of Marx to existential phenomenology does not seem to have been widely noticed if indeed it has been previously noticed at all. In reading the history of philosophy, it would seem that one of the most persistent themes in the period after Descartes is a revolt against the strictures of his view, an attempt to break out of the Cartesian framework. From Vico, whose importance was only recognized later, onwards, the struggle against Descartes's thought took place in many regions of later philosophy, especially in German idealism, where we can discern a continuing concern to relativize the original distinction between thought and being through emphasis on an anti-Cartesian concept of an active subject.

A well known instance is Kant's insistence that the subject's production of the object is the condition of any knowledge at all; the result of this is that, at the cost of understanding the subject in anti-Cartesian fashion as an active being, objectivity can be shown to depend on subjectivity. Nevertheless, a variant of the Cartesian difficulty recurs elsewhere in Kant's position, in particular in Kant's well-known inability to understand the manner in which the phenomenal and noumenal realms, distinguished within the epistemological side of his theory, are in fact to be related within ethical activity. It is this Kantian form of the Cartesian problem that further recurs within existentialism.

The precise relation of Sartre and Merleau-Ponty to preceding moments of the philosophical tradition is a complex historical problem that cannot be discussed here. And there are further a number of important differences between the two positions that inform the way in which each of them approaches Marxism. But there are at least two similarities that should be noted as relevant to the present context. To begin with, although this is more the case for Sartre than for his existentialist colleague, both being from a quasi-Cartesian concept of subjectivity as different, not in degree but in kind, from objectivity. This similarity generates a specific, quasi-Cartesian problem, namely, how can we comprehend the interaction between man and his world if in the final analysis they are unrelated? It is, I believe, through his own difficulty in responding to this concern within the context of his position that Sartre turns to Marxism as a source of an imperfectly formulated theory of action, which presumably can be made to speak to this issue. And in similar manner, it is the awareness of Sartre's inability to resolve this difficulty within the limits of his position that also impels Merleau-Ponty, although in different fashion, in the same direction. But although the dialogue that arises in this way between Marxism and existentialism is in fact significant, its nature is intrinsically limited, for reasons I shall specify below, by the sense in which existentialism continues to accept a modified form of the Cartesian view of human freedom. For if we prescind for a moment from his Marxist followers, Marx, whether rightly or wrongly, on this point as on others as well, adopts a firmly anti-Cartesian stance.

If we turn now to Sartre, we can see at once that his early writings, including *Being and Nothingness*, demonstrate virtually no acquaintance with Marxism, a fact that Sartre has himself confirmed on more than one occasion. Nevertheless, the ensuing attempt to come to grips with Marxism, which began in the mid-1940s, continues as a central theme in unmodified fashion in Sartre's thought for more than three decades until his recent death and hence remains one of the leading themes of his entrie position. Sartre's specific approach to Marxism, although not necessarily the Marxist response to it, is largely determined, I believe, by the prior existence of his own philosophical position and in particular by a problem arising within it. Sartre, to be sure, is clearly engaged in a valuable effort, in Marxian terminology, to discover the rational kernel in materialist mythology, in other words, to turn right side up the materialist dialectic that in the writings of Marx's dogmatic acolytes is standing on its head. But, to employ Sartrean terminology, everything happens in his encounter with Marxism as if it provides him ultimately with an occasion to resolve a difficulty in phenomenological ontology.

Critics of Sartre's phenomenological ontology have often noticed a residual dualism in it. Indeed, it would appear that there is a certain tension between Sartre's desire to overcome various forms of dualism and the dualistic approach he employs in *Being and Nothingness*. The book, to be sure, opens with an attempt to replace a variety of forms of dualism with the single concept of the phenomenon, which betrays an interest in monism. But dualism immediately reappears on several levels: within the phenomenon viewed as an opposition between finite and infinite perspectives, between consciousness and being or for-itself and in-itself, and further within consciousness, in the distinction between its thetic and positional and nonthetic or nonpositional levels.

Sartre, to be sure, is not unaware of this problem, whose solution he envisages, but does not provide at this time. As early as the Introduction, he remarks that although he has distinguished two separate realms of being, that of the prereflective cogito and that of the being of the phenomenon, neither can be fully understood until their relation between themselves and with being in general has been elucidated. Certainly the later discussion of other topics, such as transcendence, solipsism, and the relation of being to being, contribute to this end. But in the Conclusion, Sartre returns to the problem of a hiatus at the core of being. Here he states that the necessary reunion between the elements cannot be effected because the reciprocity of the relation prevents us from grasping it in its integrity. This remark is, of course, consistent with Sartre's insistence on the distinction between the being of the phenomenon and the phenomenon of being. But light can nevertheless be shed on this problem through a theory of action concerned with what Sartre calls the "transcendent efficacy of consciousness" as a clue to the relation of being with being. This latter task is the province of existential psychoanalysis, an anti-Freudian approach whose aim is precisely to produce a synthesis of consciousness of being. But (and here I am admittedly reading between the lines in terms of the later evolution of Sartre's position), although existential psychoanalysis will enable us to furnish a concrete analysis of the individual human project in irreducible terms, it is no substitute for the concrete general theory of human action, whose first, albeit imperfect, statement can be found in Marxism.

From this perspective, whose presupposition is a certain continuity, despite evident evolution, between earlier and later phases of Sartre's thought (for instance, in the concept of freedom), the successful extension of his theory of phenomenological ontology would seem to require a theory of action on at least three levels, namely, those of (1) the individual, (2) the group, and (3) the interaction of both individual and group in human history. The first element is furnished, by existential psychoanalysis, in several shorter studies such as those on Baudelaire and Genêt, in Sartre's own autobiography, *The Words,* and in his ongoing account of Flaubert; it is sketched successively in *Being and Nothingness* and *Search for a Method,* and it is developed at massive length in the unfinished *Family Idiot.* The latter work represents the most developed attempt in Sartre's corpus and, despite Proust's accomplishment, perhaps in the entire literature, to reconstitute completely an individual life as a project through an analysis of its basic components. At the same time, this instance of existential psychoanalysis serves as an example of the kind of concrete historical analysis lacking in the rigid dogmatism of Marxist writers such as Lukács, but which Marx has made available in his own study of the *Eighteenth Brumaire.*

The second element, which is provided by the encounter with Marxism, takes place in several interrelated stages, including criticism and reformulation of Marxist theory on theorectical and practical planes. As early as *Existentialism is a Humanism* (1945), intended as a voluntary vulgarization of his own work for a wider audience, Sartre begins to shift his attention from the isolated consciousness, as necessarily condemned to freedom, to the group, in his claim that the desire for individual freedom necessarily implies that for all men. This statement fits closely with his view of Marxism in *Materialism and Revolution* (1946) as a humanism whose goal is to bring about human liberation of all oppressed people through force. This text, which exhibits greater Sartrean sensitivity to problems of Marxism than I had previously recognized, and perhaps more so than is apparent in his later writings, is further doubly characteristic of Sartre's later discussions of Marxism. In the first place, Sartre is severely critical of Marxist orthodoxy, although here as elsewhere he fails to distinguish clearly between Marxism and Marx, which perhaps in turn induced him to accept uncritically certain Marxist dogmas, such as the claim that Marxism is and must be a science. Secondly, after criticizing Marxism, he immediately proposes to reformulate it, largely in terms of ideas borrowed for the purpose from his own thought, such as the concepts of freedom and situation. The attempt to reformulate Marxism on his own Sartrean basis is a recurrent theme in numerous later texts, such as *Communists and Peace* (1953), *Search for a Method* (1957), and the much longer *Critique of Dialectical Reason* (1960). In *Materialism and Revolution,* the claim is made that the resultant philosophy, much like that announced in *Being and Nothingness,* is neither idealism nor materialism but the theory of the completely free act. But the reformulated theory presumably goes beyond the original version of phenomenological ontology. It anticipates claims made later in *Search for a Method* concerning its own status, to the effect that it is a means to the eventual future affirmation of human liberty under socialism, while at the same time constituting both the philosophy of all mankind until socialism has been realized and the concrete truth of all men.

Despite their undoubted interest, the later texts on Marxism are mainly further extensions, often in novel ways, of the twin themes of criticism and reformulation already present in Sartre's earlier writings. Neither the published portion of *Critique of Dialectical Reason*, which contains the theory of ensembles preceding the discussion of history as a progressive totalization and of historical truth as a process nor the vast discussion of Flaubert in the *Family Idiot* does more than develop the project already visible in Sartre's corpus as early as *Materialism and Revolution*. The single exception might be the brief references to the view of history, the third element in the dialogue with Marxism, to be found in the third volume of the study of Flaubert, where we find passages attempting to relate the micrototalization on the level of the individual to the macrototalization on the historical plane.

If we turn now to Merleau-Ponty, we can note that in part the differences in the respective existentialist views of Marxism can be attributed to personal disparities, some of which Sartre has himself mentioned in a well-known essay written on the occasion of his colleague's death. But beyond personal facts, philosophical differences, evident in Merleau-Ponty's criticism of a position to which he was otherwise much indebted, also played a role. Although perhaps the best known of these criticisms is his denunciation of Sartre for ultra-Bolshevism, in my opinion more is to be learned, as concerns the difference in the two approaches to Marxism, from Merleau-Ponty's remarks in an early article, "The Battle over Existentialism," which appeared in the same year as the *Phenomenology of Perception* (1945), his major treatise. Here we find his dissatisfaction at Sartre's inability to relate subjectivity and objectivity and, by implication, to go beyond Descartes.

The article was meant to consider the silence with which Sartre's treatise on phenomenological ontology had been welcomed. Merleau-Ponty here approaches *Being and Nothingness* in terms of the problem of subjectivity. In relation to this problem, he distinguishes two views, of which the first tends to reduce man to a thing among things in terms of the influences operative upon him, whereas the second understands man, in so far as he possesses a mind capable of knowledge, as "cosmic freedom." Now Sartre, to be sure, desires in the first instance to present subjectivity as liberty untainted by a relation to being. But the result is a series of antitheses that leaves unclarified the problematical relation of conscience to action. Otherwise stated, an acceptable account of human being must understand the subject at the same time as his body, his world, and his situation, that is, not only as transcendent to his experience, but as directly immanent to it.

Merleau-Ponty's doctrine of the subject as both immanent and transcendent, which he voluntarily characterizes as a paradox, is the cornerstone of his own position and presupposed in his dialogue with Marxism. The claim that the subject is immanent enables him to resolve at least partially the persistence of Cartesian dualism in Sartre's position through the relationship of subjectivity and objectivity. But what it does not do is provide the theory of action, which, as we have seen, Sartre was also seeking, and in terms of which one can understand the interaction of man and nature and man and other men. Having in mind this aspect of the original Sartrean problem, itself a form of the earlier Cartesian difficulty in relating subjectivity to objectivity, Merleau-Ponty turns to Marxism.

Beyond their common interest in a theory of action to understand the relation of subjectivity to objectivity, there is a basic difference in the manner in which Sartre and Merleau-Ponty approach Marxism. This difference should be emphasized. Sartre, as already indicated, is basically concerned to reformulate Marx's position in terms of his own view of adequate theory. His interest in Marxism is hence less in it as it is than in terms of what it could become. Merleau-Ponty, on the contrary, adopts a more immanent approach, probably attributable to the pragmatic cast of his own thought that is visible, for instance, in his rejection of ahistorical apodictic truth and in his belief that theory that remains only theory is a mystification. In this spirit he turns to Marxism neither as a locus of apodictic social truth, as some Marxists pretend, nor as a merely ideological justification for political views, as some non-Marxists would have it. His aim, rather, would seem to be to discern, through comparison of Marxist practice with Marxist theory, the extent to which the former can justify the latter or, to appeal again to the well known Marxian metaphor, to ascertain whether there is in fact a nonideological kernel in the revolutionary myth.

In a sense, Merleau-Ponty's dialogue with Marxism has already begun in the *Phenomenology of Perception*, especially in the last chapter devoted to freedom. But beyond that work, this discussion can be found in four other books, written over a period of some fifteen years. In two of these works, *Sense and Nonsense* (1960) and *Signs* (1948), he reveals an extensive acquaintance, important as it is rare among philosophers, with Marxist practice, although on occasion this appears in somewhat romantic form. But for the most part, his attempt to understand the relation of theory to practice within Marxism can be found in two other books, *Humanism and Terror* (1948) and *Adventures of the Dialectic* (1955). It is my belief that, taken together, these two studies constitute stages in a continuous inquiry, originating in the *Phenomenology of Perception*, whose aim is to grasp the rationality of Marxism immanently in terms of its own criteria, in other words, to assess its interest as a theory of human activity.

In *Humanism and Terror*, Merleau-Ponty provisionally accepts the Marxist view that revolutionary violence can be undertaken with a humanist intent provided that it is self-limiting. He then raises the problem of the adequacy of Marxist theory to justify Marxist practice in terms of a specific event, the execution of Bukharin (1938) in the last of the Moscow purge trials. Consistently with his conception of Marxism as a theory of history, Merleau-Ponty transforms the political event of Bukharin's execution into a problem of historical knowledge. Rejecting the argument of Koestler that the conflict is between a revolutionary and a saint because it is rather between two views of revolution, Merleau-Ponty, in search of a better justification, turns to Trotsky. The latter suggested that, although subjectively innocent, Bukharin was in fact guilty of impeding historical progress. But in order to judge in the light of history, historical knowledge must be possible. Yet in any strict sense, as Merleau-Ponty, appealing implicitly to his own concept of the individual as free consistently asserts, the future is always open; and hence history can never yield the apodictic knowledge necessary for the sacrifice either of a generation or a single person.

The criticism of Marxism that Merleau-Ponty raises in *Humanism and Terror* is a special case of a more general concept of human history implicitly based on his conception of human being and opposed to Marxism, which he further develops in *Adventures of the Dialectic*. If we bracket the lengthy criticism of Sartre's uneasy relation to the French Communist Party, which is not strictly relevant here, two themes, formulated in terms of Merleau-Ponty's view of history, emerge from the remainder of the book. In the first place, through a discussion of Lukács's relation to Weber, he strengthens his point concerning the unavailability of historical knowledge. Weber's position is held to contain an unresolved dualism between "objective understanding and pathetic morality" for which Lukács substitutes a concept of epistemological apodicticity that arises within history itself. Although, on strictly historical grounds, Merleau-Ponty's reading of Weber's influence on the constitution of Lukács's thought seems questionable, this in no way detracts from the acuity of the criticisms of it he advances, in particular of the incoherent attempt to attribute epistemological primacy to a given social class. But I am less certain about Merleau-Ponty's second point. Proceeding from the epistemology of history to its ontology, he formulates a criticism of the concept of revolution as such that is intended to undercut, it would seem, its very possibility. Lukács suggests that our knowledge of history will enable us to escape from it through the revolutionary act, and Trotsky proposes that the relative failure of one or another revolution to attain its goal follows from a reluctance to extend the revolutionary process to its ultimate fulfillment. Now, turning the latter's theory of permanent revolution against the concept of revolution as such, Merleau-Ponty objects here, in a moment of apparent theoretical isolation, that is unusual for him, that any revolution must necessarily fail because its participants will always be coopted by it and hence deflected from their original goal.

So far I have summarized the main outlines of the existential turn to Marx in terms of a shared concern to grasp the relation of subjectivity to objectivity, a problem inherited from Descartes, through a theory of human action. If we turn now to the problem of dialogue, we can immediately note that in a certain sense the question is moot because in one form or another the dialogue between them has been underway for decades. But from another perspective, the issue of the extent to which such discussion can be meaningful must be faced. For discussion to be meaningful, the views in question must partially overlap, and in significant fashion. For if they fail to overlap, they share no point in common, and conceptual interaction has no basis for occurring; but if they totally coincide, there are no differences, so any discussion can only resemble a celebration. On the other hand, if the points they have in common are insignificant, they cannot serve as a framework for meaningful dialogue.

If dialogue among partisans of a given tendency, for instance among Kantians or Platonists, is more frequent than that between representatives of different tendencies, such as between Aristotelians and Hegelians, it may be that the latter form of discussion requires as its precondition implicit recognition of the merely relative value of one or another theoretical option, which not everyone is willing to admit. Despite certain exceptions, it is thus not unexpected that both Marxists and phenomenologists have mainly been hesitant to enter into direct debate. This reluctance is especially evident in Marxist quarters, where perhaps the strongest and certainly most informed attack on existentialism has been launched by Lukács.

Lukács' most detailed study of existentialism can be found in his book, *Existentialism or Marxism* (1947), which dates from his period of Stalinist orthodoxy. Although the language may be unfamiliar, it is interesting to note that Lukács bases his objection on a form of the already-mentioned Cartesian ontological distinction. The struggle between idealism and materialism, which ended in the victory of the latter through Marx's position, has been revived in the imperialist epoch, most recently by existentialism, through the emergence of the so-called third alternative, which pretends to surpass the old dichotomy. But one cannot go beyond the choice between the relative priority of being over thought or thought over being. The existentialist view of the inseparability of existence and consciousness falls back into idealism through its refusal of the materialist doctrine of the priority of existence over consciousness. In the same way, the problem of knowledge has been resolved through what Lukács calls the dialectical theory of human consciousness as reflecting an exterior world existing independently of the subject. It follows that a meaningful dialogue between Marxism and existentialism cannot occur, because the latter is only a new form of a position that has already been vanquished and whose problem has been solved by Marxism.

In response, it must immediately be noted that Lukács' objection rests on the distinction drawn by Engels, in quasi-Cartesian fashion, between idealism and materialism. But the distinction in this and, I suspect, any other form is problematic; and in any case it is not descriptive of post-Kantian idealism where, beginning with Fichte, idealists of all kinds regularly sought to supersede the alternative in question. In view of the Marxist origin of Lukács' objection, it is of particular interest that a similar tendency is present in Marx's thought, for instance in the reference in the *Paris Manuscripts* to humanism. Presumably Marx's own position here is neither idealism nor materialism, as we find again in the *Grundrisse*, in his description of experience as the outcome of an interaction between a mind that thereby becomes conscious and a world that as a result is known. But because it is only in terms of the experiential interaction that it is meaningful to speak of the subject-object distinction in Marx's position, the distance of his own thought from later Marxism, which here remains Cartesian, is apparent; and there is, further, a substantive parallel between Marx's account and some forms of post-Husserlian phenomenology, as I have argued elsewhere.

Other a priori Marxist objections to existentialism are possible, have been raised, and will continue to arise as long as Marx's epigones maintain the quasi-religious attitude that precludes critical examination of Marxism and alternatives. In the present context, the significance of Lukács's criticism is that its examination reveals a similarity on this point between existential and perhaps other forms of phenomenology, which deny a Cartesian view of subjectivity as passive and weaken the Cartesian ontological distinction between thought and being, and Marx's position, as well as a dissimilarity between Marx's view and Marxism in general. But it would be hasty to infer that, because Marx, like the existentialists (although perhaps not Heidegger), rejects the "established" view of what Marxists since Engels have always seen as the watershed problem of philosophy, therefore unrestricted agreement, if not between Marxism and existentialism, at least between existentialism and Marx, is now possible.

The intrinsic dissimilarity between Marx's view and phenomenological existentialism, and hence the basic constraint on their dialogue, can be stated in terms of their respective understandings of subjectivity against the background of the Cartesian framework invoked above. If we prescind from further discussion of Marxism, it should immediately be noted that there is a strong anti-Cartesian element in Marx's overall position, which can fairly be described as a form of philosophical anthropology. This is especially true in Marx's stress on man as an active being, the producer of himself and his world, and further in his concept of ideology, or the limitation of social awareness through social being. But although Merleau-Ponty, the later Sartre, and perhaps the early Sartre as well, recognize the restriction of activity by situation and in that sense are anti-Cartesian and close to Marx's view, in an important sense they remain Cartesian, in particular in their fidelity to the belief that nothing external to me can restrict consciousness, because consciousness and being are different in kind. To state it otherwise, Marx and the existentialists, in the final analysis, are operating with different and irreconcilable concepts of human being, which for the latter is understood in almost traditional terms through its rational capacity but for the former is subordinated to the comprehension of man as practically active and only then possibly rational in a theoretical sense.

I should like to close with a general observation. If the differences between positions are less fundamental than they are often depicted, it should not therefore be inferred that there are not differences in kind, which constitute a kind of philosophical watershed. Such differences, which cannot, I suspect, finally be relativized, concern the decision as to whether to understand human subjectivity in isolation or as relative to the social context; and it is precisely this difference that is illustrated in the dialogue between the different perspectives considered here.

9. Kant's Proto-Phenomenology

RICHARD F. GRABAU

Introductory Remarks

Kant, of course, was not a phenomenologist in any strict sense. He neither used a descriptive method nor did he practice anything like the phenomenological reductions Husserl put so much stock in. Besides, Husserl himself makes clear, the philosopher who would seem to be the spiritual forerunner of phenomenology as Husserl practiced it, is Descartes, not Kant. The notion of *Evidenz*, which plays such a dominant role in Husserl, is more closely related to Descartes' idea of something being so clearly and distinctly presented to the mind that it cannot but assent to what is so presented than to Kantian types of necessary condition arguments.

In fact, Kant is often criticized or compared unfavorably to their own practice by phenomenologists. Husserl took him to task for not being radical enough in his questioning, illustrated by his unacknowledged dependence on the very empiricism he is attacking as he formulated his alternative.[1] In addition, Kant is typically and unfavorably mentioned in two other connections. First, it is held that for Kant the mind imposes a set of pure concepts upon reality, thus somehow distorting it and giving rise to all the problems of synthesis, whereas for phenomenologists experience comes already structured and organized. The task is to describe those structures and organizations and, in doing so, get to basic rather than superficial or merely sedimented ones. Second, it is observed, usually by phenomenologists of existentialist persuasion, that Kant has an inadequate notion of the knowing subject in that it is an abstract ego without life or history and without the worldly projects characteristic of concrete, existing subjects. As a result, the world that is the object of this knower's attention is not the concrete world of human projects but a derived and abstract world, merely a totality of entities in an abstract space-time continuum. To an extent, Kant is of course subject to this kind of criticism; but it is also in danger of masking important insights and connections.

In spite of these criticisms, it seems to me that there is a profound and natural kinship between Kant and phenomenology, both in motivation and in result. Husserl and Kant both desired to undercut the unproductive conflicts that reigned in philosophy and make out of it a critical and strict science. In addition, many of the insights that Kant first had are similar enough to some of the dominant and most characteristic ideas of phenomenology to be called at least proto-phenomenological. At the same time, of course, there are important differences that raise questions that have not yet been fully resolved by phenomenologists. Chief among the latter is the problem of the *questio juris*, (question of right) that Kant introduces at the beginning of the Transcendental Deduction of the Categories. Kant did not think description could get to universal and necessary knowledge and hence grounded his results by showing them to be conditions of the very possibility of experience rather than pervasive features of actual experience. In this paper I want to discuss a few of the similarities between Kant and phenomenology. First, the reinterpretation of the nature and role of concepts and intuition in experience resulting from Kant's Copernican Revolution results in a prototype of the phenomenological idea of consciousness as intentional. Second, what is intended is a world structured by relations and vectors and constituting a horizon. Philosophical knowledge is knowledge of the structure of that horizon. Third, when one attends to Kant's second and third Critiques as well as the first, one begins to see an analogue of the phenomenological idea of region and perhaps even of the idea of an ultimate unity of these regions, which is what the phenomenological idea of the life-world or the world of ordinary, concrete human projects represents. In this similarity there are also deep differences. The unity of standpoints or regions in Kant, for example, is a task (*Aufgabe*), not something given in the primordial structure of experience if one could only get down to it in its purity.

Intellect, Intuition, Intentionality

The relation of consciousness to its objects had always been a problem for modern philosophy. For Descartes the mind was a thinking substance whose contents were ideas of varying degrees of clarity. They had certain relations among themselves evident to the mind contemplating them, but the ideas might or might not have any reference to something outside the mind. Descartes had to demonstrate the existence of God in order to guarantee the application of clear and distinct ideas to objects. Kant, of course, thought that move did not work; Descartes, and rationalist philosophy generally, fell into what he called dogmatism, namely the claim to knowledge or the assertion of the existence of something on the basis of mere concepts. In part, the *Critique of Pure Reason* was written in order to limit this kind of claim of pure reason.

The empiricists were no better off, except they ended up in scepticism. For them the objects of experience just were the impressions and the ideas they left behind as traces. Everything else had to be traced back to its original impression. The result was that things like enduring selves and physical objects were "feigned," as Hume put it, on the basis of associations between the ideas and impressions. In Kant's estimation, not only did that leave philosophy in the scandalous situation of not being able to account for our certainty about the external world, but it begged its own starting point by being unable to account for the very associations between ideas that were the basis of all further constructions. In short, there was no unity of consciousness.

Kant resolved this problem by his Copernican Revolution; in his first presentation of it he states both the reason for it and what it consists in:

> Hitherto it has been assumed that all our knowledge must conform to objects. But all attempts to extend our knowledge of objects by establishing something in regard to them *a priori* by means of concepts, have, on this assumption, ended in failure. Let us therefore make trial whether we may not have more success in the task of metaphysics if we suppose that objects must conform to our knowledge.[2]

With this "trial" philosophy underwent a profound change, a shift in the very way of posing and answering questions. Such an enterprise involved sailing on uncharted seas, and Kant himself occasionally used this metaphor to explain the difficulty and obscurity of what he was about. In a completely new inquiry standpoint, the words change their meanings. Fresh issues emerge or old ones take on new aspects. With such a profound shift in standpoint, it is not surprising that Kant left much obscure or that because of the remnants in his presentations of the old way of philosophizing, inconsistencies seem to abound in his philosophy. The patchwork theory may be an exaggerated account of these inconsistencies, but the feeling one has that many of Kant's conclusions undercut the grand architectonic scheme in terms of which he formulates his whole project makes it a tempting theory.

> Time after time Kant delves beneath the surface of his system and grapples with the problems which lie there. As he pushes the argument deeper

and deeper he makes discoveries which, if their consequences be accepted, require the reshaping of the entire philosophical enterprise. Not simply new answers, but new questions, a new vocabulary, a totally new orientation are demanded. And Kant, in order to preserve his grip on a system too vast even for him to control, could not carry through that revision. So it is that after the profound speculations of the Deduction, Kant continues to use a system of organization which his own argument completely undercuts.[3]

Wolff cites as an example the inconsistency between the architectonic version of the relation between concepts and judgments according to which one starts with concepts, proceeds to judgments, and then on to inferences, and the critical view according to which concepts must be defined in relation to judgments rather than the other way around. Another example can be cited from the Transcendental Deduction. There Kant starts off by assuming a Humean analysis of sensation and experience. Sensations are discrete and distinct from each other, mere atoms of experience, so to speak. Kant's task was to show how this manifold of atomized units gets combined together. His answer is they are combined by the action of the understanding operating with concepts it itself originates. That in turn raises problems about how pure concepts can apply to things so foreign to themselves as Humean impressions.

The trouble with this is that the Transcendental Analytic eventuates in an account of experience that is much more organic than this. Awareness is not a matter of apprehending discrete data and then doing something with them. Appearances rather present themselves within the forms of space and time and the horizon of the unity of consciousness. Independent of the threefold synthesis of apprehension, reproduction, and recognition, it is hard to see what it might mean to be aware of sensations; rather it seems there would be no consciousness at all. In some sense (not explained), Kant says that it might be possible for "appearances to be so constituted that the understanding should not find them to be in accordance with the conditions of its unity."[4] But elsewhere he suggests that in such a situation they would be a mere "rhapsody," and would be "for us as good as nothing,"[5] "a blind play of representations, less even than a dream."[6] At other places he suggests that understanding and intuition are not completely unrelated faculties but have a common root,[7] which suggests a much closer relation than Kant's way of formulating the problem presupposes.

In various places, when discussing the nature and role of concepts, Kant says:

> In whatever manner and by whatever means a cognition may relate to object, *intuition* is that through which it is immediate relation to them and to which all thought as a means is directed.[8]

Objects are given to us by means of sensibility, and it alone yields us *intuitions*, they are *thought* through the understanding, and from the understanding come *concepts*. But all thought must, directly or indirectly, by way of certain characters, relate ultimately to intuitions. . . .[9]

We demand in every concept, first, the logical form of a concept (of thought) in general, and secondly, the possibility of giving it an object to which it may be applied. In the absence of such object, it has no meaning and is completely lacking in content, though it may still contain the logical function which is required for making a concept out of any data that may be presented.[10]

Therefore all concepts, and with them all principles, even such as are possible *a priori*, relate to empirical intuitions, that is to the data for a possible experience. Apart from this relation they have no objective validity, and in respect of their representations are a mere play of imagination or understanding.[11]

We therefore demand that a bare concept be *made sensible*, that an object corresponding to it be presented in intuition. Otherwise the concept would, as we say, be without sense, that is, without meaning.[12]

The pure categories are nothing but representations of things in general, so far as the manifold of their intuition must be thought through one or other of these logical functions.[13]

And finally,

. . . all categories through which we attempt to form the concept of such an object (of intellectual intuition) allow only of an empirical employment, and have no meaning whatsoever when not applied to objects of possible experience, that is, to the world of sense. Outside this field there are merely titles of concepts, which we may admit, but through which (in and by themselves) we can understand nothing.[14]

Many other passages making roughly the same points could be cited; but those given will perhaps suffice as the textual basis for the thesis I want to suggest, namely that Kant in his Copernican Revolution developed an intentional notion of consciousness in a sense not far removed from that associated with phenomenology.

They also serve to bear out Heidegger's emphasis in both his major discussions of Kant on the centrality of intuition in Kant's philosophy.[15] For Kant, says Heidegger, cognition is primarily intuition.[16] Thought is in the service of intuition.[17] Knowledge is, as it were, "thinking intuition." Heidegger's reason for stressing intuition is to underscore the essential finitude of human knowledge. Although it is not unrelated to finitude, I want to bring out the idea that for Kant intuition is not only the mark of the finitude of knowledge but is also the paradigm way consciousness is related to an object. Other ways either presuppose intuition or are in some other way parasitic upon it. For Kant, consciousness is intuitive consciousness.

Knowledge for Kant involves, as everyone knows, two sources: concepts and intuition. By the one objects are given, by the other they are thought. Both must be present for there to be experience. But the texts justify the claim that conception and intution are not two completely independent and juxtaposed sources that happen to cooperate so as to produce knowledge. Each of them stresses the fact that all thought must ultimately relate to intuitions, no matter how remotely or indirectly "by way of certain characters." Without such relation they are "empty," "without meaning," and "completely lacking in content." They are not even concepts but "only the title of a concept," mere "logical functions," "a mere play of the imagination or understanding." It appears that concepts for Kant cannot be viewed as "objects" of the mind's awareness, or at least not primarily so. They are instead, as it were, vehicles of that awareness. Not themselves mental contents, concepts are rules for the organization or synthesis of a manifold that must always be given in intuition.[18] A concept thus by itself is only a function of unity, not an independent or transintuitive representation of an object. The latter always involves intuition, however remotely.

Kant saw that reinterpreting thought in this way required a reconstruction of logic. Much of the Transcendental Analytic is taken up with the distinction between general logic and what Kant calls transcendental logic. The former had to do with the rules that govern all thought in complete abstraction from the objects that are being thought about. Transcendental logic, on the other hand, has to do with thinking in so far as it is thinking of objects. As Heidegger pointed out,[19] this involved a reinterpretation of judgment from a mere relation between several concepts to a view of it as a "manner in which *given* modes of knowledge are brought to the objective unity of apperception."[20] That is, judgment must be defined in relation to intuition; it becomes thus a procedure for connecting in advance in one consciousness the given manifold of intuition. In interpreting judgment in this way, Kant dethroned pure thought from the position it had for rationalism and tied it essentially to intuition. Only in relation to a possible intuition do concepts take on any meaning at all.

This analysis shows the critical doctrine of concepts. Now, illustrating the tension between particular results of Kant's analyses and the general framework in which he organizes his whole project, Kant persists in talking as though concepts had reference independent of intuition. Kant's achievement was so fundamental that not even he, as Heidegger says, was able to jump over his own shadow.[21]

Intentionality, Horizonality, and A Priori Knowledge

Phenomenologists have developed elaborate descriptions of human experience. What they describe, it is important to note, is not the empirical details of objects that present themselves in our everyday or even scientific experience. That would be an endless task, a mere random groping, and hence unproductive. By either such moves as Husserl's reductions or Heidegger's attempts at hermeneutical presentation of *Dasein* in its ordinary being-in-the-world, the attempt is made to get at a description of the horizon within which things present themselves. Objects are not simply presented to consciousness; they are presented within a context which has a structure, albeit these structures are not at all times thematically present. Phenomenology is a description of these structures that are then considered as a priori conditions of the representation of empirical things, allowing them to appear with the meaning they have. Husserl's description of perception, for example, is not a report about what is perceived but of what it is in principle to perceive. The attempt is to reveal the essential nature of that modality of awareness. The same can be said of Heidegger's analysis of Dasein.

Both Husserl and Heidegger thus give transcendental analyses in Kant's sense, however different from Kant's the actual working out of these analyses are. "I entitle *transcendental* all knowledge which is occupied not so much with objects as with the mode of our knowledge of objects insofar as this mode of knowledge is to be possible a priori."[22] Kant's transcendental analyses consist of two stages or steps or levels whereas those of phenomenologists have only one. Kant, that is to say, not only lays out the a priori structures of experience, a procedure which is analogous to phenomenological description. He then goes on to prove them, that is, to show they have an application—which in his case consists of showing them to be the only conditions for the possibility of experience.

Kant's transcendental analyses yield a horizonal view of experience. In this aspect, too, Kant develops a proto-phenomenological view. He points out that sensation is by itself simply a modification of our sensibility; if that were all there were to it, it would be without meaning. What gives meaning is that such modification occurs within a structured horizon. This is why the idea of pure intuition is so crucial in Kant. Kant held that there are two levels of intuition, pure and empirical. Empirical intuition is relatively unproblematic; it involves the senses and is the intuitive presentation of ordinary objects in the world. Pure intuition, on the other hand, has to do with the form of empirical intuition; and in addition it provides a manifold of its own for the operation of the categories or, more exactly, the categorial principles

Kant builds out of them. These do not determine objects directly; empirical concepts do that. Instead, they determine pure intuition. Intuition—structured by the pure concepts of the understanding—comprises an antecedent framework or horizon—Kant calls it a pure scheme[23]—in which any empirical objects appear and to which, so to speak, they must conform. Empirical objects can be seen as special determinations of pure intuition thus structured by the categories, just as Kant says that natural laws can be seen as special determinations of the categorial principles.[24] This does not mean that empirical objects or natural laws can be deduced from their pure prototypes—only that they must conform to them:

> Pure understanding is not, however, in a position, through mere categories, to prescribe to appearances any general laws other than those involved in nature in general, that is, in the conformity to law of all appearances in space and time. Special laws, as concerning those appearances which are empirically determined cannot in their turn be derived from the categories, although they are one and all subject to them. To obtain any knowledge whatsoever of the special laws, we must resort to experience.[25]

The determinations of pure space and time, but especially pure time, through the categories, present an antecedent horizon of objectivity in conformity to which empirical intuition and conception carry out their work. Much more could be said in this context. But the basic point has been made: what Kant calls the original unity of apperception is essentially an openness to objects. It is also an a priori structured relation to objects and represents a context for apprehending and interpreting presented material. On this conception not only is the epistemological gap left by Hume and Descartes closed, but awareness of the world is seen to have a horizontal, vectoral character. A priori knowledge is of that horizon, those vectors. However greatly Kant may differ from phenomenological practice as far as method is concerned, the similarity of his concept of experience to the phenomenological notion of a world held together by the connective tissue of intentionality is apparent.

In this connection one final point of similarity might be noted. Both Kant and Husserl put much emphasis on transcendental subjectivity as the locus or ground of the unity of experience. As a result, they have often been interpreted as providing essentially idealistic interpretations, in that they present analyses of transcendental consciousness. But in the case of both philosophers, that is a hasty judgment. For Husserl consciousness, whatever its modality, is always consciousness of a world. If it is aware of itself at all as an interiority, it is only against the background of the primary awareness of a world to which it may constitute itself as other. In Kant's case, as the Refutation of Idealism and associated passages make clear, self-awareness is always awareness of self aware of things. He took great pains to disassociate his philosophy from the dogmatic or problematic idealisms of Berkeley or Descartes. Self-awareness entails awareness of a world of objects obeying universal and necessary laws and is constituted over against that world.

Examples and Reinterpretations

In light of his representation of experience in terms of an a priori structured horizon within which appearances present themselves and to which they all must conform, Kant had to reinterpret many things. Specifically, he had to give new meanings to the ideas of reason consistent with his new doctrine that concepts must function within experience. He also had to deny any positive meaning to the concept of the thing-in-itself. The reason is that the thing-in-itself can never be presented in itself, that is, in utter independence of the conditions of human experiencing and knowing. Its presentation to human intuition, and thus under the categories, just is appearing. Consequently, Kant makes the thing-in-itself into a limit concept, to curb the pretentions of sensibility.[26] Similarly, the ideas of reason, namely God, Soul, and World are reinterpreted by Kant in light of his doctrine of intuition. No longer can they directly refer to objects, for no object conforming to them can possibly be given in intuition. But they do have a function in our textured experience. They relate indirectly to objects by way of directing the understanding in the empirical regresses that constitute the advance of both scientific knowledge and ordinary experience. Thinking of things-in-themselves or the ideas of reason beyond their mere limiting and regulative functions involves the use of analogy with objects that can be presented in intuition,[27] and always with the danger of leading us into transcendental illusions because they are so easily misused. There is no harm in this, says Kant, as long as we remain alert to what we are doing and do not fall prey to the illusion. Thus, when they are used beyond intuition, they are parasitic upon the way things appear to us and hence upon intuition. Both of these notions thus take on phenomenological meaning in the ways they relate to the structured matrix of human experience.

Even practical reason can be interpreted on this model, although limitations of time preclude any more than a bare indication here. Kant distinguished practical reason from theoretical reason in that the latter determined a priori only the form and categorial structure of objects of experience, which must be given in intuition, whereas practical reason determined the existence or actuality of these objects as well.[28] But this determination is not the direct creation of an object in the act of knowing it that Kant describes God's awareness as being. Instead, the determination is by way of an imperative. The moral law presents itself to finite beings such as human beings not in the form of a descriptive law, but as a command. We are commanded to bring our wills into accordance with the moral law. In discussing the categorical imperative, Kant uses the idea of a world where all persons as a matter of course act the way we are proposing to act as a way of illustrating what he means by universalizing a maxim. In a sense, what we do in moral action is strive to bring about a state of affairs where what is presented in intuition is not at odds with perfect conformity with the moral law.[29] Thus, the moral law as imperative cannot even be adequately formulated except with reference to the background of intuition. A perfect being (God) would apprehend the law as descriptive, not as a command; but that is due to the fact that his or *her* intuition, if it can be called that, is original or infinite and not passive and receptive as is the case with human intuition.

These examples show the priority and centrality of Kant's proto-phenomenological view of pure experience as an a priori horizon of objectivity that sets the structure for all appearing and the context within which everything else must be interpreted.

Regions, Modalities, and Unity

Phenomenologists have not only developed description as the fundamental method by which one tries to undercut theoretical constructions and sedimentations; they have also noted in the process that experience exhibits a plurality of modalities. In addition, they have endeavored to relate these modalities to each other. In Husserl the life-world constitutes the horizon of all horizons, that matrix out of which special regional modalities emerge and in the light of which they must be interpreted. It is the life-world that gives unity to experience. For Heidegger the structure of Dasein's being-in-the-world serves as the background against which more specialized and derivative regions, such as that of science, must be understood and ultimately judged.

Kant, too, developed a philosophy in which the idea of region plays a central role. In a sense, the whole critical philosophy just is a critical inventory of the human mind and its powers of knowing. But because consciousness for Kant, as for phenomenology, is never without its object, this philosophy also constitutes a world analysis as well. The most obvious instance of this is in the Transcendental Analytic, where Kant spells out the particular a priori principles that organize experience. Kant held that the principles he developed were not only those presupposed by the physical sciences of his day, thus constituting a region of scientific objectivity of whose dimensions and features we are a priori aware; but that they were also entailed by consciousness itself and thus constituted the structure of ordinary experience.

But this horizon or region of scientific and ordinary experience is not the only one in Kant. There are others, although exactly how they are to be conceived and how they related to the original unity of apperception of the first Critique and its structures remains obscure. Only mention will be made of them here to illustrate the fact that Kant had a conception of subjectivity or transcendental framework that went beyond the purely abstract structures of the transcendental unity of apperception, and which allow us to say he has a notion of the regional character of experience. First, there is a moral self who finds him-herself standing under obligations determined by the moral law in a world in which moral action must be possible because it is required. The categorical imperative constitutes the synthetic a priori principle of practical reason. Hence the world for Kant is constituted not simply as a collection of physical objects in abstract space-time. It *is* that, of course; but it is also a world of persons and rights and obligations. Kant even said something about the primacy of practical reason and having to limit knowledge in order to make room for faith based on the demands of practical reason. Although he did not spell it out in the detail one might like, such a move is the beginning of an attempt to relate the regions of experience to each other. The Kantian subject cannot be dissolved into the bloodless abstractions of the transcendental unity of apperception, nor can the world to which it is essentially related. The moral self in fact comes very close to the phenomenological idea of praxis and constitutes a world structured in terms of its demands and categories.

Secondly there is the aesthetic self and an aesthetic world. The third Critique takes as its task transcendental deduction of such aesthetic categories as that of the beautiful and the sublime. It develops a doctrine of reflective judgment, which is how Kant characterizes aesthetic judgment. Reflective judgments are judgments upon which universal agreement can be expected, although they are not based upon determinate categories. A work of art pleases by calling into action a free play of faculties that ultimately results in harmony. Universality can be expected here for aesthetic judgment rests on the cognitive faculties of sense, understanding, and reason, which are the common heritage of all people. Genius, says Kant, is a particular power, unpredictable and indeterminable by concepts and rules by which nature, that is, a natural talent in us, gives the rule to art. And finally art itself is said to be a symbol of morality. As was the case in Kant's ethics, the world that is the correlate of the aesthetic subject is structured in its own particular way. Great art gives us insight into reality; which is probably why we value it and keep coming back to even a familiar piece from which we can still learn more.

I mention these items from Kant's ethics and aesthetics to illustrate the fact that for Kant transcendental subjectivity was not a purely theoretical matter. Man has many postures and stances in the world, and all of them must be given their due. Kant is in this respect an antireductionist. Although it is also true that he did not in any definitive way work out the relations between the domains or horizons of subjectivity–perhaps it is not too un-Kantian to say "ways of being in the world"—it is also true that he did not deny the fact that human beings have many ways of intentionally relating to the world. Kant himself sums it up in his famous remark in the *Logic*, where he says that the three primary questions,

1. What can I know?
2. What ought I to do?
3. For what may I hope?

ultimately boil down to a fourth: What is Man? The Critical Philosophy is Kant's attempt to answer this fourth question.

While noting the similarities between Kant and phenomenology, one should not lose sight of the differences. Two examples might be mentioned here. First, for Kant there is little or no distinction between the world of science and that of ordinary perception. Science and common sense are much closer to each other than for many phenomenologists. Indeed, for Kant the structures of the first Critique, although limited, are basic. Kant would probably insist that the features of readiness-to-hand that Heidegger thinks are primoridal structures of the life-world depend upon the a priori principles about space, time, and the categories laid down in the first Critique. It is because space has the geometry it does that distances can be "too far" or space separate us from our projects. It is because things have the causal and substantial relations they have that they can serve as tools or be obstacles to our practice.

A second difference involves the unity of the regions. Earlier I mentioned that for Kant the unity of the regions is not given but is a task to be accomplished. There are hints as to how this is to be done, but they are little more than hints. For one thing, there is the already mentioned idea of the primacy of practical reason. In addition, the *Critique of Judgment* was said by Kant to provide a kind of bridge between the worlds of nature and freedom developed in his other two Critiques. Little more than suggestions and hints are given. But the idea remains that for Kant the unity of experience is a desideratum, something to be realized in the developing course of experience, not something given to be uncovered by archaeological explorations.

Husserl thought that the crisis of the European sciences had something to do with the tendency of one region, that of mathematicized science, to be emphasized as the standard of all thought and arbiter of all truth and reality. Heidegger believed, too, that Being transcended any one of its ways of making itself evident, mentioning specifically, especially in his late writings, the way of science and technology as a legitimate and in our time prevalent region of Being's self-announcing, but pointing out the dangers in confusing Being with that way. In his notion of the plurality of regions of human experience, the limitation of knowledge to make room for faith, and the idea of the thing-in-itself, the same can be said of Immanuel Kant. He is a natural ally of the phenomenological movement.

10. Kant and Phenomenology

GEORGE A. SCHRADER, JR.

At first glance the relationship between Kant and phenomenology seems altogether unproblematic. What Kant construed as "mere appearance"(*Erscheinung*), Husserl and subsequent phenomenologists have interpreted as the "self-presentation of being." Whereas for Kant phenomena constitute a surrogate for being-in-itself, barring access to the latter, to phenomenologists phenomena provide direct or indirect access to being. When Husserl proposed the slogan "zu den Sachen selbst" (to the things themselves), he meant to challenge idealistic theories that seek the explanation for appearances in conditions that must be *inferred*. Phenomenology as a rigorous science sought to provide an alternative to theories based upon speculation, inference, or conjecture. It was not only the phenomena/noumena distinction that was called into question but, also, the appeal to transcendental conditions for the *explanation* of what is given. The elaborate transcendental arguments to which Kant devoted so much to his effort are both unnecessary and useless if appearances can be self-illuminating. If, as Husserl believed, phenomenological description can satisfactorily dispense with explanatory theory, transcendental metaphysics is no more essential to our understanding of the world than the speculative metaphysics it had displaced. Yet, ironically, Husserl came to adopt more and more the language of transcendental philosophy. How are we to account for the fact that although rejecting the substance, he retained the language of Kantian idealism? Kant's relationship to Husserl and the phenomenological movement is obviously more complex than the initial repudiation of Kant's transcendental method would suggest.

It is much easier to compare Kant with Husserl than with other phenomenologists. The reason is that, in spite of their differences, Husserl segregated the cognitive from the evaluative in much the same way as had Kant. In rejecting this split between theoretical and practical reason, subsequent phenomenologists challenged a fundamental thesis shared by Kant and Husserl. The bracketing of the "natural standpoint," so central to Husserl's phenomenological method, echoes Kant's limitation of experience to the space-time world. It was not simply the natural standpoint that was suspended but the moral, aesthetic, and religious as well. Even as Kant excluded volition and feeling from the objective space-time world, Husserl excluded non-noetic modes of intentionality. In that respect Husserl followed in Kant's footsteps.

There is, however, an interesting difference in the way they interpreted the empirical world. Although in the *Critique of Pure Reason*, Kant did not consistently distinguish between objects of common sense and physical science, his primary concern was with scientific cognition. His claim that his categories are constitutive both of common sense and science confuses the argument of the Deduction. Experience for Kant is not a collection of impressions, because it includes objects and relations. But neither are the objects considered all of the same order. The everyday world of cats, dogs, ships, and houses is vastly different from the world of Newtonian physics. Yet Kant treats them as if they were ordered by a common set of principles.

This ambiguity in Kant's treatment of objects witnesses to a fundamental problem about experience. It is all of one piece such that it can accommodate the objects of common sense and science? And, if not, which is primary, the world of common sense or science? Insofar as Kant took the scientifically ordered world as his starting point, experience is saturated with theoretical elements. Yet in this regard there is no essential difference between science and common sense. Both do and must extrapolate from given data in conceptualizing objects. For Kant the natural standpoint is common to the everyday and the scientifically structured world.[1] Husserl and Kant seem to agree about this feature of common sense and science, though they do not adopt the same posture toward it. Kant thought it essential to include the extrapolated element as constitutive of the object world; Husserl, on the other hand, hoped to dispense with it altogether. In any event, we are confronted with the same problem of "bracketing" whether it is a naive empirical or sophisticated scientific experience that is in question.

The intent of bracketing is, of course, to suspend interpretation for the sake of an unbiased look at the data. One might perform an *epoché* on the "scientific standpoint" for the sake of a phenomenological account of science. There is, indeed, a place for such an account of science; but there are also built in limitations. To the extent that science has a different conception of knowledge and theory than the phenomenologist, the epoché is bound to fail. The "natural" or, in this case, "scientific" standpoint is absolutely crucial to the world to be studied. To be understood in its own terms, it must be permitted a mode of theorizing that the method of phenomenological reduction disallows.

The relation between the worlds of common sense and science is problematic for Kant in that no clear rules of translatability are provided. Husserl, on the other hand, evidences a decisive preference for the everday or "lived" world. The presumption of his method is that we can, through reflection, bring to explicit clarity those essential structures that are at the foundation of common sense and, perforce, of science. Phenomenology as a rigorous science aspires to be the foundational science and, thus, to mediate between common sense and scientific truth. One of the difficulties with this program, which has yet to be fulfilled, is that the everyday world is shot through with conjectural and even speculative elements. There are at least two issues at stake here: (1) is it possible to account for the phenomena of the received world without appeal to conceptual or formal principles that are not given as essential features of that world? and (2) is the received world itself free of elements that derive from theoretical constructions? The key word in the first question is the term *essential*. Kant tried to show that the a priori categories and principles of transcendental philosophy are *necessary* for the possibility of experience. And that is tantamount to the claim that they are *essential* to it. Yet, as we shall see, Kant was not committed to the rationalist doctrine of essence. It is a theoretical claim, indeed a metaphysical claim, on Kant's part that the rational structure of the empirical world represents the contribution of human understanding. Because those principles themselves can be ascertained only through a reconstruction of experience that could go wrong, they cannot be regarded as the essence of the sensible manifold. Formal principles have a different status and a different origin for Kant than for Husserl. With respect to the second question, Kant believed that science legislates to nature and, hence, contaminates the data with which it works. The empirical world *for us* reflects the sedimentation of quite elaborate and sophisticated theory. As I suggested earlier, this fact, if true, presents a stumbling block to any program of pure description. The attempt to clarify experience soon becomes ensnared in the network of theory and, hence, is forced either to employ an appropriate method in exploring it;[2] or it must deny its origin through an arbitrary reduction of experience to a manageable immediacy.

Heidegger met this issue straight on, arguing as he did that the immediate world of everyday concerns is prior to any scientific representation of experience. Although the scientifically structured world cannot be accounted for within the parameters of the everyday world, the scientific world view is nonetheless parasitic upon the latter. Even so, Heidegger could not escape the problem to which we have alluded earlier, namely the sedimentation of scientific and other forms of theory into the everyday world. It is not only science that poses a problem, but theology, Freudian psychology, and Marxist social theory. The possibility of a successful *epochē* would require that history be stopped—and that is not possible! It is by no means obvious that the world as scientifically conceived can be understood simply as a modification of the everyday (common sense) world. We may require a larger conception of a world in which both modes of experience are encompassed. Nor can such an encompassing world be satisfactorily conceived of as the "region of regions" within which all meanings cohere in harmonious unity. Schizoid features of such an encompassing "world" require a more critical treatment.

In his attempt to carry out an existential analysis (*Daseinsanalyse*), Heidegger gave phenomenology a definite transcendental turn. Like Kant, Heidegger sought those constitutive principles that are necessary for the understanding of the everyday world. The ontological level of meaning in terms of which the ontic is to be understood is, as with Kant's categories, more "suggested by" than derived from the world as we find it "initially and for the most part." In effect, Heidegger substituted a "metaphysics of existence" for Kant's "metaphysics of experience." He not only gave transcendental analysis a distinctively Kantian turn but reintroduced the phenomena/noumena distinction as a fundamental working principle. Little is left of Husserl's original program to develop a science of essences.

Although both Sartre and Merleau-Ponty professed to follow Husserl, neither of them actually did so save in the loosest fashion. The structure of the "pour-soi" (for-itself) is not arrived at by the method of phenomenological bracketing, but through highly imaginative speculation. Anxiety or dread is no more directly given in experience for Heidegger and Sartre than for Freud. Each of these thinkers made brilliant use of the concept to illumine everyday experience, but they could hardly claim that it represents the *essence* of the human condition. Heidegger and Sartre borrowed heavily from Kierkegaard; Heidegger acknowledges his debt to Kierkegaard on this point. Sartre was additionally indebted to Hegel for such key terms as "in-itself," "for-itself." The phenomenological moment in the thought of Heidegger and Sartre consists in their concern for the world as "lived"—and for that emphasis they were clearly indebted to Husserl. The fact remains, however, that the world as lived is not so immediate that it can be severed from its theoretical underpinnings—or superstructure, depending on how one looks at it.

123

Merleau-Ponty's *Phenomenology of Perception* is a rather curious work in that it polemicizes unceasingly against bad philosophy and psychology. What sense does it make for a phenomenologist to polemicize? If we follow Husserl's example, it should make absolutely no sense at all. Merleau-Ponty polemicized precisely because bad theories had infected the world to be analyzed. He sought through his polemics to refute bad theories, bad not just in detail but in type, in order to remove them from the scene. Positively, Merleau-Ponty wanted to disclose the rational structure of the lived world. But his polemics drew him into historical dialogue and, thus, into consideration of an array of theoretical principles that had been involved in the constitution of the lived world. He was thus divided between his commitment to a phenomenological analysis of the everyday world and a dialectical treatment of conflicting theories that were adumbrated in that world. Marvelous book that it is, it is flawed by the author's futile attempt to freeze the temporal flow and, especially, to sever the everyday world from its origins. Merleau-Ponty's attempts to make use of transcendence as, for example, with respect to the concept of nature, as a critical principle inevitably fail because of his attempted *epoche*. A consistent phenomenological program programmatically must dispense with a critical stance toward the world.

To return to Husserl, with whom we are primarily concerned in this comparison with Kant, it is illuminating to consider his relation to Descartes. Husserl not only challenged Kant's transcendental idealism as a philosophical method but returned to Descartes for his philosophical model. His aspiration was, as Husserl informs us, to carry out the Cartesian program with the fullest possible consistency. This return to Descartes is necessary because Kant and others had taken philosophical inquiry off its proper course. Instead of achieving the certainty for which he sought, Kant had left us in a state of total uncertainty about being-itself. The issue, as Husserl perceived it, was perfectly clear: human reason is either capable of intuiting reality and bringing it to perfect clarity or it is not. In his return to Descartes, Husserl affirmed precisely the rational ideal that Kant had so vigorously denied.

Unfortunately, Husserl's readers have not been equally clear about Husserl's relation to Kant. Because they read Kant as essentially a Cartesian,[3] they do not construe Husserl's reversion of Descartes as posing a systematic problem. If Kant were in fact a Cartesian, to go back to Descartes would not require a repudiation of the critical philosophy. How phenomenology is related to Kantian philosophy thus turns on the question whether Kant was a Cartesian. In spite of what appears to be a recapitulation of the Cartesian *cogito* in Kant's Transcendental Deduction, the appearance is completely misleading.[4] Kant and Husserl differed radically with respect to the need for and the character of *theory*. Husserl's return to Descartes was intended to bypass Kant's elegant transcendental arguments for the primacy of the 'I think' and the "transcendental unity of apperception." To leave them, as did Kant, as nothing more than "necessary conditions for experience" is, in effect, to leave them without ontological foundation. In any case, Kant did not *begin* with the certainty or self-certainty of a Cartesian consciousness, but argued for the necessity of such a consciousness as a principle essential to the explanation of empirical knowledge. On any other reading, Kant's refusal in the Paralogisms to draw ontological conclusions about the substantial unity or identity of the cognitive subject is nothing short of bizarre. In fact, Kant was only insisting rigorously on the strictures entailed by his method of argumentation. A transcendental necessity cannot be converted into an ontological necessity. Descartes began with a certainty with which Kant could not concur even granted the success of his transcendental argument for the "abiding and unchanging 'I'."

Kant's readers have had trouble with his treatment of the 'unity of apperception' because it is not individuated or particularized. It is a *principle* rather than a *substance* and cannot easily be identified with an empirical or ontological ego. The fact is, of course, that the universality of the 'I think' takes precedence over individual manifestations of it; it is the correlate of an experience and a world that is taken to be objective, public, and intersubjective. Kant never argued from the universal validity of *my* own consciousness to the objective reality of the experienced world. Thus, from Descartes's perspective, Kant's argument in the Deduction of Categories is upside down, arguing to precisely that certainty that should have been established at the outset. As Richard Kroner pointed out long ago, Kant uses the term "us" far more frequently than the term "me" in the *Critique of Pure Reason*. So far as his account of empirical knowledge is concerned, the transcendental "we" is prior to the "I." In this instance as with all transcendental principles, the unity of consciousness is a *presupposition for* rather than a *deliverance of* experience. It can, therefore, be arrived at only obliquely by a *reconstruction* of what is given.

The Copernican revolution, so-called, in philosophy, which Kant sought to consolidate and systematize, reversed the principle of certainty that had characterized classical philosophy. For post-Cartesian philosophy, it is the *senses* rather than reason that provide the *touchstone* for certainty and truth. Kant typifies this reversed perspective in his repudiation of intellectual intuition. His argument against intellectual intuition turns on his conviction that all concepts are *discursive* and, hence, that to speak of a nondiscursive concept is a contradiction in terms. So far as its form is concerned, every concept is "made" (*gemacht*), Kant informs us.[5] A concept is essentially a rule of synthesis or combination that enables us to grasp a multiplicity in a comprehensible unity. The German term for concept (*Begriff*) derives from the word *greifen*, which means *to seize* or *grasp*. Here as in other cases, language may well be misleading. It *suggests* rather than *demonstrates* that conceiving is basically an act of grasping, combining, or synthesizing. Plato had argued in the *Theaetetus* that several instances of a quality such as whiteness can be perceived only if there is a universal form that is instantiated in each occurrence. Kant basicallly accepted the argument of the *Theaetetus* but reinterpreted the required universal. Instead of viewing the universal form as a conceptual entity to be intuited, Kant construed it as a rule required by the human mind in effecting a unity in the manifold. The universal is, as Plato argued convincingly, formal and ideal and not given in sensation. But, on Kant's reinterpretation, it is a logical or epistemological rule rather than an ideal entity. We can perceive a line, so Kant argues, only by *drawing* it. And, by the same token, we can perceive whiteness only by "running through" many instances and combining them in one quality.

The point to be emphasized here is that Kant rejects the classical doctrine of intellectual intuition as theoretically inadequate to account for itself. To claim that one can intuit a form or idea is to view the form as ontologically independent of the act of intuition. If one argues that human consciousness is transparent such that the form can be immediately and faithfully given, one offers no explanation how apprehension of the form is possible. This amounts to claiming that apprehension occurs without a *medium*—which, on Kant's assessment of it, is a contradiction in terms. Curiously enough, for Plato it was precisely the *sensible mediation* that has to be set aside for the sake of a pure vision of formal structures. As Hegel put it, for classical philosophers "knowing is unessential to truth." For Kant, on the other hand, knowing is a form of mediation and hence indispensable for the constitution of truth.

Philosophers have long been divided on the issue of whether concepts are necessarily discursive. A goodly number have found Kant's argument compelling and will have no truck with the intuition of forms, essences, or ideal entities. Others have found Kant's rejection of intellectual intuition and his alternative account of conceptual form unconvincing and even mystifying. The fact that Husserl based his phenomenological program on the possibility of eidetic intuition attests to his disavowal of the Kantian critique of classical theory. The question here is whether Husserl's appeal to eidetic intuition can be reconciled with a discursive theory of concepts. And, if they cannot be reconciled, whether Husserl can succeed in avoiding the difficulties that Kant ascribed to classical idealism. The feature of Husserl's theory that is most interesting and most relevant to this issue is his conception of intentionality. If, as Husserl argued, for every act of consciousness there is both a form of the object intended and a form of the intended act, cognitive apprehension of eidetic form is *not unstructured*. There is in fact a *medium* for the perception of objects, even though this medium is characterized as intuition. What this means is that the intuition of essences is not a pure immediacy. The specific form of the intending act is as essential as the determinate form of the object intended. Moreover, the form of the act logically entails the object form. By structuring intuition and assigning it intentional form, has the need for a discursive theory of concepts been obviated? Or, put differently, has the distinction between intuitive and discursive thought been eliminated?

In the Aesthetic, Kant presented sensible intuition as if it were immediate. He insisted upon space and time as the two forms of intuition, without making it sufficiently clear that they were forms of intuiting as well as forms of the intuited manifold. Having repudiated intellectual intuition, he could permit only sensible intuition as a source of empirical knowledge. The obvious problem raised by the Aesthetic is how we can intuit a line, let alone a geometrical figure, in pure sensible immediacy. In his more candid moments, Kant informs us elsewhere in the *Critique* that without the contribution of the understanding, the deliverances of sensation would be a "mere play of presentations, little more than a dream." As we work our way through the more complex exposition of the Analytic, we discover that conceptualization is necessary even for the most elementary synthesis of the spatial manifold. Although intuition and conceptualization are different in kind, intuition without conceptualization is blind and, presumably, impossible. Space and time are not concepts, but neither are they unmediated unities which are directly given to consciousness.

It is not time and space that are given in sensible intuition or even in pure intuition, but only times and spaces. Insofar as space and time are pure forms, they cannot be given and, hence, cannot be intuited. The revision of the doctrines of the Aesthetic in the Analytic and Dialectic was demanded for the sake of consistency and coherence in Kant's overall account of perception. There cannot be two lines, one we draw and one we intuit, any more than there can be two spheres or two tables. The one we perceive is the only one that counts so far as existence is concerned. And we perceive the object only by virtue of the fact that we have combined it into a recognizable unity. But does this mean that in elaborating and developing his theory of sensible intuition, Kant effectively abandoned it? We have learned a great deal about the structure of peception and the rules and principles that govern synthetic ordering into intelligible unities. The pure sensible content, however, seems to have eluded us pretty completely. In that respect it is much like Husserl's "hyle," the sensible instantiation of eidetic form. If discursive thought has no content of its own and sensible content no intrinsic conceptual form, it is exceedingly difficult to explain how thought attains sensible content or sensible content acquires intelligible form.

It is precisely here that Kant's theory faces a crisis. Because there is no common measure between that which is sensibly given and that which is conceptualized, any connection between them is inevitably somewhat arbitrary. Kant's epistemology has an unstable center that threatens either to collapse into an identity of form/content (Hegel) or to break apart into a conventional juxtaposition (positivism). Kant was never willing to sacrifice either his empiricism or his idealism and, hence, held these factors together in an uneasy alliance. A crucial difference between Kant and Husserl is that Husserl construes eidetic form as the *essence* of the material content in which it is embedded, whereas Kant regards form as a rule of combination or synthesis. This difference reflects their divergent standpoints vis-à-vis Descartes, namely that ideal form represents *either* the clarification of the sensuous (Husserl) *or* the superimposition of order (Kant). To make good on the claim that intuited forms are the essence of the real requires that we regard phenomena as things-in-themselves. Kant and Husserl would, of course, agree on the requirement, but not on the possibility of its being met. This issue turns on the question of intellectual (eidetic) intuition, a possibility that Kant denies as vigorously as Husserl affirms it. Their difference on this issue is reflected, also, in their conceptions of "reduction." Kant scaled down the claims of reason to apprehend the essence of what is precisely because it lacks the power of intuition. Thus, Kant's reduction of reason (classically conceived) to understanding represents a shift from essence to rule, from teleology to causal order. We can get to the "things themselves," so far as Kant is concerned, but only as phenomenal objects that not only do not but cannot "show themselves."

Originally Kant's attitude toward intuition in the *Critique* was inconsistent in allowing an intuition of forms in the Aesthetic although denying it in other portions of the *Critique*. He met that problem eventually by revising his view of the perception of space and time in the Analytic, holding that we intuit only spaces and times. Moreover, the sensible intuition of spaces and times requires the assistance of understanding. Unfortunately, Kant left both his earlier and his revised views of intuition standing in the completed *Critique*.

Husserl's concept of the noesis would seem to answer Kant's objection to the doctrine of intellectual intuition, namely that it requires a form of apprehension and hence cannot be purely immediate (intuitive). It does, indeed, acknowledge Kant's point and attempts to make good the deficiency. The difficulty is that we are then back with the old problem of the conformity of thought to its object. The noesis/noema distinction simply reintroduces the idea/object distinction to which Kant had originally addressed himself. Unless, so Kant believed, the forms of thought and the object are identical, no account of our knowledge of objects can be given. A further difficulty with Husserl's theory is that the noetic/noematic structure must itself be grasped through an intuiting consciousness that has its own noesis. Because the appropriating consciousness is fully independent of the original (appropriated) consciousness, the same problems of correspondence between object and intending act arise. Here as in so many other places, Husserl reverts to classical realism in the formulation of his theory.

No comparison of Kant with Husserl can ignore the fact that both of them relied heavily on a programmatic "reduction." Kant's reduction, as we have already noted, involves a shift from reason to understanding. What might otherwise seem a tragic loss of autonomy on the part of reason is presented as a triumph. The conviction that reason can ascertain the intelligibility of the world is supplanted by the claim that it can order the world content. This reduction has pregnant implications for Kant's conception of theory and, especially, explanation. His paramount aim in the *Critique of Pure Reason* was, as he informs us repeatedly, to explicate the necessary and a priori conditions for the possibility of experience. These conditions are not and cannot be given in experience precisely because they are a priori. But they can and must be thought or conceptually entertained as the structures whereby the given is comprehensible. It is for this reason that Kant refers to a priori conditions as *transcendentally ideal*. As theoretical, they are necessarily ideal and, hence, normative for possible experience. Although Kant disavowed the traditional aim of reason to delineate ultimate conditions of intelligibility, he did not surrender the demand for *explanation*. Starting with the phenomenal world, he sought to isolate the various factors that compose it and specify how they combine to form a world. Kant never argued that we have compelling evidence of a self-identical consciousness that is free of schizoid features and certain of itself as an unabridged identity. Thus, he made no attempt to meet Hume on his own ground so far as the problem of self-identity is concerned. Nor, as Kant informs us, is there any reason to believe that there has ever existed a pure moral will of the sort required by his moral theory. In his moral theory as in his epistemology, his conception of the human subject is *theoretical,* which means that it is designed to clarify and explain our experience of ourselves while admittedly going beyond that experience.

We need not concern ourselves with the legitimacy of transcendental arguments. Such arguments claim that necessary conditions can be established for any given experience, for example, science, art, or morality. One of the more difficult problems confronting transcendental analyses is the avoidance of circularity. In Plato's case the very first move toward a priori forms explicitly posits an ideal standard that objects and events can only approach asymptotically. Yet, ontologically and normatively the form is held to be prior to its instantiation. Like Plato, Kant acknowledges the ideality of a priori forms, but assigns them a different status. Though ideal, a priori forms are held to be constitutive of experience and, thus, necessary for its possibility. Kant was quite candid about the idealism intrinsic to his transcendental mode of explanation. As a theory of scientific or objective cognition, it is an ideal representation of an experience that has already been idealized (synthesized, ordered, combined). Empirical data never conform perfectly to empirical rules, nor empirical rules to categories. Experience represents a compromised idealism—the accommodation of reason to existence. Reflection on experiences reveals the necessary a priori structure without which it would not be possible (comprehensible); but it does not disclose the essence of that which is given (presents itself). Curiously enough, in view of their different ontologies, Kant and Plato are in agreement in denying that rational form represents the essence of the empirically real. For both of them rational form is at least somewhat alien to the content it serves to order. Husserl's idealism, on the other hand, construes eidetic form as the essential structure of the given. This conviction follows from Husserl's commitment to the rationalist (Cartesian) metaphysics for which explanation is basically clarification.

The one point where Kant's transcendental procedure might appear to be phenomenological is in the initial descriptive account of experience. The forms of understanding must, Kant argued, first be exhibited in experience fairly completely before we can formulate them systematically. This means that Kant is committed to an *unreduced* mode of experience as a beginning point for his method of analysis. In that respect his epistemological theory seems to rest on a phenomenological foundation. Because the theory cannot be any more certain than the data on the basis of which it is postulated, phenomenological description appears to take precedence over explanatory theory. It might thus be possible, as Husserl evidently believed, to bracket Kant's theoretical paraphernalia and concentrate on the unreduced world of experience that he sought to explain. If the description is fully illuminating, explanation becomes unnecessary. We might thus dispense with the phenomena/noumena distinction and lay bare the structure of things themselves.

The empirical world for Kant is *unreduced* but not immediate. Experience for Kant is not a collection of sense date (*Vorstellungen*) but neither is it a self-articulated and self-combined totality. Thus, the reflection of experience reveals the principles in accordance with which it has been ordered (constituted) but not the intrinsic or essential structure of the empirical (phenomenal) world per se. It is precisely here that Kant's distinction between "reason" and "understanding" is so crucial. Scientifically oriented cognition has renounced the unattainable and hence vain ideal of intelligibility in favor of a comprehensible (causal) order. Experience thus reflects the categories of understanding rather than the logos of being. The reduction represents a trade off of manageable appearance for unattainable reality. Husserl's reduction (*epochē*) takes quite a different form.

To focus the difference between them we might consider the concept of an object—an idea of central importance both to Husserl and to Kant. According to Kant, the concept of an object-in-general is a theoretical notion required for the recognition of any concrete empirical object. The recognition and, hence, a fortiori the description of an object requires the transcendental concept of an object-in-general. Because the concept of an object is a theoretical principle, experience is theory laden insofar as it exhibits objects. In point of discovery, the empirical object is prior, though logically the pure concept of an object in general enjoys priority. The empirical object is impossible apart from the concept around which it is organized. It is not the case, however, that the empirical concept is intuitively given. We can apprehend the empirical object *dog* only by thinking the object, which means combining certain data in a specific unity. The concept is not directly given but must be analyzed out of the experience by a process of reflective abstraction. We can ignore the particular content that characterizes a given dog and concentrate on the rule that enables us to recognize this particular object. The empirical object neither exhausts the concept nor perfectly embodies it. Yet it can accurately be said to *exhibit* the concept. As we move to formulate the concept and, especially, to specify the categories it presupposes, we have commenced an *explanation* of the concept and, hence, have embarked upon the pathway of theory. In doing so we are presumably retracing our steps, as it were, and reconstructing the process through which the object was originally constituted.

This is an ideal reconstruction, of course, because no claim is made that an actual empirical process of constitution can be traced back to its point of origin. The argument is not that we can see with immediate clarity and certainty the pathway along which the empirical object has been constituted, but that it *had to be* constituted in this way if it is to be comprehensible. It would be tempting to hold that Kant relied upon what Sartre has termed a prereflective cogito in accounting for the possibility of reflective analysis. But, alas, that is more a Hegelian than a Kantian idea. Kant came very close to that idea in the Deduction in arguing that the 'transcendental unity of apperception' is a necessary condition for any and every moment of consciousness. It remains problematic, however, precisely how the conditioned consciousness is related to its conditions, save that they presuppose a formal principle of unity.

Kant characterized his philosophy as transcendental idealism. He did not begin with the intuition or, indeed, the certainty of a priori forms or principles but arrived at them subsequent to a meticulous examination of experience. Such forms are held to be constitutive of experience, that is, necessary for its possibility. They are not intuitable nor available to direct inspection even after they have been systematically formulated. His method is, as he indicated, both analytic and synthetic, regressive and progressive, depending upon whether one moves backward to constitutive principles from the totality of experience or forward from transcendental principles to the empirical world. The analytic method is not, however, a *metareflection* that simply reads off formal elements and structures. The analysis itself must employ the very principles it seeks to discover. *Extrapolation* from and *reconstruction* of experience is an essential part of the analysis.

In spite of their obvious differences, Husserl credits Kant with the first clear perception of phenomenology. Phenomenology is, Husserl tells us, "the longing of the whole philosophy of modern times."

> The first to perceive it truly is Kant, whose greatest intuitions first become quite clear to us after we have brought the distinctive features of the phenomenological field into the focus of full consciousness. It then becomes clear that Kant's mental gaze rested on this field, although he was not yet able to appropriate it as the centre from which to work upon on his own line a rigorous science of Essential Being. (*Ideas*, vol. 1, par. 62)

The Transcendental Deduction in the A edition of the *Critique of Pure Reason*, Husserl continues, "moves strictly on phenomenological ground; but Kant misinterprets it as psychological, and therefore eventually abandons it of his own accord." This is, I think, an astonishing statement on Husserl's part. It signifies that Husserl either misunderstood Kant quite badly, or misinterpreted his own phenomenological procedure. In construing the A Deduction as in the tradition and style of the Cartesian cogito, Husserl simply misread it.[6] Kant's procedure could be squared with the method of Descartes only if Kant were to alter radically his conception of theory and explanation. The fact is that Kant modeled his philosophical efforts on precisely the sort of scientific methodology that Husserl wants to bracket and eventually dispense with. The exposition of consciousness and self-consciousness in the A Deduction is an integral part of Kant's transcendental metaphysics. If one could have started with it as an intuitively given certainty, the Deduction need not have been written. If anything, the B Deduction makes this even clearer—which is why Husserl evidently prefers the A version.[7] Perhaps Kant should have adhered to the method of the Cartesian cogito, but the fact is that he did not. Husserl credits Kant, in this instance, with an insight which he never had.

But even though Kant was not a Cartesian, perhaps Husserl was a Kantian in certain fundamental respects—which might account for his accolade to Kant. In characterizing the phenomenological reduction, Husserl states that "we shut off the whole of physics and the whole domain of theoretical thought" (*Ideas*, vol. 1, par. 41). This statement seems by implication to dismiss Kant's entire philosophy insofar as it was modeled on physics and committed to explanatory theory. Even the A Deduction is a piece of theoretical reconstruction rather than an exercise in phenomenology. Yet, surprisingly, Husserl goes on to state in the next sentence that the syntheses that belong to perception are to be retained. "We remain within the framework of plain intuition and the syntheses that belong to it, including perception." Does this mean that Husserl incorporates the Kantian transcendental paraphernalia bodily into his phenomenological program? "Plain intuition" is not very plain if it includes these syntheses. Perhaps the way in which Husserl thought that Kant anticipated phenomenology was in Kant's exposition of the structure of consciousness. In any event, that was surely one of Kant's more important contributions to the understanding of perception. If intentions can be active and synthetic, Kant's theory of transcendental consciousness could be termed "intentional"—in which case there is a definite affinity between Kant's theory and Husserl's conception of intentional consciousness.

Although the afffinity can hardly be doubted, there is still a fundamental difference in their interpretations of intentional structures. For Kant they are elements in a theory of perception, arrived at by transcendental analysis. For Husserl they are intuitable structures that are brought to prominence through the phenomenological reduction. Thus, if the Kantian syntheses are to be retained by phenomenology, they must be *reinterpreted* as inner structures of an immanent consciousness rather than transcending features of a consciousness that is never self-transparent. Otherwise the bracketing required by the phenomenological reduction simply eliminates these forms as theoretical posits. It would seem that either Kant or Husserl misunderstood his own method. Either Kant was a phenomenologist without being fully aware of it— as Husserl suggests, or Husserl was actually a Kantian under the guise of a phenomenologist.

A strong case can be made out, in fact, for the thesis that Husserl became progressively an advocate of a Kantian form of transcendental philosophy and that his alleged "descriptions" were actually theoretical proposals for understanding perception and other forms of experience. A plausible way of reading Husserl is as a neo-Kantian who was somewhat confused about his method. The regional ontology Husserl outlined could easily be construed as domains of experience, each with its own categorial framework (e.g., as with Stephan Körner). The difference between C. I. Lewis, an avowed Kantian, and Husserl fades away as soon as we bracket Husserl himself and suspend judgment about our reflection on experience. To the extent, however, that the everyday world is systematically incoherent,[8] reflecting as it does the archeological deposit of innumerable theories, no analysis of it promises to make it transparently clear. It is for that reason that any reflection on experience is forced to choose principles of interpretation and, hence, to make use of theoretical maxims in the description of phenomena. Or, put differently, every description necessarily idealizes by selecting, excluding, stressing, ignoring, and so forth.

One of the more troublesome legacies of Kant's transcendental philosophy is the concept of the thing-in-itself. Virtually every philosopher since Kant has taken exception to that doctrine. Yet, without it there could be no *Critique*. If the world constituted by the cognizing consciousness is equivalent to being itself, no transcendence of experience is possible. Kant's critics and detractors have never tired of pointing out that he should have considered the possibility of alternative categorial schemes. Indeed he should and, in that respect, his theory is not critical enough. But neither is it possible to change categories while leaving experience unaltered. If categories and conceptual forms are *constitutive* of the empirical world, there is no substantial world on which to hang the garments of theory. Yet Husserl ties his eidetic forms even more tightly to empirical contents than does Kant. The claim that in explicating intentional structures one is only *describing* the immanent world of consciousness implies that no alternative description is possible. If an alternative description were possible, that would testify to the fact that it is a *theory* of experience rather than a *description*. But this has the questionable import of marrying form to content so tightly that no alternative description is permitted. A description would be corrigible only with respect to clarity or confusion. And that is basically a rationalist rather than an empiricist commitment, namely that those ideas that are clear and distinct constitute the structure of truth.

There are at least two basic issues at stake here with respect to the nature of reflection. There is, on the one hand, the question how experience is constituted, and especially, whether there is a primordial rational constitution of the experienced world. And, in the second place, there is a question how the reflecting consciousness is related to the experience reflected on. Is there, as Sartre has argued, a prereflective cogito? If there is and must be such a cogito for reflection to be possible, the reflecting consciousness must, as Merleau-Ponty puts it, *reenact* the constitution of the empirical world. The reflecting consciousness cannot then be neutral with respect to the experiences it appropriates because it has already been involved in their constitution. This means, in effect, that a pure metareflection is impossible, whether for phenomenology or any other philosophical program. Though Husserl's phenomenological program begins with experience, it depends crucially on the assumption that the experienced world is rationally constituted and, thus, can be rationally assessed. Because description and constitution logically entail one another, the possibility of rational description that focuses on the structure of ideal essences assumes that experience has been rationally constituted in the first place.

This presupposition is either dogmatic, a fundamental assumption that is taken to be self-evident, or it is subject to interpretation and challenge. If rationality is open to question, we cannot infer from the supposition that the world is rational what structures it exhibits. Nor can we assume that it is thoroughly or completely rational with respect to its form. Indeed, the question of form is only another facet of the question about rationality. The assumption that experience exhibits and requires pure eidetic forms for its possibility can be equally as dogmatic as the supposition that it is thoroughly rational.

Both Kant and Husserl were rationalists. In the *Metaphysics of Morals*, Kant makes the quite immodest claim that philosophy actually begins with his transcendental program.[9] Whatever came before was only an anticipation of the true philosophy. Kant's dogmatism with respect to the transcendental a priori rests on his assumption that experience is eternally constituted, albeit for a contingent world. Critical in his address to speculative philosophy and even to empiricism, he sought to replace criticism with the *certainty* of transcendental principles. This had the effect of locking him into the science and morality of his day. The one point where he retained the principle of critique was in his distinction between appearances and things-in-themselves. If that distinction were to be surrendered, experience would be absolutized in the form in which it is most immediately available.

For better or for worse, this is precisely the move which Husserl made, namely to dispense with the phenomena/noumena distinction for the sake of an immanent and transparent world of consciousness. Husserl's empiricism is even more tenuous than Kant's, a mere excuse for the appearance of eidetic forms. Husserl's commitment to the logic of eidetic structures is thoroughly rationalistic and dogmatic to the degree that it is in principle immune to critique.

The existential turn in phenomenology that followed so closely upon the heels of Husserl's work, reinstituted the phenomena/noumena distinction, though with definite Hegelian overtones. Heidegger was uncomfortable with a descriptive analysis of the everyday world that took the apparent (phenomena) as the ultimately real or true. By reintroducing a conception of being beyond appearance, Heidegger gave phenomenological inquiry a hermeneutical turn. Although Sartre professes to follow Husserl's phenomenological program, in fact he makes use of a thinly veiled speculative method in elaborating the structure of his own ontology. In general, the existentialists follow in the footsteps of Kant, Kierkegaard, and Hegel in their analysis of the conditions of human existence. Heidegger's existential conditions are clearly transcendental in Kant's rather than Husserl's sense of that term. Whatever Husserl's phenomenological program may have suggested to Heidegger, Sartre, and other of the existentialist philosophers, it failed to persuade them that the conditions of existence are transparently available to the reflecting consciousness. Initial concentration on unreduced experience summons new flights of imagination and speculative efforts designed to *explain* the everyday world. Pure description can at best trace the lineaments of the world as given; it cannot render it self-illuminating. Only a dialectical phenomenology on the order of Hegel's could have much promise of achieving that goal, and Hegel's program itself is not altogether convincing. An explanation that does not surprise us and require us to alter our view of that with which we started is of little philosophical interest. To give up explanation altogether in favor of an immanent world of consciousness would be to close off the mystery that generates inquiry. There is a conspicuous and recurrent conflict between the desire for certainty and the concern to understand the world as it is in itself. Philosophical truth and rigorous science may well be incompatible. Husserl's phenomenological program is philosophically interesting only because it is problematic.

To summarize: Whatever their similarities may be, Husserl is mistaken in viewing Kant as a naive but somewhat confused phenomenologist who glimpsed a verdant garden that he could not harvest. Kant and Husserl held radically different assessments of intuition. Kant believed that intellectual (conceptual) intuition is impossible, whereas Husserl relied upon it as the primary element in his phenomenological method. Their differing interpretations of intuition are correlated with quite different conceptions of phenomena. For Kant the phenomenon is essentially a construction that reflects the legislation of human understanding in response to the solicitations of experience; for Husserl, on the other hand, the phenomenon is a pure self-presentation that needs only to be freed of the layers of speculative veneer that occludes the vision of the reflecting consciousness. It is not possible to reconcile Kant and Husserl simply by lopping off the thing-in-itself. The reason is that they differ fundamentally in their conception of the phenomenal object. Experience as given is far too fragmentary to provide us with those rational principles we need in order to understand it. Every interpretation of experience, so far as Kant is concerned, requires an extrapolation from that which is given. The issue between them here is that Kant is a limited rationalist whereas Husserl is an avowed Cartesian. In spite of Husserl's extensive use of transcendental language, his version of transcendental philosophy is radically different from Kant's on the decisive issue concerning the nature of theory. For Kant no *epochē*, however successful, can hope to dispense with the need for explanation. Kant and Husserl began with different assumptions and pursued radically different goals.

Still, Husserl has offered some extremely interesting materials for interpreting and even modifying Kant's philosophy. This is particularly true with respect to the Aesthetic of the *Critique of Pure Reason*. One can make use of Husserl's analysis of the intentional structure of consciousness to interpret the perceptual consciousness. Not only that, but if one construes Husserl's descriptions as theoretical proposals, they can be taken as explanatory of experience. To read Husserl in that way would be to view him more as a transcendental philosopher in Kant's sense than a pure phenomenologist. I am inclined to read Husserl in the latter fashion; indeed, I see no viable alternative. Because Kant was anti-Cartesian, Husserl could not both return to Descartes for his method and assimilate Kant's transcendental philosophy. It was Husserl rather than Kant who was confused on this point.

PART 3

PHENOMENOLOGY OF MEDICINE

11. Flirtations or Engagements? Prolegomenon to a Philosophy of Medicine

RICHARD M. ZANER

Medicine and philosophy, Edmund Pellegrino notes, have had a "vexed history" (1974, p. 6), one oscillating between affection and antagonism. Not since classical Greek times, however, has there been anything like the "ideal of Paideia," that remarkable synthesis in which philosophy and medicine were "the major determinants of the dominant image of man" (ibid., p. 9).

Yet, no sooner was that zenith of comprehensiveness reached than matters sharply declined, and both disciplines fell into schisms. Medicine may well have suffered most, for it became a kind of leaf unhung and at the whims of whatever philosophic winds happened by: influenced by Aristotle and then the skeptics (especially Carneades and Pyrrho), medicine became *empiricism*; then by Plato (especially his *Timaeus*) and the Neoplatonists (especially Plotinus), it became *dogmatism*; later by Epicurus and his ethics, it became *methodism*. The advent of Galen (130 A.D.-200A.D.) saw a monumental effort to achieve a new synthesis of philosophy with Hippocratic medicine, now in the light of his own discoveries in anatomy and physiology. This sweepingly ambitious aim, however, as Oswei Temkin has shown (1973), was plagued with internal contradictions; and the effort was consequently a failure. Nonetheless, the impact of Galen's work was considerable, exercising an authority in medical matters for the next thirteen hundred years. In the Middle Ages, Galenism became diffused by numerous elements of Christian theology, gnosticism, and so forth. Eventually it came under fire from the violent and colorful Paracelsus, whose own vision—a concoction of Neoplatonism, alchemy and astronomy— spawned a host of medical romantics and mystics and seems as well to have given philosophy a dark name for much of subsequent medicine.

What gradually occurred was an increasingly powerful insistence that medicine return to the best insights of the Hippocratics and even Galen: to clinical observation, to careful study of the natural history of diseases, to a fund of empirically verifiable data. And for that insistence, a natural ally was the newly emerging natural science. Even though it was a philosopher, Descarates, whose dualistic conception of mind and matter gave credence to that tendency, philosophy continued, except for brief and ultimately ineffectual interludes, to have connotations of Paracelsian flights of fantasy for medicine (Risse, 1971, 1972). Thus, Pellegrino points out that,

> in the twentieth century, medicine has emerged completely from its centuries-long domination by philosophy . . . largely as a result of its increasingly impressive and unprecedented empiric and factual base. To-day, medicine is a strong, independent discipline, rich in theoretical and practical accomplishments. It has turned from philosophic pursuits and it is wary and skeptical of any significant re-engagement with its formerly fascinating partner. (ibid., pp. 11–12)

Contemporary medicine, wedded to a scientific and clinical vision, is a "fusion of the neo-Hippocratic spirit with a new, matured Cartesian conviction that human illness can be described in physico-chemical and quantified terms" (ibid., p. 11). And, with what must seem a kind of well-deserved historic, if not poetic, justice, philosophy plainly limps along, not only solipsistically fascinated with its own metaphoric navel but generally ignored and even maligned: a decided outcast, poorly paid and without detectable impact. Uncertain of itself and puzzled, dubious of its role in humanity's current crisis, philosophy, Pellegrino acidly remarks, "has become lost in the intellectual omphaloskepsis in which its positivist and analytic bent have culminated" (ibid., p. 15).

Still, Pellegrino and others of us envisage a more significant prospect on the horizon, for if a judicious and well-informed encounter between medicine and philosophy can at all be achieved again, we stand to realize "a new cultural synthesis, rivaling that of ancient Greece" (ibid., p. 20).

Dependent in part on the willingness of persons in both disciplines to listen well to one another, each from its own clearly delineated strengths and weaknesses, this genuinely new prospect rests to an even greater extent on something else: namely, that both are, as Pellegrino says,

> deeply concerned with the most fundamental aspects of man and his existence. For centuries, medicine has probed his body and his biological and social reality, and philosophy has concentrated on man's thinking

and knowing—speculating on his nature and his actions as a moral and artistic being. In its own way, each discipline has, in every era, wrestled with learning what man is about. (ibid., pp. 5–6)

But in our times, in an age wherein the image of man has suffered a paralyzing fragmentation and man, as Max Scheler remarked in 1928 (1961, pp. 5–6), has become as never before in human history deeply enigmatic to himself, philosophy and medicine have inherited a unique and central responsibility: caring for and critically understanding the nexus of human life. Clearly, the prospect and challenge to develop a philosophy of medicine is an urgent and necessary one, new to both disciplines. It requires on the part of philosophy a healthy respect for clinical observation, immersion in the particular and specific, and a sober regard for the constraints thereby imposed on inquiry. This prospect is by no means merely one more of the already burdensome plethora of "philosophies of"—science, art, religion, and so forth, which can be found in the curricula of every department of philosophy. What is at stake here is more profound and difficult than the easy phrase "philosophy of medicine" conveys. At issue is "the central question of all human culture—the problem of man" (ibid., pp. 24–25), and both disciplines must confront it as "a cultural necessity" (p. 21).

To do so, however, requires a clear perception of reality. And *reality* here has a number of different facets: on the one hand, the crisis, as it is called, in our understanding of human life; on the other, several remarkable but too infrequently noticed features about medicine as a human enterprise. I have only touched on the first, and not even mentioned the second. A word, then, about the first, then more on the second.

1. We hear a good deal today about all manner of crises. One thinks, for example, not only of Max Scheler's "crisis of man," but of crisis variously in science, religion, ecology, international affairs, and the like. Beyond this, Eike-Henner Kluge insists that "we live in a time of profound moral crisis," as a consequence of which views on morality "are more confused—even contradictory—than at any other time in history" (1975, p. vii). More specifically, Peter H. Schuck points out that "it has been certified on the highest authority that America is in the throes of a 'health care crisis'" (1974, p. 95), certified not only by Presidential statements but by the Committee for Economic Development (1973)—whose issuance of one of its reports seems to make it all quite official! Revealing economic, political, as well as technological parameters, the health care crisis has perhaps more poignant dimensions for consumers: access to primary health care services, especially by the innter-city poor and those in rural areas; the quality of health care and

considerable variations from hospital to hospital; the costs of health care; the "drastic decline in primary physicians (particularly general practitioners) and the corresponding growth in the specialties and sub-specialties" (Schuck, p. 99); and the fact that the level of health in this country is quite low relative to that of other industrialized nations (pp. 97–99).

The talk of crisis in medicine is by no means empty. But what is rarely appreciated is that its source lies in the very history that at once helped to make modern medicine possible and yet that it believes it has left behind. Consider only this, for instance: the very philosophical vision—that is, Descartes's dualism—which seemed to give license to medicine's eventual marriage to the natural sciences, initiates on the other hand the basis for much of the current crisis. Everything, Descartes says, is either matter or mind, and nothing is both. But this metaphysical stance was coupled with another thesis: the only way genuinely to know the material world is mathematics, conceived as the science of quantitative measurement. Thus, everything that proves to be nonmaterial is thereby nonquantitative and so is no proper part of the world of bodies—of science. It is rather, as is said, "in the mind." Thus, with a single stroke was the observable opulence of nature, especially biological nature, stripped of precisely what gave it not only meaning but its very richness and diversity. Nature was reduced to the level of sheer quantity and motion; not only was *life* thereby rendered utterly enigmatic, but human life suffered an internal schism hitherto unknown. For even though there have been other dualisms (e.g., gnostic), none had proclaimed the utterly indifferent, indeed alien, character of nature: pure, sheer quantity in motion (Jonas, 1966, pp. 211–234). Moreover, even though everything was taken to be either matter (body) or mind (soul), and nothing both, even Descartes knew well that not only he himself but all other human beings were indeed both, at once mind and body. But the Cartesian framework, its inner logic, could not comprehend that very thing!

Nor have most subsequent efforts fared any better. Either they remained entrapped in the same dualism, or they assumed one or another form of monism: idealism (denying reality to matter) or materialism (denying reality to mind). Subsequent postdualistic monisms, as Hans Jonas has brilliantly demonstrated (ibid., pp. 7–26), are born of the Cartesian sectioning and ineluctably bear the marks of that parentage. If idealism leaves us wondering about our actual bodily placement in the social and material world (body, and idea merely, seems to have neither weight nor biologic wherewithal), materialism makes of mind but a spectral presence, a mere ghost in a machine. Neither of them, any more than their common parent, dualism, can comprehend the specific and obvious wholeness of the human being as embodied and alive in the social and material world.

The price medicine paid for its marriage to the natural sciences has not been light, for all its otherwise obvious benefits. For so long as it is conceived in the Cartesian tradition, self-consciously or not, it inherits the painful and well-known problems inherent to that, not only regarding the conceptual understanding of the body but also the entrenched relativism affecting so many discussions of the ethical problems in medicine. If nature, after all, is thought to be nothing but material particles in motion and definable by mathematical formulas, then everything not so construable must be cast aside or into the "merely subjective." And so far as mathematical measurement became the paradigm of knowledge itself, anything not amenable to that mode of expression had to be regarded either as reducible to quantitative data (if it were to be knowable), or if not that, then taken as nonexistent or insignificant—that is, without efficacy and thus able to be ignored as such. But this includes, after all, the entire range of values and thereby that of life. The only recourse was to regard values, thus life, as mere subjective phenomena. That subjectivism is, now as then, a radical impasse from which there is no exit, as is clear from the history of modern empiricism or rationalism—except by rejecting the very terms of the discourse. And, as should become clear, certain features of medicine itself make that rejection necessary.

The understanding of human life is thus historically little more than a puppetlike caricature; man came to view himself as severed, compartmentalized, and notoriously at the mercy of whims, deceptions, seductions, and fancies, fit precisely for the psychoanalysis that was still to come but was already noticeable on the horizon. Indeed, the psychiatrist J. H. van den Berg has argued, in an important convergence with Hans Jonas, that the emergence of Cartesian dualism is no historical accident, not merely one of the many metaphysical viewpoints that arbitrarily pop up in the historical panaorama. Cartesian dualism, Van der Berg seeks to show (as does Jonas), has profound connections with the develoments in biology and medicine before and during Descartes's times. With the first anatomical intrusion into the human cadaver (by Mundinus, in 1306), and continuing in a sequence of decisive events to the present day, "human existence," he argues, "has in a very specific sense been impoverished" (1977, p. 134). That anatomical intrusion had the synchronic force of initiating the actual separation of mind and body (opening the body is effectively openly *displaying* the body) and thereby introducing the cultural subtexture for the body-soul dualism that was later to give it conceptual credence and in turn receiving legitimacy for itself. Correlated with that, there became evident an elemental "distress" affecting the "soul" itself, an internal schism. Scarcely a century after Descartes, this shows up and is formally dubbed "neurosis" by George Cheyne (1733). A few decades later, the abnormal state of mind termed "magnetic sleep" by Mesmer (1780) and the "double" by Richter (1786) is even more prominent. By 1843, prior to the advent of Freud, Kierkegaard was to lay out the incredibly complex entanglements of that decisive disease of the soul, despair. The path explored by Freud and subsequent psychoanalysis was effectively prepared. So-called mental illness, in short, is an *historical emergent.*

Van den Berg argues that this historical rending of the human context is synchronously matched by other cultural events: for example, in painting, with the "emancipation of the landscape." The "environs," the surrounding world, of human life becomes split off from human life, and thus is the soil also prepared for and the seeds of estrangement planted in that context. Within this setting there could now occur the initial cultural form of modern alienation: industrialization and its unique modes of reification of human life, human work, and modes of human interchanges. Given this, what George Cheyne called "the English malady," that is, neurosis, could make its first appearance: "Neuroses can be regarded as the pathological consequence of a world which has been steadily turning away from man" (ibid., p. 133).

Thanks to this historical uncovering of what he calls *anthro-pathology*, van den Berg shows how the entire issue of "mental health" receives a new significance: ". . . the most important symptom that there is something wrong with our *mental health* lies in the word *mental*. Yes, if we are asked to live *mentally*, that is as a *soul*, in a strange anatomical body, in a strange chemical-physical world, nobody can expect us to live mentally in good health" (p. 135). "Health," that integral "healing" whose root meaning is *wholeness*, literally encompasses everything about us: "*health of the unity of man and his landscape, man and his body*" (p. 135). To talk of mental health, thus, is already to endorse that internal schism and the ontological bifurcations that have their source in early medieval medicine, painting, and philosophy. Thus does darkness come to govern, and we come to be haunted by faint, wispy traces of ourselves.

A second point about modern medicine can now be made, but again with necessary brevity.

2. Even brief consideration of modern medicine makes it plain that the lowliest practitioner has at his disposal a truly incredible arsenal of regimens, procedures, techniques, and a huge variety of specialists, not to mention the array of pills, balms, salves, and other medications and anesthesias, exotic or mundane, on prescription or over-the-counter—

any of which can readily be brought to bear on even the smallest of complaints. We have inherited, and continue to contribute to, a technological cornucopia of mammouth proportions, an overspill that sometimes promises to become an overkill. The success of the marriage between medicine and biomedical science, formally endorsed in the context of Cartesian metaphysics, has been remarkable—whatever the price of that marriage. But there are serious problems nonetheless.

One particularly sensitive facet of medicine owes its peculiar poignancy, though not its origin, to that abundance of techniques, therapies and medications: namely, medical *error*. Regardless of the Cartesian commitment to certainty, mathematically conceived, the practice of medicine bristles with regions of ignorance, matched perhaps only by that of patients over their condition and what is practiced on them. The margin of error: the present state of medicine surely makes this far more salient than ever before. But we must be clear at precisely this point: for medical fallibility is by no means solely a matter of plain negligence or of limitations due to the "state of the art." For as Samuel Gorovitz and Alasdair MacIntyre have suggested, medical practice is far more opaque than is normally understood, most especially on the sources of error. Medicine, to the extent that it is a science, is focused on *particulars*, and however much a medical theoretician may wish to detect regularities and concomitances in his subject-matter, it is simply mistaken to regard such statements of regularities as universals. Indeed, one must insist, they point out, that

> precisely because our understanding and expectations of particulars cannot be fully spelled out in terms of lawlike generalizations and initial conditions, the best possible judgment may always turn out to be erroneous, and erroneous not merely because our science has not yet progressed far enough or because the scientist has been either wilful or negligent, but because of the necessary fallibility of our knowledge of particulars. (1976, p. 62)

As regards different types of individual—hurricanes, dolphins, or people—the kinds of predictive power and corresponding lawlike generalizations by which we know whatever it is we do about these individuals will necessarily differ. We always face regions of ignorance as regards any type of individual—variations in environmental context, specific factors about its history, specific configurations of physical and other mechanisms operative in it (ibid., p. 58). Some of these factors, moreover, themselves vary in unpredictable ways (for example, the environmental context of people even within a particular culture). Thus, the types of generalizations available for each type of individual are in principle "generalizations prefaced by 'Characteristically and for the most part. . . .'" (ibid.). That signifies that every science of particulars incorporates a *necessary fallibility*, having nothing to do with negligence or the state of the art.

That medicine is such a science, quite as much as meteorology or sociology, biology or political science, seems perfectly clear. Hence, like other sciences, it includes this mode of fallibility. To what extent it is present in medicine, as opposed to other sciences, is of course a crucial question. It is bound to have significant ramifications for a patient's image of the physician as well as for social and legal policies. These are surely real and important problems to be explored. They do not concern me here, however.

What does concern me are the implications of the point that H. Tristram Engelhardt, Jr., has emphasized about medicine as a human enterprise.

> Medicine is the most revolutionary of human technologies. It does not sculpt statues or paint paintings: it restructures man and man's life. . . . In short, medicine is not merely a science, not merely a technology. Medicine is a singular art which has as its object man himself. Medicine is the art of remaking man, not in the image of nature, but in his own image; medicine operates with an implicit idea of what man *should* be. . . . The more competent medicine becomes, the more powerful it is, the more able it is to remake man, the more necessary it consequently becomes to understand what medicine should do with its competence. (1973, p. 445)

The point here is not so much, as the usual conundrum has it, that the physician and the biomedical scientist "play at being God." Perhaps they do; but then so do we all in our own ways: in the use of other technologies, in common crimes, in suicide, in war, in making moral decisions about abortion or euthanasia, or even in telling or not telling the truth. The point is that "the laws and concepts of medicine are in their very nature caught up with values and human goals" (ibid., p. 451).

Indeed, such central concepts as health and disease are quite obviously value concepts. "Health," as "well-being" or "wholeness" (Kass, 1975), invokes specific goals and enmeshes us in considerations of their desirability, attainability, and possible alternatives—that is, in value choices. But the same is true of disease: considered as an undesirable condition, one to be rectified or cured, it inevitably evokes value considerations of the first order.

But more than this is at issue here: the very "progress" of medicine results in sometimes profound changes in human life and *consequently in medicine itself.* Given medicine's ability to enable fewer babies to die at birth and to keep more people alive afterwards, the resultant population explosion helped to bring about man as an urban animal, drastically different from before. But in light of this, Engelhardt points out:

> . . . medicine was forced to find ways of bringing the nature of man, in particular his reproduction, under rational control. The result is a profound change in the nature of man, a full separation of the social and reproductive aspects of sex. But also, medicine itself is changed, and it is no longer just treating specific ills of specific people. It is engaged in remaking man in general—after all, fertility is not usually thought of as a personal disease. Indeed, in the natural Darwinian context, the highest premium is given to fertility. But the success of medicine reversed natural priorities and produced the social disease of overpopulation. As a consequence, medicine is now "treating" fertility and population dynamics. (ibid., pp. 446–447)

Indeed, it is worth pointing out that just this effective separation of sexual from reproductive activity brings about wholly new kinds of moral issues impacting family structure, educational policy, child rearing, population planning, and even such a sensitive issue as the right to reproduce. And it seems perfectly clear that such enhanced technical prowess must inevitably figure prominently in altering human life and human society.

But specifically *modern* technology, Hans Jonas has rightly insisted, brings with it decisive changes from what was hitherto possible. He notes even in classical times the "awestruck homage to man's powers" (1974, p. 5) in Sophocles' *Antigone* and that unique celebration of man's "violent and violating irruption into the cosmic order" and his "restless cleverness" and "building" (ibid.). Still, there is, he continues, "a subdued and even anxious quality about this appraisal of the marvel that is man. . . . With all his boundless resourcefulness, man is still small by the measure of the elements: precisely this makes his sallies into them so daring and allows those elements to tolerate his forwardness" (ibid.). For all his invasions of nature's various domains, their encompassing nature is left unchanged and undiminished: "They last, while his schemes have their shortlived way" (ibid.).

With modern technology, however, all this changes. For with the drastically altered scale of technological invasion in our day, what has become starkly clear is the discovery of the "critical *vulnerability* of nature to man's technological intervention—unsuspected before it began to show itself in damage already done" (ibid., p. 9). And what this kind of power brings in its wake has only barely begun to be realized— how profoundly the very scope of human action has changed, the expansion of the artificial environment, and even the ways by which the boundary between "city" and "nature" has been obliterated (ibid., pp. 10–12), and still other far-reaching consequences. Of more immediate import here, of course, are the impacts in and by medicine and biology: for it is currently plausible not only to conceive and practice genetic control of future men (taking our own evolution in hand), nor only to conceive and practice behavior control on individuals and entire populations, but even the idea of controlling our own mortality is no longer inconceivable.

Clearly modern technology has brought profound and qualitative changes in its wake and gives Engelhardt's point actual force.

This shift in medicine is of great significance, for it shows quite clearly just how medicine is, as the father of modern pathology, Rudolph Virchow, says, "a social science in its very bone and marrow" (quoted in Jonas, p. 448). With contraception, genetic manipulation, abortion, in vitro fertilization, transplantation, massive innoculation programs, or even cosmetic surgery, medicine has effectively become an *active agent of social change and change of individual persons.* All of which, be it noted, invokes values and goals concerning the wellbeing of man. That is, medicine is (and has been all along, although never so clearly as today) engaged in remaking human individual and social life; and for the most part the value judgments that have guided medicine have remained unassessed, uncritically accepted, but silently and powerfully guiding its course—whether it be a matter of developing a particular drug or technology, exploring new surgical techniques, or even dietary plans.

Medicine is a wholly singular enterprise. Pellegrino expresses this in his contention that medicine is at once the most humane of the sciences and the most scientific of the humanities (1970, pp. 31–36). Engelhardt, emphasizing with Virchow that medicine is a social science, contends that, philosophically understood, medicine is the actual bridge between the natural and social sciences (1973, p. 451). And both stress that the role of the philosophy of medicine is not at all to bridge the gap between the value-free and the value-involved sciences but rather to *understand* the actual bridge—that is, medicine. Even more, Engelhardt points out that

> . . . one must recognize that medicine can make a potentially unique contribution to the humanities: a domain of reality where value and facts coincide, where theory is praxis, where man himself is defined, remade, and redefined. . . . In the end this is the issue in medicine: the problem of discovering proportion and measure so that its Promethean endeavor can be undertaken without the hubris which invites tragedy. Here medicine needs to become critically self-conscious and philosophy attentive to the

central human enterprise of medicine. . . . Man has become more technically adept that he is wise, and must now look for the wisdom to use
that knowledge he possesses. (ibid., p. 451–452).

Here is a point of fundamental concern for ethics, especially for medical
ethics. It is one also made by Hans Jonas in his recent work in ethics:
the classical distinction between the "is" (fact) and the "ought" (value)
seems to break down, and consequently any purported medical ethics
must take cognizance of this decisive fact about medicine (see Jonas,
1977, esp. pp. 193–195).

Both Engelhardt and Pellegrino have, it seems to me, real insights
into the place and necessary presence of philosophy in medicine, and
about medicine itself. And both have made important contributions to
the conception of the tasks of a philosophy of medicine. What remains
to be done is the labor of actual philosophical study of these issues
and many more connected with them. Although I surely cannot do
that, here I do want to mark out two points I take to be necessary
ingredients to that task.

First, given, as Gorovitz and MacIntyre have suggested, that medicine
incorporates a region of necessary fallibility, we need now to recall
that medicine is an enterprise that *at once changes the nature of its
particulars*—human beings—*and thereby changes itself.* Medicine does
not merely study and explain a certain range of phenomena; its very
"study" (theory) is both an acting-on and an affecting (praxis) of what
is studied—even in the apparently more remote cases of research in
physiology, neurology, and the like. As such, medicine is unique in a
way even beyond that marked out by Pellegrino or Engelhardt and
differs in a way as well from the sort of science of particulars analyzed
by Gorovitz and MacIntyre.

The kind of fallibility at issue here must on the one hand distinguish
medicine from every other science of particulars and on the other
inevitably give the changes in man that medicine brings about a unique
kind of emotive and valuational force. My point can perhaps be
expressed this way: like the social and humanistic disciplines, medicine's
principal object is man himself, individually and socially. Unlike being
an object of study by the former, however, to be brought as a patient
within the focus of medicine is not simply to be observed and explained
(whether well or badly) but *to be changed thereby*, whether trivially or
more seriously.

Not only this, however: for as medicine "remakes man," in Engelhardt's phrase, medicine itself undergoes changes—again, whether trivially or more profoundly. Hence, medicine is not only a science of
particulars but is a science which, unique among the sciences, *itself*

changes as it changes its "objects"—human beings. Such changes, however, we recall, are brought about within the nexus of medicine's *necessary fallibility*.

It is not only, then, that medicine is so singularly involved in value questions but also that these value questions are uniquely significant. To express the point here as sharply as possible: *it lies within the power of modern medicine to alter, perhaps radically and irrevocably, and for better or ill, our very capacity to reckon with and understand medicine itself—and thereby our ability to understand ourselves.* Medicine is thus a *critical* discipline and not only in view of the current crises mentioned earlier but rather precisely because man himself is always at issue in every medical encounter, every medical decision—as is the physician himself! The "logos" of *medicine itself thus commits it to having to be philosophically self-critical.* Philosophy, to put it bluntly, understood as that discipline that must by its very nature be self-critical, is found *within* the very nature of medicine.

A second, and final, point now emerges. The presence of technological power, we may say, elicits or at least encourages the use of that power. For power of the sort modern technology puts at our disposal, especially in medicine, must wither if left unused and dormant. As Hans Jonas points out, "There is no other way of exercising the power than by making oneself available to the use of the things as they become available. Where use is forgone the power must lapse, but there is no limit to the extension of either" (1966, p. 193). This of itself, of course, calls for judicious and circumspect deliberation concerning the place of values in a world of use.

But there is another side to this, not usually appreciated. An enterprise possessing such technological power—a *power whose use is defined*, as I suggested, *by its ability to cancel out all cognizance of its use*—also elicits social prominence and prestige for and to itself within the community of its practice. It invariably provides and encourages (as part of its very power) influential ways for those outside medicine to understand, view, and even "image" themselves. Not only does medicine, in short, encourage those in the wider culture to view themselves in medical ways, but also to pass these ways on to others through education, the media, and other more indirect ways.

Thus, what we are constantly induced to think and to feel about ourselves, our lives, is heavily influenced by the sheer presence of modern medicine. It is an influence considerably enhanced by the fact that medicine frequently has to do with the ultimate issues facing human beings: life, death, impairment, disease, guilt, failure, that is, with human beings in respect to what precisely *defines their humanity*. To be impaired is to suffer a lessening of autonomy, of one's ability to choose (one's associates, for example), of one's self-image, in short of one's freedom to act on one's own. A "complaint" quickly becomes a "sickness," an "illness," and readily then a "disease"—and thereby medicalized: one readily learns to see oneself as medicine sees one. But so, too, for the sense of one's "life," my life, my very body: what are these, for medicine?

Here we touch on exceedingly intricate regions. Consider, for example, the body, which is, after all, the main concern for the bulk of medicine. Typically, of course, this is regarded as a strictly biological affair, wholly innocent of values and other "unscientific" things (cf. Hellegers, 1973). Values, goals, and the like are no proper part of physical or medical science but are rather, it is said, metaphysical and ethical. What, then, is this body biologically speaking? Or, rather, to try to keep matters brief here, what is the body that is at the center of medicine's concern? Here, a slight indirection will help to make the point. Paul Ramsey (1974) made the following observation in another connection:

> In the second year anatomy course, medical students clothe with "gallows humor" their encounter with the cadaver which was a human being alive. That defense is not to be despised; nor does it necessarily indicate socialization in shallowness. . . . Even when dealing with the remains of the long since dead, there is a special tension involved . . . when performing investigatory medical actions involving the face, the hands, and the genitalia. This thing-in-the-world that was once a man alive we still encounter as once a communicating being, not quite as an object of research or instruction. Face and hands, yes; but why the genitalia? Those reactions must seem incongruous to a resolutely biologizing age. For a beginning of an explanation, one might take up the expression "carnal knowledge" . . . and behind that go to the expression "*carnal conversation*," an old, legal term for adultery, and back of both to the Biblical word "know" . . . Here we have an entire anthropology impacted in a word, not a squeamish euphemism. In short, in those reactions of medical students can be discerned a sensed relic of the human being bodily experiencing and communicating, and the body itself uniquely speaking. (p. 59)

Concerned here to evoke the "felt difference between life and death," Ramsey emphasizes that this difference makes itself felt even in the case of the cadaver: thing-in-the-world though it may be, it is not merely that, for it is still encountered as "once a man alive" and not simply as an object of research or instruction. To be sure, the incommensurable contrast between life and death is met most dramatically with the "newly dead" (e.g. in the emergency room): if the cadaver evokes gallows humor, the mangled body lying on the emergency room stretcher awakens dread and awe. Both, however, suggest an almost haunting presence of once enlivened flesh—bodily gestures, attitudes,

151

movements, stances—which a "resolutely biologizing age" too easily seems to ignore or to suppress.

Such encounters with corpses (newly or long dead) suggest, indeed, that there are no clean divisions—neither empirically in medicine nor substantially in metaphysics—possible between biological and personal life. Which is not to say that there are no differences in significance or logical status. It is to say, on the other hand, both that what Ramsey has pointed to is a positive phenomenon standing in need of an accounting and that this remains deeply enigmatic from the perspective presented often by biomedicine. Labeling terms such as *self, person*, or *dignity*, as "unscientific" (as Hellegers and others do) does nothing to elucidate their sense. Neither does it formally recognize that the animate organism treated or investigated by a physician or researcher is in no way *simply there* on the examining table but is a far more complex affair: in some determinable sense, varying with age, biological wherewithal, and circumstances, it is the body belonging to and experienced by a someone, a person. The cases of the fetus, the severely handicapped neonate, the comatose patient, or one under relatively complete anaesthesia, are, doubtless, problematic ones. Perhaps they must be conceived as *limiting cases*, those where the processes of embodiment are either not yet able to be more than minimally or only globally (undifferentiatedly) articulated or have been too severely curtailed to permit *the embodying function*. Perhaps, even, some organisms will never be able to be fully experienced by the one whose organism it is (or was). Nevertheless, however one eventually comes to understand them, much less to treat them, it needs to be pointed out that they are as much "sensed embodiments" as the cadavers Ramsey talks about are "sensed relics" of the once embodied human being bodily experiencing and the body itself "uniquely speaking"—that is, considered as a person's embodiment.

Pointing to this phenomenon, Ramsey is clearly at odds with any "mind/body" dualism—either philosophical or medical—which certainly seems implicit to our "biologizing age," to our modern medicine, which, as Pellegrino remarks, is based in part on a more matured Cartesianism. In an ultimately not very successful effort to surmount the dualism, Ramsey refers to St. Augustine's claim that "the body is not an extraneous ornament or aid, but a part of man's very nature" (ibid., p. 60). In the case of the alive human being, body and soul are "conjoined and closely intertwined," they "interpenetrate" each other. Thus, Ramsey insists, "for Biblical or later Christian anthropology, the only possible form which human life in any true and proper sense can take here or hereafter is 'somatic'" (ibid., p. 60).

These suggestions raise profound issues, in light of which views like that of Hellegers become most problematic. Let me mention but one here. The effort to divide out human *biological* from human *personal* life (the one to medicine, the other to ethics) may well signify, para- doxically and ironically, that such a biomedical theory has in effect taken the *dead body*, the cadaver, as the model for the human live body. This suggestion is by no means outlandish. As Hans Jonas masterfully demonstrates, in classical times, and its panvitalism (the belief in the ubiquity of life),

> . . . it was the corpse, this primal exhibition of "dead" matter, which was the limit of all understanding and therefore the first thing not to be accepted at its face-value. Today the living, feeling, striving organism has taken over this role and is being unmasked as a *ludibrium materiae,* a subtle hoax of matter. Only when a corpse is the body plainly intelligible: then it returns from its puzzling and unorthodox behavior of aliveness to the unambiguous, "familiar" state of a body within the world of bodies, whose general laws provide the canon of all comprehensibility. To ap- proximate the laws of the organic body to this canon, i.e. to efface in *this* sense the boundaries between life and death, is the direction of modern thought on life as a physical fact. Our thinking today is under the ontological dominance of death . . . All modern theories of life are to be understood against this backdrop of an ontology of death, from which each single life must coax or bully its lease, only to be swallowed up by it in the end. (Jonas, 1966, pp. 12, 15).

Not a live body, one animated and experienced by a person, but only a dead one seems even remotely capable of being spliced off from the person. Yet, even though death is no longer the profound shock it had to be within panvitalism but is now a constitutive principle and the accepted norm for bodies "in a universe formed after the image of the corpse" (ibid., p. 15), as Jonas remarks, Ramsey's quick reminder is perceptive. Even with the corpse, that is, we face a "sensed relic" of the once-embodied and communicating person—whence, of course, the otherwise quite unintelligible gallows humor, and that special ten- sion, and even the felt reluctance or hesitancy on encountering corpses in coffins or cadavers on carts.

It seems unavoidable, indeed, that such a biology can only be a science (*logos*) without life (*bios*). The point is that no science of life, of animate being generally, much less a medical science, can be con- sidered well-grounded, epistemically complete, or even intelligible unless it can *systematically* and *consistently* take into account that the human body is most fundamentally a live organism embodying a human person and is experienced precisely as such by the person in accountable ways. Or, at the very least, such a science *must not in principle exclude* this.

The materialism, dualism, mechanism, positivism, which subtly infuses so much of modern biomedicine, in short, renders not only its own fundamental *issue*—"life"—highly problematic; it also, and more significantly, leaves the living human body deeply enigmatic.

And this is quite enough for me to make the point I set out to make: precisely to the extent that medicine's powerful presence in our culture positively induces persons in the wider culture to view themselves in the ways medicine itself views them and human life, and the latter includes a concept of the alive body as based on the dead body (the cadaver), so are we encouraged to view ourselves: as mechanisms and thus as fundamental enigmas. We are led eventually to the conviction that our everyday, life-worldly understanding and experience of our own alive bodies are fundamentally wrong, specious, and thus to think that our own most fundamental experiences are yet fundamental deceptions. Not trusting ourselves, thus, we perforce are led to place our trust in others—in experts in the body—to tell us about ourselves: whether, for example, our complaints are really diseases in need of professional treatment and cures. In short: coming to view ourselves in the ways medicine views us, and our bodies, we come to be alienated from ourselves and our most intimate experiences.

I have suggested, then, that given what Pellegrino and Engelhardt have argued about the nature of medicine and its relations to humanities and social science and given what Gorovitz and MacIntyre have pointed out regarding medicine as a science of particulars, a philosophy of medicine begins to assume some more definite shape. In particular, it must take cognizance of the real singularity of medicine as a discipline which at once changes human beings (and itself changing thereby), and thus presents a field wherein fact and value coincide, and which does so fallibly. Appreciating that, but at the same time the very real power of medicine in our times, I suggested in a specific case some of the consequences of that power.

I have in no way wanted to suggest, however, that medicine should be deprecated; I have suggested that a viable philosophy of medicine leads to important critical considerations that must now inform medicine quite as much as biomedicine has traditionally informed it. Philosophy, in a word, must be understood as having a status for, and an essential place within, medicine on a par with biomedical science; and working thus as equals, we can begin to have some real hope that Pellegrino's ideal of a "new Paideia" can actually be realized.

12. The Facticity of Illness and the Appropriation of Health

MARY C. RAWLINSON

An appropriate phenomenology of medicine would provide accounts of health and illness both useful for medical practice and appropriately applicable to human being, as opposed to merely mechanical, organic, or animal being. A concrete determination of the nature of human health and illness or disease persists as the central problem in the philosophy of medicine. I will argue that the concept of health now operative in medical practice is in fact not very "healthy" in that it violates rather than expresses the essential nature of human being. Concepts of health and disease function not merely descriptively or explanatorily in medical practice but evaluatively and prescriptively. I will argue that these concepts of disease are derived from a concept of health that functions as a regulative ideal in medical practice and that this concept of health describes not mere physiological states but a system of possibilities for being and doing in the world. Concepts of health and disease in medicine apply to socio-historical human *subjects*; and, thus, if these concepts are to be appropriate concepts of human health and disease, they must take this subjectivity into account.

Medicine, in conceptualizing health and disease, tends to think of the human subject as a "functioning physiology" and assumes as a definition of health the absence of limitation and dependency. Being human, however, is a subjective event conditioned by an essential limitedness and dependency. A more appropriate concept of health, then, would involve the appropriation or acceptance of this limitation and dependency of which illness is a primary manifestation. Illness, then, would consist at least in part in the resistance to limitation, and the appropriation of limitation would itself be a therapeutic event. Finally, I will argue that medicine, in conceptualizing its own practice, fails to recognize the denial of limitation as an etiological factor and the appropriation of limitation as a therapeutic event precisely insofar as medicine fails to recognize the subjectivity of its subject by taking the human body as a mere corporeal thing, rather than as a living, intentional embodiment. As analysis of embodiment itself would provide adequate concepts of health and disease.

The argument requires a clear distinguishing between illness and disease. Illness refers to the experience that we undergo when our own individual everyday embodied capacities fail us. Illness obstructs our ordinary access to the world and presents the body not as a system of openness onto the world but as an impediment in our encounter with the world. In illness our embodiment seems unreliable and unpredictable. Illness constricts time and space by filling it with the pain and concerns of illness. Furthermore, in illness the future either short-term or long-range takes on a brittle quality. One finds plans disrupted and possibilities withheld. Thus, illness constitutes a disruption in the ordinary continuity of our experience. Ill being resists integration into the fabric of our experience. In illness, then, one discovers *one's self* as an obstacle in one's own project of encountering and relating to the world. Illness involves necessarily an experience of alienation, of being set against one's self through falling prey to possibilities one does not own.

Illness distorts our ordinary relations with others. It involves some degree of unusual incapacitation and dependence; we cannot do for ourselves what we are ordinarily capable of doing and require extraordinary assistance from others. Furthermore, illness isolates. The ill person's concern for her own welfare absorbs the scope of her attention such that she is not open to or available for encountering others. Moreover, others actively isolate the ill persons for several reasons, only the most obvious of which is the fear of contracting the illness themselves. Illness, as Susan Sontag so persuasively argues in her recent "phenomenology" of illness, almost always carries a stigma that is frequently associated with the assumed cause of the illness or the belief that illness indicates a pathetic weakness of will.[1] The stigma, however, and the attendant turning away from the ill person most often results because others seek to avoid what illness presents, namely our own mortality, frailty, and susceptibility to certain anonymous possibilities.

Finally, illness humiliates. In illness one is in an extraordinary way no longer in control of one's embodied capacities. Consequently, one finds one's self at the mercy of others to regulate, manipulate, investigate, and, perhaps, restore those capacities. In the relation to those individuals aiding us in the restoration of those capacities, we submit to exceptional probing, prying, and even violence. Illness, then, generally results in certain surrenders of one's autonomy and integrity of person in the hope that this surrender will be useful in the effort to recover those capacities that the illness obstructs and threatens.

Given this analysis, certain sorts of unpleasant experiences or limitations are clearly not illness. Being unable to run a six minute mile does not constitute illness nor does having an unsightly visage; though, each could be characterized as a physical limitation. Physical handicaps such as blindness or paralysis do not necessarily constitute illnesses insofar as such handicaps can be integrated into a free and productive encounter with the world. Illness, rather, threatens and obstructs not only particular modes of responding to the solicitation of the world but our very capacity to respond. The future of a handicapped person who has accepted the necessary limitations of his debilitated condition may be quite solidly and openly constituted, whereas the ill person's future always seems to some degree foreshortened and tenuous. Finally, anxiety understood as the confrontation with our responsibility for our participation in the world or such difficult experiences as grief or disappointment do not constitute illnesses insofar as these are not obstructions to our involvement in the world but in fact modes of appropriate participation in the world. Zaner has described human life as a certain situated "possibilizing"[2]; we might describe illness as an inability to exercise this possibilizing or as an obstruction of it.

Disease, on the other hand, is not an experience, but a theoretical entity, a concept. Three points are crucial here: (1) concepts of disease function evaluatively and prescriptively rather than merely descriptively or explanatorily; (2) concepts of disease apply not to physiologies, mere organisms, but to embodied persons situated socially and historically and constituted by certain possibilities for involvement in the world; and (3) specific normative medical judgments depend upon strictly non-medical judgments about what possibilities are in fact constitutive of human being such that one ought to have access to them, that is, concepts of disease function correlative to a concept of health articulating what the structure of human being is.

Zaner, Engelhardt, Wartofsky, and others have already argued convincingly that concepts of disease function primarily evaluatively and prescriptively in medicine.[3] No concept of disease merely describes a physiological state or merely accounts for the origin of certain physiological facts. Concepts of disease correlate facts in such a way that expectations of undesirable developments justify a certain course of intervention in the life history of the patient. Medicine is not reducible to the science of physiology. It is not enough to *know* and *explain* the physiological facts; in medical practice one wants to *do* something as well, namely, alter the facts. Concepts of disease are in short, as

Engelhardt claims, plans for "coordinating phenomena for the purpose of prognosis, diagnosis, and therapy."[4]

One cannot make a diagnosis, prognosis, or prescribe a course of therapy without knowing something, in fact a good deal, about a patient's history, and by knowing his history I do not mean something like knowing what his lab results were a year ago or knowing to what pharmacological agents he is allergic, though that may be relevant information too. In order to diagnose, predict, and prescribe as physicians do, one needs to know something about a patient's style of life, patterns of behavior, family history, occupation, personal relationships, expectations, capacities, propensities, and so on. Concepts of disease in medical practice apply not to organs or even organisms, rather concepts of disease describe and evaluate certain social, historical, and cultural situations. If we consider the person as a mere biological organism, medical practice itself becomes impossible. "Medical facts," as Wartofsky argues, "are *themselves* socio-historical facts."[5] For this reason, specialization in medical practice, the propensity of physicians to concentrate on organs and organs systems, rather than the socio-historical situations of persons, in part constitutes an impediment to good medical practice, an impediment which must be offset by what Wartofsky calls the "socialization" of medical practice itself.[6] Thus, we find in medical practice today trends indicating a return to generality or "sociality" such as the development of family practice programs or programs in general internal medicine and a growing emphasis on the health care team as the deliverer of health care, rather than the individual physician. These trends indicate that the subject matter of medicine is not itself "specialized," that is, appropriately dissected into organs and organ systems. Physiology might appropriately treat the person so, but medicine—given its own evaluative and prescriptive character—cannot. For medical practice to proceed effectively, the patient must be treated as a whole, the embodiment of a particular socio-historical situation with all its implications.

Concepts of disease change over time, and a parade of all too familiar examples remind us of the destructive effects of inappropriate concepts of disease. Homosexuality, masturbation, liveliness in children, aggressivity and intellectual interests in women, political dissidence, and even the running away of slaves have been determined as disease states or indications of disease states during the recent history of medicine. Given the prescriptive function of concepts of disease, inappropriate determinations of disease can and have served as the justification for programs of repression and violent violations of persons' integrity and autonomy. In his essay on the "disease of masturbation"—which in the late nineteenth century accounted for, among other things, instances of dyspepsia, epilepsy, vertigo, deafness, memory loss, impotency, and rickets, and which was treated by such radical procedures as clitoridectomy and castration—Engelhardt concludes:

> Medicine turns to what has been judged to be naturally ugly or deviant, and then develops etiological accounts in order to explain and treat in a coherent fashion a manifold of displeasing signs and symptoms. The notion of the "deviant" structures the concept of disease providing a purpose and direction for explanation and for action, that is, for diagnosis and prognosis, and for therapy. A "disease entity" operates as a conceptual form organizing phenomena in a fashion deemed useful for certain goals. The goals, though, involve choice by man and are not objective facts, data "given" by nature.[7]

Given that concepts of disease account for what is wrong with a present state of affairs, these concepts are implicitly accounts of what ought to be the case. Concepts of disease usually function correlatively with some notion of "the normal," which in some cases merely articulates a colloquial notion of what most people seem to find publicly acceptable or which, somewhat more respectably, represents a statistical analysis of a population's characteristics and behaviors. Neither notion enjoys any firm footing in an account of the necessary structures—the limitations and possibilities—of human being. What do we mean, in fact, when we say in medical practice that 120/80 is a "normal" blood pressure or that "100" is a "normal" glucose level? Certainly, we do not mean that this is the blood pressure or glucose level that most people exhibit; rather, the usage indicates that we have made some prior, that is, premedical, determination concerning what kinds and levels of activities ought to be available to us and that *normal* and *abnormal* are defined by their correlation with the accessibility or obstruction of certain possibilities already determined as constitutive of healthy human being. For example, medicine determines a blood pressure value to be abnormal only in virtue of its association with conditions such as stroke or congestive heart failure in which everyday activities such as climbing stairs or running for a bus become difficult or impossible. Such usages of *normal* and *abnormal* may be convenient *and* acceptable in medical practice, given the recognition that these notions in themselves cannot function as appropriate concepts of health and disease but are derived from concepts of health and disease already, however implicitly, in hand. Normative statements when strictly medical are always made relative to some already accepted account of health.

In medical practice the concept of health articulates the goal of therapy; thus, that concept always regulates the intervention prescribed by a concept of disease. The concept of health that regulates determinations of disease describes not merely the absence of disease, nor even a complex of optimum physiological states and values; rather, medicine's operative concept of health involves judgments about what capacities, activities, and modes of experience ought to be available to persons. Any concept of health describes a way of being in the world, a structure of possibilities for being and doing in relation to what is. The development of a concept of health, insofar as that concept involves claims about what it means to be a human being and what possibilities are appropriate to being human, is not strictly speaking a problem for medical science; rather, it is a problem in the philosophy of medicine. Determinations of disease, of abnormality, definitions of hypo- and hyper-states, of optimal values and acceptable ranges can be made only on the ground of judgments concerning what state of well-being ought to obtain for strictly nonmedical reasons. Concepts of disease always are regulated by a concept of health that articulates what is to be accepted as appropriate human experience given the meaning and structure of human being. A state of affairs is appropriately determined as a disease state, then, because it obstructs, threatens, or steals possibilities appropriate to us as human beings. Concepts of health and disease are necessarily open to philosophical criticism as they are founded on an ontological account of the human person. Medical concepts of disease will be appropriate prescriptive accounts of illness only if medicine is informed by a philosophical analysis of the structures of human experience, an analysis that would itself account both for the possibility of falling ill and the possibility of intervening therapeutically.

What, then, is the concept of health operative in medical practice? And what ought it to be?

Let me return to the analysis of illness with which I began. One might object to an attempt to develop a concept of health from an analysis of illness; however, I want to suggest that the event of illness is significantly like the event of the "broken hammer" that Heidegger describes in *Being and Time*, namely, an event in which one is confronted by structures of experience that in one's everyday way of comporting one's self remain merely assumed and implicit. When our embodiment fails us we are confronted by the opportunity to countenance the meaning of embodiment. In illness our body presents itself like the broken hammer with a certain "obstinacy" (*Aufsässigkeit*) and a certain "urgency" (*Dringlichkeit*).[8] We discover that as embodied we have enjoyed a capacity to surpass ourselves in intending the world meaningfully. Embodiment ordinarily means reaching for, going toward, attending to what is present, and, in short, existing essentially as a capacity to encounter what is other. In illness we discover this possibility as obstructed by the obstinacy of the body that urgently demands our attention as a prelude to any further worldly involvement. Thus, we discover as well that embodiment manifests not only the capacity of the self to go beyond itself claiming its future in responding to the solicitation of the world but also the profound binding of the self to the context from which it moves and the incapacity of the self to fully account for its own being. What illness most poignantly manifests is precisely the facticity necessarily constitutive of human being.

Heidegger states that "the concept of 'facticity' implies that an entity 'within-the-world' has Being-in-the-world in such a way that it can understand itself as bound up in its 'destiny' with the Being of those entities which it encounters within its own world."[9] And, "throwness" expresses the facticity of the self's "being delivered over." Facticity means that the being of the human subject cannot be understood simply or primarily by reference to the willfulness of subjectivity; it means, in short, that any human history is also a destiny described by the subject's fateful involvement with what is other. "Throwness" indicates the way in which at the heart of our experience we discover an anonymity—conditions and possibilities of which we cannot claim authorship and which our individual will can neither fully control nor shed. Illness makes accessible in an extraordinary way precisely this structure of limitation; we are called to confront the lack of independence that permeates our being. The insistence and intransigence or opacity of embodiment in illness indicates the incapacity of the human self to achieve any absolute perspective on itself and simply that the self is not in the end its own ground.

Heidegger argues, however, that

> *facticity is not the factuality of the factum brutum of something present-at-hand, but a characteristic of Dasein's Being*—one which has been taken up into existence, even if proximally it has been thrust aside. [Furthermore,] as an entity which has been delivered over to its Being, it remains also delivered over to the fact that it must always have found itself—but found itself in a way of finding which arises not so much from a direct seeking as rather from a fleeing.[10]

The self always "finds itself" in its facticity "whether explicitly or not"; that is, not only facticity but also the appropriation of facticity necessarily constitutes human being. Facticity must in some way by each of us be "taken up." Human beings always, for example, find themselves the subjects of certain desires; and these desires are in themselves anonymous and prepersonal, instinctual desires as Freud would say. *Human* desire, however, involves not only the fact of desire but also the interpretation and criticism of desire. Desire becomes *human* desire only when it is understood, however, prereflectively; and the objects with which we satisfy our desires represent, as Freud argued, these individuating interpretations.[11]

Ordinarily the structures of limitations that facticity names and our appropriation of those structures remain merely implicit serving as the background to the figure of our daily experience. Moreover, we ordinarily seek to avoid, evade, flee, or turn away from these limitations and our responsibility for their meaning. Facticity and interpretation as structures of human experience themselves present the possibility of the alienated experiences of falling and fleeing. We are, due to the very nature of our experience, subject continually to the self-deception of ignoring it. Nevertheless, any denial of facticity constitutes a self-denial, for facticity names structures of limitation defining possibilities that we are.

Illness, however, threatens any everyday appropriation of facticity. As I have argued, in illness our ordinary embodied encountering and appropriating the world and the facticity of our embodiment are thematically at issue, whereas ordinarily they remain merely implicit and operative. The evasiveness of our everyday understanding of facticity is threatened by illness. Furthermore, how we interpret illness manifests our understanding of facticity itself insofar as the limitations of illness signify the facticity of embodiment.

One cannot do this sort of "applied" philosophy without soiling one's hands, so to speak, with the facts—and it is to the facts that I now turn. I have claimed that the concept of health now operative in medical practice is inappropriate because it denies facticity and ignores its appropriations as a factor in health and illness. How is this manifest in medical practice?

Studies of physicians themselves seem to indicate a denial of facticity and a refusal to accept limitation in their own lives. Physicians as a group exhibit an exceptional fear of death. Studies suggest that fear of death serves as a relevant variable in the choice of medicine as a career. Feifel, for example, concludes that one must admit "the implication that a number of physicians utilize the medical profession, through which the individual secures prominent mastery over disease, to help control personal concerns about death."[12] Bressler's recent study of "Suicide and Drug Abuse in the Medical Community" notes that "each year the equivalent of an average-size medical school graduating class commits suicide . . . [and that] equally alarming is the incidence of drug abuse and alcohol abuse by physicians, even when it does not involve suicide."[13] Suicide and use of addictive agents was found to correlate with "role strain" characterized by an unrealistic sense of what he or she the physician can accomplish, "an exaggerated sense of duty and obligation," and feelings of shame and inadequacy because he or she has quite naturally failed to meet these unrealistic requirements. Drug-using physicians exhibit the startlingly naive belief that they are immune to drug addiction and capable of using addictive drugs in a "safe way." Furthermore, studies suggest that physicians suffering severe emotional stress find little assistance in their medical colleagues. Bressler states:

> It is his colleagues who have the greatest difficulty in accepting him as a patient, and instead of providing him with the psychiatric referral that would be used for almost anyone else, they are more likely to treat him as a social outcast. . . . Time and again in clinical practice, estimable and well-meaning physicians have been observed exacerbating the condition of a disturbed colleague who has made a suicide attempt by keeping quiet about it and merely exhorting the colleague with a 'Pull yourself together and straighten yourself out'. As a result, seeking the professional help he needs becomes more and more difficult and even degrading, and the tendency to conceal or deny his condition is only reinforced.[14]

The physician's characteristic attitude toward weakness and dependency seems to indicate a denial of limitation both in himself or herself and in medical practice itself. The studies exhibit as well the disastrous results of the denial of limitation.

The concept of health regulating concepts of disease in medical practice, too, appears to consist in a denial of limitation. Limitation itself becomes conceptualized as disease, a state to be eradicated. As such, certain concepts of disease involve violations of human well-being, rather than prescriptions for the nurturance, maintenance, and restoration of that well-being.

Consider, for example, the "disease" of old age. Although aging may not be techically classified as a disease, it is at least considered to be a morbid process worthy of its own subspecialties in medicine and psychiatry. Shader's current *Manual of Psychiatric Therapeutics* summarizes the etiology of psychiatric disorders in the elderly: "Old age is characterized by the necessity of dealing with losses. Self-image and self-esteem wither as the external world, which once was the domain of the patient, gradually becomes less familiar through the loss of occupation, friends, social and cultural functions and physical capacities."[15] Note that the "necessity of dealing with losses" is described as the primary cause of psychiatric problems in the elderly. The aged are expected to be "rigid" and "inflexible," and it is surprising when they are not. Furthermore, the standard psychiatric textbook—edited by

Alfred M. Freedman, Harold I. Kaplan, and Benjamin J. Sadock—states that

> . . . persons who retain a youthful, vigorous problem-solving view of life tend to make a better adjustment in old age than those who accept old age as a time of diminished resources and agility or of relatively stereotyped behavior. Persons who although themselves chronologically aged, feel that the aged do not need protection, but are likely to be healthy or socially vigorous, are relatively well adjusted, even when their own physical status and socio-economic condition belie their conviction.[16]

Note that health is explicitly contraposed to the need for protection. "Healthy" old age involves a refusal to accept old age and the maintenance of a "youthful" attitude. Dependency is raised to the level of a symptom; elderly patients, we are told, exhibit "dependency striving," a "search for another presumed to be stronger and capable of helping and maneuvers to hold the other in a helpful or potentially helpful relationship." Old age surely exhibits medical problems peculiar to it; any period of life does. However, in the medical literature we find old age *itself* treated as a medical problem, as a state to be eradicated through the inculcation of youthful attitudes and the maintenance of youthful physiques. We should recall at this point Engelhardt's well-argued claim that "Medicine turns to what has been judged to be naturally ugly or deviant, and then develops etiological accounts in order to explain and treat in a coherent fashion a manifold of displeasing signs and symptoms."[17] Medicine conceptualizes old age as a disease state not because aging in fact means being ill but because aging manifests our facticity all too clearly. The "necessity of dealing with losses" and "dependency" are certainly not peculiar to old age, though perhaps those conditions of our experience are less easily evaded by the elderly. Medicine's conceptualization of aging as a morbid process provides a category of disease, which when criticized appears as ludicrous and as destructive in its prescriptive force as the disease of masturbation.

This way of thinking about aging not only creates disease but also genuine illness. The characteristic psychological disorder of the aged is agitated depression accompanied by pronounced anger. Suicide rates reach a peak in the seventh decade. The anger is self-directed, and the depression involves a profound self-rejection. The depressed elderly person refuses certain limitations that he or she nevertheless *is*. And it is to this self-denial, the refusal to appropriate aging itself that is encouraged by the medical account, that we must look for an etiology of the peculiar psychiatric disorders of the aged. Illness arises not in the "necessity of dealing with losses" or dependency, but in the refusal of possibilities necessarily constitutive of the elderly person's experience. Just as the physician's own resistance to limitation works destructively upon his own well-being, so, too, this self-denial in the aged engenders illness.

This self-denial obstructs the aged person's access to the positive possibilities constitutive peculiarly of old age. The medical account ignores these special enjoyments of aging: it does not speak of the wisdom or at least sobriety of long experience, the satisfaction of having endured and accomplished, the relief from the striving to succeed, the pleasure of decreased responsibility, or the peace of contemplation. Self-acceptance, the acceptance of aging itself, frees the elderly person from the anger and agitated depression of self-denial *for* these positive experiences of well-being. Yet, the medical account of aging and medicine in general gives no mention of the appropriation of limitation as itself a therapeutic event.

Medicine treats an embodied subjectivity, a socio-historical human being, and never a mere organism. No set of facts, physiological or behavioral, can ever be an adequate account of the health or illness of human subjects. Any diagnosis and prognosis, any determination of disease, must take into account the subjectivity of the subject involved; that is, the health or illness of a patient always depends to some degree on the self-understanding of the patient, specifically the appropriation of limitations or the acceptance of facticity. This analysis applies obviously in a variety of cases from ulcerative colitis and irritable bowel syndrome to conversion hysteria. I am arguing, however, that the appropriation of facticity is not merely *sometimes* relevant to health; rather, it is in any case relevant, and, therefore, ought to inform and regulate determinations of disease. Any time medical practice fails to take into account the way in which a subject appropriates physiological facts, medicine ceases to treat *human* subjects and treats instead a mere biological organism, thankfully—because it seems to make things easier—reduced to the level of a mere thing. In reflection, to take the body as a thing is certainly possible and sometimes appropriate; to *treat* the body as a thing in medical practice, however, violates the character of the embodied subject, given medicine's essentially evaluative and prescriptive functions. Furthermore, this reducing of the person to bodily thing exhibits a lack of self-understanding on the part of medical practice: as I have argued, if the body were merely a body like any other thing in the world, rather than an embodied social, historical, self-interpreting subject, medical practice itself would not be possible.

Simply because we can in reflection take the embodied subject as pure consciousness on the one hand or as merely physical on the other, we are not justified in thinking that this subject ever *is* merely mind or merely body. The dichotomy between mind and body is resolved in human experience, though medical practice and medicine's account of itself, as well as a venerable tradition of Cartesian philosophy, indicate that we do not yet understand this actual resolution very well. The human subject is thought now as mind and now as body, that is to say, in its different "aspects"; and, in our thinking, the dichotomy of the mental and the physical remains external to the nature of the human subject and, therefore, unresolved. What embodiment names is a phenomenon that is neither mental nor physical nor is it merely mental-and-physical. It is altogether different from either of those modes.

What must be appropriated by medicine is precisely the subjectivity of its embodied subject. Medicine can employ a concept of health that fails to recognize facticity and the therapeutic function of its appropriation only because it does make the body over into a thing. The body, rather, poses finite possibilities of encountering the world. It is the kind of consciousness humans are. The self confronts these finite possibilities in itself and constitutes its identity in interpreting and appropriating these possibilities. Thus, medicine is possible: not only can we reflect on and describe philosophically the embodied possibilities for worldly involvement that constitute human being; we can also evaluate individual embodiments according to the way in which possibilities are obstructed and prescribe methods of intervention that restore capacities by removing those obstructions. Self-interpretation, the appropriation of those possibilities that one *is*, always figures, then, in health and illness. One may responsively and responsibly accept and embrace the possibilities necessarily constitutive of one's being, or one may deny and refuse these possibilities. The first choice is a prerequisite for health; the second, a generator of illness. We can fall ill not only because as factical beings we are subject to certain anonymous possibilities like the intervention of infectious agents but also because as beings whose identities are constituted in self-interpretation, we can deny, reject, distort, or violate possibilities that we nevertheless are. As any good physician knows, a successful treatment of illness and a restoration of health depends in all cases upon the patient's acceptance of that illness and its limitations. Illness, then, means being obstructed, and one mode of obstruction is self-denial. Health refers to any state, experience, or choice that nourishes one's capacity to respond freely to the possibilities constitutive of human experience; and the appropriation of facticity is always a requirement for health.

13. *Illness and Health: Alternatives to Medicine*

ARLEEN B. DALLERY

My paper is partly a commentary on the two preceding papers and partly a contribution to the discussion of phenomenology and medicine. I shall present two general criticisms of each paper: (1) Zaner's approach to the phenomenology of medicine is not sufficiently historical or dialectical, and (2) Rawlinson's discussion of health and disease omits the societal context of the construction of concepts of disease and health. I shall argue that a pretheoretical or phenomenological meaning of health cannot serve as a regulative ideal for medicine. This pretheoretic notion of health, however, is being promoted in alternative strategies of healing; for example, self-help groups and lay communities.

My own independent contribution, here, is to provide the dialectical counterpart to Zaner's understanding of medical praxis and to extend Rawlinson's phenomenology of illness to a social dimension. By describing the experiential structures of self-help groups and the Woman's Health Movement, I show how these groups promote a pretheoretic notion of health and revise the role of medicine in the promotion of human well-being.

Zaner

Both papers are splendid introductions to a new phenomenology of medicine that sees medical science as cultural praxis, rather than as applied biology or physiology. Both Professor Zaner and Professor Rawlinson take the view that medical judgements and practices are essentially normative and prescriptive. Medical concepts of health and disease require philosophical scrutiny because they ought to be regulated by a pretheoretic concept of health or human well being that is proper to human beings as embodied subjects in a social historical world.

What is taken to be normal or "healthy" functioning in an organism is measured relative to human abilities of the person to do expected or desired activities, socially and ontologically. Disease ascriptions do not just refer to physiological or psychological processes as abnormal or dysfunctional, but they presuppose values, norms, or social expectations, according to which these psycho-physiological processes are measured as dysfunctional or abnormal.

Zaner, however, takes a more radical approach than other normativists when he states that medicine not only reflects and promotes prevailing social, aesthetic, or moral values but also directly changes us, our bodies, our own self-interpretation. This is a theme later developed by Dr. Rawlinson. Through its therapeutic interventions and its theoretical constructs, medicine affects and alters human individuals. Zaner means that we begin to see ourselves in medical ways: we come to see the person as a dualism of mind and body, the lived body as a physiological object, our embodiment as a set of organ systems or a thing. As Dr. Zaner says, "coming to view ourselves as medicine views us . . . we come to be alienated from ourselves and our most intimate experiences" (Zaner, p. 154). (Surely this would apply to alienation from one's body and alienation from the natural experiences of pregnancy, childbirth, aging and dying, which have become medicalized processes.) In Zaner's language, medicine and the employment of its technology change man and man's images of himself.

For example, the pernicious dualism of mind and body, part of the Cartesian legacy, would suggest that recovery from a disease would mean only bringing up the functioning of an organ to statistically normal levels. More broadly conceived, on a conception of the person as both an embodied and cultural entity, recovery from illness would mean not only a change in body functioning but reintegration of the person to a social and cultural matrix. Restoring a person to health is more than getting rid of a disease or an impairment of proper organic functioning, as social workers and physical therapists already know.

On Zaner's view, medical practice not only reflects prevailing ideologies and social norms in its therapeutic interventions, but it *changes* our experience of self, others, and world (Zaner, p. 149). Although I am partly in agreement with this view of medicine, I feel that the view is exaggerated and one-sided.

On this point *I would submit that much current philosophy of medicine is not sufficiently dialectical*; philosophers seek to *define* the value-laden and hidden ontologies of the science and *practice of medicine:* how medicine promotes an image of man and even changes our experience of our lived body. But, current philosophy of medicine stays too much on the side of medicine. It does not describe how medical knowledge and practice are now encountered—not by society which is too general—but by relatively new medically dependent groups, the aging, the chronically ill, the dying, as well as the subculture of women. These significant therapeutic communities have contributed to an awareness of the limits of medical intervention and to the limits of the image of man promoted by contemporary medicine. This has been done by using practices known more popularly as the "demystification of medical knowledge," "equalizing the doctor/patient relationship," "changing the experience of medical care," "getting our bodies back." What these practices commonly promote is the construction of a norm of health of persons and the overcoming of the alienation and self-interpretation foisted by medical practice and other social, cultural structures. These forms of social praxis include medically dependent self and mutual care groups, lay communities, and individual self-care. Let me repeat, what these groups have in common is the practical promotion of a pretheoretic notion of health, under which medical intervention is subsumed and regulated. I will return to these groups later.

Rawlinson

There are two basic themes in Dr. Rawlinson's reflections on medicine. (1) Medical judgements of health and disease should be grounded in a phenomenological concept of health. (2) Unless medicine is grounded in an appropriate conception of the meaning and structures of human being, it will tend to view all life limitations (aging, death, etc.) as diseases.

I shall briefly follow the development of these themes in her paper to show that (1) the social context, which she neglects, is essential in the construing of what is or is not a disease; (2) a purely normative view of medical judgements neglects the descriptive or objective component of medical judgements.

Rawlinson develops an insightful phenomenology of illness as being brought up against the limitation of one's body, its obstinacy, opacity, and obduracy. Illness reveals to us the limitations of our facticity that is usually surpassed in our agency in the world. Illness is also characterized as a closure of possibilities, a shortening of time and space. These are valuable insights, which I will later extend further.

From this account of illness, Rawlinson develops a phenomenological notion of health as a regulative ideal for the health and disease concepts of medicine. Health is the acceptance of limitation and the capacity to respond freely to possibilities. On her account, diseases should be correlated with illness as precisely those processes that steal, obstruct, or threaten possibilities (Rawlinson, p. 160). Concepts of disease change and are also improperly applied by medicine. To construe social deviance or what is ugly or undesirable to society as disease would be an improper extension of the term, unless there is an illness experience attached to it. Because of its ascriptions of disease to various states of affairs, medicine also "creates illness" in those who appropriate medical interpretations of their own life events (Rawlinson, p. 164).

A great deal of illness, she claims, is to be understood as the denial of ontological or life limitations. Aging becomes an illness for human beings owing to their denial of this ontological limitation.[1] People do not want to be old, to age. Such denial is fostered by medicine itself, which sees aging as a morbid process requiring medical intervention. In a self-fulfilling way, old age *becomes* an illness for those who seek to deny this experience and refuse the possibilities of aging. Because one's identity is based on self-interpretation, the awareness of one's own possibilities, the aging person can only accept the identity promoted by medicine as dependency, loss of memory, regression to childhood—truly an alien identity.

Assuredly the limitations of death, menopause, adolescence, as stages of the human life cycle, are ontological limitations, part of human being or human becoming. If much illness is owing to the denial of these limitations, then Dr. Rawlinson is correct in stating that therapeutic intervention begins with the acceptance of these limitations and the *possibilities they generate.*

But when is depression in the elderly not just an expression of the denial of aging but a symptom of a correctable neurophysiological process? Medicine can alleviate the effects of artereosclerosis, while regarding aging as normal. Does Dr. Rawlinson's purely normative account of disease leave room for this possibility? I believe that she overstates her case that a concept of health as absence of disease or even absence of symptoms inevitably leads to absence of limitation or that medicine seeks to remove all limitations. Her purely normative account of disease dangerously loses the descriptive component of disease judgements, that there are dysfunctional, physiological processes that are correctable.

At any rate, I think that Professor Rawlinson's attempt to root and limit medical judgements of disease and health in an ontology of human being lacks the element of social mediation. Social changes produce different construings of what is a disease and what is no longer a disease. It is society that construes various processes as diseases, not medicine. What is taken as a disease is relative to social expectations of activity and conduct and evaluations of what is an acceptable limit. Society constructs its own stock of possibilities. According to Caroline

Whitbeck, a disease is "any psychophysiological process which interferes with what people expect to be able to do or wish to do."[2] Of course, there must be shared knowledge and assumptions of what it is possible for humans to do.

Medicine is thus empowered to intervene to alter this process (even though it may not be undesirable for its bearer). Medicine does not autonomously construe or interpret processes as diseases, although it does label, classify, and explain them. Medicine also establishes that a psychophysiological process is not statistically normal; this provides the descriptive component of medical judgements. Medical norms are thus relative to social norms, which may or may not be rooted in an acceptance of such ontological limits as aging, death, and the other stages of the human life cycle.[3] Philosophy's critical move here is to establish what limits those persons who are human should accept. As Engelhardt puts it, what is a reasonable expectation in regard to freedom of action on our part and what is an instance of hubris.[4]

At this point, I would like to combine the two criticisms of both papers. I claimed that Zaner's perspective on medicine is not sufficiently dialectical and that Rawlinson's theory of disease concepts loses the societal basis of interpretation of disease processes. Both argue that phenomenological reflection is necessary to make medicine critical of its hidden ontologies, of its lack of cognizance of itself and of human subjectivity. Indeed, philosophical assumptions are already impregnated in medical practice as it promotes uncritically an image of man, systems of aesthetic and ethical values, and self-interpretations based on medical judgements.

I now want to show that there are social forms of praxis, namely, *therapeutic communities*, which are dialectically opposing the above practices of medicine. I shall refer to these groups as intersubjective or lateral healing strategies and I shall outline how a pretheoretic notion of health is promoted in their practices. The two groups are the lay community of the Woman's Health Movement and such medically dependent self-help groups as Alcoholics Anonymous, Make Today Count (cancer patients), Recovery Inc. (mental disorders). In thematizing the experiential structures of these groups, my objective is to show that (1) the philosophical critique of medicine which Drs. Zaner and Rawlinson call for is already embedded in their practices, and (2) the self-interpretation of participants in these groups is exactly rooted in seeing oneself as an embodied subjectivity in a specific social and historical context.

Self-Help Groups[5]

In 1935 the self-help movement began with Alcoholics Anonymous; it now includes such disease category groups as stroke, diabetes, schizophrenia, obesity, and chronic pain. Perhaps, a general name can be attached to them like "groups facing life limitations." These groups of sick individuals are paradigmatic of promoting health through agency rather than participating in the sick role. It is precisely in their responsiveness to the situation of chronic illness that members of self-help groups are capable of acceptance and transcendence. Part of human agency and autonomy is the construction of new norms of adequate individual functioning and appropriate aims. Living with a chronic disease means establishing norms or expectations that will be more limited, in some respects, than prevailing social ones. Such revised norms are constructed through the interaction of members of these groups.[6]

The experience of these self-help groups can be described in terms of the categories of facticity and possibility that Dr. Rawlinson has furnished.

1. A profound and utter sense of limitation is surely a component of the experience of chronic illness in which illness becomes one's facticity—not a temporary discontinuity in one's life. Such an experience—perhaps incommunicable—is what often is articulated in group discussions. Through speaking together, others validate one's own experience and allow one to appropriate it.

2. Self-interpretation is mediated by others. Self-help groups of ill persons are expressly dealing with acceptance of the limitations of their own facticity. At the same time, one's possibilities that are closed off in the experience of illness are opened and attested to by others. What is possible for others may also be possible for oneself. Self-interpretation or self-understanding, in the terms of the possibilities we already are, is mediated by others as they express in their actions possibilities that may be open to us. Each one becomes a standard for the other.

3. We can define these encounters as reciprocal relationships. If illness is characterized by a sense of isolation and utter dependency, then self-help groups, by contrast, foster reciprocal relationships that are different from the asymmetrical, role-structured relationships within the health-care system. Each one's experience counts for the other person. Here is also an acceptance of otherness, of dependency: coming to terms with one's illness cannot be done alone. These are groups in which people grow older together (in Alfred Schutz's terms); they are time-binding relationships, a community of patients as agents in their own promotion of health.

4. What is health for these people? Health or well-being is healing or making whole in Zaner's terms; it is also "possibilizing" in Rawlinson's terms. Self-help groups are therapeutic communities that integrate a person to his embodiment, however failed or frail it is; and they integrate the person to a revised or redefined social and cultural situation. They are essentially normative through intersubjectively projecting norms of possibility for the participants.

It should be apparent that the outcomes of self-help groups, as well as the practice of the Woman's Health Movement, cannot be evaluated with medical criteria of health as absence of disease or statistically normal functions.[7] Health, as I am using the term, is compatible with disease—even with dying; the pursuit of health is an open-ended task with no unique goal. More dynamically health is responsiveness to human limitations, whether ontological (aging); social (stress); or personal (illness). The transcending self is recreated in the appropriation of these limitations. The wholeness and integration of the person is tested and contested in these experiences of limitation.

WOMAN'S HEALTH MOVEMENT (WHM)

I now will consider the WHM as a lay healing community. Caroline Whitbeck, in her paper, "Health: The Transition From Patient to Agent," argued that the WHM was a paradigmatic example of self-care and that its practices expressed the promotion of a pretheoretic normative concept of health as wholeness or, in her terms, as psychophysiological functioning. What I want to add to her interpretation of the WHM is the way in which appropriately relating to one's body or one's embodiment is integral to health in this sense.

In books such as *Taking Our Bodies Back* and *Our Bodies, Ourselves*, the phenomenological theme, although not explicitly stated, is overcoming alienation from one's body. Such alienation is partly the result of women's encounters with gynecological medicine, though its sources lie in the wider social cultural context on which one's self-interpretation and relation to one's body is based. I shall just briefly describe the structures of female embodiment and some of the ways in which alienation from one's body is overcome.

For women, the facticity of one's body is especially compelling, since one's identification with it is either too close or too distant. As sexual object or distant, it is to be mastered, thinned down, adorned, displayed; one may even play with one's body in the change of fashions. There is a certain distance between subjectivity and one's body. Up against the body as biological organism, as signifying one's gender, it is a different story. The body is unknown, a mystery, a series of processes whose origin is deep down in the recesses of one's being. One's body is now opaque to oneself, although it is only for one's self.

It is precisely this opacity of the body that is cleared away when women explore the inner orifices of their body in self-help clinics. It is equally the body as object for oneself and for others—that distant displayed body—which is grasped and held close in the activity of masturbation, another suggested practice. We've come a long way since the disease of masturbation! The lived body as touching and touched, seeing and seen, is created in these experiences. An appropriation of one's embodiment is achieved through these and other practices, thereby overcoming alienation from one's body.

Another practice of promoting health in the WHM is a preventive one: creating community, a modality of healing that is lacking in a purely dyadic doctor/patient relationship. Epidemiological studies have shown that the social environment may contain stress factors that can predispose people to the onset of physical and psychological disease and disorders. The Woman's Health Movement has provided a system of social supports, a temporary minicommunity for women going through various stages of the human life cycle. A culture of shared experience with unifying norms is constructed in such groups as Widow to Widow, Women in Transition, and so forth. Traditionally, cultural strategies and rituals were used to navigate through such stressful situations as grief and bereavement. Belonging to a cultural matrix enabled one to respond appropriately to crises or insults. Culture, in this sense, is a protective cocoon against the onslaughts of a disorganized social or physically threatening environment. Because contemporary society is noteworthy for the lack of a unifying cultural matrix, many people go through extremely stressful situations without fully understanding why they are experiencing such turmoil. There are no shared rituals or codes to "explain" their private experiences.

Here is where an epidemiological theory of disease, in terms of social environment, may be confirmed by the practices of the WHM. For it has provided a preventive care system of social supports for some women who have suffered or who are likely to suffer life crises. Let's consider this possibility: An epidemiological study might be done on the effectiveness of the WHM preventive role in reducing morbidity or predisposition towards disease among its members. But which criterion of health should be used: medical ones or the ones coming out of the practices of the WHM? The medical criteria of health might be epidemiological: the health status of a population in terms of morbidity rates, mortality rate, and longevity rates, visits to the doctor per year. The other would be closer to Whitbeck's concept of health in terms of integrative functioning. Is it really possible to measure promotion of health in her sense in terms of a population? Conversely which criteria of health should be used to measure treatment outcomes in self-help clinics when interpersonal contact is part of the therapeutic effort? Is it even appropriate to ask if self-care is better than medical care?

What I am suggesting through these questions is that the nonprofessional, supportive healing strategies should not be judged by the criteria we apply to specialized knowledge-based therapies. Nor should medicine be judged by the criteria used in nonprofessional supportive healing strategies.

As I have reviewed the medical and social science literature on self-help and self-care groups, the common theme is that the healing praxis of these groups is a complete enigma to medicine. By this I do not mean irrational, mystical, or cultish. Rather, the evaluative criteria that are used by medicine to measure its own outcomes cannot be applied to these healing communities.

Similarly, the causal explanations used by medicine to account for events and states of affairs cannot be employed to understand these intersubjective self-help encounters. Indeed, as one commentator pointed out, to understand what is going on in these new social groups would require detachment from causal intellectual constructs and participation within these reciprocal relationships. Such relationships, however, are contrary to the institutionalized role of the physician/researcher.

The healing strategies of self-help groups and lay communities cannot be evaluated by the health criteria of professional medicine. Similarly, the healing strategies of medicine cannot be evaluated by the pretheoretic notion of health, promoted in self-help and lay communities. One seeks to restore normal psychophysiologic functioning; the other seeks to integrate the person to a social-cultural world. Rawlinson claims that medicine should be regulated by this ideal, but that is because she does not see that there are alternative strategies to the promotion of health as human well-being.

I have also attempted to show that the experiential structures of these healing communities express self-interpretations and practices that are liberated from medical constructs. In describing them I have attempted to complete Dr. Zaner's reflections on medical praxis.

PART 4

PHENOMENOLOGY OF

ART AND AESTHETICS

14. Sketch for a Phenomenology of the American Experience[1]

JOHN M. ANDERSON

I

It is at least an interesting story that Columbus was blind to the unknown continent, that he never knew he had discovered America, that at the time of his death he believed he had found a westward path to the East; for in his inability to see anything but what his hopes and aspirations suggested to him, in his inability to enter the New World while he searched for the East Indies, Columbus typifies Western man.[2]

Yet Columbus understood the conflict between his hopes and what he might have done; he occasionally spoke of himself as an unhappy man because he could not yield to the strange land he had come upon. Thus, on Sunday, October 21, 1492, he noted in his journals some events of the day spent sailing in the waters of the West Indies:[3]

> At ten o'clock I arrived here, off this islet. If the others already seen are very beautiful, green and fertile, this is much more so, with large trees. . . . Here there are large lagoons with wonderful vegetation on their banks. . . . The songs of the birds were so numerous and of so many kinds, that it was wonderful. There are trees of a thousand sorts, and all have several fruits; and I feel the most unhappy man in the world not to know them . . .

Aware of his own failure, Columbus set the task of responding to the unknown continent for those who were to come after him.

Who, then, essayed this task? Those who mined the earth? But they have worked to tear ore from the ground in insensate struggle and darkness. Those who built the trails, roads, and railroads that enabled men to cross an unknown continent? No, for their frenzied activity has made possible only travel by everyone everywhere. Those who raised the houses, factories, and cities across the land? But these, surely have hidden the mystery of the continent for man and things behind the pall of noise, smoke, and action produced in the driven effort to master and control. No, these men have not addressed the task Columbus set.

Perhaps it was someone like Thomas Wolfe who properly understood the task. He tells of his memories:[4]

> . . . the look of an old iron bridge across an American river, the sound the train makes as it goes across it; the spoke-and-hollow rumble of the ties below; the look of the muddy banks . . . an old flat-bottomed boat half filled with water stogged in the muddy bank . . . the sight of a little wooden shed out in the country two miles from my home town where people waited for the street car, and I see and feel the dull rusty color of the old paint and see and feel all of the initials that had been carved out with jackknives on the planks and benches in the shed, and smell the warm and sultry air so resinous and so thrilling, so filled with a strange and nameless excitement of an unknown joy, a coming prophecy . . .

Then Wolfe adds, ". . . and from that moment of my discovery of this America, the line and purpose of my life was shaped. At any rate from this time on I was engaged in writing." The unknown calls to us through our senses. It hails us in sight, hearing, taste and touch, arresting us in beauty. It is the artist's task to gather this appearance as both the evidence of his own freedom and as the harbinger of the New World.

Columbus did not even begin the task he set. This seems an oversight, for he might have reported his journey as the first of many movements west yet to come—as the prototype of the yet-to-come exploits of Mike Fink, Paul Bunyan, and other heroes of the moving frontier. To be grasped as a response to an unknown continent—unknown not only because old categories, old forms, old modes of response are inappropriate to a continent too rich to be structured, formed, and built, but also because it calls men through the strange beauties of a rich phantasmagoria of sights, sounds, flavors, smells and textures—the journey Columbus made, needs to become a myth. Would not this myth be easy to tell? Was not Columbus chosen by the queen to carry her banner into the West? Did not his stature increase to overcome impossible difficulties set in his path by evil men? Tossed about by random winds and held immobile by strange calms, did not he find the compass within him sufficient to plot his journey to make the West East and the East West? Did not his genius enable him to pick a free course through the dark and unknown waters past the lairs of sea monsters, through nets of seaweed cast into his path by inscrutable forces to stop him—even to kill him?

Certainly anyone who stumbles upon the shores of an unknown continent is aware of where he is only through its gift to him of his own nature as free and can only penetrate that unknown land through the use of this freedom in art. The task Columbus sets us of exemplifying our freedom and of gathering the beauties of the senses to reflect in the freedom of their selection the inexhaustible riches of the unknown, of thus becoming the brave new men who as free also stand within the New World, can begin only in stories and plays, songs, music, picture, and dance; only in art that presents our freedom as the freedom of autonomous artistry.

II

Columbus was en route to the East Indies; but tried and found equal to his trials, he stumbled upon an unknown continent. Seized by sights, sounds, tastes, textures and smells, he senses their deep significance; but he did not know how to respond to this evidence of the unknown and to disclose the truth it holds for man. He could only return to his boat; set sail for Spain; and, once there and imprisoned, die in chains.

The failure of Columbus's life is that he did not respond as an artist, that he did not begin to gather at least some of the beauties he experienced to attest the freedom of man and to hint at the discovery of the New World. Then other artists might have continued his beginning by developing art to speak the freedom of man and adumbrate the articulation of language to preserve this freedom. So others must do immediately for him what he might have done for them. They must retell his story, at once making sure that when Columbus stumbles upon the shores of an unknown continent, he moves freely to awaken some sleeping princess or other who, in waking, returns from the New World as the sign of what is to come for all men. They must let him do what, say, Walt Whitman did when confronted by the beauties of the senses—that is, yield to them and offer the freedom of his genius to write the poetry that presents the truth of his own nature as free, ". . . I think I will do nothing now but listen / To let sounds contribute to me / is this then touch quivering me to a new identity?" And having shown Columbus coming to a new identity in the articulation of the free rush of such experience, they might let him encounter the bluebells in the woods of the new island upon which he landed, and work to bespeak his own significance in the freedom of his response as did Hopkins.[5]

> . . . they stood in blackish spreads . . . in your hand they baffle you with their inscape, made to every sense: if you draw your fingers through them they are lodged and struggle with a shock of heads; the long stalks rub and click and flatten to a fan on one another like your fingers themselves would when you passed the palms hard across one another, making a brittle rub and jostle like the noise of a hurdle strained by leaning against; then there is the faint honey smell and in the mouth the sweet gum when you bite them.

They might even let him paint a picture that attested his freedom in the developing articulation of an infinity of hidden color tones gathering the sensuous evidence of the unknown into that freedom which when this language speaks, calls the things of the New World.

Many come upon the unknown continent through the accident of rising to an occasion that demands much of them. But only if they act as artists can they begin, only then are they aware they must build a free path along which to gather the mainifest beauties of the unknown continent into the truth and so participate in that articulation that calls to things to help men to come to stand free not only as brave new men, but in the New World.

III

It is one thing to search for the East Indies and discover an unknown continent in the West. Stumble upon an unknown continent any man may, and no doubt, as in crisis, each of us has when he rises to his full stature as free. Anyone can catch the alien flame— the wave of a hand, the flash of a smile, the green line of a sunset, the presence of the big sky, the glint of gold, the glare of a place in the sun. Each of us does come upon beauty and may blow this spark into the flame of a haunting image. But many take the broad highway toward this vision. There are many tales of the horror of fulfilled vision; fulfilled literally and in detail, but devastatingly—say the story of the wish for power granted the children in Henry James's *Turn of the Screw* or a story of the flaming hopes of youth that are fulfilled in the ashes of middle age.

Certainly the true journey west is not this mistaking of a vision as fixing the broad highway toward a specific goal. The true journey west must be the journey on which the alien spark of beauty flames freely again and again to illumine a narrow and wandering path along which the evidenced riches of the unknown continent are gathered to enable man to articulate his freedom. Columbus did not trust the unknown; but knowing that he would like to trust it, he limned this journey as a task that art alone can begin, for only through art can man come to trust the unknown. Unlike other men who want only to control it, the artist is as intent upon yielding to the unknown in his action as upon forming it. A water color can and often does include unwet paper; a sculpture, primal stone; a musical composition, noise; a novel, brute existence presented but not handled by its words. Art develops as much through acceptance of the unknown as through the development of its own explicit structures. In art, forming can be a free process exemplifying trust.

Because the artist is aware that his forming is dependent on that which he is not, he becomes aware, too, that his work is not consummated in the mastery forming might afford but in the always partially emergent and yet still hidden unknown to which he yields in order to respond freely. In yielding, the artist comes to trust the unknown emerging as given to him in the course of his work; and he expresses this trust in his projection of the art work as an unendingly open receptacle for the free moments of beauty that successively culminate the joint enterprise in which he and the unknown participate.

The artist can attest his trust repeatedly. Thus, in retelling the tales of Paul Bunyan, he can present each incredible achievement of Paul and his blue ox as a free response to a situation emerging unexpectedly from the unknown; a response, that is, which is addressed with intensity to the occasion, which claims no finality, which spontaneously meets a challenge somehow. He need not offer an explanation of Paul's confident self-reliance, Paul's trust; but he can offer the forest as a symbol of the horizon within which Paul's free responses occur and are supported. Paul acts always within its scope when responding to challenges emerging from its dark obscurity. He acts, because he trusts the forests freely and affirmatively as did Mike Fink within the expanse of the rivers, as did Davy Crockett along the edge of the early frontier, and as do the tellers and retellers of these tales, the artists, within the horizons that their art works constitute as well as symbolize.

Or consider Martha Smith who sustains a lifetime of wandering. In looking back over the course of her life of pioneering begun in the 1890s, she sensed in her own life her trust of the unknown continent and rightly sought to express this in its irresistible beckoning. She, her husband, and children repeatedly move west, literally of course (although sometimes west is east) but also, as the genius of her art constitutes it, freely in the spirit of the deep comedy of an affirmative human life.[6]

We were going to God's country. With a husle and busle to get things ready. With 5 litel children and the oldest only 10. We did not realize what we were getting into. Old Missouri was after all a pretty tough place, I hated to leave it for it was all I knew. But we were going to God's country—to a new land and get rich. / So there we were on the Red River across from Texas. And was we ever happy and ever so tired from 33 days drive. / The dug out was so full of centipeads that we had to sleep with a bucher knife under our pillows at night to kill the centipeads—this was existing. Next morning the first thing to do was move the beds and sweep the dead ones out. But that was pioneering in God's country. / We bought some land in Texas. / Another goose chase to Oregon. / We decided then to go back. We did a lot of thinking and a litel talking. We had been living back there in Oklahoma for 3 years when H. H. had a stroke. My beloved died. We had spent 48 years together hunting for God's country. Before he died we learned something. Something terribly important. We learned that God's country isn't in the country. As we looked back we knew that all the time we was hunting for God's country we had it. We worked hard. We was loyal. Honest. We was happy. For 48 years we lived in God's country.

Martha Smith, the artist, symbolized in her story as a pioneer, did not become something in particular nor was she destroyed. She moved at random across the land into the West. Each move was free. Together or singly these moves did not result in any particular success, in any particular modification and determination of her character. She became free not because she became a hero or a mother or a wife or played any other role; but because she played no role. That is, not because her life came to have a specific pattern but because it expressed in a significant way something deeper about human nature than anything she was or became: that man is always becoming, that his truth is the freedom attained in his participation with the unknown and attested in the projection of the horizon of the developing art work as the locus articulating unending emergence of free moments of beauty.

This suggestion is confirmed by the fact that the events of her life are also the moments of beauty culminating successively within the horizon of her art work. These significant events, as falling within the horizon of this art work, are a sequence of moments of beauty, that is, yielding and forming, culminating in moments of harmony between the artist and the unknown as contingent evidence of their joint enterprise. These moments fall, in principle unendingly, within the horizon of this or any other art work projected as the horizon of the unknown.

IV

In the American experience the rejection of Europe, the discovery of the unknown continent, the movement into it, all the tasks of responding to its richness, can be grasped as the random walk of comedy, that free walking in which man accepts the unknown again and again along a path symbolized as a walk without a goal, as a walk on which he can meet and respond to unexpected events and circumstances only as best he can, never with certainty nor with complete control; as a walk that must be taken self-reliantly as Emerson says it—that is, on the assumption that somehow one's responses will carry on to the next free moment—and in nature as a part of herself as Thoreau says it—that is, without humanizing or controlling nature and so progressively limiting the possibilities remaining open and losing the truth of this freedom.

The journey west is one symbol of this path—it is a walk on which one can meet and respond to unexpected events and circumstances freely without loss of freedom. This path need not be literal pioneering interpreted by art as the journey west. In *Huckleberry Finn* Mark Twain interprets a journey down the Mississippi River as the journey down the river of life itself in the terms of art. Charlie Chaplin makes the path something still different—using the rush of film itself to interpret the movement of life as act. And so does Buster Keaton. Keaton's *Cops* is an example of American life judged by the standard of the freedom possible in art.

Witness an American life lived as free action falling within the horizon of an art work.[7]

Buster's girl tells him she won't marry him until he is a successful business man. We see him talking to her through bars—as if he were in jail; but on hearing her rejection, Buster turns away and we see the bars were merely the gate to her father's estate. Buster has been judged and found wanting by the standards of the Old World in which the paths of life lead upward—but must all wind along the road to her father's mansion and the single goal of success.

For better or worse, Buster is now free. Turning away from this old path, he stumbles upon a billfold containing some money; repeatedly attempts to return it to the man who dropped it; but every time he tries, he gets the money back by another accident. He is forced to move off on the path of freedom.

Half understanding this and offered a bargain on some furniture by a fellow who doesn't own it, and "buying" a horse and wagon from another fellow who happens to be standing beside them, he accepts the conditions of this path. Continuing along it he loads "his" furniture on "his" wagon with the help of the owner of the furniture, who thinks he is the van driver sent to move the household, and starts off down the street to nowhere in particular.

On this random journey atop the load of furniture, he wanders into a parade of policemen, a parade of law and order typical of the Old World. But even in the midst of this panoply of the forces of control, Buster manages to proceed freely. A bomb thrown by an anarchist at the policemen lands on his cart, so he pulls out a cigarette and uses the burning fuse to light it. He throws the bomb away like a used match. It explodes in the ranks of the policemen. They then recognize his freedom as a threat and begin to chase him.

He raises a parasol and huddles under it to escape a wetting from a broken fire hydrant, and the police pass him unnoticed. He is caught between two groups of policemen dashing at him from opposite directions and climbs a tall ladder leaning against a high fence. The ladder becomes a seesaw pivoted on the fence. When one group of policemen pulls it down, Buster moves away from them; and helped by the other group to pull it down, keeps the seesaw in precarious balance with the unwilling aid of the forces of law.

Almost caught again and again, he escapes by finding holes in the fence of order. Finally he runs into the police station followed by all the cops and then simply steps out from behind the front door that has hidden him, locks the cops in jail, and proves that, paradoxically, freedom is possible in the very citadel of the law.

Thus, having managed to distinguish the New World from the Old and having saved the New World from becoming an Old World by catching the forces of law and order in their own net, Buster assumes he has finally succeeded and again asks his girl to marry him. But she, who still lives in the Old World, says no—that his achievement has none of the finality of success.

He then does the only thing he could do; he disclaims success and acts in the spirit of pure freedom: for love. He gives his love what she wants. He unlocks the door to the police station and lets the cops out again. They emerge file upon file to conceal the New World he has rediscovered. He must now journey without hope of freedom unendingly through the Old World, or so it seems. Yet he is saved from this fate. The cops continue their eternal chase of Buster and in their insensate lust for order grind him beneath their feet into the dust of the road to success.

His dust is collected, and a tombstone erected in his memory. Descending into his grave he uses the tombstone, like the bomb he used to light his cigarette, as a rack upon which to hang his hat at a free and precarious angle; the sign that freedom can be attained by ignoring the patterns inherited from the past and by entering the future without plan.

The action of art that gathers the beauties developing in the course of man's confrontation by the unknown is not restricted to myth, to film, to folklore, or to true stories of the frontier. The forming and yielding resulting in the freedom attained in an artwork might well be reflected in the words of any artist who says:

I always try to give people something they do not expect and, in fact, will reject. I'm subversive. I present man as made up of all the ordinary elements of human life, yet put together in such a way as to be free, and so incredibly, unendingly becoming what he is not. But surely one must believe what is incredible. The only possible explanation for the incredible is that it is the truth.

Of course I have to make my audience think I'm giving them the world they long for: the pleasant details, the idyllic scenes, the progressive developments. People seem to accept only what they already want! But when they are busy accepting what they long for, I mix in something radically new—again and again—and they are fooled into trusting this too. They are pulled, the fools, by the beauties falling within the horizon of the art work into trust of the unknown, and the things of the New World begin to emerge for them in spite of all their efforts to attain the particular things they desire.

This artist could be a director of films, a painter, a composer, a sculptor, or any one who takes the artistic act in which he engages as ultimate and who expresses his trust in the unknown by projecting the horizon of an art work as the locus in which free action can occur as such. But even a member of an audience, an appreciator, might say something very much the same.

Of course I go to see or hear art that I recognize. I re-read books and poems. I like to remember phrases and forms. It's easiest to respond to the things I've learned to know, to be fulfilled by what I anticipate. But then I always find odd and new things, things I don't know; and their emergence transfixes me. And so art for me is a kind of foolish adventure, awakening me to each new day, days in which things bespeak possibility. So that the wife who serves bread and wine on the table by the fireside foretells what is to come. Such things are not what is but a perspective on all that could be. They are ringing bells tolling the unending path of man's freedom, ringing in the New World.

The possibility of this path along which man and things become unendingly what they are not, is articulated by the projection of the horizon of an art work and the sequence of significant events that take place within it. A motive dot (within a film screen) could suggest this; so could a meandering line (within the frame of a painting); or an elusive phrase with variations (in the performance of a symphony); or the random walk of a fool (within the story of a novel). Whoever and whatever moves in art can limn this path as such movements culminate in successive moments of free response falling in principle unendingly within the horizon of the art work.

Still, this path is only suggested in the projection of the horizon and the symbolic events that characterize the content of the art work. Even in the context of the horizon of the art work itself, the free moments of beauty falling within it only adumbrate the possibility of the artist's unendingly becoming what he is not, foretell, that is, those moments in which the artist's collaboration with the unknown culminate in the contingent harmonies that as beauties are the significant steps on man's unending path. This foretelling is the truth of man, his freedom. Yet art foretells when this truth is spoken, a deeper truth, even, than this.

V

In *Moby Dick* the sea is the reflexive symbol of the horizon of Melville's art work. His novel begins when men turn away from the already known land to gaze at the mysterious sea. All the form developed in the novel, as the depiction of the craft of whaling, plumbs the sea as if to penetrate and be near its secret. Yet it is art, not knowledge, that illumines in this way; art that projects itself as a metaphor, the sea, reflecting itself through this symbol as the horizon that, like the space of a geometry, is one with whatever emerges within it.

Art, as the sea, attracts men from the knowable patterns and specific forms of ordinary life. Art pulls Melville into the craft of fiction as the sea pulls Ishmael into the craft of whaling. And art supports fiction only with the deepening ambiguity in which Melville's writing develops beyond a novel to elicit the meaning of the unknown, as the sea supports whaling only with the deepening ambiguity developed in Ahab's consuming effort to capture the White Whale, his pursuit of its meaning.

Thus, the meaning attained at the end of the novel is not merely the attraction of mystery so effectively suggested by the projection of the metaphor of the sea at its beginning. Beginning Melville tells us:[8]

> There now is your insular city of the Manhattoes . . . Its extreme down town is the battery, where the noble mole is washed by waves . . . Look at the crowds of water-gazers there. . . . But look! here come more crowds, pacing straight for the water, and seemingly bound for a dive . . . Surely all this is not without meaning. And still deeper the meaning of that story of Narcissus, who because he could not grasp the tormenting mild image he saw in the fountain, plunged into it and was drowned. But that same image, we ourselves see in all rivers and oceans. It is the image of the ungraspable phantom of life.

Lines toward the end of the novel tell us we have not only approached the mystery but that our journey has somehow reached its goal: "Now small fowls flew screaming over the yet yawning gulf; a sullen white surf beat against its steep sides; then all collapsed, and the great shroud of the sea rolled on as it rolled five thousand years ago."[9]

In these penultimate lines, we are told that all the particularity and individuality that is hidden in the inchoate waters of the sea, all that emerges from the unknown, floats precariously on its surface, as precariously and as transiently as the waves themselves. How are we brought to awareness of this illusion as unqualified?

First, of course, by following Ahab's quest for the White Whale, which in its negative quality of whiteness, lacks all particularity and individuality, like the quest for the meaning of the sea, a meaning that can be attained only when man seeks it explicitly and persistently beyond any appearance. Ahab's life consisted only of incidents in his quest to wrest from the sea its secret, to fix the meaning of the unknown. His efforts doubled at each step along the way, his powers focused more and more upon this one goal, defining the broad highway to this end. But in so fixing his path, Ahab set for himself the impossible task of identifying with the unknown—impossible because he could only do this by capturing it, by exercising a power which though continually extended could never be infinite. Inevitably the unknown captured Ahab, using the finite particularity of the very harpoon and line that carried his power to capture it. That harpoon, finally set firmly in the back of the sounding White Whale, accidentally caught a loop of its following line around his throat and pulled him down.

Melville was willing, as too often artists are not, to allow his art to develop fully the illusion integral to it. He does not settle for saying what men already are, nor for projecting the world of men as built of finite elements into a happy place in the bounded clarity of a high sunlit valley. Melville does not spin a vision of recollections or hopes but builds an illusion floating in the wash of the unknown.

In Ahab's quest there is no reference to the unknown and no human response to it, no disclosure of its meaning as in any way human. Ahab's world is separated from the unknown, pulled out of it. It is imaged as a world that has a fixed boundary, a line beyond which its elements are no longer distinguishable, beyond which elements exist potentially but are not actually fixed. This is the line that Ahab casts as he attacks the unknown and dies, and his world dies with him. It is the line beyond which the image of his world is utterly meaningless.

Yet Melville develops illusion in a more fundamental way than Ahab. Ahab's pursuit takes place not only on the sea but in art developed freely by Melville's genius to project itself as the horizon of the unknown, as the paradigm of illusion. Ahab is not the only symbol of Melville's art in its quest for the meaning of the unknown. There is also Ishmael.[10]

EPILOGUE
"And I only am escaped alone to tell thee." Job

The drama's done. Why then here does any one come forth?—because one did survive the wreck.

Ishmael speaks for the artist who faces and accepts the unknown, who sees whatever lies on the finite side of the line between man and the unknown as utterly illusion, but lives to write books and stories, works in which the unknown is approached through illusion as a task to be undertaken again and again. Ahab blindly faced and attacked the unknown. It became an obsession and his fate. Ishmael was not only living a life but telling a story. Like the artist he symbolizes, Ishmael crossed the line into the unknown by deliberate chance. He wandered knowingly down to the oceanside and signed up for a whaling voyage, intending to take advantage of the miracles bound to turn up in its course. He responded freely to whatever occurred and discovered behind the free manifestations of the unknown, the tormenting, mild image not only of himself as free but that of the freedom of emerging things as well:[11]

> It was our business to squeeze these lumps back into fluid. A sweet and unctuous duty! No wonder that in old times sperm was such a favorite cosmetic . . . After having my hands in it for only a few mintues, my fingers felt like eels, and began, as it were to serpentine and spiralize.
>
> As I sat there at my ease, cross-legged on the deck; after the bitter exertion at the windlass; under a blue tranquil sky; the ship under indolent sail, and gliding so serenely along; as I bathed my hands among those soft, gentle globules of infiltrated tissues, wove almost within the hour; as they broke to my fingers, and discharged all their opulence, like fully ripe grapes their wine; as I snuffed up that uncontaminated aroma,—literally and truly, like the smell of spring violets; I declare to you, that for the time I lived as in a musky meadow; I forgot all about our horrible oath, in that expressible sperm, I washed my hands and my heart of it; I almost began to credit the old Paracelsan supersition that sperm is of rare virtue in allaying the heat of anger: while bathing in that bath, I felt divinely free from ill-will, or petulance, or malice, of any sort whatsoever.
>
> Squeeze! squeeze! squeeze! all the morning long; I squeezed that sperm till I myself almost melted into it; I squeezed that sperm till a strange sort of insanity came over me; and I found myself unwittingly squeezing my co-laborers' hands in it, mistaking their hands for the gentle globules. Such an abounding, affectionate, friendly, loving feeling did this avocation beget; that at least I was continually squeezing their hands, and looking up into their eyes sentimentally; as much as to say,—Oh! my dear fellow beings . . . Come; let us squeeze hands all round; nay, let us all squeeze ourselves into each other; let us squeeze ourselves universally into the very milk and sperm of kindness.

Is this then man given away by himself, quivering to a sense of new identity? Is this the sign that the freedom of the artist can be told by stepping with supreme trust into the unknown at any opportunity? Is this trust which Ishmael, the story teller, evidences the key to the freedom of the artist, so that the whaling ship *Rachael* searching for her children finds not them but the artist? "On the second day, a sail drew near, nearer, and picked me up at last. It was the devious-cruising *Rachael*, that in her retracing search after her missing children, only found another orphan."[12]

But is the freedom of the artist merely that of the ordinary orphan? Melville seems not to take this orphan's estate too poorly. Indeed, Ishmael attests its splendor:[13]

Would that I could keep squeezing that sperm for ever! For now, since by many prolonged, repeated experiences, I have perceived that in all cases man must eventually lower, or at least shift, his conceit of attainable felicity; not placing it anywhere in the intellect or the fancy; but in the wife, the heart, the bed, the table, the saddle, the fire-side; the country; now that I have perceived all this, I am ready to squeeze case eternally. In thoughts of the visions of the night, I saw long rows of angels in paradise, each with his hands in a jar of spermaceti.

Are these, then, the things of the New World, the things that are the estate of the artist who trusts the unknown? Surely the freedom of the art of squeezing sperm, of art itself, bespeaks man's truth as his freedom. Why, then, should it not also discover more? Discover, that is, not only the free man of the New World, but also the things of the New World as freely emerging from the unknown? Why should art not bring to presence what it is in the unknown that supports the trust of a free man, the freely emerging things that signify all the possibilities that the unknown offers man? These things, if art could bring them to presence, are not the things fixing the determinateness of what has already happened but the thinging that attests not what has been, but all that might have come to be or might still come to be. Some of these things named by Ishmael, the fireside, the table, the bed, the heart, and the wife; these things, if they could be brought to presence, would embody freedom not only as man's truth but as themselves true, and together with man, the truth of freedom.

VI

The unknown continent has evoked deep artistic response interpreting American life and culture. Why? Because those Americans confronting and seeking to live in an unknown continent have adumbrated the deepest task of art itself, because artists have seen the men living in the unknown continent as symbols of their own efforts to yield to the unknown and through this to show the way to freedom. It has been the American genius to have faced the frontier and tried to be free and the merit of the American artist to have seen his own genius adumbrated by this effort, to have used its particular mode as a symbol to present in art the fuller significance of this freedom.

Even so the American artist has not succeeded in the very difficult task of clarifying the deeper significance of this path that his art can state so much better than a life of practice. Despite the artist, Americans have too often mistaken the significance of freedom as the path to power or the path of progress. The American artist, like artists anywhere, demands response; and the fuller significance that his art bespeaks can be evident only to those who respond to his results with the same care, with the same yielding forming, with which he contributes to creation.

To walk the path that leads beyond the settlement into the wilds may be to walk freely; but to walk this path is not of itself to express its significance. In her literal pioneering along the frontier, Martha Smith could not have been moving within a horizon projected as open to all free movements. Only in artistic anticipation of and, then, in the art work that was the origin of the book that is her autobiography could this horizon have been projected and brought to presence. In her book this horizon is symbolized by the moving frontier within which her acts of pioneering are presented as free, but it came to presence as the horizon of an art work itself, as the locus of her free acts as artist. Falling within this horizon, the yielding creative forming of Martha Smith and of any artist develops and builds a path of free movement telling the truth of man, telling Martha Smith and those whose response to the book rebuilds this path that nothing that happens along it is irrevocable; that nothing that happens along it determines the future, that along this path the future is and always remains open to all the possibilities there might be.

Art is symbolized in human action—the facts of autobiography or the contexts of novels; representations and the emotional significance of colors, lines, or spaces of a painting; the humanly significant movements and patterns of the dance—it offers these expressions as reflexive symbols of its own nature and development. Thus, although it offers a variety, even an untold variety, of such humanly significant circumstances in the objects produced by one artist and, again, in the work of different artists, all these can be symbols of the one task of art. When viewed from the perspective of its humanly expressive content, each art work (and resulting art objects) is different; yet when understood in the terms of the horizon each projects, all art works (but not all art objects) are essentially the same. They are the same as constituting the horizon within which the free acts of artistic yielding and forming can fall, as *the* horizon opening to the unending free acts which, as falling within this locus, generate the random path of freedom that moves into and within the unknown. It is this path, whatever the details of its human content, that emerges in art to attest that freedom which is the truth of man.

This presence and not the literal details of the symbols used is the fundamental concern of the artist. Similarly, the appreciator approaches art most fundamentally concerned not about this art object or this artist but about the free path that he may be able to rebuild in his own way. Both artists and appreciators project the horizon of art and participate within it by moving along the path of man's freedom and so contributing to art's speaking the truth of man.

Because art speaks the truth of that freedom that is man's being, it reveals the literal aspects of human movement along this path as appearance. The events of autobiography, the movements of dance, the representation of drawing, the melodies and harmonic development of music could all be different than they are and still serve their function. Indeed, the artistic representation of this variety as imaginative efflorescence is essential. Were the free path of art actually generated by the determinate events, patterns, and literal circumstances that the artist uses to symbolize its development within the horizon of the art work, this path could not be presented as the truth of man. Then its free movement would be lost to the literal existence of determinate pattern and repetition.

The artist whose efforts creatively form and yet yield to the materials with which he works participates in free movement in those moments when contingent harmonies attest the junction of his efforts and the support of this material: those moments when he accepts the gift to which he responds with the gift of his own nature. Such free movement has, always, a determinate context, but this determinateness is an accident of no special relevance. But the world of art is not a world of particular men and literal things, it is a world of illusion and possibility. Indifferent to what in particular men and things are and, so, representing man and things imaginatively only, it is a world of whatever is the occasion for the free action in which man seeks and finds *his* truth. Though the artist is able to bring man to his truth in the art work, he cannot do this for things. This explicit lack of discrimination within the given support of man's freedom constitutes the blind illusion of art. Illusion serves as the imaginative facade attesting all possibilities that might come to be in the free becoming of the unknown bringing man to presence as free. Illusion avoids any qualification of this freedom by determinate pattern or particular circumstances, including the terminal finitude in the art object. Thus, the origination of man's freedom remains entirely implicit in art and its world appears as ephemeral and transient as the stillness of the freedom it brings to presence as man's truth. The ephemerality of the world of art can always be ignored in favor of the intoxication of the development of the art work that brings man to presence as free. Yet as we hear art speak of one task, that is, the task of any and of all art work: the task of bringing man to presence in his truth, as free, we begin to participate in language, and to endeavor to hear in its speaking the truth not only of man but the truth behind the transience of the world of art, the truth of its existence as illusion.

The artist and the appreciator enter into the speaking of art as language when they seek not only to speak the truth of man but to distinguish those things whose truth originates this freedom. The fire, the table, the bed, are things that in the truth of their being are as free as man is in the truth of his being. Such things support man's freedom not merely as illusory, as mere symbols of the contingent harmony of the free becoming of the unknown and man as free, but in their disclosed natures, as offering support in different ways and so in their own truth; they bespeak another world, a different world than that which art offers as illusion carved on a facade. Indeed, in *Moby Dick*, Melville seeks constantly for such things as may embody the illusory world of art and provide its true content.

Language speaking is adumbrated by the speaking of art; but it comes to presence beyond art. Artistic response to the unknown projects the horizon of art as the locus within which free acts fall and brings these to presence as the human path of freedom, the truth of man. In the art work, this path remains, at best, the path along which man's freedom emerges, the path that speaks the truth of man's being as free, as the truth disclosed by illusion. Yet the literal immediacy of its presentation tends to obscure the awareness that things, too, may be true. The task of language is to grasp the horizon of art as the horizon of the unknown. It is the task of speaking the unending becoming of the unknown as the truth of things as well as the truth of man.

If art is at once the silent bell of the wine glass and the stroking of the wand along its rim that calls forth the primal vibration that gives voice in the choir of man's song of freedom, the speaking of language makes that bell repeatedly sound the true names of things as the contrapuntal chords of the chorale of thanksgiving for all that the free becoming of the unknown could come to be: the free men in the New World.

15. Affectively Possible Worlds: A Sketch for a Theory of Aesthetic Experience

CYRIL W. DWIGGINS

She was the single artificer of the world
In which she sang. And when she sang, the sea,
Whatever self it had, became the self
That was her song, for she was the maker. Then we,
As we beheld her striding there alone,
Knew that there never was a world for her
Except the one she sang and, singing, made.
(Wallace Stevens, "The Idea of Order at Key West")

I

One of the problems entailed in sketching a theory of aesthetic experience is to get clear what one wants to talk about. Aesthetic experience is usually described in consummatory terms, as something positive. But I take it that the experience of the incomplete, the unfinished, the mediocre, the ugly, is also aesthetic.

Surely I would not wish to call an object ugly solely because I had not experienced it with some evident pleasure. Jarrett puts it more strongly. An object is ugly not simply if it fails to arouse "aesthetic interest"; it is ugly if it first arouses and then disappoints or frustrates that interest.[1] Immediately the problem reasserts itself. Reduced to the use of the adjective *aesthetic* for both the ugly and the satisfying, we are caught in the endless round of attempting to define objects in terms of the experiences we have of them, then of defining the experiences as being of those objects.

Where we can talk of *interest* there is some sense in using words such as *disappointment* or *frustration*. We are interested when we have positive expectations of an object or a situation, disappointed when those expectations are not met, frustrated when they are systematically dashed. But what is it I expect? When are my expectations met? When is aesthetic experience 'successful'?

The vagueness is not dispelled by calling an aesthetic experience "successful" when it is accompanied by or results in some form of pleasure or satisfaction. Almost anything may give pleasure to at least someone, granting the appropriate combination of personality and circumstance. Moreover, the element of pleasure or satisfaction introduces the problem of taste before one has the theoretical strength to deal with it. This is especially true if one wants to draw a sharp distinction between the experience of the aesthetic elite and the experience of the masses. What is the aesthetic value of bread, circuses, dumb show, noise? Or does wine have aesthetic value? Tea? Sex? Perhaps the distinction between "high" and "low" pleasure is significant. But I must assume *at this point* that the mere fact that I happen to derive pleasure from the experience of an object does not *necessarily* mark either the object or my experience of it as aesthetic.

What does seem significant? My satisfaction (when and if I have it) is had simply by giving the object my attention. I say "simply," even though the giving of attention may entail a high degree of preparation or effort. My attention may be prolonged or condensed in an intense moment of insight or may be a network of repeated acts of attention. These differences are incidental to the main point: I am attentive, and this satisfies me.

What sort of attention? Perceptual or at least (to hedge all bets) quasi-perceptual. Even though I may be helped or sustained by acts of analysis or memories of prior experiences, I am in the *presence* of a concrete something, or the something is concretely present to me.[2] (More precisely: the object and I are mutually present to each other because my focused attention is an opening of myself to the object.)

I am in some form of emotional engagement with the object. There is no other way it could be capable of disappointing me.

I also experience a being-*in*-something, whether I seem to be "in" the object itself, as in musical experience; or in something the object presents, as I do when I live vicariously in the situation presented by a novel; or copresence in something *with* the object, a presence of *in-dwelling*, as in the experience of sculpture or architecture. (Ultimately all modes reduce to in-dwelling.)

The object seems to be nothing but a pure object of experience. There is nothing I "do" with or to the object except to experience it. To the extent that I experience the object aesthetically, the experience itself is the only "use" the object has for me. Consider the way I might experience a painting if I were a visitor in a gallery and the way I might look at it if I were a mover or an insurance agent or a shipping clerk. I can look in several ways at once. Consider the difference between *seeing* and *looking at* or between looking at a painting as a thing and looking at a painting as an art object or between looking at clouds as weather indicators and as landscapes in the sky. (These are not, of course, mutually exclusive.)

Aesthetic experience may not be limited to the experience of objects in the usual sense (persons, things, events). In my experience of the painting, I may be aware of more than I concretely see. The painting may be the *vehicle* of the experience, but it does not necessarily exhaust what I am made aware of by means of that vehicle. What I mean here is: I cannot yet say whether *what* I experience is limited to the aesthetic object narrowly taken, even though it seems clear that what I experience comes to me as a *result* of, or as *accompaniment* of, my direct experience of that object. If the painting makes me dwell in a world, it is not because I imagine myself placed within the frame but because I begin to experience the painting and myself as cohabitants in a world appropriate to our encounter. Music and architecture seem to be more direct paths to this sense of indwelling.

II

In the attitude of pure attention, I am prepared to let the art object have its way with me. According to Jarrett, this attitude is one of "attentive, self-contained regard for the *qualities* of an object . . . often described as contemplative and as savoring, or negatively as non-practical, nonanalytic."[3] Notice that this is a description of an *attitude*, not of an aesthetic experience as such. True enough, in aesthetic experience I am especially attentive to the qualities of the art object; but aesthetic experience is *of* something more than these qualities. The qualities are of something that is *present*; but something more is *presented*.

Ortega y Gasset insists that perception of lived reality and perception of artistic form require "different adjustment of our perceptive apparatus."[4] I submit that this "different adjustment" is what Todes calls sensuous or perceptual abstraction.[5] I *normally* perceive things as cohabitants of the world in which my practical concerns are rooted and exercised. In this sense *normal* perception is *practical* perception, and it is *concrete* in the way that my everyday living is concrete to me. But perception can also be *abstract*, when what I perceive is seen as somehow detached from my everyday world. This is what happens in aesthetic experience. It is only when I begin to perceive an object *as though it belonged to some world other than the one in which my practical concerns are engaged* that I begin to experience that object in the aesthetic mode. Yet I also realize that the object does in fact reside (physically, at any rate) in the everyday world. I am explicitly aware of the "as though" in the case of art; I am explicitly aware of the art object's *being* art.[6]

Todes describes this abstract mode of perception in terms of "skillful inhibition." Perception is a multi-staged effort: we look for, before we see; listen for, before we hear; taste before we eat; sniff before smelling. But we can also maintain the attitudes of looking and listening "even after what is sought presents itself. Thus, one hears sounds, but *listens to* music. And one sees things, but *looks at* paintings. . . . This state of rapt attention is achieved by looking-at or listening-to things seen or heard with that attitude of attentiveness normally reserved for looking-for and listening-for things not yet seen or heard. . . . In all these cases of skillfully inhibited perception . . . one becomes aware of *qualities* rather than things."[7] I do not disregard the things; I regard them differently. The things are now important precisely as bearers of their qualities, just as the violinist and the violin are musically important chiefly because of the sounds they produce. They have ceased to exist in their everyday identities because I have ceased perceiving them in the context of my everyday concerns.

Perception is our knowledge of the *existence* of things, of their *reality*, that is, of their presence in the "real" world. "I imagine X" is consistent with "X does not exist"; "I *perceive* X" is *not* consistent with "X does not exist". Normal perception comes to completion with the sense of a thing's existing as part of the real world. This completion is missing in abstract perception. What is given in abstract perception is first given as detached from the horizon of the everyday world, and it is for the instant a sheer presence without a context.

But this is intolerable. Perception *means* seeing something against a ground or a horizon, within a context, within a world. If I perceive anything at all, I can do so *because* I am able to see it against some ground or within some world.

III

The presence of world or horizon or context in every experience is such that the proper noematic correlate for any act of experiencing within a given context must always be a figure displayed within that context, always figure-on-ground, never figure as such or ground as such.[8] Further, no act of consciousness *within* a given context or ground can intend that ground directly. But the act that *constitutes* a context or ground (and which we might call a *grounding consciousness* relative to any figures that are to appear) is not within that context. In the case of a particular subworld, the grounding consciousness is ordinarily taken to be a commitment to the end that rules the subworld, which is intended as a figure against the horizon of the life-world. I commit to the end, and my commitment opens up a field in which figures related to that end can appear, like the motor space that opens up beneath Merleau-Ponty's hands when he sits at his typewriter or the "expressive space" that opens up for the experienced organist as he takes the measure of a new instrument with his whole body and "settles into the organ as one settles into a house."[9]

On the other hand, intending any figure *within* the field of commitment intends the field itself (including the ordinary commitment) nonthematically, as ground: just as the organist has incorporated the keyboard, stops, and pedals into his own bodily space, so that he does not need to locate them objectively in order to play. The act of reaching for this or that stop or pedal is performed with no thought of where they are, no more than I need to determine where my hand is before I can move it. To put this same point the other way round: there is never a *thematic* consciousness of the subworld itself so long as I am directly intending a figure within it. My habitual commitment to the subworld's end continues to constitute the subworld a ground for any figure related to that end.

As for the world—"the world simply," in Husserl's phrase—we are *constantly* conscious of it but only as a horizon, never directly or thematically: the world is *pre*given, not given. World and thing form an inseparable noematic unity, and from this point of view the awareness of world as ground is nothing more than the world-intending dimension of any awareness of a thing *in* the world. But we should not presume that such a *noematic* unity precludes the possibility or even the need for different sorts or levels of consciousness on the noetic side: "Felt, willed, and conceptual meanings [together with perceptual meanings] mix and mingle in primordial world experience. Feelings vitalize concepts, concepts organize feelings, and both feelings and concepts are colored with volitional dispositions. It is not as though there were three separate sources of meaning, emanating from three separate psychic powers, but rather there is one source, world experience, contextually differentiated, expressing meaning in three interrelated modes."[10] World-intending may not be *separable* from object-intending, but its "focus of attention" is different; and insofar as world-intending can be distinguished in this way from object-intending, it seems clear that world-intending must be an object*less* modality of consciousness.

IV

In this light Heidegger's discussion of mood in *Being and Time* takes on fresh significance. For Heidegger moods (*Stimmungen*) disclose the world as the pure "wherein" of dasein. Mood is the sheer sense of how I am *in* the world—the sheer sense of being situated in a particular way—and I must have this sense before I can address myself to anything within the world, just as I must have a sense of where I am at this moment before I even think of moving elsewhere.[11] But the correlate of *Stimmung* in Heidegger's analysis is a world in which there is no "elsewhere," at least not yet, or for that matter anything else at all. Mood is a *global* sense of being-situated and has to do only with in-being as a whole (*als Ganzes*), without reference to anything other than the world and myself. Feeling myself in a mood—fearfulness, boredom, anxiety, elation, depression—is finding myself in a world, open to whatever can appear in it, because my mood is my here-and-now attunement (*Gestimmtheit*) to the world as a general situation. "The ontological core of finding-oneself-disposed-thus (*Befindlichkeit*) is a disclosing directedness toward the world that makes it possible for us to encounter something that can stir us."[12] It is only in a world that we face in a fearful (or fear*less*) mood that anything threatening can appear, and this is true not simply in a psychological sense. "Indeed, from the *ontological* point of view and as a general rule, we must leave the primary discovery of the world to *pure mood*."[13] The discovery is primary because what is discovered is not something against the world-horizon but the horizon itself, more precisely a *sense* of the horizon that is not determined by the sight of any figure against it but by how it feels to *be* a figure against it; and the mood is "pure" (*bloss*, naked) because it is not a response *to* a figure but the figure's own pure sense of being in its ground, as yet a pure openness to other figures.[14]

This conception of moods opening us to the world and the world to us lends considerable force to the suggestion that the world is pregiven precisely as *felt* meaning and that the grounding consciousness of "the world simply" is precisely a form of affect, which I shall call, for want of something better, primordial affect. The correlate of primordial affect is *the* world, in itself prior to all objects and subworlds but always pregiven as the ultimate ground of a particular object or subworld. "There are, as a matter of fact, no affective *states*," writes the young Sartre. "Reflection yields us affective *consciousnesses*. Joy, sorrow, melancholy are consciousnesses. And we must apply to them the great law of consciousness: that all consciousness is consciousness *of* something."[15]

But what is it that affect is consciousness *of?* The French phenomenologists have been fairly consistent in holding that affect properly intends a world of some sort rather than an object as such. Even if a feeling seems to be directed toward an object, it is toward an object transformed, suffused with an *affective quality* which is at the same time a quality of the world at this moment and constitutive of the sense of the object for feeling. A grinning face suddenly appears at the window; I feel "invaded by terror." My world is transformed; I am suddenly plunged into an ambience in which this face is somehow *appropriate*—a magical world, in Sartre's phrase, in which distance and the solidity of physical obstacles cannot protect me from this grinning threat. The face appears behind the window ten yards away, but its menace is immediately present to me. This is possible, writes Sartre, "only in an act of consciousness which destroys all the structures of the world which might reject the magical and reduce the event to its proper proportions. For example, the window . . . is no longer perceived as that which must first be opened. It is perceived as the *frame* of the horrible face. And in a general way regions are set up around me *on the basis of which* the horrible manifests itself. For the horrible *is not possible* in the deterministic world of instruments."[16] The horrible can appear only in a world full of danger, but also one in which no routine handling of the danger, no ordinary recourse against it, is effective. But the horrible is not an object. It is the constitutive quality or tonality, the affective texture of such a world. This quality manifests itself in objects, but my horror is not so much *of* these objects as it is of the world that grounds their possibility.[17]

Sartre's debt to Heidegger is evident here, but unlike Heidegger, Sartre emphasizes the intentionality of feeling almost at the expense of the fact that it *is* feeling, a being-affectively-*moved*. Ricoeur, on the other hand, insists on both the affective and the intentional aspects of feeling.[18] Feeling does bear upon something beyond itself; but this very bearing upon something else, toward the lovable or the hateful or the horrible, is equally a bearing of the world inward upon the self. In feeling, affection is intention. The moments of interiority and exteriority coalesce. This piece of music will always have its developmental structure, its tonality, whether it is listened to or not; but it will not have its sadness unless it is heard as sad. To hear the music as sad is to hear it *sounding like sadness feels*, to hear it as an external counter of my own sadness or of the sadness that *can* be mine. Yet the sadness of the music is not over against me, displayed like a specimen for observation. I am *in* this sadness. It is around me; it has become a world for me, a horizon that extends beyond the edges of the music, just as the sadness I may feel within me (or may imagine myself to be feeling) extends beyond the music, even though the music may be its *focus*. The music is thus a figure against the ground of this sadness; or rather the music and I are fellow figures in it. Feeling is the sheer sense of the world in which I find myself, insofar as it is also the world of the object that now fixes my attention.

For Ricoeur feeling is "the manifestation of a relation to the world which constantly restores our complicity with it, our inherence and belonging in it."[19] If feeling is at the same time an intention toward the world and an affection of the self and therefore a paradox, the paradox is resolved by recognizing that the affection of the self is its sense of inherence in (and therefore its being toward) the world. But if by feeling I intend the world itself as I inhere and belong in it, I am intending my own ground; yet the ground can appear only *as* ground, not thematically, and it is clearly not the case that it always appears as *my* ground as such because I do not intend myself thematically in every act of feeling. My terror at the face in the window is not directly a consciousness of my being terrified.[20] The ground appears to me only as the ground of some object that I experience as grounded in the world of this moment with me, as fellow figure; or in those cases in which my feeling does bear directly upon myself, the world appears as grounding the object I have become for myself at this moment. Feeling too has its cunning. As Ricoeur says, it "seems to play the game of the object."

V

An affective quality is, on one hand, the object's reflection of my own inwardness, which is in turn my complicity, my attunement with the world at this moment. Such qualities, writes Dufrenne, "can be pregnant with a world, since a world . . . is precisely a response to a certain attitude, the correlate of the subjectivity that manifests itself in the affective quality."[21] On the other hand, an affective quality is a demand made by the object for placement together with me in a world to which it is native. To borrow an example from Dufrenne, "A certain kind of wolf exists 'for' the Siberian forest as the forest does for the wolf."[22] There is an affective quality which constitutes an essence common to both the wolf and the forest, an essence which encompasses them before they are themselves, and which has, so to speak, differentiated itself into them. The same relationship exists between subject and object. Ultimately "we must subordinate both the subject's attitudes and the object's aspects to a primary being which contains and produces them both."[23]

In this way subject and object are seen to encounter each other on a common ground. I perceive the object against its horizon only because the horizon is also mine. This is the source of an object's ability to modulate or transform my sense of the world. The object appears bearing the affective quality of a world other than the one I now feel; I take up the new quality and instantly my horizon has been altered. To be more precise, I should say that the object in this situation is ambiguous: it appears in the first instance in my present world but seems to belong in another world. Its very alien quality is an invitation to enter that other world; and if I take up the invitation, then "at a single stroke," as Merleau-Ponty would say, the object and I stand together within the new horizon.

My feelings, then, are the experiential ground from my side. They are my awareness of the setting in which the object is displayed insofar as that setting is felt as one in which the object and I cohabit. Affect is my intentional insertion into the setting, into this or that world, and therefore into *the* world. "This music is sad." A world in which things sound like that, if I am in it, is a world in which *I* am sad. Each encounter with things is the coming-to-presence of the world in which they are grounded and to which our feelings have already testified.

VI

In both science and aesthetic encounters, we detach, abstract, take materials or data out of their habitual contexts and put them together in new ways by seeing them in alternative contexts. Or one could say that the data *demand* this or that context or that by reconfiguring the data, we *make* them demand a new context (but then it is still the data that make the demand).

For the scientist the alternative context is his theory, which describes the general sort of world in which his data might be intelligible. His data present themselves as enigmas to thought and demand the construction of a world context that allows him to think consistently with them. Aesthetic data, on the other hand, present themselves as enigmas to feeling—affective enigmas—which resist absorption into the deterministic world of instruments and demand the generation of an affective world sense that allows me to feel consistently with the datum and thereby to perceive it *in* its difference from the everyday. I am confronted by a thing, a gesture, an utterance that seems to have its meaning *elsewhere*. By refusing to participate in the affective essence of *my* world, the datum invites me to enter *its* world. If I respond to the invitation and take up the affective quality that this alien presence ambiguously evokes, I have provided it with a world context appropriate to its demands and at the same time experience that context as an affective sense of the world simply: as *a* world distinct from my everyday world.[24] I do not mistake this world, therefore, for the everyday; it stands only as an affective possibility over against the feeling, empirically constant and constantly realized, that grounds the world of instruments. Without abandoning that feeling or that world I begin also to share in the alien's affective aura. I neither leave the everyday nor refuse the alien; I inhabit two worlds at once, and each illumines the other.[25]

But how does the aesthetic datum engage my feelings? How does it display a distinct affective essence? I suggest that it does so by solely and directly guiding my experience of it, there being no aim apart from the will to experience and no guide other than the structure of the datum itself.[26] In pragmatic perception my projects dictate. (Where can I grip this to lift it? How shall I crate this to ship it?) But in aesthetic perception, solely the structure of the datum itself and not the demand of instrumentality controls the flow of my experience. I let the datum "have its way with me." Its parts demand now this sort, now that sort of attentiveness. Its perceptual configuration creates in me a flow of bodily *resonances*, a rhythm of responses by which I progressively take up the datum or rather by which I *perform* it as though it were a choreography.

Specific gestures pick out objects *in* a world. Bodily resonances are not yet gestures, but ways of "having my body" that locate me in the world of the object. The aesthetic datum is thus an object that controls my sense of being *placed* (*Befindlichkeit*, to use Heidegger's term), which is essentially object*less* in itself (although always tied to the object) and which reaches beyond the object to the place in which the object and I encounter each other.[27]

The art object or the ordinary thing experienced aesthetically is not the ultimate object of aesthetic experience; it is only the vehicle, the aesthetic datum, and the datum is a perceptually abstract *medium* through which a *world* is presented. The ultimate object of aesthetic experience is the affectively possible world presented by the datum. "Precisely because it dwells and makes us dwell in a world we do not have the key to, the work of art teaches us to see and gives us something to think about as no analytical work can."[28]

The happiness that lies at the heart of aesthetic experience is grounded in the identity of aesthetic experience with the experience of one's own freedom. From this point of view, art's ultimate gift may be to help me experience the world as that which stands over against my freedom, as opposed to that which merely dictates my necessities, and thus to have a sense of my deepest self as free rather than slave. Every aesthetic encounter is a call to transcend the habitual limits of the "real," to experience the other possibilities inherent in the very stuff of our everyday experience, much as an experienced climber might contemplate the possibilities of a rock face he has never seen before and may never in fact scale.

Affectively possible worlds are not fantasies, although they may engender fantasies. The point is that we can be led to see that the real is as fantastic a construction as what we formerly took to be fantasy and to see the world to be as much capable of spawning the fantastic as it is of housing the ordinary. The experience of metaphor helps us see that the real is nothing more than our own real*izing* of the always fluid possibilities that go to make up our conventional and pragmatic fixities. Makers of metaphors, poets most of all, thus provide us with paradigms of sight. Not without some reason did the artist replace the religious prophet in nineteenth-century Europe. But the reason was not that the artist is blessed with second sight, as was supposed by those who wished to make the artist himself the object of aesthetic contemplation by worshipping at the shrine of genius; rather the artist is blessed with *first* sight, which convention seeks to dim in the rest of us: a vision of the real as only one possibility of *the* world.

The ultimate interpretation of aesthetic experience lies in the recognition that we are constantly seduced by the call of things to dwell with them in their own time, space, and ambience. We pass so easily from one possibility of world feeling to another that we can lose sight of both the passing and of the fact that these lapped-over worlds are distinct from each other. If we regain this awareness, we regain (or retain) our playful freedom in the face of the congealments, however much needed, of the everyday. The everyday is not necessarily an enemy of freedom; but freedom can become snared by the illusion that the everyday world is the same as *the* world. It is the overcoming of entrapment in the everyday that makes us simultaneously aware of our own freedom and of the radically conventional nature of what we so often take to have been forever given.

The possibilities grasped in aesthetic experience, and particularly in art, are not substitutes for the real. Rather they reveal that balance of immanence and transcendence that alone *is* the real for us: constantly in our bodily situations, constantly capable of going beyond them by seizing in new ways on the strengths that sing in our dreams.

PART 5

PHENOMENOLOGY OF LANGUAGE

16. Does the Transcendental Ego Speak in Tongues?

or

The Problem of Language for Transcendental Reflection in Husserl's Phenomenology

RONALD BRUZINA

Some years ago in Paris, during a small weekend conference on the topic, "The Meaning and Limits of Philosophy," Paul Ricoeur made a remark about language that I think is most apt here today. He was thinking out loud about the peculiar property of the human communicative system to be able to deal with itself, to have a second order of operation specifically upon itself as a signitive system, to possess a *reflexivity* congruent with the power of reflexion we call thought. He said:

> Now if human language has always carried this possibility of "speaking about speaking," of speaking about language and its own institutions, of reflecting them, in other words, of reflexivity, still one can imagine people or civilizations who have not used it. But once we have begun to use

The study on which this paper is based was done during a year of research made possible by a fellowship from the Alexander von Humboldt Foundation in 1977–78. I wish also to express my thanks to Mrs. Susanne Fink for permission to draw quotations from the manuscript of Professor Fink's Sixth Cartesian Meditation and to Professor Samuel IJsseling and the Husserl Archives at Louvain for similar permission regarding Husserl's *Nachlass* materials. Finally also I wish to thank Professor IJsseling and his staff for their kind help in correcting the quoted materials in accordance with the final edited version of the respective texts.

it, we find ourselves in a way facing something that can have no origin [*un "ingénérable"*], in Spinoza's sense when he says of the third order of knowledge, once it is born, once it appears, it is eternal, it cannot not have been, although it is contingent that a mind attain to it. But once this contingency is passed, that state is ineluctable and inexhaustible.[1]

Two thoughts are prompted by this remark. In the first place, it has become a *precondition* of serious work in philosophy that one's inquiries in any area have a center and base in attention to language. That we first and last consider the role of language in all that we do is no longer a viewpoint that needs to be explained. Rather, *not* to begin with a recognition of the overarching role of language would need explanation and justification. *Not* to base one's study in a first under- standing of how language works in a methodology that draws from its analysis is to be astonishingly naive and hopelessly blinded by a fictional ideal of sublimely pure intellectual superwordliness. And so, for ex- ample, when we read Descartes from within this perspective, we are astounded by a glaring naivete in his *Meditations*. We smile and cluck our tongues at the obviousness of something he never notices and never remarks on, namely, that the process of reflection inwards towards a source of certainty in his own consciousness is all done in *words*, in words for a listener/reader, for himself in the first place, as the pseu- doother that is no other, and then for the genuine other to whom he finds no adequate access—except, of course, in these very words, a fact about which he is again silent.

On the other hand, perhaps we smile and chide Descartes *too quickly* for this *great unsaid* of his, which is that he worked his *thinking* in *saying* it, or indeed *writing* it. For even if the structuring of what we think is done by its articulation in language, this does not mean necessarily that the thinking or the saying in which meaning is posited need be given an *origin* as thinking or saying anywhere other than *in a sheer spontaneity*, neither in the history or causative mechanisms of an entity one might call mind, whether biologically or psychologically considered, nor in the history or causative mechanisms of a system called language. And if nothing else, Descartes reaches and explores the cogito precisely as that which is *uncaused as thinking*, however much it may in the end be caused as *substance*; Descartes's cogito is something that can have no process of origination outside itself. It is the sheer spontaneity of self-recognition that is ineluctable and inex- haustible once it is active. And this is to be true regardless of the form it takes in being spoken or regardless of whether one is attentive to the *fact* of its being spoken. In other words, for the basic truth of the cogito, the great unsaid *did not have* to be said.

That, of course, does not solve all problems, and it doesn't solve at all in particular those problems that have to do with showing how the verbal expression of this self-recognitional self-activation of the cogito *can indeed appropriately articulate it.* And this brings me to the specific subject I wish to explore in my paper. For if the sense of an insight, particularly one as fundamental as Descartes's cogito, is such that it *challenges* the concepts, terms, and frameworks that existing language and given cognitive perspectives offer, then those concepts, terms and frameworks may well be simply *inadequate* and *misleading,* and hence they will be *ineffectual* in articulating that insight—unless they be *transformed* as they are being used. And how is the other who listens or reads to *recognize* the *transforming/transformed* meaning when it appears entirely clothed in a language secured by familiar and normal significances? One could suggest that precisely because of this difficulty, originator philosophers like Descartes simply *have not been understood* and that the history of philosophy after such thinkers is the history of the attempts to understand that which originated in their thinking. Language *fails* the matter to be grasped; and so we have ever new attempts to say what has not and perhaps *can* not be adequately said. But let me pass over that idea and move more directly to my specific subject, which is this difficulty of articulating a radical insight that challenges normal sense when the normal-sense language in which one would articulate it is seen as recalcitrant to it; and specifically I wish to treat this issue directly in the way it arises for Husserl's transcendental phenomenology, which, as we all know, tries to recover and radicalize the basic insight first formulated by Descartes as *Cogito ergo sum.*

II

The question of how to express adequately what progressively radical self-refining insight grasps is one that Husserl is plainly aware of throughout his career. It is first discussed in one of the opening sections of the *Logical Investigations.*[2] Thereafter, throughout Husserl's works both published and unpublished one finds a similar concern and awareness expressed.[3] For the most part, however, this concern is motivated by a *methodological* purpose, namely, to make clear why phenomenology must incessantly return to matters already discussed and critically redo their treatment. Husserl's concern is not guided by a preoccupation with the phenomenon of language as such, though he certainly recognizes its importance. Rather he wishes to put his readers on the alert against thinking naively that because there seem to be words for what he is investigating, words that may well be philosophically well respected, those words don't need further clarification, or that the meaning these words are now meant to carry comes across quite well with a minimum of intellectual awareness and knowledge on the reader's part. But the issue to be raised is not one simply of methodology, of how to proceed for maximum clarity and effectiveness in using an instrument that one can assume is in principle adequately endowed for the task required of it. The issue is one of *theoretical* possibility, of whether the "instrument" in question, human language, *is* adequately endowed to express the insights claimed and whether serious difficulty regarding *that* possibility could mean a serious reservation regarding the very possibility and legitimacy of those same insights in general.[4] To put the matter more directly: how can a transcendental phenomenology achieve its understanding as the joint work of many communicating thinkers if the only language in which that understanding can be articulated is not itself transcendental? Can there be such a thing as a *transcendental language*? If so, how? If not, then can such a thing as a transcendental philosophy even be admitted?

I wish to jump right to the very center of this issue by a most interesting pair of statements, whose source I must explain before quoting them. The most concise and thorough discussion of the whole matter is found in a long unpublished essay written by Eugen Fink in 1932 as his last contribution to the task of revising the *Cartesian Meditations* that Husserl had asked him to undertake. Fink had entitled his essay "The Idea of a Transcendental Doctrine of Method," as an essay to be included as a sixth Cartesian Meditation. In addition to the lucid and incisive analysis of fundamental problems in the project of transcendental phenomenology that Fink provides—to my mind a brilliant theoretical discussion—the interest of the work is heightened enormously by the extensive marginal comments by Husserl himself. The interplay between Fink's discussion and Husserl's remarks is absolutely fascinating, particularly because there is not always agreement between the two.[5] The whole text clearly merits close study, something that will be possible when the text and its notational materials finally appear in the Husserliana *Dokumente* series.

It is in this manuscript, in a section entitled "Phenomenologizing as Predication," that the following statement of Fink's occurs:

> If the naivete of predicative explication is overcome through advances in phenomenological knowledge and mundane concepts are more and more freed from the natural associations that adhere to them, still it can never happen that the divergence of [equivocal] meaning that is present in every transcendental sentence between the natural sense of words and the transcendental meaning that is indicated in them be removed. Rather there will always remain an intrinsic conflict and contradiction in every

transcendental predication. Indeed, it is not even a *desideratum* that this divergence altogether disappear. The idea of a transcendental language that would just not need the mediation of natural language is in itself absurd.[6]

Husserl, now, writes the following note specifically to the last sentence just quoted, although it obviously continues and confirms the whole train of thought Fink here formulates.

Even if the phenomenologist should want to invent a new language, he would for that purpose still need natural equivocal language as the first expression of his phenomenological ascertainments, as their most direct expression. And the indirect new language would precisely for that reason be again equivocally defined.[7]

Throughout this section of Fink's manuscript, dealing as it does directly with language, and Husserl's comments and notes on those pages, it is unambiguously clear that a serious conflict exists and *has to* exist between the normal framework of meaning in the natural language the phenomenologist must use and the transcendental framework from within which the phenomenologist seeks articulation in that language. As a result, when words are used by the phenomenologist to express specifically transcendental phenomenological assertions, they must undergo a *transformation of their meaning*. Husserl himself states this as explicitly as one would want in a marginal remark to a paragraph where Fink speaks of the way in which language, used after the *epoché*, still retains the "expressive character that applies solely to beings,"[8] (that is, things taken in a precritical ontological attribution). Husserl says, "The human habit set (being in the world) changes the sense being has in it to the habit set of the transcendental I—this is something I, the observer, assert, and become at once thematic as observer; again I assert this and still speak natural language, but in transcendentally altered sense."[9] Even more explicit is another comment on the same page and pertaining to the same point in Fink's discussion; and this comment is more helpful for the direction to take treating the overall problem. "A phenomenological language only has meaning, only has possibility, in principle as transformed natural language, just as the transcendental phenomenon world only has meaning as the transformed ontological meaning world."[10]

It is the radical change in value framework achieved through the *epoché* and the transcendental-phenomenological reduction that governs the radical change imposed upon an articulative system: to be fit for the expression of transcendental-phenomenological insights, it must not allow ontological attribution in accord with the natural attitude to operate.

How deep-grained, how misleading and contrary to phenomenological realizations, ontological attribution of this kind is, is a topic for treatment on another occasion. Beyond the many declarations of the overall principle, it can be seen in those occasional more specific discussions Husserl offers coupled with his *practice* whereby concepts are progressively formed in the course of a specific phenomenological analysis. What I wish to do here is *assume* that principle and proceed to consider the *effect* it has on the question of how language can be transcendentally appropriate. And the chief effect of this principle lies in the positing of a *dualism of meaning for the very same words* when they function as the medium of articulation for transcendental phenomenological insight.

The expressions used by Husserl and Fink in respect to this dualism are not minced. As to the intensity of the dualism, they speak of "divergence," "tension," "conflict," and then even "rebellion": a "constant rebellion" on the part of "natural habit . . . against phenomenologizing."[11] The more interesting terms, however, and the ones that raise the problem more directly are the ones that attempt to characterize this dualism itself. For Fink, the two frameworks of meaning stand in a certain *"analogical"* relationship by which natural language terms can only be *"inadequate"* to express transcendental phenomenological meanings. Husserl is more severe. In place of "inadequacy" (*Inadäquatheit*) he prefers to speak of a "split in two" (*Zwiepältigkeit*) and a "doubleness of meaning" (*Doppeldeutigkeit*), even if there is a "parallel" between the two elements in question.[12]

What are we to make of this? The difficulty seems obvious enough. If in the interest of a radical philosophic position, an expression is to be taken in a sense *different in kind* from the meaning it normally has, and if that normal kind of meanings is the communicative basis in the expression for the articulation of the *new* meaning, then what assures one of getting that *new* meaning *through* the normal one?[13] As Fink points out, what is to prevent the statement of some specifically transcendental point from being understood in such a way "that the natural, original sense of the words overcomes the transcendental meaning that is therewith analogically indicated, stifles it, and covers it over," the result being simply *mis*understanding?[14]

We have here, now, a good example of the way in which the resolution of a difficulty depends centrally upon the way in which the difficulty is represented, upon the way in which elements of a whole philosophic position have to be first searched out in the very conception of the relevant factors that are seen to give rise to the problem. For the whole difficulty in the present case takes on a very different character depending upon (1) the conception one has of the *way* in which radically different meanings in a same expression *are different*, and (2) upon the conception one has of the way in which a subject speaking *depends upon* or is *constrained by* linguistic forms. The whole tenor of the discussion that Fink pursues regarding this problem requires background treatment of exactly this sort in order to see how a resolution might be anticipated, a resolution that Fink is *calling for* rather than providing.

1. Regarding the way in which meanings can be different, the first thing that has to be made clear is that the difference at issue here is a very unusual one. Between a *transcendental* order of meaning for some expression or assertion and a *mundane* (or normal) order of meaning for the same expression or assertion, the difference for Husserlian phenomenology is *not* one wherein discrete parcels of meaning are separated off one from another so that one "unit" of meaning stands as utterly *closed off* from the other, as if in a wholly disparate, separate sphere. The difference is rather one of taking a *same* meaning "*differently*." A same meaning is "*transformed*" in being taken, or expressed, with transcendental value, it is not *replaced*. The same meaning is kept but *with a different value*, namely, as no longer presupposed to include inherent reference to fixed existence somewhere in the autonomous order of being called the "natural world" but rather is taken exclusively within the horizon of (phenomenological) phenomenality, that is, as relating exclusively to intentional appearance modes in the experience of radically reflecting subjectivity.[15] The crucial consideration here is simply that expressed in the marginal remark of Husserl's quoted earlier; namely, that the transformation of *language* in phenomenology parallels the transformation of *world* in the phenomenological reduction. "A phenomenological language only has meaning, only has possibility, in principle as transformed natural language, just as the transcendental phenomenon world only has meaning as the transformed ontological meaning world."[16]

Before leaving this point, however, one further consideration is needed. It seems to me that the idea here in Husserl's thinking has to be that unless the first or normal sense of some particular phenomenon—in this case the world and the language to articulate our awareness of it—held within it the *implicit potential* of a transcendental transvaluation of its meaning, that transformation of it would not be possible. And the way this transformational potential is positively implicit in the naive awareness we have of the world right in the natural attitude is through its *presuppositional bearing*. Being presuppositional, being unquestioned, being taken for granted, the world as the massive global plenum for all our movements and perceptions becomes the most radical of puzzles once questioning turns *upon it*. And to turn questioning upon it, to require explanation of the privileged presuppositional status for this plenum and our awareness of it, is to open up the *transcendental* as a dimension of possible meaning.[17]

Still, one must ask, if this is so, if that dimension of reflection and meaning called transcendental is thus implicated right in the naive and mundane and is a kind of *transformational repetition* of it, why then is there in both Fink's and Husserl's discussion so strong an emphasis upon *difference*, indeed, upon *conflict* between the two? The reason has to be this, that the move from the naive and mundane to the transcendental is not an *easy* transition; it goes against the unquestioned *settledness* of "natural" understanding, which after all is a deeply set *presuppositional* stance. To reach and maintain the radically questioning and reconsidering viewpoint of the transcendental is a constant *struggle*, not an easy step made once and for all. In the end, terms that emphasize difference, even to the point of speaking of duality, need to be modulated out of the basic *affinity*[18] that obtains between the "warring" orders of meaning, the natural, naive, or mundane and the transcendental in Husserl's phenomenological sense.

2. Regarding now the way in which a subject speaking *depends upon* or *follows* language in articulating thought, the point to consider here is how linguistic forms are *determinants*, the way in which the formative articulative power language offers is a *possibilizing* factor rather than a *constraining* one. Rather than consider linguistic expressions as rigid capsules or molds within which anything subject to them takes on sharply contoured, invariant form, words, especially *in combination*, are instead nodes of variously determinate *potential*. In the framework of a Husserlian phenomenology, one can rather speak more properly of words as embodying *nodes of intentional determination* that provide *articulation possibilities*. In point of fact, words in sentences are not sequences of units isomorphically picturing a train of "ideas" existing alongside them, but are the sequentially expressed form of an intentional project, whose "content" is actual only in the movement of that project through that articulative form. To put it in other terms: The sentence has actual meaning only *in being consciously spoken* (or *mutatis mutandis*, in being listened to),[19] and the meaning thus actual only in the speaking (or listening) is not reducible to a formal sequencing of lexical or grammatical parts of the sentence linguistically considered. To put this same point in yet another form, one closer to Husserl's own in the First Logical Investigation: for expressions to have meaning, they must be actualized in their specifically determined usage by the *intentional act* of a speaking subject. Only then is the meaning *potential* of a sequence of expressions (which very much owes its ability to offer

meaning differentiations to the *differential forms* that the linguistic system provides) *decided* as a specific saying (as the determined set of *these* words in *this* assertive usage), only *then* do the words actually *have meaning.*[20]

III

In the end, for Husserl and for Fink the whole framework for understanding the way in which language acquires transcendental validity for its meanings lies not in the analysis of language as an overarching, predetermining foundation for the whole order of reflection and thought but in the analysis of the intentional activity of subjectivity as taking form in and relating to the total horizon of world, of the spatio-temporally experienced plenum. Notice it is not enough to say here that what is basic is the intentional activity of subjectivity *simply put.* It is rather the analysis of subjectivity in its *"enworlding" process* (*Verweltlichung*) that is needed. Only therein can the function of language be made clear both with respect to being a "medium" of articulation and communication in the ordinary sense and, more importantly here, as functioning in the *intersubjective constitution* of the genuinely *scientific,* in Husserl's comprehensive sense of the "scientific." But that whole set of issues is a *very* large topic which I am not prepared to try to represent here. I should add, however, that the largest part of Fink's manuscript (namely, the section that follows the one under discussion here) is devoted to this very matter, and it is to these pages that Husserl makes his most extensive comments.[21]

The need for language on the part of the transcendentally reflecting self is based, then, on the necessity for subjectivity even in a transcendental stance to be enworlded, to be embodied as an in-the-world phenomenon, even with the presumption that this embodiment will be taken in a mundane or natural attitude way. Yet I cannot simply make mention of this whole topical body of findings and problems without at least drawing out one overall lesson of great import; and it is this. The use transcendental reflection makes of language in such a way that the language used can never become fully transcendentally appropriate[22] is an example, and perhaps the paradigm instance, of the general paradoxical exigency that transcendental subjectivity can only fully accomplish its project by *compromising itself as transcendental.* A return or recourse to modalities that retain an unreduced mundaneity is unavoidable. And what better demonstration can there be of this paradoxical situation as a condition not only that cannot be avoided but that is to be *exploited* in the interest of transcendental realization than the massive fact of Husserl's own output in *words written?*

On the other hand, this singular emphasis upon the need for an "enworlding" on the part of subjectivity even in its transcendental exercise needs proper balancing. Correlation to and progressive form-taking within the horizon of world are indeed basic, but so also is the intentional agency of the constituting I. The phrase rolls out easily, particularly because it represents the centerpiece of Husserl's phenomenological project and its constant repetition there needs no supplementing. But what does it mean in the context of the concern for language that we have been exploring here? Begin with a statement of Fink's on this and Husserl's addenda (in brackets) to it: "Phenomenological sentences can accordingly only [really] be understood if the *meaning-giving situation* of the transcendental sentence is always repeated, that is, if [the *epochē* is vitally and actively held to as another way of taking the world in the usual bearing and] predicative explicating terms are always verified by the [really transcendental] phenomenologizing intuition."[23] The same point is asserted in a paragraph exclusively of Husserl's writing in *Ideas I*, where the language one uses is said to have to "coincide with what is intuitively given."[24] Now what I want to draw out here is not the intricate *structure* of this multi-"leveled" activity,[25] important as that is, but rather the overall *lesson* it is meant to demonstrate. And that lesson is simply that the assertions made in language, that is, the points articulated through adaptation of the signification potential of linguistic expressions, is governed ultimately by the intentional thrust originating in the I pole of subjectivity.[26]

Two things are being said here. In the first place, there is a constitutive *autonomy* asserted for the intentional agent; and, secondly, the maintaining of that autonomy in *the act of speaking* is defended, notwithstanding the socio-historical constitution of language as a system of differential forms for the articulation of meaning. It must be made clear, however, that the autonomy of the speaking I-subject here claimed is the power of governance for the *assertion* made *in* words, for the whole *actual* assertion *unit*: no more than that is claimed.

The meaning *potential* of words taken abstractly outside an actual instance of use, is clearly not under the autonomous governance of the speaker. All that is an expressive medium, so to speak, "at the disposal" of the speaker and awaiting the speaker's actualizing choice. Its origins lie in the workings of the complex conditions of history and society, within which the single I may be a contributing factor, but only within the dynamics of a transindividual situation.

At the same time, what is being claimed here is not that all conscious goings-on are acts explicitly springing from a totally controlling I-center.

Consciousness can have anonymous processes within it and can be conditioned by structures that are not egological (e.g., cultural and historical traditions (functions of temporality) at psychological or even biological "levels").[27] The consciousness in question here, however, is consciousness as *rational subjectivity*, as rational intentionality in thrust toward the *truth* of the world. In the project of *reason* aiming to understand itself and its world in the bearing of one upon the other, consciousness is uncompromisingly "egological", that is, I-centered and I-activated. And the I of *this* intentioning, that is, ultimately, the I of *transcendental thinking*, is irreducibly *autonomous and spontaneous*. It operates *under no compulsion*; it is accountable for the acts of "*seeing*" and *asserting* to no one and nothing but itself. It is in view of this, then, that Fink, in critical representation of Husserl's position, and Husserl himself, will speak of the sheerly *instrumental* status of language with respect to the "transcendental observer" (*der transzendentale Zuschauer*) in the rendering of phenomenological reflection (*das Phänomenologisieren*) in linguistic form.[28]

In the end, then, to return to some thoughts pursued at the beginning, the cogito retains a radicality and irreducibility in Husserl's phenomenology—which is no news to anyone—but it does it as well even in the face of the need for language on the part of the I who thinks, even in the face of the need to be in the world. The I is an "*ingénérable*". Once active, it will seem always to have been. Far from owing origin to anything else, it will itself be the agency of activation that gives life and significance to whole dimensions of human consciousness, in the present case, to language as meaningful discourse in the pursuit of rational knowledge. The I of the long reflective enterprise of Husserl's phenomenology will not give up its transcendental aims, will not consign itself to silence, and will not go away.

17. The Poetic Function in Phenomenological Discourse

DAVID LEVIN

Introduction

Consider the following observations, collected from well-known works by Maurice Merleau-Ponty and Martin Heidegger:

"[E]very perception is a communication or a communion, . . . the complete expression outside ourselves of our perceptual powers and a coition, so to speak, of our body with things." (*Phenomenology of Perception*)[1]

"[I]n a sense, to understand a phrase is nothing else than to fully welcome it in its sonorous being." ("The Interwining—The Chiasm")[2]

"All flesh . . . radiates beyond itself." ("Eye and Mind")[3]

With regard to our experience of space, "is it not of its essence to embrace every being that one can imagine?" (*Phenomenology of Perception*)[4]

"[T]he mouth is not merely a kind of organ of the body understood as an organism—body and mouth are part of the earth's flow and growth in which we mortals flourish, and from which we receive the soundness of our roots." ("The Nature of Language")[5]

Perception is "a gathering which clears and shelters." ("The Anaximander Fragment")[6]

"The genuine greeting offers to the one greeted the harmony of his own being." ("Andenken")[7]

If these are, as I very strongly believe, not only genuine examples of phenomenological discourse but also examples of the kind of clarity, rigor, and accuracy we may find in the *best* of such discourse, then it seems to me that we need to give further thought to the orthodox claims that phenomenology is a purely descriptive science. For these eight textual fragments, as well as others we shall consider later, seem to be *neither* merely descriptive, in some straightforward sense of that term, *nor* so transparently true that their truth can stand without some attempt to interpret their experiential evidence and dynamics. And, what is more, although we may find it disconcerting, we must admit that these formulations say what they have to say with as much clarity and precision as we might wish. They mean what they say and say what they mean.

Confronted with such observations in texts that presume to articulate truthful descriptions of human experience that are optimally clear and explicit, I found myself compelled to rethink the task of phenomenology not only in relation to the transcendental method and the realm it presumes to open up but also in relation to the dream of humanism, whose ideal of the human being depends upon an understanding of the nature of human experience.

In this essay, then, I will begin with a brief statement of my philosophical "faith": how I understand the transcendental calling of phenomenology and how I practice phenomenology as a powerful guardian of the dream we name, echoing an earlier renaissance, the dream of humanism. However, the main focus of this paper will be on the problem of truth and description. At the center of the problem, this focus finds a troubling question concerning the origin and function of poetic language in phenomenological discourse. In the process of articulating our response to this question, we will find ourselves deeply challenged by precisely that critique of phenomenology, a critique itself phenomenological, to which Husserl never ceased to summon us.

Humanism and Transcendental Phenomenology

In Appendix IV published with Husserl's *The Crisis of European Sciences and Transcendental Phenomenology*, there is a text with the title: "Philosophy as Mankind's Self-Reflection: The Self-Realization of Reason." It is in this text that Husserl proclaims the underlying entelechy of phenomenology, vigilant guardian of philosophical humanism. Phenomenology, at once method and source of self-understanding, holds the power, he says to make us "blessed."[8] The humanism in phenomenology, then, consists in the capacity of this method, as a method of self-awareness and self-understanding, to contribute not only to our satisfaction but to guide us toward a well-being that really fulfills our human nature.

When Goethe declared that "the highest joy of man should be the growth of personality," he meant by that a growth in which the individual personality blossoms, but blossoms and flourishes in *response to* the deepest inborn needs of human nature—needs each personality *shares* with all others and which can reach fulfillment only in consonance with the natural unfolding of each and every being.

Phenomenology puts itself in the service of humanism *whenever* its articulation of human experience is aimed at a self-awareness and self-understanding that respond to the inborn needs of human nature and challenge us to deepen our awareness and develop our ownmost potential for being. Considered experientially, this potential lies in, and indeed essentially constitutes, the very *depth* of experience. But the true nature of our experience is that this depth is our openness. Openness *is* our nature, our potential for being. Thus, *humanism requires a phenomenology of depth*, a phenomenology capable of being true to our essential nature and serving us by deepening and opening up our experience of being. If now we introduce the method and realm of the transcendental in terms of a phenomenology of experiential depth (depth phenomenology, for short), then we will begin to appreciate why, and in what sense, humanism must insist on a *transcendental* phenomenology.

But what does this mean? To begin with, it is at least clear that the sense of "transcendental" in question here depends on how we are to understand the notion of *experiential depth.* Although I agree with Husserl that humanism requires a transcendental phenomenology, I differ from him in my understanding of what it is that humanism thereby requires. Consequently, I also differ from him with regard to the nature of the transcendental realm and the method of access. For me, phenomenology is *transcendental* insofar as it cherishes the process of deepening and opening and nurtures with methododological guidance a continuing movement of *self-transcendence.* Putting this point another way, I want to urge that it is by the evidence of deep transformations in our experience *and by this alone* that we should judge whether or not a phenomenological practice is a transcendental reflection or has become what Merleau-Ponty calls "a radical reflection."

It is possible to recognize with Husserl that the transcendental method gives access to a hidden or deep realm of experience that functions according to inwrought principles of its own order without being obliged, in effect, to reify this realm as an object of thought (*eidos*) and conceive it in the form of a transcendental Ego. I want to suggest that the idea of the transcendental Ego is basically the idea of the human being in its inexhaustible depth and ultimately ungraspable otherness and that it is the "source" of our being only in the sense of bearing the richness we are and the reserve of our becoming. Perhaps, then, we can characterize the transcendental much more simply and radically albeit still in relation to knowledge, as the inexhaustible depth and openness of the implicit treasury of human experience. The transcendental thereby becomes an existential challenge, a project, an infinite task, because self-knowledge (or self-understanding) can never coincide with the sheer openness of meaningful existing. Transcendental method serves to remind us that the human being is rooted in, and emerges from, an inexhaustible, ungraspable, perhaps unfathomable source of being, hidden from us in the depths of our own irreducible otherness. "Transcendental Ego" is just a name for a never-ending method of reflection and for its access to a being that ultimately eludes it. We must not let this name mislead us. As Merleau-Ponty points out, we must construe the transcendental method to be not a means of establishing "an autonomous transcendental subjectivity," but rather a gesture that initiates for us, "the perpetual beginning of reflection, at the point where the individual life begins to reflect on itself."[9]

From this standpoint, "A philosophy becomes transcendental, or radical, not by taking its place in absolute consciousness without mentioning the ways by which this is reached, but by considering itself as a problem."[10] We may be tempted to think that Husserl could easily accept this. But we need to listen to Merleau-Ponty with care, so we can hear his way, in the Preface to his *Phenomenology*, of radicalizing the Husserlian "problematic": "The phenomenological world is not the bringing to explicit expression of a pre-existing being, but the laying down of being. Philosophy is not the reflection of a pre-existing truth, but, like art, the act of bringing truth into being."[11]

Now, it is my contention that the questioning of method Merleau-Ponty initiates in these passages will ultimately require us to *abandon* the Husserlian vision of a "rigorous phenomenological science"—and also, of course, his paradigm of a "pure description." Is this vision, this paradigm, the residue, perhaps, of an older kind of rationalism, an intellectualism, as it were, which settled, unnoticed, into a principle more in keeping with logical positivism than with a phenomenology true to the vital and creative dimension of experience? Because Merleau-Ponty's articulations of experience clearly *achieved* a "poetic" effect, an effect he undoubtedly cherished and sought, though it often must have emerged spontaneously, it is extremely unfortunate that he was not stirred to consider the possibility that there *might* be an intrinsic or essential relationship between, on the one side, the poetic ambiguity, the sensuous reasonance, the play of meaning, which is so strikingly characteristic of the experiential approach to phenomenological articulation that we find in both Heidegger and Merleau-Ponty, and on the other side, the question concerning the method of description, or the conception of description, which strongly shapes—and in certain respects distorts—the orthodox phenomenological approach to experience.

To be sure, even the orthodox Husserlian paradigm of simple phenomenological description will help us to focus on our experience and bring it into expression. We may fruitfully adhere to it for purposes of a surface phenomenology, a phenomenology of the everyday experiential surface, the so-called natural attitude. But how does description relate to the depth and openness of experience? How does it relate to a potential for further change and growth? How does it take account of the dynamic movement involved in the process of reflecting and languaging? How does it recognize the dialectical relationship between experience and its reflection, experience and its expression? If a phenomenological description is insightful, it will arise from a process of opening, a process *experienced* as an opening; and it will generate experiential shifts, accompanied by newly emergent meanings.[12]

It will become apparent if we thoughtfully experience what we are doing when we attempt to describe human experience, that the most powerful, most insightful descriptions of phenomenology never truly *fit* "the experience": there is always a resonance, an ambiguity, a free elusiveness in the descriptive meaning. The description seems to straddle the experience, like a cowboy riding a wild horse. This "play" is actually essential, because experience is not an already predetermined "thing in itself". The (felt) sense of the description invariably undergoes spontaneous, involuntary shifts, taking hold only in a rich dissemination.

Beyond, or beneath, the reflective surface of everyday experience, we can contact another dimension of our being: experience in its wild vitality and unbounded depth. (In feeling we find ourselves in touch with much more of our being than we can know in a cognitive way. This is *Vor-Verständnis*.) And in this depth, this openness, there takes shape our potential for being. Humanism reminds us of this vital potential. Our potential, that is, for being ourselves; our capacity for being *true* to ourselves. Humanism, as I understand it, also reminds us that the human being (*Da-sein*) is essentially an ecstatic process of opening, opening out from a center. So phenomenological description in the service of humanism must not only *acknowledge* this openness; it must also *stay* with it in truthful harmony because openness to being is (and can be intensely experienced as) the center, or heart, of our essential nature. And this means that phenomenological description must (resonantly) express and facilitate this process, deepening, enriching, enlivening, and opening up our experience of being. Description that does not challenge and inspire us to *continue* the natural process of meaningful growth cannot be true. If there be any truth, then, in the transcendental method, it must be that the transcendental is not just a method for understanding the facticity of experience but that it is also a way of enjoying, or appreciating, the intrinsically creative and open nature of experience, because appreciation of this nature is a necessary condition for true and authentic existential knowledge.

Language and Existential Authenticity

If our phenomenology is to be true at all, it must be true to our *potential*, our *depth*; it must penetrate beneath the surface of familiar, habitually organized, and standardized experience. Now, a transcendentally deep phenomenology, which will be addressed to our ownmost potential for deepening and heightening and opening up the meaningfulness of human existence, is a phenomenology that affirms existential *authenticity*, and guides each one of us into the process of becoming a being capable of being (true to) one-self. Crucial, then, is the *way* in which phenomenology articulates, or brings to language, the treasures of human experience. Under what conditions, then, is language transcendentally appropriate? Well, what is a transcendental "employment" of language? When is it functioning transcendentally, in contrast with its standard "mundane" functioning—the functioning, that is, of the "natural attitude"?

Because the task of phenomenology necessarily involves the languaging of our experience, it is crucial that we work with a conception of the languaging process that understands and appreciates the nature of experience (especially its inherent changingness and the *need* for this changingness to be cultivated), and which therefore commits us to a way of languaging that really *encourages* existential authenticity. That is to say, in order to be true at all, our way of languaging *must* be true to our (transcendental) potential for being. It must have a transcendental and no longer a mundane relationship to our experience. If existential authenticity is—and involves respect for—our potential, then being true to experience *requires* that the languaging actively encourage the *movement* toward authenticity. Furthermore, it is important that we *experience* the languaging of our experience *as making room* for authentic change and growth. Both Heidegger and Merleau-Ponty understand the subtleties that constitute the inner relationship between our languaging and our experiencing.

In *The Visible and the Invisible*, for example, Merleau-Ponty asserts that, "language is not only the depository of fixed and acquired significations."[13] Indeed, "the words most charged with philosophy are not necessarily those that *contain* what they say, but rather those that most energetically *open* upon Being."[14] Languaging that is true to experience and therefore also true to our deepest experience of languaging itself is languaging that touches and opens up the transformative process. Authentic languaging is always challenging; and it attempts to facilitate authentic existential transformation. It functions, then, in a way that Merleau-Ponty would characterize as an "initiating gesture".[15] When authentic, that is, when true to its own nature, "speech is [always] an originating realm," a movement within experience "which brings it into existence, in the first place for ourselves, and then for others."[16] Authentic languaging is thus altogether different from "secondary speech," the speech "which renders a thought already acquired."[17]

Authentic languaging—language functioning, you might say, transcendentally—gets *involved* in the potential for growth implicit in our reflection-upon experience. It not only *contributes* to the unfolding of experience in a dynamic of self-fulfillment, but it also *responds* to those changes, thereby making way for a further explicitation, a further unfolding and enrichment. And it is *this*, I submit, that chiefly distinguishes mundane from transcendental language. Their difference is therefore not so much a question of their different contents of meaning (different *Sinne*), as it is a question of *their way of relating* to the experiential process; i.e., their *Weise* (way). The transcendental reduction does *not* change the *meaning* of our words in any ordinary sense, or way; rather, it changes *how our words relate to our experience.* (Here I find myself at odds with more orthodox phenomenologists like Mohanty and Bruzina.)

When we understand the intrinsic creativity of the languaging process, the process of expression and articulation, we realize that authentic languaging remains true to the potential in experience for authentic existence only because it stays in touch with the experiencing from which it emerged and because it has the power to carry our experiencing forward.[18]

It must not be supposed, however, that the languaging of experience to which the humanism of a depth phenomenology is committed can be exclusively, or even primarily, concerned with the cognitive content—the "thought," I mean. The *way* in which experience is languaged—and this includes such things as intonation, resonance, warmth, and vitality—is at least as important as the *content of thought* in facilitating the transformative opening of experience. "I begin to understand a philosophy by feeling my way into its existential manner, by reproducing the tone and accent of the philosopher. In fact, every language conveys its own teaching and carries its meaning into the listener's mind."[19] Just consider, for a moment, whether a philosopher whose tone is experienced as cold, unfeeling, and dogmatic could possibly teach the truth of a life dedicated to compassionate service. Also consider whether the thinker could accurately convey experiences of great beauty, experiences felt with great joy, in the affectless tone of current professional journals.

Concluding this all too brief discussion of authentic languaging, I submit that if we remain true to our deeply felt *experience* of truth as that which opens and initiates growth, we must concede that the sole criterion of phenomenological truth is to be found in the *movement* toward existential fulfillment. Thus a phenomenological articulation is true if and only if it addresses the surface actuality of our everyday experience in such a powerful truthful way that it moves us to realize, or fulfill, our deepest wholesome tendencies, opening us up to further realms of existential meaningfulness that become explicit for us on their own terms. Phenomenological truth must speak to our authentic *becoming* and not only to our everyday state of *being*. It must also penetrate beneath the factual surface of everyday experience—which remains, of course, bound to the familiar, the habitual, and the standardized—in order to touch our authentic way of being in its unfathomable transcendental depth and intrinsic creativity.

Languaging and Truth

The analysis I have attempted to make thus far points to the conclusion that we must give up the correspondence theory of truth and the conception, which goes together with this, of how languaging relates to experience. Truth does not consist in a mirrorlike correspondence, or *adequatio*, between, on the one side, the phenomenological articulation, and on the other side, a fixed, "ready-made," and objectively determinate experience. Rather, it is an experiential opening: that which fruitfully opens up the experiential process, letting it unfold according to its own inherent structural, or situational dynamic. Truth (*alētheia*) is unconcealment. Unconcealment is an opening. The opening is what sets being *free* in the space that it clears. The truth is a gathering recollection of this freedom in openness.

We must give up the notion of a "descriptive" truth that simply corresponds to the facts: externally, inertly, and without any feeling of personal communication. I suggest that we need to embrace a poetizing truth, that hermeneutically discloses and opens by touching, moving, changing, freeing us—in short, a truth that helps us to *develop* and in that way also to *preserve* our potential for being. Because the correspondence theory of truth does not do justice to the openness, depth, and changingness of experience nor to the way in which languaging, as the expression and articulation of experience, emerges from it and carries it forward, that theory of truth actually *inhibits* any gesture toward authentic experiential expression. The correspondence theory creates a vast unbridgeable chasm between experience and language, both of which it posits as massive unchanging structures.

It is, I think, significant that, in his discussion of phenomenological discourse, Merleau-Ponty speaks of "the occult trading of the metaphor," and of "transfers and exchanges." If we make explicit what this seems to imply, we find ourselves drawn into the realm of the poetic—which is where, I believe, all authentic languaging of experience moves us. For authentic languaging always involves us in a creative dynamic and a creative relationship with experience. There is a reason, indeed, why authentic, inwardly truthful languaging, sincerely issuing forth from the experience that flows into it and attaining fulfillment by its grace, will have a *full-bodied sound*, the "ring of truth." For authentic languaging issues from the *whole* of our being, which it itself has brought into a newly emergent unit and integrity and even moved to a new stage of integrated unfolding. So authentic languaging will always manifest, will always be audibly evident, in the poetic qualities of its sounding forth: because meaning is necessarily incarnate in a sensuous element that resonates with the full-bodied truth of experience, authentic languaging participates, like the words of the poet, in the occultations, dissemi-nations, and ambiguities Merleau-Ponty speaks of. Authentic phenom-enological languaging, languaging that is true to the nature of experience, cannot be other than resonant, vibrant, and dispersed in the *play* of echoes and ambiguities. The experiential meaningfulness of a word arises through its resonance, its bodily felt sense, and can be deepened when our listening really gives it the space, or silence, in which to reverberate and take hold of us. The more deeply phenomenological discourse touches our feeling, the more the meaning of that discourse resonates and echoes; and the more it resonates, or echoes, the more it eludes objective clarity and descriptive precision. Authentic lan-guaging, in fact, can be true only on condition that it opens up and somehow spans a space for change, movement, and growth. But that entails its irreducible ambiguity inasmuch as the phenomenological languaging must hover freely over that experiential space: the space *between* where one is at present and where the languaging of that present moves one. To this ambiguity, then, there corresponds an auditory space, wherein the poetizing word of phenomenological dis-course can echo and reverberate.

The Poetic Function in Phenomenological Discourse

Metaphor and Description

The claim I have attempted to establish in the preceding section is that phenomenological description must resonate with poetic freedom and even partake of ambiguity in order to remain true to the character of experience. For the truth itself, from an experiential standpoint, is irremediably ambiguous and resonant with many tenses, voices and moods. In the realm of experience, all description becomes, in an important sense, metaphorical.

What is metaphor? Etymology tells us that the metaphor carries, transfers, transports: the metaphor is essentially *ek-static.* (The allusion to the experience of being ecstatically transported is intended.) In the context of an experiential phenomenology of existence, this means that the metaphor is the catalyst in a process of existential transformation. On this account the metaphor functions as pivot, always speaking ambiguously: that is to say, simultaneously addressing us in regard for *our present state of being*, or state of awareness, yet also addressing us in a sensitive, feeling way that not only initiates experiential change but even leaps ahead of us so that it can also speak meaningfully to us at the point where the metaphor is taking us.

The phenomenologies of Heidegger and Merleau-Ponty offer an astonishing abundance of metaphors. Many phenomenologists do not seem to know what to do with them. Can we really *work* with metaphors in a serious way? Can we let them play with our awareness? Can we let their creative play with us deepen and expand the meaningfulness of our experience? There is, I think, a way of thinking with metaphors— a way that can make a significant difference. Phenomenology needs to make a place for the metaphorical nature of experiential language.

The problem of description has for me this import: that I want to know how I can articulate experience in a way that recognises the depth and changingness of experience and remains true to its unrealised potential for continuous meaningful development. You might say, to state the matter succinctly, that I want to know how to describe experience truthfully.

Truthful discourse must open and disclose; but it must protect and preserve our potential for being; must restore experience to its bodily felt wholeness; must also serve at the same time to *conceal* the elemental roots of our experience of being in an unfathomable existential depth that cannot be *reduced* to what can be known and fixed (fixated) in true objective descriptions without destroying our sense of life. Phenomenological discourse, as poetizing and metaphorical, is therefore necessarily hermeneutical: not only because experiential truth is bound by its contexts and determined by self-deceptions, but also because such discourse *protects* experience against every form of totalization, fixation, reduction, and objectification.

It might be pointed out here that Heidegger and Merleau-Ponty have already shown the way. I would concur. But I would also hasten to point out that their practice of working with experience will only show the way insofar as we already know how to *read* them in an experientially appropriate and responsive manner. On the basis of extensive commentarial research, it is my conviction—a conviction, mind you, that has caused me no little distress, even anguish—that readers of Heidegger and Merleau-Ponty do *not* really know how to work with their texts in an experiential manner and that with regard, in particular, to the metaphors and other poetic forms of articulation, most readers do not realize the need for taking metaphorical languaging to communicate the deepest experiential truths. When Heidegger says, for example, that language is the "house of Being" and that we are devoted "shepherds," he is addressing us in language empowered with creative, transformative energy, language intended to bestir us to think. Thinking, here, involves our willingness to open up to what is being said so that the words can touch, penetrate, and claim us. Thinking involves a process of focusing, in which we bring the words into our experiential space: a space where we allow the sound of phenomenological truth to reverberate, a space where the words can propose their meaning in a noncoercive manner, and we can respond to them deeply and freely. (When words can echo and reverberate freely, their meaning is correspondingly deepened.)

Basically, we need to listen carefully and openly, need to be open to letting the metaphors carry our experience forward where they want to (or can) take us. We need to put to one side our interpretations, preconceptions, and our readiness to explain or, indeed, do *anything* with the metaphor that would take us away from the directly felt response, the experiential response, to what the texts are offering. This experiential approach to responding is extremely difficult; it demands of us, perhaps, more than we can give. But the effort must, I believe, be made. Heidegger himself warns us repeatedly (for example, in *What Is Called Thinking?*) against interpreting his metaphors and other poetic features of his languaging as mere embellishments of style and rhetoric. "It would mean," he says, in "The Nature of Language,"[20] "that we stayed bogged down in metaphysics if we were to take the name Hölderlin gives here to 'words, like flowers' as being [merely] a metaphor." For he realises that it is all too easy to use Heideggerian language correctly and thereby deceive ourselves into thinking that we understand when in fact there is no authentic apprehension of the *experience* to which the words point and of which they were originally (i.e., for Heidegger himself) an authentic expression and flowering of his experience.

To read Heidegger—and Merleau-Ponty too, for that matter—in an authentic and therefore experiential way is to *accept* their metaphors as irreducible, irreplaceable, and literally truthful evocations of their experience. If we read their metaphors as stirring fictions rather than as profound truths, that simply reflects the shallowness of our own experience—and our discomfiture, our defensiveness, when confronted by a human existence fearless enough to risk madness itself in order to enter the labyrinth of meaningfulness in which our human experience is situated. Thus, when Heidegger speaks, for example, of a "flash of lightning" or when he speaks of "the heart of opening," it is *crucial* that we take him at his word. For these are the words he has thoughtfully *entrusted* with the treasure of his experience. These, and these alone, are the words that finally emerged from his own experience with thought and which moved and transported him to another experiential place. These are the only words he found to formulate his experience and communicate it to others with as much clarity and exactitude as he could muster or as the experience itself made possible. Consequently, it would be a misunderstanding to contend that the argument presented here is an attempt to substitute ambiguity, metaphor, poetry and myth for clarity and truth. Only if one adheres, for instance, to a Cartesian notion of clear and distinct ideas or believes that feeling is a confused idea, will the poetic formulation of language necessarily sound like confusion and obfuscation. So we must be extremely careful not to betray or deny what he says he has experienced simply because we feel ourselves unable to accept or understand such experience. Above all, we must be constantly alert to the possibility that we may attempt to distort or repress what the philosopher has to say because we are too frightened by its experientially demanding reverberations and feel the need to protect ourselves from them at all costs.

Responding in an existentially authentic way, that is, in a personally self-developing and self-fulfilling way, involves, of course, much more than taking the metaphors to heart. For those of us who, as scholars, are accustomed to thinking in a way that is detached from experience and especially from feeling, such responding involves an entirely different way of reading phenomenological texts and relating to their articulations. In reading Heidegger's phenomenology, for example, I have found it helpful at certain points to ask myself: "How do I feel about this?" "Does this feel right (good)?" "What do I need to hear (next)?" "What do I want (what would I like) to hear (next)?" "Where does this move (take) me?" These questions facilitate a process of focusing that directly connects the phenomenological description (perhaps the metaphor) we are reading with our own experiential unfolding. And it does so in a way that encourages, even perhaps inspires, further unfolding. Thus, deeper and deeper experiential meanings gradually emerge and become real for us.

The Poetic Function

In *Being and Time*, Heidegger writes; "In poetical discourse, the communication of the existential possibilities of one's state-of-mind can become an aim in itself, and this amounts to a disclosing of existence.[21] I would like to let these words guide us in our thinking. I would like to allow them to echo through my own words and reverberate creatively through the channels of our experience.

If we read Heidegger and Merleau-Ponty with the carefully listening inner ear of thought, it is possible to understand how and why their way of communicating—their way, in fact, of bringing deep experience to expression in language—is poetic or has a poetic ring: by necessity, not by choice. First of all, every true philosopher will speak with his (or her) own unique voice. (We have already heard Merleau-Ponty say as much. But we should also consider, here, what Heidegger says about the importance of melody, pace, ring, and tone in the communication of thinking.)[22] According to both great thinkers, the philosopher's *way* of speaking cannot be separated from the cognitive *content*, the thought; in fact, what is being said *depends* upon the way it is said. (Cartesian rationalism has strongly influenced our sensibility in this regard.) Thus, for example, we certainly cannot articulate the need for compassion or the need for cultivating feeling and sensibility nor can we expect to communicate that need in words that are themselves bereft of warmth, kindness, and good feeling. Many philosophers do not appreciate the extent to which the truth of our teaching is rooted in feeling and needs to be made manifest in this rooting. There must be an exemplary (and thus audible) consonance between the *what* and the *how*, between the cognitive truth and how it feels. Not appreciating this, many philosophers will find it especially difficult to understand how poetizing (what Heidegger calls *Dichtung*) could be called the true vocation of the philosopher and of the experiential phenomenologist, above all.

This needs explaining. Why is poetizing, poetic speaking, necessary? Basically and most simply my answer is that phenomenologically focused and reflective articulations of experience cannot be other than poetic: first, by expressing and conveying—in short, embodying—the beautifully good (bodily) feeling that spontaneously arises with the saying of that which is true to experience; and second, by virtue of this truth (this being-in-truth), disclosing a more open space in which to open (*ek-sist*). Poetizing addresses and lays claim to our potential for being; and like a metaphor, it carries us forward. Any experiential articulation that (1) is *rooted* in a truly felt experience, (2) *emerges* from that experience in a felt movement of self-expression, and (3) *maintains its contact* with the original, spontaneous thrust of experience even in the phase of completed expression, will at least *tend* to be (tend to *sound*) poetic. In phenomenological discourse, therefore, the deepest transcendental truth of an existentially authentic languaging of experience will be articulated with the sensuous resonance, the emotional spaciousness, and the elemental openness of the poetic word. (Robert Romanyshyn argues that perception itself is metaphoric.)

It may help to bear in mind here what Heidegger has to say, in "The Nature of Language," about the importance of actually "undergoing an experience with language" and letting our experience speak for itself.[23] He also enjoins us to let ourselves be *transformed* by our participation in that process. The truthful languaging of our experience can be nothing but poetic under these circumstances because *this* is how languaging *naturally* embodies and reflects the originary, creative spirit of the experiencing we have entrusted to it. If I undergo an experience that brings me profound insight, that is, a deeply integrating personal self-knowledge, then the languaging of that experiential movement will spontaneously resonate with my feelings of pleasure, satisfaction, and fulfillment. The voicing of a phenomenological "description" will naturally ring out with the audible excitement of discovery; and it will be possible to hear the singing quality that accompanies my sense of mastery and accomplishment. The joy in creativity is something that can always be heard. This is surely part of what Heidegger means when he says that singing and thinking are neighboring branches of poetizing.

The *essence* of poetry is that it is moving. Poetic language is language with the power to touch and move us; language with the "ecstatic" power to open and transport us. When languaging is in communication with a touching and moving experience, an experience of opening and deepening, it is natural, simply natural, that it sound (and resound) with the qualities of poetic song.[24] Likewise, when that which is to be communicated is brought forth for others in a way that touches and moves them by directly appropriating their experience, it is certain that the power of the communication, the very beauty in the act of *sharing* a phenomenological articulation, is responsible for, and resides in, its poetic quality. The sound of poetry is the sound of its truthfulness, its goodness to our experience. The poetic quality is also related to the fullness, or reach, of its experiential meaning, which we hear in, and hear as, an audible resonance, the deep, *fullbodied* sound of the truth, which reverberates through experience. Speech that is true to experience *opens* up that experience, making "space" for that speech to resonate. But the resonating itself *deepens* the meaning, the felt sense, of the original speech, so that the opening may continue. The poetic quality thus corresponds to the audible joy in the opening process of self-expression, a joy that is heightened and intensified when the articulation really focuses and channels *the whole body of one's being* into a newly emergent meaning that is communicated and shared with others.

The *beauty* of experiential articulations thus manifests the *good feeling* that is involved in the trueness of the entire expressive process. The beauty especially resides, however, in the responsive, communicative, and sharing dimension, where authentic teaching will always spontaneously take place. But the good feeling is not merely in response to *beauty*; it is fundamentally a response to the experiential *opening*, which is nothing other than the taking place (*Ereignis*) of truth. "Saying sets all present beings free into their given presence."[25] The truth will set us free. That setting free is an experiential opening. (In *Being and Time*, Heidegger speaks of our *Freisein* [being free].) *Whenever* such an opening takes place, whether it be in oneself or in another, something beautiful is felt. *So the poetic quality is a function of the experiential truth.*

I would like to stress here that I have not been referring poetic beauty to the emergence of some specific kind of cognitive content. The content articulated may very well, of course, be itself a source or stimulus for "poetic" experience. But what I want to argue is that the main source of "the poetic" is not the cognitive *content* but rather the poetizing *process* as such, the process, that is, of metaphoring experience. The process itself is a poetic one, for the creative movement of carrying a meaning forward and completing its melodic phase in the formation of a new integrity, a newly emergent personal whole, is the most fundamental determinant of poetizing. When phenomenology poetizes, it remains true to the experiential *process* while reflecting and bringing it to articulation; and it remains true precisely because it is *creatively and harmoniously related* to that process, which it touches and moves with the beauty and good feeling that spontaneously arise wherever the truth is spoken. (The truth always clears a free space, a space for freedom, exploration, discovery, growth, wisdom. The truth is an opening; but, as the root of the word for truth (*das Wahre*) reminds us, the truth is also a protecting and preserving. Poetizing discourse is true to the needs of experience; it opens precisely *in order to* protect and preserve our deepest, ownmost potential for being.)

Having made this point, however, I do wish to concede that the poetic quality is also, at least in the work of both Heidegger and Merleau-Ponty, a function, in part, of the emergent *content*. In Heidegger's case, for example, the emergent content concerns the manifesting of an experiential relationship to the Being of beings. As Heidegger says, in "The Anaximander Fragment", "Thinking of Being is the original way of poetizing . . . Thinking is primordial poetry, prior to all poesy . . . The poetizing essence of thinking preserves the sway of the truth of Being."[26] And the intensity, strangeness, and beauty of Heidegger's languaging originate, at least in part, in the ecstatic openness of this relationship. In the case of Merleau-Ponty, the emergent content is, in essence, the realm that he variously characterizes as the prepersonal, the anonymous, the primordial: the stratum of holistic experience that underlies the polarized duality of subject and object; the stratum of intensely erotic, or libidinal, energy, that Freud would call the locus of primary process experience. Thus, it becomes quite understandable why the languaging of a newly emergent content in Merleau-Ponty's phenomenology should bear with it the sound and the sense of the poetic. For it cannot be denied that languaging that "recovers" for reflection this dimension of experience is perforce dipping into the very source of poetry—the holistic continuum of existential feeling. What Heidegger calls "the original speech of language"[27] is language that, in the poetizing work of Merleau-Ponty, has taken up into itself the integrative power of libidinal feeling and the integrative power in feeling of the erotic *dream*, the reverie of being human. Merleau-Ponty understands this well when he says that "speech or gesture transforms the body."[28]

The Making of Truth

Throughout this discussion, I have implicitly relied upon a distinction that I must now make explicit: the distinction, I mean, between *being true to* and *being true of*. If we return to the question that originally motivated our thinking, namely, the fact that many of the phenomenological descriptions that Heidegger and Merleau-Ponty offer us seem not to be *true of* our everyday experience as we live it "in the natural attitude," we are finally in a position to shed some light on the paradox, or problem.

It is not at all accidental that the articulations that seem to be farthest from being obviously true (prima facie true) of our everyday (surface) experience are precisely the articulations with the most poetic ring. Indeed, our discussion suggests that this is exactly what we should expect. I would like to suggest that poetizing articulations in phenomenological discourse not only may be, but must be untrue, that is, not *true of* our "surface" experience; and that their untruth in this respect is correlative with their being *true to* the depths of our moving experience. It is, I believe, precisely because such articulations *are* true to these depths, that is, offer transcendental descriptions that are both *true of* these depths and *true to* their a priori potential, that they have the full-bodied ring of poetizing truth. For articulations true to these depths issue *from* those very depths; and it is the depth of experience that always sounds forth in poetizing. Poetizing formulations resonate by *echoing* the depths from which they come and to which, moreover, they give the fulfillment of expression.

Our interpretation of the poetic function in phenomenological discourse invites us to appreciate that, and also how, a poetizing of experience is intended to possess the power, almost magical, to *let happen* and *make true* what it describes by touching us in a *prereflective* manner (i.e., by eliciting our *felt sense*, a *Vor-Verständnis*, of what it lies within us to become), opening up our essential capacities and our preunderstanding of them and really moving or transporting us. Articulations that are not true of our experience *become* true by moving us to change in ways that *make* them true. *And they possess this power because of the fact that they were all along true to the ownmost nature of our being—a nature with which we are primordially endowed.* (*Mythos*, as that which can "make appear," therefore has according to Heidegger not only phenomenological truth but also for that very reason a tremendous therapeutic power.)[29]

When a phenomenologist poetizes, that is, when he describes human experience with high regard for its deepest inborn potential, the description is certainly functioning *descriptively*, from a transcendental point of view. But what about its relationship to the *surface* of experience that is characteristic of human life in the natural attitude? We have already determined that the articulation fails to be true, fails to describe. I submit that the transcendentally true descriptions of poetizing phenomenology also function *normatively*, or *prescriptively*. And they function this way precisely in relation to the surface. First of all, as we have noted, phenomenological poetizing touches and moves us: it brings about meaningful experiential changes if we "let ourselves be *told* what is worthy of thinking" by listening closely to the *singing* of our own experience.[30]

Depth phenomenology cannot, in fact, avoid the truthfulness of a poetizing reflection; nor, therefore, can it avoid entrusting transcendental descriptions to what I am calling "the poetic function." But because poetizing is true to our innermost being and because this innermost being is in need of recognition, development, deepening, and opening, deeply true phenomenological description will inevitably function in a *prescriptive* manner. Describing the transcendental depths of our being is also at the very same time to embrace and espouse the realization and unfolding of this potential for being. By describing in a poetically touching and moving way what our experience primordially *is* and therefore *could become*, we are *inspired* to undergo the transformations that would fulfill our nature and bring to us and our world an expanding horizon of perhaps unfathomable meaningfulness.

Let us consider the prescriptive character of poetizing more closely. We already have some sense of how poetizing affects us—how it produces transformations. Can we clarify this process any further? In answer I would like to suggest that the poetizing descriptions of transcendental, or depth, phenomenology serve as visualizations, imaginative projections. That is to say, they simultaneously describe our as yet unrealized deep potential for being and also make it possible for us to imagine and deeply feel that potential in its more developed stage, or phase. But, by helping us to put ourselves into that experience through the power of the imagination, poetizing actually brings us nearer to that way of being. Nearer in two respects: first, because we are *already living in* that experience for as long as the poetizing enthralls our imagination; and second, because the schematism moves us *deeper* into that open transcendental realm of experience. The point is that we need a *sense* of the goal, a *feeling* for it, in order to know how to move closer. The poetizing descriptions of depth phenomenology *prescribe*, schematize for us, the goal to be attained. They belong to the conversation of culture.

Is this prescriptive process coercive? I think not. The truth is often demanding and hard to accept; but it can never be coercive. The poetizing is simply prescribing the fulfillment of tendencies it has contacted and recognized as *already* manifest, *already* operative in our experience. The description can have prescriptive force *only* if the fulfillment of its truth is already implicit in the experience being described. Consequently, *if* any transformation may be said to come about, we can be sure that it does so only *by virtue* of the successful *appeal* of the image. Without that appeal, the image would simply present itself in its otherness as a description of a profoundly different awareness, a profoundly different way of being. The prescriptive power exists *only* for the one who *recognizes* himself (or herself) in the poetic, metaphoric image and feels the attraction of that image as an existential project. Does this analysis dangerously subjectivize the truth? I do not think so. Each person can, and should, test and confirm for himself (or herself) whether or not a significant shift, an important experiential transformation, has taken place.

My last thought, then, is that the noble task of phenomenology is no less a work of hermeneutic art than it is a positive science of description. What else could phenomenology be, when it is devoted to realising, through the suffering in its absence, the vision, and the conversation, of a renewed humanism?

18. The Destiny of Transcendental Philosophy

J. N. MOHANTY

I

1. Transcendental philosophies are not all of the same sort. They share a common philosophical motif in so far as they are "transcendental," but otherwise they differ a great deal among themselves as much as idealisms or empiricisms do. This common motif is the search for a *foundation* for knowledge, thinking, and experience. But not every foundationalism is transcendental philosophy. For example, many of the logical empiricists who held the view that the edifice of knowledge rests on basic, protocol sentences are far from being transcendental philosophers. It would seem then that only certain kinds of foundational thinking are transcendental. Foundationalism as such, then, cannot constitute transcendental thinking. Perhaps we should say that the foundation sought after by the transcendental philosophies should be priori. A formalistic philosophy that first sets up an a priori uninterpreted system and then assigns to it an interpretation comprehensive enough to include large features of experience, would still not be transcendental, for such an uninterpreted system would not be a *foundation*; it would rather be a formal-conceptual framework that illuminates, at most, certain formal structures of the world. But one may also seek to provide an a priori *metaphysical* foundation for experience, in which case we also would not have a transcendental philosophy. If we exclude formal and metaphysical attempts at providing experience with a foundation, we have to say that in the long run a transcendental philosophy looks for the foundation in the a priori structures of the experiencing *subject*, leaving aside for the present how precisely this subject is to be understood.

2. Transcendental philosophies differ among other things, regarding:

(i) what it is for which they claim to be providing a foundation;
(ii) the nature of the foundational principle, in this case, the *structure of subjectivity*; and
(iii) the *access* to the transcendental, foundational principle.

2.1 With regard to (i), I want to distinguish between two kinds of transcendental philosophies: those that set out from a body of scientific *knowledge* (or at least cognitive claims) and seek to lay bare the a priori conditions pertaining to the structure of the knowing subject, which make such knowledge possible; and those that do not restrict the explanandum, the "fact" to be accounted for, to a body of truths, to a system of knowledge, but would rather set out from the meanings and structures of meanings that characterize the way we experience (and, in addition, also *know*) the world and ourselves and ask how such meanings are possible. The contrast is between the conditions of the possibility of *truths* (of a certain sort) about the world and the conditions of the possibility of meanings, or, what amounts to the same, of modes of interpretation. The first is the Kantian, the second the phenomenological enterprise. Because the concept of meaning is prior to and presupposed by the concept of truth, the second sort of enterprise is more fundamental than the first. Also, because it is free from the commitment to a certain historically accomplished body of *knowledge* (such as Newtonian physics or Euclidean geometry, in Kant's case) as having a privileged status, it is also free from a naivety that vitiates the first, that is, the Kantian transcendental philosophy.

2.2 With regard to (ii), likewise, there is a fundamental distinction to be made. Because the concern with justifying a body of knowledge requires *critical* standards, the Kantian transcendental philosophy becomes critical philosophy; it appeals to a set of *principles*; its concern with subjectivity is only to the extent this transcendental subjectivity is the source of the principle that constitutes scientific knowledge (and correlatively, the world of science). This is what some neo-Kantians have called *prinzipien-theoretisch* transcendental philosophy. The best I can do is to quote from Cassirer: "The essential content of the Kantian doctrine does not consist in the ego, nor its relation to the external object, but that to which it relates in the first place, i.e. the legality and the logical structure of experience." The concrete 'I' is the subject as much of true knowledge as of error. But if we are looking for the subject of true knowledge, then we have to stop with the normative autonomy of logical principles.

It is different however with a philosophy that wants to throw light on the constitution of our meanings, concepts, and modes of interpretation or even on the constitution of the world insofar as a world is structure of meanings. The subjectivity that is to provide the foundation for meanings, that is, in which meanings are to find their origin, has to be a concrete, temporal, and historically developing life. Such a transcendental philosophy sets out to evaluate cognitive claims by a set of principles but to describe the nature and origin of those claims by tracing them back to their origin in appropriate modes of intentionality.

If the logical-critical principles are discovered by a method of reasoning known as, and in contemporary literature much discussed under the heading of, transcendental *arguments*, the concrete subjectivity of a phenomenological transcendental philosophy uses a method of reflection to lay bare the founding stratum. Thus the modes of *access*, in the two cases, to the foundation they look for are different. In the one case, it is by a transcendental *argument*, in the other by an appropriate *reflection*. The reflective procedure claims not to argue (from the alleged fact to the conditions of its possibility) but to bring to intuitive evidence the constituting intentional experience. The phenomenological transcendental philosophy may then be called, as contrasted with the Kantian or *prinzipien-theoretisch*, *evidenz-theoretisch* transcendental philosophy.

3. Now briefly to weigh their relative merits and weaknesses. Because one wants, in philosophy, not merely to appeal to evidence but also to give reasons, which amounts to giving good arguments, for one's position, the neo-Kantian transcendental philosophy conforms to this expectation. Phenomenology's claim to render the foundational stratum of subjectivity *evident* has always aroused the suspicion of evading that requirement of a good argument and a sound reason. In fact, however, the matter is more complicated than that. In the first place, for phenomenology the ultimate rationality lies in intuitive insight and not in the logical concatenation of propositions constituting a proof. The reason for this is not far to seek. It is not that the proof is deficient qua proof. It lacks not logical rigor but philosophical radicalness. It *assumes* the validity of logical principles, which a transcendental philosophy cannot presuppose without relapsing into just the naivety it wants to avoid; a transcendental philosophy based only on formal-logical reasoning (of the sort "p only if q") cannot be "*transcendental*" in the strictest sense; just as, it would seem, one based on intuitive evidence alone would be transcendental but not, as such, good *philosophy*. I think a major problem for phenomenology, as a transcendental philosophy, is how to combine the appeal to evidence with criticism. But the criticism a strictly transcendental philosophy would need to make room for will not be in the interest of *justifying* any existing body of knowledge but will *examine* the claims of conceptual frame-

works to be the transcendental foundation. Here Husserlian phenomenology has to learn from the Hegelian.

4. Transcendental philosophy has undergone another change as a consequence of the foregoing, a change that was already foreshadowed in the Kantian philosophy. The search for a foundation has often been, in the philosophical tradition, a search for an *apodictic* basis. The paradigmatic example of such a foundation is the Cartesian cogito. It has to satisfy two requirements. In the first place, it has itself to be an item of knowledge, generally construed as a proposition. Added to this, it has to be apodictically true in some familiar sense of *apodicticity*. Now, it goes without saying that such a transcendental thinking tries to emulate the model of mathematics. The change, I suggest, that Kant foreshadowed consisted in a rejection of this mathematical model and in introducing a new concept of necessity that is to be sharply distinguished from the formal-logical necessity. The fact that formal logic was to be founded in transcendental logic made it impossible to extend the modal concepts belonging to the former to the latter. Transcendental necessity, if we can call the new modal concept by that name, refers back to the *a priori* structure of subjectivity as it happens to be *in fact*, not as it must be by logical necessity. We have here a sort of contingent necessity. I am aware of the paradoxical nature of this expression, as also of the fact that the notion of contingency itself may look like a formal-logical concept. The important thing to note is that we are led back in Kantian transcendental philosophy to the ultimacy of a *fact*, the structure of subjectivity as it happens to be.

4.1 What I am proposing, then, is this. Once we do not want from transcendental philosophy that it provide an apodictic foundation for a given body of scientific knowledge but would rather have it return to that concrete, temporal, and historical life of subjectivity in which all our meanings, theories, and conceptual frameworks have their origin, a different sort of transcendental philosophy emerges. It is such a phenomenological transcendental philosophy and its concept of transcendental subjectivity that I want to defend in the rest of this paper against some recent criticisms.

II

5.1 There is one sort of criticism that I will not consider in this paper. This criticism, which in various forms and with differences in emphasis is to be found dispersed in the writings of Martin Heidegger, Michel Foucault and Jacques Derrida amongst others, appeals to a certain reading of history, especially of history of ideas, in order to argue that the age that made a certain type of philosophy (in this case, transcendental philosophy) possible is now past, making it now impossible to return to that kind of philosophy. This historical critique, *persuasive* though it may be, derives its main philosophical weakness from the fact that it is based on a highly selective reading of history, a selective concatenation of facts, which is only one amongst many other possible readings and whose validity is assumed rather than established.

5.2 Another line of criticism, with which we all are familiar, takes transcendental philosophy to task for according primacy to consciousness, the inner and the subjective, on the ground that this implies metaphysical idealism. Heideggereans have wanted to impress upon us that consciousness is representational, and that a philosophy founded upon primacy of consciousness cannot recover the original access to being. It is only a philosophy that accords primacy to *Dasein* understood as being-in-the-world, that can undercut the very possibility of the realism-idealism issue. However, the fact of the matter is not as simple as that. Even so acute a Heidegger scholar as Hans-Georg Gadamer recognizes—in fact, he is the only Heidegger scholar, to my knowledge, to have been able to see this—that in this regard Husserlian phenomenology is as much beyond the realism-idealism dispute as is Heideggerean fundamental ontology. If consciousness is intentional and so is a directedness towards the world, it does not have an inner where things *could* have their habitation. Intentionality is not representational.

6. Challenges to transcendental philosophy are challenges to the concept of consciousness as *transparent* as well as to the concept of reflection as capable of achieving coincidence with the reflected upon. Ultimately, both these alleged assumptions on the part of the transcendental philosopher are traced back by the critic to a *metaphysical* understanding of being as presence, as object and then as subjectivity. Consciousness is not only that to which the world is presented as an object; it is also present to itself. Today it hardly needs to be argued that man's original relationship to the world is not that of a subject to its object, and that in the very heart of consciousness there is an opacity that reflection cannot dissolve by its luminousness. Heidegger does not merely replace the primacy of consciousness as presentational by the primacy of care as prospective, for if he had merely done that his thinking would still have been transcendental *in structure* (as it was in *Sein und Zeit.*). He goes beyond this by advancing what Gadamer calls the principle of "the interinvolvement of disclosure and concealment." According to this principle, every presencing is necessarily an absencing and every manifestation is a concealment. Such a principle, if universally valid, renders all *Letztbegründung*, all alleged insight into

the ultimate foundation, impossible. Heidegger's real overcoming of Husserl, then, lies—as Gadamer has correctly pointed out—not in overcoming idealism for the sake of a realistic ontology, not in undercutting the very realism-idealism controversy, not even in overcoming the alleged universality of objectifying acts (for Husserl himself had been able to do so in his discovery of horizon intentionalities), but in rejecting the very possibility of a laying bare that is not also a concealing. This, then, is the final death blow to all attempts at a *Letztbegründung*. Note that it is not an issue about rationalism versus irrationalism. It is not as though experience and knowledge have to be founded on an irrational basis rather than on rational principles. Even the irrationalist claims ultimate, if not rational, insight into the foundation. The more radical critique denies *all* such insight, and so renders the idea of ultimate foundation vacuous and pointless.

6.1 Against this powerful critique, I will pose the following questions. First of all, I want to challenge the legitimacy of the principle of intervolvement. Is it an empirical generalization? Is it an *a priori*, eidetic truth discovered by phenomenological reflection? Or is it an analytic truth based on conceptual analysis? I do not think that any of these alternatives are acceptable to the Heideggerean. If he tends to fall back on exegesis of classical texts, I will question if that is a legitimation of an ultimate principle. If he appeals to the more homely phenomenological findings such as the perspectival character of all perception; the impossibility of adequate givenness; the temporality of consciousness that does not permit reflection to coincide with the reflected upon; the situatedness and finiteness of man that does not permit him omniscience; the roles that the Freudian libido, the class interest and ideology of Marx, or bad faith play in the life of consciousness, then we find ourselves facing more manageable problems— problems that transcendental philosophy of the sort I am espousing is, I believe, capable of taking care of.

7. For the purposes of this presentation, let me confine myself to the three recalcitrant phenomena: language, body, and history. Each of these presents a challenge to transcendental thinking, each resists the gaze of reflection and announces itself as an autonomous other. In each case, however, I would want to argue, consciousness can proclaim itself to be the source of this otherness just because each of these phenomena, taken as an other, is constituted in an inmost feature of what I call transcendental subjectivity.

7.1 We begin with language. If language is not merely an instrument of communication but shapes our thoughts and our world and embodies through its lexical as well as syntactical features sedimented interpretations of the community, can we say that inasmuch as the philosopher uses it he can ever be certain of that ideal of presuppositionlessness that transcendental philosophising requires of him? Can transcendental subjectivity be nonlinguistic? If not, how can it help being contaminated by the hidden presuppositions, cultural as well as metaphysical, of any given language?

These are large issues, and it is indeed awfully difficult to see what the stakes are. I will only make a rough and preliminary statement of my position. I want to say that consciousness is both linguistic and nonlinguistic. Language may be looked upon either as the linguistic system (*la langue*) or as speech (*la parole*). As the former, it is an objective system of lexical elements built out of an inventory of phonemes and syntactical and semantical rules. Such a system may be perceived diachronically or synchronically. At any given time, we are presented with a logical system with an ideal being of its own; at the same time, it is undeniable that the system had a genesis, a course of development, a history. In so far as *this* is concerned, we have taken care of it in the context of our discussion of historicity in general. What I say of language would equally well be true of cultures in general: the objective structures are, in the long run, constituted in subjective acts. This thesis, I am aware, runs contrary to a predominant philosophy in continental Europe today. The structuralists have insisted on the priority of objective structures, so that in speaking, for example, I follow rules that I find, rather than generate. To this my response is: in any historical epoch, when I speak, I take up language (lexical and formal) already constituted, which is true of any historical acquisition. But that which I inherit *was* constituted by acts of speaking. It is not the hypothetical first beginning of a language that we are after. It is rather the fact that what are today anonymous structures, appearing to be objective, self-subsistent entities, had their genesis in acts. One could formulate the same in the form of a counterfactual: were there no speaking consciousness, there would have been no language.

In according this primacy to speech, we are in the company of Husserl and Wittgenstein. But speaking, apart from being a rule-governed behavior, is an act of consciousness; it is an intentional act. Not only is speaking an act of consciousness, it has a universality that does not belong to any other sort of act, which is borne out by the fact that all other acts are "expressible." I may even go further and say that in speech, the domain of consciousness is mapped onto itself. The speech act, in its relationship to nonlinguistic acts, constitutes a most interesting structure, not merely of empirical consciousness but also of the transcendentally purified consciousness. If consciousness is permeated by linguisticality, it also always escapes it. Consciousness of speaking, which accompanies speaking, is not linguistic (I do not say, "I am speaking").

This explains what has been called by some writers as the transcendental character of language. Language is transcendental only in so far as linguisticality permeates transcendental subjectivity. I do not think transcendental philosophy can stop with the communicative, dialogical structure, as Karl Otto Apel would have us do, for we can raise the question: how is communication possible?

7.2 The same strategy helps us to deal with body and history. Tracing back the constitution of body, we are led to a corporeal stratum within transcendental subjectivity (e.g., the kinaesthetic consciousness "I can move myself"), just as the constitution of "history" leads us back to the living present-sedimentation-inheritance-reactivation structure of the life of consciousness. It is with regard to the latter that I want to add a few remarks.

7.3 True, the philosopher is a human being, entrenched in time and history. It is also undeniable that transcendental philosophy, by its very conception, is a philosophy from a radically critical standpoint. As such, it would seem as though the possibility of such philosophizing is *a priori* denied to man. But in drawing this conclusion, one overlooks two things. In the first place, it is not the case that the whole being of human consciousness is exhausted in its being in time and in its historicity. Secondly, it is not a matter of exclusive disjunction: *either* all at once and without the least trace and risk of failure one achieves the transcendental point of view *or* one does not do so at all. Regarding the first: consciousness has both temporal and nontemporal aspects. In its nontemporal aspect, it is self-revealing; this self-revelation is not an event that has its temporal horizon. Furthermore, the meanings that consciousness confers are logical unities and retain an identity through time; one can return to them again. There is still something more to be hopeful about: if consciousness were nothing more than temporality and historicity, we could not know that very structure. We would not have been able to determine such an essential structure. A formal structure remains invariant amid the temporal and historical flow. Moreover, we not only determine these eidetic structures, we also can in reflection relive in our consciousness the essential stadia in history. Heidegger does it in his thinking of Being; Husserl does it in reactivating the essential process by which Galilean physics originated. The fact that history can be relived in its essential structure, that sedimented acquisitions can be reactivated (otherwise they would not be acquisitions) shows that consciousness always transcends its own historicity, that it is not a perpetual dissipation of itself, but always gathers itself up: in its own transparency in the logical meanings it secretes and in its ability to relive and reactivate the past.

7.4 To argue as Foucault does, that the radical discontinuities that characterize history resist the process of appropriation of history into transcendental philosophy, is to overlook that the thesis of *radical* discontinuity, if maintained consistently, would even make Foucault's own task as a surveyor of that history impossible. The concepts of continuity and discontinuity are so vague and relative that arguments founded on them, as on the alleged facts of radically different conceptual frameworks, are in the long run either trivial or analytically valid *or* just incapable of doing the job they are meant to do.

8. Underlying these responses is a certain conception of the distinction between the mundane and the transcendental that should have been obvious by now. We no more need the myth of two worlds. The transcendental *is* the mundane, only freed from that self-forgetfulness, that naivety, and that self-interpretation that constitutes mundaneity. This accounts for the fact that each of the phenomena (consciousness, body, language, and history) may be viewed either as mundane or as transcendental. I have argued that the concept of consciousness may be so formulated that it would be the most inclusive of the four and contain within itself the constitutive origins of all mundaneity.

This seeming collapse of the distinction between the empirical and the transcendental is the destiny of transcendental philosophy.

PART 6

PHENOMENOLOGY OF RELIGION

19. The Problem of God in Sartre's *Being and Nothingness*

ROBERT R. WILLIAMS

Edmund Husserl's lifelong struggle against positivism and his quest for foundations led him to the discovery of the life-world as the foundation of all human praxis, including the theoretical and scientific. His discovery that the so-called objective world of science was founded upon and presupposed the life-world led to a further unsettling question: How can the "objective" and "true" world of science be founded upon the "subjective-relative" life-world? Traditional philosophy, including Kant's transcendental philosophy, had passed over this problem and so was carried on in a naive mundane mode. Husserl was compelled to take up the question of the origin of the world as the foundational philosophical problem. Husserl demanded a systematic tracing back of all the so-called objective disciplines to their foundation in the life-world and called for an ontology of the life-world—inaugurating a new series of phenomenological and existential investigations. However, there is an ambiguity pervading this effort: What is the foundation ultimately attained through phenomenological *Rückfragen* (regressive inquiry): is it the life-world? or is it a transcendental constituting subjectivity? or neither? Further, is the philosophical result of this *Rückfragen* a corrective of the philosophical tradition from its positivistic subversion? Or is it a thorough dismantling of the tradition, more radical than positivism? Such profound ambiguities frustrate efforts at a coherent interpretation of Husserl's philosophy, and reappear in the appropriations of Husserl by his successors.

The above-noted ambiguities pervade assessments of the significance of phenomenology for religion, philosophy of religion, and theology. Does the return to the life-world imply the elimination of God along with objectifying metaphysics? Or does God and Transcendence continue in the pursuit of the question of the origin of the world? If so, in what way? The issue appears in connection with the famous *Kant-*

studien article by Eugen Fink,[1] when Fink sought to determine the meaning of the concept "constitution." Paul Ricoeur in commenting on the Fink article, interprets the question of the origin of the world in the following way: "Is the most radical subject God? Or does the question of the 'origin' scientifically elaborated by transcendental phenomenology, dissipate the natural man and problems of religion as if they were myths?[2] To identify transcendental constituting subjectivity with God takes phenomenology in the direction of absolute idealism. Not only is this a metaphysical dogmatism, it invites the existential protest that human being is more than an Idea. On the other hand, to identify transcendental subjectivity as human and to treat God as a construct or projection of human subjectivity appears to reduce theology to anthropology. Moreover, this humanism is no less metaphysically dogmatic than its idealist opponent. The dilemma gives rise to the question whether there may not be a third alternative.

When Sartre develops his interpretation of phenomenology and seeks to move from phenomenology to ontology, he appears to take the second course outlined above. Religion and theology are to be deconstructed and treated as elements in the human project. Sartre pits Husserlian intentionality—interpreted through the Hegelian concept of negativity—against Husserlian "idealism" and its doctrine of the transcendental ego. The result is an interpretation of consciousness as a pure transcendental field, which is at the same time pure transcendence of itself towards the world. Yet this pure subjectivity is identified as human subjectivity, and so Sartre "draws the consequences of a coherent atheistic position."[3] Sartre thus charges classical metaphysical theism and metaphysical idealism with a heteronomous objectification of human subjectivity and seeks to correct them both in the name of autonomy: nothing is or can be prior to transcendental consciousness or the for-itself.

However, phenomenology is not a simple elimination of the problem of God. When phenomenology takes its existential turn and investigates prereflective intentionality, Sartre finds that human being is the being whose fundamental project it is to be God. The desire for being constitutive of human being as nothingness is a desire for God. The problem of God is thus displaced from the search for a transcendent metaphysical absolute that is the origin of both human being and the world to a striving for absolute being on the part of human being. Sartre's atheism is paradoxical in that it involves a theological anthropology. Although Sartre thinks that the desire to be God is a useless passion, human being cannot be genuinely free unless this passion is first understood and mastered.

In what follows, I shall examine first Sartre's claim that the prereflective or non-thetic cogito has a preontological comprehension of the being of God. Sartre's description of consciousness as essentially religious appears to approximate theological descriptions, such as those of Friedrich Schleiermacher. However, Sartre offers an interpretation of consciousness opposite to that of Schleiermacher; and this raises a cluster of issues concerning phenomenology, the foundational status of the prereflective cogito, theology as bound up with the non-thetic cogito and the move to the ontological level. Second, I shall examine Sartre's discreditation of the prereflective cogito as an illusion, and his extension of this discreditation to its theological referent. This in turn raises questions concerning Sartre's claim that intentionality is an ontological proof.

The Prereflective Preontological Comprehension of God

Sartre appears to follow Husserl in granting a certain priority to the natural attitude, which is a pretheoretical involvement and engagement with the world. Sartre thus speaks of a nonpositional, prereflective consciousness that is completely self-transcendent and immersed in the world and bound up with mundane objects, tasks, and so forth. Such a consciousness is not self-consciousness; it is rather so completely transcendent to itself and immersed in its tasks/objects that there is no reflective gap and no reflection present in it. Hence it is nonpositional, prereflective, and thus written as consciousness (of)————. To be sure, it can be reflected on and explicated by reflection, but only retrospectively. It is not unconscious, but rather nonpositionally conscious of itself as intending the world and mundane objects.

When Sartre seeks to recover the content and significance of such nonpositional nonthetic consciousness, he says that human being is nonthetically conscious of itself as the origin of its own nothingness but not the origin of its own being. Hence, human being is prereflectively conscious of itself as radically incomplete: it cannot prevent itself from existing (= throwness) and yet it is absolutely responsible for its being. However, in order to grasp itself as incomplete, contingent, human being presupposes a sense of completeness, totality, perfection of existence; in short it presupposes a being that is its own foundation or God. Human being "rises in being as perpetually haunted by a totality which it is, without being able to be it . . ."[4] This shows that prereflective human engagement with the world is fundamentally theological.

The fundamental value which presides over this project is . . . the ideal of a consciousness which would be the foundation of its own being in itself by the pure consciousness it would have of itself. It is this ideal which can be called God. Thus the best way to conceive of the fundamental project of human reality is to say that man is the being whose project it is to be God. Whatever may be the myths and rites of the religion considered, God is first "sensible to the heart" of man as the one who identifies and defines him in his ultimate and fundamental project. If *man possesses a pre-ontological comprehension of the being of God*, it is not the great wonders of nature or the powers of society which have conferred it upon him. God, value, and supreme end of transcendence, represents the permanent limit in terms of which man makes known to himself what he is. To be man means to reach toward being God. Or, if you prefer, man fundamentally is the desire to be God.[5] [My emphasis]

Despite his odd retention of traditional philosophical and theological vocabulary that is overlaid with theoretical, objectifying concerns, Sartre apparently means to locate the preontological comprehension of the being of God in the prereflective cogito. The preontological comprehension of God is not an inference nor a projection, for those are reflective acts. God and the prereflective cogito form an irreducible dyad in which both are equiprimordial. Thus Sartre writes:

Shall we say that it [viz., the preontological comprehension of God] is a being relative to consciousness? This would be to confuse it with the object of a thesis. This being is not posited through and before consciousness; there is no consciousness of this being since *it haunts the non-thetic self-consciousness*. It points to consciousness as the meaning of its being . . . inasmuch as consciousness enjoys being a consciousness (of) being, *this being is there*. Consciousness does not confer meaning on this being as it does for this inkwell or this pencil; but without this being . . . consciousness would not be consciousness. . . . On the contrary, consciousness derives for itself its meaning as consciousness from this being. This being comes into the world along with consciousness, at once in its heart and outside of it; it is absolute transcendence in absolute immanence.[6] [My emphasis]

The foregoing passages sound as if Sartre were in the theological business of tracing theological consciousness to its origins in human experience and locating within experience the original prereflective foundations of theology. The Transcendent is not a being of reflection, the result of an inference or theoretical act of projection/postulation; rather it is copresent and equiprimordial with nonthetic consciousness. God is the ultimate and permanent limit in terms of which human being is conscious of itself and its world.

However, Sartre is far from the theological enterprise; he seeks its inversion. The idea of God is impossible, he says, in reference to

Descartes and Spinoza, and the conception of God as necessary being. In reference to the copresence of God with the nonthetic cogito, Sartre maintains that the presence of God is a phantom or pseudo presence. "Everything happens as if the world, man and man in the world succeeded in realizing only a missing God. Everything happens as if the in-itself and the for-itself were presented in a perpetual state of disintegration in relation to an ideal synthesis. Not that the integration has ever taken place, but on the contrary, precisely because it is always indicated and always impossible."[7] The desire for God and reference to God constitutive of the prereflective, nonpositional cogito, are dismissed as useless passions.

Sartre's Antitheism

Sartre contends that God, understood in the classical sense as necessary being, is impossible. It is not clear whether Sartre thinks that this is the sense of God disclosed as the intentional correlate of the prereflective cogito or whether he is simply taking aim at Spinoza and Descartes. In any event, Sartre does contend that whatever the being disclosed as the correlate of the prereflective cogito, it is not a genuine transcendent being but only a limit principle of human consciousness. Despite Sartre's retention of the word *god*, his position is antitheistic in the sense that the word *god* refers simply to the highest human ideal, limit, and so forth. Hence god has no independent being or reality status beyond the human project: ". . . the being towards which human reality surpasses itself is not a transcendent God; it is at the heart of human reality; it is only human reality itself as a totality."[8] Sartre's controversial claims are part of his appropriation of Husserl's phenomenology and attempt to move from phenomenological description to ontology. Although Sartre follows Husserl in granting primacy to the prereflective cogito, he departs from Husserl in his discreditation of the prereflective cogito and its preontological comprehension of God. The being intended by the prereflective cogito is not a genuine, but a spurious, illusory transcendence. And the ontological turn of phenomenology moves not in the direction of a supreme transcendent being but rather in the direction of the ontological dualism of being and nothingness. Accordingly, we shall examine Sartre's discussion of the prereflective cogito, and then his move to the ontological level.

THE DISCREDITATION OF THE PREREFLECTIVE COGITO
OR NATURAL ATTITUDE

In the *Ideas*, Husserl provided a classic description of the world of the natural attitude, which is naively but constantly presupposed by consciousness in all its modalities. He showed that consciousness is naively immersed in its surrounding *Umwelt* and that it rarely thematizes its general thesis, namely the thesis of the world. Instead, this thesis is constantly lived and taken for granted. Already in the *Ideas* and later in the *Crisis*, the world is the horizon of consciousness, cointended and copresent in all concrete thematic intendings, and hence foundational. This means that while the naivete of consciousness is an obstacle to be overcome, such overcoming does not displace but rather clarifies the horizon of consciousness, or the world. Hence world-intending is a transcendental structure and condition of possibility of experience. Far from being "lost" through the phenomenological reductions, the world is constantly presupposed as the general thesis of consciousness, which is thematized and clarified through the reduction. Far from being a loss of the world, the reduction is the very possibility of grasping the thesis of the world as a transcendental condition of experience. For Husserl as for Heidegger, consciousness cannot grasp itself as worldless, but only as in correlation with the world. The world is the general horizon of all praxis and constituting activity of consciousness and hence equiprimordial with consciousness.

Sartre takes over the Husserlian account of the natural attitude, and follows Heidegger in giving it an existential interpretation. Specifically, the naive immersion of consciousness in its *Umwelt* is now seen as more than an epistemological obstacle to be overcome; it involves a deficient mode of being in the world, namely the inauthentic. In *Transcendence of the Ego*, Sartre maintains that the phenomenological reduction that discloses the thesis of the world is not primarily an intellectual act performed on the natural attitude to overcome its naivete. Rather the epoche is understood as motivated by a prior, constitutive anxiety (*Angst*). This means that the act that discloses the world of the natural attitude is not a neutral reflective act, but rather the attempt of consciousness to flee from its own transcendental constitutive activity. In short, the disclosure/constitution of the world of the natural attitude is the flight of consciousness from itself, its anguish at being free and indeterminate. The world of the natural attitude is constituted as an anonymous public world in which values are ready-made, pregiven to the human being. Moreover, the human being projects itself into this world as an object in the world, namely the ego. The function of the world of the natural attitude and the transcendence of the ego as a mundane object is to conceal from human consciousness its own constituting activity, its freedom and responsibility for the world.[9]

In *Being and Nothingness* Sartre continues and expands his interpretation of the prereflective cogito and its natural attitude. The disclosure of the world is motivated transcendentally by the attempt to flee from transcendental freedom and the accompanying responsibility: ". . . the responsibility of the for-itself is overwhelming since it is the one by whom it happens that *there is* a world."[10] Such transcendental constituting freedom is refused, and the for-itself seeks to lose itself in the anonymous public world. "All this happens as if the For-itself had a Passion to lose itself in order that the affirmation 'world' might come to the In-itself. Of course this affirmation exists only for the For-itself; it is the For-itself itself and disappears with it."[11] It is evident that Sartre here departs significantly from Husserl and Heidegger. Consciousness and world have ceased to be equiprimordial and copresent. The transcendental correlation between consciousness and the world-horizon (Husserl) or the unitary phenomenon of being-in-the-world (Heidegger) has been replaced by Sartre's dualism between the For-itself and the In-itself, of two absolutely different and separate regions of being which cannot be unified. The world is not equiprimordial with and copresent to consciousness; rather it falls on the side of consciousness. It is a response of consciousness to the featureless and meaningless in-itself. The world *comes to* the in-itself through the transcendental creative agency of the for-itself.

In comparison with Husserl and Heidegger, Sartre is a philosophical conservative in that he retains the Cartesian primacy of the cogito.[12] To be sure, the cogito is not to be understood substantially but as pure negativity. And it is not absolute: the Hegelian absolute spirit is scaled down to the size of an individual consciousness, and in this scaled-down version it becomes the absurd *contingent foundation*. The for-itself is the foundation of its own nothingness but not its being. However, as the foundation of its own nothingness, the for-itself is the transcendental foundation and source of its ideas, values, world, and God. Sartre puts it thus: "As a being by whom values exist, I am unjustifiable. My freedom is anguished at being the foundation of values, while itself without foundation."[13] It is precisely the constitutive anguish and insecurity of being a contingent foundation which gives rise to the flight from freedom and the loss of self in the world.

Sartre's discreditation of the natural attitude that deprives it of foundational status consists in showing that the natural attitude is transcendentally constituted and that such transcendental constitution is itself motivated by flight from freedom. The self seeks to lose itself in the world by making itself into an object, an ego. It seeks to confer objective ontological weight upon its values, its world view, by tracing such to a supreme necessary being that is the ultimate foundation. To the extent that all such postulations are transcendentally motivated as flight from freedom, they are illusions. The project of being God is the supreme form of flight and the supreme illusion: "Thus the passion of man is the reverse of that of Christ, for man loses himself as man in order that God may be born. But the idea of God is contradictory, and we lose ourselves in vain. Man is a useless passion."[14] The Kantian system of transcendent Ideas—self, world and God—is traced back to transcendental consciousness itself. Further, they are grasped as relative to transcendental consciousness, in the sense that the only ontological foundation any of these has is transcendental freedom itself. Hence, they are meant to serve as instrumentalities of the flight from freedom and responsibility. Sartre thus inverts the classical metaphysical tradition by insisting that nothing is prior to transcendental consciousness[15] and that nothing comes to transcendental freedom from the outside.[16] The primacy of the cogito also deprives the life-world and prereflective consciousness of any foundational status. All dependence, receptivity, naivete are to be considered as self-caused and self-inflicted. Even if human being finds itself thrown into the world, it is still responsible for this primordial situation. "In fact we are a freedom which chooses, but we do not choose to be free. We are condemned to freedom, as we said earlier, thrown into freedom, or, as Heidegger says, 'abandoned'. And we can see that *this abandonment has no other origin than the very existence of freedom*"[17] [My emphasis]. Human being is thrown into the world, but there is no transcendent "thrower." The origin of throwness, as the origin of the world, can only be freedom itself. The primacy of the *cogito* spells the demise of the foundational status of the life-world; it is an epistemological mistake to take it seriously as a genuine disclosure to being. The critical deconstruction of the life-world to its origins in transcendental consciousness spells the demise of God as a transcendent absolute. In this sense the preontological comprehension of the being of God credited to the nonpositional, prereflective cogito is an illusion.

CRITICAL EVALUATION

Despite his critical disagreement with Husserl (that Husserl did not go far enough in grasping the significance of intentionality) and his accusation that Husserl is an idealist, Sartre is more philosophically conservative and more of a Cartesian than is Husserl. Sartre appropriates the Cartesian form of the phenomenological reduction presented by Husserl in the *Ideas*—which Husserl later criticized and rejected.[18] In the Cartesian form, the reduction appears as a *loss* of the transcendent existence of the world and a gaining of an absolute apodictic certainty of transcendental consciousness. Sartre retains the notion of the reduction as loss but inverts Husserl: what is lost—or, better, fled from—is transcendental freedom. The disclosure of the world of the natural attitude is the loss of the self and the distortion/concealment of the self from itself by constituting itself as a mundane entity, or the ego. The problem then becomes how to regain one's transcendental purity, put a stop to flight, assume responsibility for oneself and one's world, and so forth.

Further, Husserl rejected the Cartesian way of the reduction because he saw that it was too simple a step to the transcendental region—as if the entire transcendental region could be attained at a single stroke. In fact, Husserl came to see that the *full* transcendental region is not and cannot be attained at all through the Cartesian way: for all that is attained is transcendental consciousness, and this gives rise to the twin illusions of solipsism on the one hand and the complete transparency of consciousness to itself on the other, losing sight of embodiment and historicity. Husserl was thus led to formulate two alternative ways of pursuing the reduction, through psychology and through the critique of the positive sciences. In the latter critique, the foundation of the life-world and the problem of the origin of the world became central. The effect of the way of performing the reduction through the life-world is to show that the transcendental region is far more complex than an individual ego. The life-world itself is part of the transcendental region, equiprimordial with consciousness. Yet even this is not the ultimate stratum of the transcendental region: the world is not primordially "my" world; it is there for everyone. Hence, the very meaning of world is essentially tied to and bound up with the problem of the other and intersubjectivity. The transcendental region is not attained all at once; it is a multi-strata complex that is comprised of several elements or strata, which are uncovered only gradually by moving from founded to founding strata. The transcendental ego is not *the* single ultimate founding stratum, but at best *equiprimordial* with the world and other coconstituting transcendental egos. Moreover, it is far from clear whether this is as far as intentional analysis can be pushed, or whether there is a yet more ultimate founding stratum, to wit, God; hence, the problem of God. One point is clear, however, and that is that the world and the other are not reducible to the act-intentionality of an individual ego. Conversely, because the transcendental ego cannot grasp itself as worldless, its constitutive activity and freedom are not absolute.

In contrast with Husserl's gradual departure from Cartesianism,[19] Sartre appears philosophically more conservative in that he maintains (1) the primacy of the cogito, (2) the complete transparency of consciousness to the world, which is recoverable completely in reflection, (3) negativity as the essence of intentional constituting activity. Hence, all essences, determinate structures, values, and so forth, are expelled from consciousness to the world. Even the ego must be regarded as a mundane entity, alien to consciousness and masking it from itself. As transcendental field, consciousness is pure negativity or pure nothingness. Conversely, the natural attitude is the primal fall of consciousness from its transcendental a-cosmic purity into the world, immersion in the world, and the consequent impure reflection.[20] The transcendental correlation between consciousness and world (Husserl) or the unitary phenomenon of being-in-the-world (Heidegger) is displaced in favor of the ontological dualism of being and nothingness. This means that being-in-the-world is not a unitary phenomenon at all, but a contradiction. Being-in-the-world is not an ontologically neutral structure of human existence that can be concretely modified toward authenticity or inauthenticity. Rather being-in-the-world is itself the primal existential contradiction, or Fall. "It is not then through inauthenticity that human reality loses itself in the world. For human reality, *being in the world means radically to lose oneself in the world through the very revelation which causes there to be a world . . .*"[21] [My emphasis]. Sartre's existential version of the primacy of the cogito means that the prereflective cogito's allegedly preontological comprehension of the world, values, and God are all forms of flight and so are illusions, epistemological mistakes.

If being in the world means radically to lose oneself in the world through the very disclosure of the world, then Sartre does not have a transcendental consciousness any more. Instead, transcendental consciousness has become a-cosmic; its relation to the world is one of negation and exclusion, and this is why it excludes all dependence, receptivity, and passivity. Michael Haar writes:

> As pure transparency, pure escape from itself and from the in-itself, spontaneous consciousness is freed in advance from any possibility of density, opacity, primitive involvement . . . with respect to the world. It may certainly decline towards the in-itself and be alienated or "glued", but its essence is to be detached. As a metaphysical principle, consciousness could never be compromised by complicity with the world; from it comes openness to the world that it dominates and masters, and this excludes any situation of truly primal and irrecoverable passivity.[22]

Is the for-itself a-cosmic in principle, such that to find itself thrown into the world is the primal fall? Sartre appears to flirt with this possibility when at the end of *Being and Nothingness* he asks whether to take freedom itself (instead of God) as the supreme value and end of transcendence implies an escape from all *situation* or whether it implies a fuller and more concrete situatedness of the self in the midst of the world.[23] Sartre does not answer this question. However, the ontology of *Being and Nothingness* seems to point in the direction of the former alternative and to exclude the latter possibility. The for-itself is the foundation of the world and values, and is itself without foundation in that nothing justifies the adoption of any particular value. This seems to make the for-itself a-cosmic in principle, and render impossible ethical distinctions between various ways of being in the world. All are manifestations of the primal fall of being-in-the-world, and it follows from Sartre's own ontology that all human actions are equivalent and doomed to failure. This is to raise the oft-debated question whether Sartre's ontology does not undermine any ethics, including his own, and conversely, whether Sartre's ethics does not require a different ontology from the one he presents in *Being and Nothingness*, in which situation is not a contradiction or diminution of the for-itself.[24]

Sartre's Ontological Proof

The preceding discussion brings us to the problem of the ontological turn of Sartre's phenomenology. The critical question is whether Sartre's move from phenomenology to ontology is phenomenologically justified and grounded or whether a preconceived ontology is dogmatically imposed on the phenomenological descriptions. This is a subtle question, and there is no neutral ontologically "objective" position from which such a judgment can be rendered. Moreover, phenomenological method was instituted in the first place as a protest and corrective to certain theoretical prejudices present in the traditional metaphysics. Hence phenomenology seeks to "get beneath" such prejudices. On the other hand, phenomenology is not antiontological, for it clarifies the givens with which ontology must deal, particularly anthropo-ontology. In this sense it is a moment in philosophical method, and makes possible new sorts of ontology. As such, that is, as an initial, clarifying moment in philosophical method, phenomenology is compatible with several different possible ontologies and not synonymous with any. Thus it seems to be possible to accept a philosopher's phenomenological investigations without necessarily being committed to or having to accept his particular ontology. That is, the philosopher's descriptions may indeed have ontological import but point to a different ontology from the one he identifies and provides.

Against the above background, Sartre's ontological turn takes the form of a discussion of the so-called ontological proof. Actually there are two ontological proofs running through the pages of *Being and Nothingness*: the traditional argument for the existence of God (Anselm, Descartes) and the novel interpretation of intentionality presented by Sartre himself. Sartre rejects the classical theological proof as presented by Descartes. In a move similar to J. N. Findlay, Sartre finds the traditional form of the argument is really a disproof of the existence of God. For the argument is supposed to establish a necessary being, a being that is its own foundation. Hence, the traditional theistic form of the proof is supposed to establish a substance that is also subject, a synthesis of the in-itself and for-itself; and this is a contradiction. In order to be the self-conscious foundation of itself, a necessary being would have to exist at a distance from itself, and this reflective distance reinstates the very contingency that the concept of necessary being is supposed to suppress. Hence the argument fails because it posits a supreme contradiction. Despite his so-called existentialism, Sartre here sounds like a rationalist.

Having disposed of the ontological proof in its traditional form, Sartre presents another concrete existential version, this time as an interpretation of intentionality. Both arguments have in common the quest for being. But there is radical divergence in the execution and the terminus, that is, the result attained. In Sartre's case the prereflective intentionality of consciousness is the ontological proof. In short, it belongs to consciousness as intentional to be a disclosure of transcendent being other than consciousness itself. "Consciousness is consciousness of something. This means that transcendence is the constitutive structure of consciousness; that is, that consciousness is born *supported* by a being which is not itself. This is what we call the ontological proof."[25] Because consciousness is essentially intentional, consciousness (of)———, it is already on the ontological plane. There is no *shift* to the ontological level from phenomenology. *Phenomenology is ontology*, and its task is the explication of the prereflective cogito.

Sartre claims that the ontological proof is valid for the whole domain of consciousness. This means that the intentionality of prereflective consciousness per se discloses the transphenomenal being of the phenomenon. However, this seems to prove too much, for the implication is that any object, simply qua intended, carries with it an ontological proof/disclosure of its transphenomenal reality or being. Sartre's ontological proof collapses Husserl's important distinction between the *noema* or object simply as meant and the real object. Not all *noemata* are meant as real; some are purely imaginary. Sartre's "proof" seems to imply that even imaginary beings have transphenomenal status. If this were so, then it is difficult to see how Sartre could consistently reject the classical ontological argument for God, particularly its restatement in transcendental form. For the preontological comprehension of the being of God that Sartre credits to nonpositional self-consciousness would be the original disclosure of divine presence. The following passage from *Being and Nothingness* would constitute a serious theological proposal: "If man possesses a pre-ontological comprehension of the being of God, it is not the great wonders of nature or the power of society that have conferred it upon him. God, value, and supreme end of transcendence, represents the permanent limit in terms of which man makes known to himself what he is."[26] If it were the case that the whole domain of consciousness constituted a single ontological proof of transphenomenal being as Sartre claims, it would, on Sartre's description of the prereflective cogito of God, disclose God as the ultimate horizon and limit of human being. And this disclosure would imply that human being stands in a relation of utter dependence on God as ultimate limit. Moreover, the transcendent need not be interpreted as the Hegelian absolute—a synthesis of for-itself and in-itself—precisely because the transcendent disclosed in the preontological comprehension of God is not a theoretical construct.

However, Sartre stands Hegel and the traditional ontological proof on its head: Sartre's ontological proof discloses not an in-itself-for-itself, but only a missing God. It points to two absolutely separated and opposed regions of being—being and nothingness—between which no mediation and no synthesis are possible. Hence, Sartre's ontological proof announces a primordial *disruption* between man and world, such that being in the world is a contradiction. Because Sartre's proof establishes disruption rather than synthesis and mediation, Sartre has little to say about the transcendent being that the ontological proof discloses. He identifies it as "the being of this table, of this package of tobacco, of the lamp, more generally, the being of the world . . ."[27] Such being is "uncreated, without reason for being, without any connection with another being . . . *de trop* for eternity."[28]

Sartre's ontological proof establishes an ontological dualism between being and nothingness, between the in-itself and the for-itself. Sartre's concept of being appears to be positivistic, namely, sheer brute fact. Not only is this a truncation and inversion of the classical ontology, it forces Sartre to a purely negative concept of freedom, or freedom as nihilation. Despite the contingent existence of the for-itself, its freedom is absolute in the sense that nothing is prior to it; and so freedom is without foundation and justification. Hence human being is responsible for all its apparent passive affection from without; emotions are self-inflicted, rather than responses to initiatives and influences from the world. Moreover, Sartre maintains that human freedom is the foundation of all values, including the ideal value of God. However, although human freedom is absolute in the sense that it can create and destroy its projected values and deals, it is also a futile and useless passion because it is nonreciprocally related to the absurd and meaningless in-itself that threatens and eventually claims and annihilates the for-itself and its values.

CRITICAL EVALUATION

Phenomenology is ontology; and the ontology that Sartre finds issuing from his existential phenomenology is a peculiar ontology of finitude, namely the dualism of an all but meaningless being in itself, *de trop* for eternity, and an a-cosmic for-itself unaccountably thrown into the world and enmeshed in meaningless schemes of its own manufacture. It is ironic that Sartre apparently finds phenomenology issuing in a version of the positivism against which Husserl struggled all his career and that called forth his efforts to found phenomenology as a corrective. From the Husserlian vantage point, Sartre's phenomenological ontology appears as a regression. Heidegger observed that Sartre does not get beyond the classical ontological-metaphysical tradition; he retains its fundamental assumptions but inverts them. As an inversion, Sartre's ontology is simply on par with the traditional view, and does not escape its dogmatism and theoretical prejudices. To be sure, Sartre is more than a positivist. His radical dualism between being and nothingness intends to be in the service of human freedom and ethics. However, in its own way, Sartre's ontology of finitude is a contemporary restatement of the ancient gnostic vision of the world, in which evil is equated with finitude, with being in the world per se.[29] Sartre reformulates the primordial disruption between man and world that lies at the basis of gnostic dualism and gives powerful expression to the ancient themes of alienation, the indifference and hostility of the cosmos, and the alien or missing God. However, despite the power of Sartre's vision, the radical ontological dualism is not a phenomenologically derived treatment of the problem of the origin of the world; it passes over that problem. Precisely at the point where phenomenological radicalism is called for—tracing the theoretical world of science to its foundations in the life-world—Sartre follows the classical theoretical ontology to its positivistic subversion. Sartre's ontological dualism of being and nothingness succumbs to the very positivism that Husserl sought to overcome.

Sartre did not explore the full range of ontological possibilities opened up by Husserl's transcendental phenomenology. This omission may be due to the fact that Sartre apparently had already formed his fundamental vision of the world prior to his study of phenomenology. Hence, it is not derived from but rather imposed on Sartre's phenomenological descriptions. In view of Sartre's negative results, Merleau-Ponty sought to reopen the transcendental-ontological problem. Specifically the latter seeks a third alternative to the ontological dualism set forth in *Being and Nothingness*.

> The openness upon a natural and historical world is not an illusion and it is not a priori; it is our involvement with Being. Sartre expressed this by saying that the For-itself is necessarily haunted by an imaginary In-itself–For-itself. We only say that the In-itself–For-itself is more than merely imaginary. The imaginary is without consistence . . . it vanishes when one proceeds to vision. . . . It seems to us on the contrary that it is necessary to recognize in it the solidity of myth, that is, of an operative imaginary, which is part of our institution, and which is indispensable for the definition of Being itself.[30]

The ultimate significance of this passage is far from clear. However, it appears that being in the world has a religious, even theological, dimension to which Sartre has failed to do justice. The In-itself–For-itself is more than merely imaginary, and is foundational for both man and world, that is, their reciprocity and correlation. This in turn suggests an ultimate receptivity of both man and world to a transcendence that is irreducible to either. Clearly Merleau-Ponty is after an alternative to the abstract philosophy of identity of German idealism and an alternative to Sartre's inversion of idealism that culminates in a radical dualism.

It is precisely such a third alternative that is presented by Schleiermacher's phenomenology or eidetics of religious consciousness. Schleiermacher anticipates the general phenomenological principle of evidence, namely, that for every thematizable state of affairs, there is a corresponding originary mode of evidence pertaining to it and through which alone it is originally presented. Hence, to disclose the original mode of evidential encounter is equivalent to the disclosure of the thing itself.[31] Schleiermacher's account of religious consciousness carries out this principle of evidence and issues in a theological eidetics. According to Schleiermacher, religion has its locus in human being in feeling, or global immediate prereflective consciousness. The essence of religion is the feeling of utter dependence. Several points deserve notice: (1)

259

The consciousness of utter dependence includes and presupposes a consciousness of reciprocal interdependence between self and world. Specifically, the consciousness of utter dependence presupposes the consciousness of freedom, which is the ability to resist mundane influences and exert counterinfluences upon the world. In Kantian terminology the ability of the human being to constitute its world is acknowledged, yet this ability is neither a useless passion nor absolute. (2) The world that is transcendentally constituted/disclosed is not only the theoretical realm of knowledge but also a social and cultural world. Hence, Schleiermacher is far from portraying the feeling of utter dependence as a subhuman, doglike passivity as Hegel charged, for only a being capable of constituting and having a world in the distinctive human sense is capable of a consciousness of utter dependence. (3) Although human being is free, human freedom is not a capacity for absolute self-origination or self-creation. Schleiermacher acknowledges the self-originating character of freedom as transcendental, yet maintains that such spontaneous freedom is not absolute but relative because human being is concretely situated in time, history, community and embodiment. (4) The consciousness of utter dependence intends a referent that is not a mundane object nor the world but transcendent to, and irreducible to, either self or world. The referent of utter dependence is a transcendent Whence. This transcendent Whence is the original referent and significance of the word *god*. God is thus disclosed through feeling in an ordinary way, prior to and independent of speculation and intellectual acts such as occur in the traditional theological proofs. To be conscious of utter dependence and to be conscious of God are one and the same, for these are the noetic and noematic aspects of the same original phenomenon.[32]

For Schleiermacher as for Sartre, religious consciousness is constituted by a preontological comprehension of the being of God, and such comprehension is not an inference, postulate, invention, or projection but an originary disclosure of transcendence (not a merely imaginary but at least an operative imaginary, to use Merleau-Ponty's phrase).

Hence, for Schleiermacher as for Sartre, the intentionality of religious consciousness constitutes an existential ontological proof. Precisely because utter dependence is both existential and ontological, it takes the place of the so-called objectifying proofs of nature theology.[33] Whatever may be the ultimate metaphysical interpretation and elaboration of this preontological comprehension, the resulting theological language will be different from objectifying and speculative metaphysical theology.[34]

If there is a point at issue between Schleiermacher and Sartre, it does not appear to be a phenomenological descriptive issue. Descriptively, Sartre agrees with Schleiermacher: human being, owing to its finitude and consciousness of finitude, is involved in a quest for being that is at the same time a quest for God. Moreover, it is the preontological comprehension of God at the level of the prereflective cogito that makes possible the quest. The dispute between Sartre and Schleiermacher arises at the transition from phenomenological description to the ontological level. The dispute is not whether the prereflective cogito has ontological import, but what import and in what ontological direction(s) it may point. Of the two Schleiermacher seems more Husserlian in adhering to the principle of evidence. However, the evidence for God is far from apodictic. Sartre shows that the reality and evidential status of the transcendent Whence can be seriously questioned. But this is hardly a new discovery: the attempt to domesticate the transcendent and turn it into a principle or deus ex machina has always called forth protest. The biblical book of Job is on record that Job's *denials* of traditional theology are closer to the truth than is traditional theology. Theology does not need Sartre to establish that the transcendent is elusive. However, Sartre takes a further step that probably contradicts the phenomenological principle of evidence when he claims that because God is a pseudo presence haunting the prereflective cogito, it follows that God is part of the human project itself, that theology is reducible to anthropology. This assertion simply refuses to concede any evidential status to the prereflective cogito, in the name of absolute self-creation and responsibility.

Schleiermacher encountered in Fichte a position similar to Sartre's and rejected it on two grounds: (1) There is no such thing as absolute freedom because the totality of our existence does not present itself as having been self-created. Human freedom is temporal, relative, situated in a world. The claim of absolute freedom (that freedom is the origin of value, the Ideas of Self, World and God) not only makes freedom a-cosmic; it is simply untrue. It is either a deception or an abstraction from the human situation. (2) Because human freedom is relative and not absolute, it is not the absolute foundation of anything. Schleiermacher breaks with the various forms of absolute freedom and autonomy present in German Idealism, although retaining a historical and limited version of freedom as relatively transcendental. Moreover, Schleiermacher would regard a god that is a projection of human freedom as ipso facto not the genuine transcendent Whence of utter dependence. Such a projection may well be a form of flight from the transcendent, a refusal of human finitude, and an attempt at self-absolutization. Sartre has no monopoly on, nor did he originate the concept of, bad faith. Nor is he alone in struggling against it.

PART 7

PHENOMENOLOGY OF

SOCIAL RELATIONS

20. Personalities Of a Higher Order

DAVID CARR

When he reaches section 56 of the Fifth Cartesian Meditation, Husserl claims he has completed the clarification of the "first and lowest level" of intersubjectivity, or of what he calls the communalization of monads, and can now proceed to "higher levels" that, he says, present "relatively minor difficulties."[1] Discussing various forms of communalization, Husserl mentions "the pre-eminent types that have the character of 'personalities of a higher order.'"[2] In using this phrase, Husserl is in effect attributing personal characteristics to certain kinds of social groups as well as to individuals. He does not follow up here on the precise manner in which such attribution is justified, and although the expression "personalities of a higher order" makes its appearance in other works (e.g., *The Crisis*),[3] they likewise lack any detailed justification of the use of such a phrase. We might thus suppose that Husserl is merely indulging in a *façon de parler*, but if we consult the manuscripts on intersubjectivity, in particular those of volume 14 of Husserliana, dating from the 1920s,[4] we find that Husserl takes this expression very seriously indeed. There we find him attributing to certain forms of community not only "personality" (199, 405) but also "subjectivity" (404), "consciousness" and "unity of consciousness" (200), "faculties" (*Vermögen*), "character", "conviction" (*Gesinnung*) (201), "memory" (205), and even *"so etwas wie Leiblichkeit"*—something like corporality (206). Of course, we often use some of these terms to characterize certain social units in ordinary speech, but Husserl goes out of his way to insist that such talk is not inauthentic (*"keine uneigentliche Rede"* [404]), no mere analogy (*"keine blosse Analogie"* [201]). He mentions the use of the term *Gemeingeist* by the nineteenth century humanists under the influence of German idealism, and the tendency of modern, reductionistic psychology, reacting against German idealism, to debunk such terminology as mystical or fictitious (404). But the attempt to reduce *Gemeingeist* to a collection of individuals is just as misguided, he says, as the analogous attempt by some of the same psychologists to make individual consciousness an epiphenomenon of matter (404).

I find it remarkable that Husserl seems explicitly to embrace in these manuscripts a conception that most phenomenologists and most other philosophers of the twentieth century have found uncongenial. Alfred Schutz, for example, rejects it in no uncertain terms, drawing on Max Weber for support.[5] Even Dilthey, who became increasingly a source of inspiration for Husserl in his later years, especially when dealing with social topics, was suspicious of the notion of a superpersonal subjectivity, in spite of his closeness to German idealism.[6]

Indeed, there is something prima facie unphenomenological about the notion. Husserl has a guarded respect for the German idealists, but he always demanded that the paper money of their high-flown conceptions be cashed in for the hard currency of phenomenological analysis. But what this means is that anything whatsoever should be analyzed in terms of its relation to the conscious life of an individual subject. The very notion of phenomenological analysis would seem to prescribe that any treatment of transindividual subjectivity would make it subordinate to the subjectivity of the investigator. Perhaps these considerations have something to do with the fact that the concrete analyses that Husserl does devote to this topic in volume 14, which are in any case not extensive, are (to me, at least) so unsatisfying.

In the following I do not intend to present Husserl's analysis, or to criticize it, though I shall draw on it occasionally. I shall rather attempt on my own to test the degree to which one can make phenomenological sense of what we may call the subjectivity of certain kinds of social units. It is clear that ordinary language often deals in such a conception, and that it has also been used philosophically. But can it be understood phenomenologically?

The approach that immediately suggests itself—and this is largely Husserl's approach—is to proceed as usual in the first person singular, adopting the phenomenological standpoint toward one's world, and inquiring after the manner in which social units make their appearance in that world. What sort of entity is the family, the university, the Society for Phenomenology and Existential Philosophy, the working class, or the United States, and how do these phenomena fit into my perceptual and conceptual world? How do they figure in my spatial and bodily surroundings, how are they encountered, how are they given? In such a context of investigation, one could then ask the crucial question: Do I experience, encounter, interact with such social entities, large or small, in ways which are importantly similar to the manner in which I experience, encounter and interact with individual persons?

Such an approach seems to present rich possibilities, but it is burdened with a difficulty that has already been hinted at. It tends to place the social unit over against me, as an object for my subjectivity, and thus suggests, for one thing, the scientific and detached attitude I might take toward a society of which I am not a member. To be sure, comparing the social unit with another person suggests other possibilities as well: struggling with it, being victimized by it, and so forth. But in these cases, the other person is still irreducibly other and "over against" me, and in this analogy an important aspect of the nature of the social unit for the individual is being left out, namely, the fact that the individual can be a member of it. Although there are many different ways of encountering another person, there is no sense, that I can see, in which one can be a participating member of another person. Yet the notion of participation seems a better avenue to the putative subjectivity of the social unit than its givenness as an object. Let us try to consider the social unit, then, not as one which stands over against me but as one of which I am a member. Thus, one would be considering the possibility of a larger subjectivity in which one participates rather than as a subjectivity that one encounters as one encounters another person.

But such an approach has its own difficulties. Does it not run up against and reveal the limits of phenomenological analysis? Where does it fit into the scheme *ego cogito cogitatum qua cogitatum*, which was Husserl's formula for the phenomenological frame of reference? A larger subjectivity in which I participate would seem to be neither cogito nor cogitatum (thought). Nevertheless, I think some progress can be made in this direction, starting with what Husserl calls the "first and lowest level" of intersubjectivity.

This first level, which Husserl has tried to account for in the Fifth Meditation, is what Schutz later called the face-to-face encounter with another conscious subject. What has clearly emerged from Husserl's analysis is that this one-to-one encounter essentially involves a third element, the common surrounding world. The other is in my world, but as a consciousness he or she is also for the world and the world is for him or her as well as for me. No face-to-face encounter, then, without something in common—meaning, of course, not common characteristics or a common essence but something particular in common: this particular place in the world in which we stand and face each other. But again, we share this common place not as two pencils share a common desk top, but rather as a single environment consciously given to both of us—and one which, by the way, also *includes* both of us among its constituents. Simplifying, we could say that the encounter with another person is first of all this: the encounter with another perspective on the world, a perspective which is not my own.[7]

Now, Husserl often compares intersubjective experience with memory,[8] and his point is this: memory offers us the example of a plurality of experiences of one and the same object. The object is both a unity and a plurality of ways of showing itself. In intersubjectivity, we also have a plurality of experiences of one and the same "object"—at least, the common environment—but this plurality, instead of being spread out in time, is simultaneous. Another and more important difference, of course, is that in memory I have not only a single object but also a single subject, that is, the plurality of experiences are all my own; whereas in intersubjectivity this is not the case. In the face-to-face encounter, though, I am *aware* of the other's experiences even if I don't *have* them; and they fit together with mine in virtue of the common object and the kinesthetic-spatial interlocking of perspectives, into a single system of views on our common environment. Furthermore, this single system is given as much to the other as it is to me.

We can now take this simultaneity of differing perspectives on the same world and consider it as itself spread out over time, as Schutz does when he considers two persons observing together a bird in flight.[9] It is odd that Schutz should have hit on this marvelous example and yet failed to grasp the richness of its implications. His striking and much-quoted phrase "we grow older together," used again in this context, I find very misleading. It suggests the clock, ticking away while our two streams of experience run along parallel to each other. Of course Schutz meant, in using the word "together", to indicate the mutual awareness of this passing time, because it is also true, but irrelevant, that I am growing older along with everyone else in the universe. But what is crucial to this example is not that, along with the bird's flight, we are aware of *objective* time passing (which is what "growing older" suggests to me), but rather that the structural features of what Husserl calls *internal* time-consciousness are shared. That is, the common object, ex hypothesi, is an event, something that unfolds in time. In order that there *be* a *common* object for us, each of the simultaneous phases of the experience of the event, my own and the other's, must bear within itself the retention of the past phases of the event and project before it the event's future. Again, as individual participant, I am aware of the intersubjectivity of the common experience in that I am aware of an interlocking system not only of perspectives but also of retentions and protentions, some of which are not my own, a single such system in which my own experiences participate.

266

It is the common object, along with the single system of perspectives and time consciousness it implies, which is the key, in my view, to what Schutz calls the we-relationship. Again I think Schutz got it wrong, because he defines this relationship simply as a reciprocal thou-orientation.[10] For one thing, each of the two parties could be thou-oriented toward the other without knowing that the other was thou-oriented toward *him*. But that's a minor difficulty, probably an oversight on Schutz' part. More important is the fact, which Schutz fails to note, that it is the common object—whether object in the narrow sense or event or even simply the common environment—which gives rise to a single system of interlocking experiences in which we both participate. It is this single system that best corresponds to most of our uses of the term *we*; it is this system, in fact, to which the term frequently applies. Comprising two or more subjectivities, it requires a third thing, the common object, in order to come into being. The object becomes this system's own object, the thing *we* see, the bird's flight *we* observe, the surrounding world which is *our* surroundings, not just mine. The we-relationship, then, is mediated by the common object. Schutz' description suggests a staring match or perhaps lovers gazing deep into each other's eyes. But in a staring match the other disappears as other, and lovers who do not get on to other things besides gazing will not have much of an affair.

Because every face-to-face encounter involves the common surroundings, and thus the common object in the broadest sense, every such encounter would seem to involve the establishment of a we-relationship, this sense that I am participating in a subjectivity larger than my own. We seem to have established the subjectivity of the social unit at too low a level. Yet Husserl called even this level *Vergemeinschaffung*—communalization or the establishment of a community. We have already discerned what we might call differing degrees of focus in intersubjective experience; and these may be seen to correspond to different degrees of communalization, even while remaining at the same level. A face-to-face encounter may be fleeting, its only object the totality of objects that is the common environment, including the participants themselves. But a common focus, that is, a particular object within that environment, can focus the we-relationship as well. Remember the famous example of what the traffic accident does to the collection of people at a sidewalk cafe. If the object is an unfolding event, like the bird's flight, it is spread out over time and the we-relationship is spread out as well.

The we-relationship is cemented even further if the common focus is not a perceived object or event but a common *objective* to be attained. Here the common object is not constituted as passively given, but is actively constituted as lying in a future to be realized. Constituted along with it are the means to its realization, the common project comprising various steps in the means-end relation, steps that are often tasks that can be divided up among the participants in the project. It was Heidegger, of course, who stressed the fact that others are encountered, "proximally and for the most part," not as entities present at hand or standing over against me, but as it were obliquely, through the common project in which we are engaged.[11] Whether or not this is the primordial or most authentic form of encounter with other persons, as opposed to other, possibly derivative forms, it seems certain that it is the key to the foundation of we-relationships that form a distinct class. The intersubjective unity of a common project is both more fragile and more concrete than that of a common perception. The observers of the bird in flight or the spectators at a football game or at the theater are fused by their common object, but they take the object to exist independently of themselves. For the participants in a common project, like a barn raising, their common object or objective is literally created by their commitment and their activity, first mental and communicative and then physical. For spectators and observers, their we-relationship seems called forth and sustained in being by the independent object. For the participants in a common endeavor, the object is called forth and sustained in being by their we-relationship. Thus, the latter form of relationship is not at the mercy of its object, as we might say, and is in this sense not subject to an outside reality. But at the same time, it receives no support for its existence from outside and is dependent on its own internal cohesiveness for its sustained existence.

It should be noted here that our attempt to attribute subjectivity and intentionality to groups by means of the we-relationship differs in at least one important respect from certain classical conceptions. In Adam Smith's notion of the invisible hand and Hegel's of the cunning of reason, groups act in furtherance of goals that are unknown to and even at variance with the purposes of the individuals who make them up. In the we-relationship, by contrast, participants are quite conscious of the ends pursued by the group; but it is still the group, and not the individuals serially or collectively, that pursues these ends.

It might be noted further that the common object, especially in the sense of the common objective, seems the key not only to the we-relationship but also to what might be regarded as its opposite, conflict between persons. Competition for a scarce supply of food, struggle over a piece of disputed territory, are cases in point. Even when the conflict derives from differing objectives, there is no conflict unless the differing objectives somehow involve the same elements, such as means. Here, of course, to say that there is a common object or objective is not to say that the objective is to be realized in common. One party's possession and consumption of the food supply is meant precisely to exclude the other's attainment of the same objective. What is interesting about these two alternatives, conflict and cooperation, is that in either case we could say with Hegel that each consciousness seeks the death of the other:[12] in the first case by eliminating him as a threat to the attainment of my objective, in the second case by submerging his independence in the common project.

There is, of course, something intermediate between these two alternatives, and Husserl saw its importance as well as Hegel. Turning up at several points in the intersubjectivity manuscripts as an example of communalization is what Husserl calls *das Herr-Diener Verhältnis*, the relation of master and servant.[13] As we might expect, there is no mention of Hegel, nor is there any evidence that Husserl acquired the term or even the idea from reading Hegel's work, though he was surely aware of its presence there. In any case, Husserl like Hegel sees this relation as significant in the formation of community or "personality of a higher order." What interests Husserl about it is that the master supplies the will and the servant provides the execution of the action;[14] but because the action is the unity of will and execution, the action cannot be said to belong to either of them exclusively but is strictly speaking the action of the rudimentary community they form.

Again we see the common third element, in this case the action, as the key to the intersubjective relationship; and again we see that the action is a single system of subjective accomplishment in which each individual sees his own activity as a functioning part. It should be remembered that for Hegel, too, this all-important human relation is mediated by a third element, that is, nature, whose mastery is the common business of the two participants. There is another aspect of the relation that Husserl notes—one that is also taken for granted by Hegel—namely, that it not merely focused on a single common project but established itself as a generalized relation—habitual, as Husserl calls it—to be applicable henceforth to all future activities.[15]

Though he does note that the master-servant relation is commonly based on power and threat,[16] Husserl does not bring out the explosive features of the relation, the internal contradictions that Hegel depicts so brilliantly. These have their source in the changing view of the servant, who first sees his own contribution to the common action as "inessential," then comes to regard himself as the true agent and the master's role as superfluous.[17] Husserl simply contrasts the master-servant relation with what he calls a "reciprocal relation."[18] But the master-servant relation has instructive force, just as it has dialectical force in Hegel. It is well known that for Hegel, in the community of mutual recognition, the master-servant relation is not simply done away with. It is *aufgehoben*, and that means both surpassed and retained. It is retained in the sense that the two functions, master and servant, are still present; but it is surpassed in that they are not vested in particular individuals or classes. Rather, each is for himself and for the others both master and servant. We can still distinguish between will (or formulation) and execution, but the individual participates in both. The genuine subject of the activity is the spirit of the community, which Hegel calls "the I that is a We, the We that is an I."[19]

For Hegel, of course, *Geist* in this sense is not only a genuinely subjective and conscious being but is even more genuinely and really so than the individual consciousness. But let us proceed more cautiously. Our task is to determine, on phenomenological grounds, the exact degree to which we can attribute subjectivity to any sort of social unity at all. Let us review what we have accomplished so far.

Beginning at the level of face-to-face encounter, we pointed out that part of the sense of the encounter for the individual, for me, is that I participate in a single system of perspectival views that is interlocked and unified in a way that is similar to the coordination of temporally spread-out views and perspectives within my own experience. The unity derives from or corresponds to the common object, whether merely as common environment or as common focus within that environment. The object is at once a unity and a multiplicity of ways of presenting itself. This is no less true of the object that is an unfolding event, like the flight of a bird. In the case of the common project, the unified system of subjective aspects consists not so much of perspective views as of actions that are functioning parts of a single total action. Again, the unity of this single system is derived from the common object— the objective in this case—but here the common object is itself dependent on the intersubjective unity. In Husserl's language, here the common object is not passively, but actively, constituted, truly created.

We have hardly mentioned communication and language so far; but it is at this point, at the level of the common project, that it commonly becomes decisive.[20] This is a vast topic, needless to say, and we cannot go into it extensively. But what strikes me here is that the role of language in the intersubjective situation is oddly isomorphic with what we have been discussing so far. Our common language, if we have one, lies spread out around us like our common environment and like it forms a vast system of interlocking potentialities waiting to be activated. When we speak, our speech acts may be indications to each other of our intentions of psychic states; but we genuinely communicate in virtue of something distinguishable from both our words and our thoughts—the common meaning and through it the common referent. When I speak to someone I say *something—about* something. And I communicate with him to the extent that he understands what I am saying, about what. Again it is the third element, the common theme distinct from, but shared by, the two speakers, which provides the unity of their different subjective contributions.

Have we arrived at any phenomenological justification for attributing subjectivity, or indeed consciousness, to any sort of social unit? I think the key to intersubjectivity, as to subjectivity itself, is temporality. Husserl and other phenomenologists have taught us that the unity of consciousness at the individual level is not an abstract or timeless ego that stands above or behind the multiplicity of experiential phases. It is nothing but the internal temporal unity achieved when each phase resumes its own past and projects its own future, the phases being linked to the temporal persistence or the temporal unfolding of whatever object it is concerned with. The unity of intersubjective experience has the same feature. The single system of interlocking views in which I participate, while it has a simultaneous unity-in-multiplicity, has a protentive and retentive unity-in-multiplicity as well, again provided by the single object. The multiplicity of conscious experiences had by the individual parties to a common experience is no more a *mere* multiplicity than the object is a mere multiplicity of private and particular appearances. It is a system of consciousness, a single one, which lasts just as long as its object is precisely a common object.

I think that in a certain sense we can attribute not only consciousness but even self-consciousness to certain forms of community. What is self-consciousness, phenomenologically speaking? Again, it is not the static conception of a self observing itself. It occurs rather when the unity of the temporal phases of experience is not only lived through but is made thematic. When I experience reflectively, or act deliberately, it means that I am not so much absorbed in the object of my experience, or the objective of my action, but am also attentive to the structure or flow of my experience itself, to the pursuit of my objective and its articulation into steps and stages, means and ends. In the case of the project, such attention is often necessary to its formulation, and often becomes necessary in the course of its execution, whether to remind myself of what I am doing or to revise my plans as I go along, perhaps in response to changed circumstances. This sort of reflection, whether prospectively, retrospectively, or both, draws together the disparate and fleeting elements and phases of my experience or activity and imposes on them—or discovers or rediscovers in them or reimposes on them— a sense, a direction, and articulated structure. Often requiring the use of language, such reflection consists in constructing as it were a *story* about myself that accounts for what I'm doing, a story that I may tell to others or merely to myself.

Now I want to maintain that something similar takes place at the intersubjective level too. It may be that only individuals tell stories, but they don't always tell them about themselves or use the first person singular. Often the storyteller speaks to, and on behalf of, the group to which he belongs; and the disparate elements he draws together into a temporally articulated whole are not the elements of his own experience only but those also of the other participants in the common project or course of experience. The experience described, the action proposed or articulated, is then not *my* action, *my* experience, but *ours*. Now to the extent that others subscribe to this account, *believe* this story about what is going on, we have, it seems to me, not merely a single object or objective, not only a single system of coordinated experience but also a single reflection or self-consciousness expressed in the single story subscribed to by all. In this way the *we* can be seen not only as conscious, not only as active, but also as self-conscious and reflective. Such storytelling may take place in conversation, in the rhetoric of the political leader, in the writings of journalists and historians. It constitutes intersubjective self-consciousness, however, only to extent that it is taken up and believed by the other members of the group.

If we pursue far enough the role of storytelling and storybelieving in communal life, we arrive at the *historical* character of social existence and the origin of historical inquiry. But this would be the subject of another paper. We hope to have shown here how it is possible, despite appearances to the contrary, to make phenomenological sense of the idea of personalities of a higher order.

21. Objectivity, Alienation, and Reflection

James L. Marsh

Within phenomenology and existentialism in the past century, one of the constant themes has been a critique of objectivity, an attempt to define and limit the claims of objective knowing. Kierkegaard's critique of the objective thinker, Nietzsche's attack on the asceticism of science, Sartre's analysis of the "look" as degrading and reifying, and the later Heidegger's overcoming of metaphysics may be taken as examples of this tendency. It is true that there are differences and even contradictions among these thinkers, but they do share a common problematic.[1]

Now, however, it is perhaps time to redress the balance. Too often, although not always,[2] there has been a slighting of objectivity in favor of subjectivity. Whereas in the nineteenth century, the academic and cultural bias was in favor of objective, conceptual thinking, now in some versions of existentialism and phenomenology, the bias has shifted away from objectivity towards a passionate, nonconceptual, nonscientific thinking and willing; for example, Kierkegaard's passionate inwardness, Nietzsche's will to power, Sartre's negative freedom, and Heidegger's meditative thinking. Is it true that any thematic knowledge of the other person necessarily degrades the other?[3] Does objective knowledge necessarily alienate one from himself?[4] Is a conceptual, metaphysical knowledge of being necessarily "murderous," as Heidegger claims?[5] These and other related questions cry out for more balanced, systematic treatment.

In past papers I have dealt with this issue mostly in a historical fashion.[6] In this paper I first distinguish phenomenologically among various kinds of objectivity and objectification, then establish fundamental relationships among kinds, and finally argue for certain consequences. What emerges from such an analysis is a limited phenomenological rehabilitation of objectivity. It is limited because, as I will show later, no objective knowledge can be total, but rather presupposes a prethematic context that can never be fully articulated. *Objectivity* is understood in this paper as the noematic or object pole of a conscious act, *objectification* as the noetic or intentional pole of that same act. *Phenomenology* is understood as an unprejudiced description of conscious experience in order to uncover essential structures in that experience. *Reflection* as understood and practiced in this paper is simply the doing of phenomenology.

The Kinds of Objectivity

The first, most obvious kind of objectivity is perceptual, the presence of a concrete, individual, sensuous thing to a perceiving, embodied subject. To perceive the table over there is to perceive an object distinct from me and yet related to me. It is distinct from me, first, because it is experienced as "there," thematic, and separable from me, in contrast to the presence of my lived body, "here", implicit, and inseparable from me. I am explicitly aware of the table as there at a distance from me here. At the same time I am vaguely, prethematically aware of my perceiving body not as object, but as subject, as my presence to the world. The table is experienced as separable from me in the sense that I can leave it behind by leaving the room, but I cannot leave my body. Indeed my body is the condition of the possibility of my leaving behind or losing anything else. It makes good ordinary language sense to say that I lost or misplaced my pen, but it is nonsensical to say that I lost or misplaced my body.

Second, the thing is given to me perspectivally, in contrast to the nonperspectival presence of my body. I only perceive the table from a point of view; not all of its sides are immediately present to me in the strict sense. There is a spontaneous anticipation by me of the cogiven, hidden sides. Because the table is only partially given, I can be deceived about it. My certainty about its existence is presumptive, not apodictic. Past perspectives are continually being related to present viewpoints; present interpretations can be either confirmed or nullified by future perceptions. This perspectival presence of the thing is different from the massive, mute, nonperspectival presence of my perceiving body. Because my body is the agent or source of perceptual activity, I cannot doubt my body. My body is the necessary condition for resolving perceptual doubt; therefore, any perceptual doubt concerning its existence makes no sense.

Third, the content of the object is experienced as independent of me, in contrast to my own acts of perceiving. It is up to me whether

I see or touch, look at this object or that, focus on the shape of the table or its color. What is not up to me is the content of the object perceived. Whether I like it or not, the table is brown, not red; rectangular, not triangular.

Fourth, the table is experienced as a unity, in contrast to multiple acts of perceiving. As I move around the table, touch it, look at it from different points of view, it still remains the same table "there." When I leave the room and return, the table is still given as the same individual table in the same place. Finally, the table is experienced as a gestalt or figure against the background of the room, house, and so on. The table is not a collection of atomistic points, but an organized whole. Each part has meaning only in relation to the whole and to the other parts, the "front" in relation to the "back," the "top" in relation to the "bottom."

All of these five aspects taken together constitute perceptual objectivity, although no one aspect taken by itself is sufficient. For instance, content can occur independently of will in my body—I can feel pain. But this content is not taken as an indication of a distinct physical thing because it is present in my body "here," inseparable from me. The other four aspects of perceptual objectivity are not present.[7]

Although the table is distinct from me, nonetheless it is related to me because it is present to my consciousness. The real table is not something hidden behind the phenomena of perception but present in and through these phenomena. Consequently there is a basic paradox in perceptual objectivity shared by all other types as well. The thing is known as independent of consciousness only because of evidence present to consciousness. Perception is perception of an object distinct from the perceiver and yet present in the perceiver's conscious experience.

A second kind of objectivity is that of the universal, present in such disciplines as science, mathematics, formal logic, and philosophy. The object here, in contrast to the perceived object, is universal, applicable to many different particulars. The scientific law $f = ma$ or the mathematical definition of a triangle is true not just of one force or one triangle but of all forces and all triangles. Because the object of such thinking is universal, it is also nonperspectival and nonimaginable. In contrast to perception, which is always from a point of view, the definition of force or triangle transcends this limitation because it is true from all points of view. The universal is a concept, not an image. If it were an image, it would be individual, not universal. Although the image of triangle always has some thickness to the lines and points, the concept of a triangle posits no thickness in lines and points.

Still a third kind of objectivity is the thematic. Here again the most obvious example is from perception, in which I actively attend to or thematize what I am perceiving. When I look at the table to determine its color, I am actively attending to that and only implicitly, vaguely aware of other things in the room forming part of the background. If a piece of music catches my attention, then the table slides into the background and the music now becomes the theme. Thematization is present on all levels of conscious experience. Other examples are the working out of a mathematical proof, in which I actively attend to the argument and its conclusion; and daydreaming, in which I imagine myself in Bermuda enjoying a winter vacation.

A fourth kind of objectivity is factual, the objectivity arrived at through the *yes* or *no* of judgment. When I affirm that the bread is on the table or that f = ma or that Columbus discovered America in 1492, I am affirming facts. This kind of objectivity gets one beyond what is merely conceptually true to what in fact is so. A mathematical definition of a triangle is conceptually true, but that there are some triangular things is a fact. Factual truth also gets us beyond what is merely hypothetical or possible. When the scientist entertains the theory of relativity as a hypothesis, he is considering the merely possible. When he verifies such a hypothesis, then he knows a fact.[8]

A fifth kind of objectivity is alienation. When, without prior provocation, I call a person a name, slap him, or shoot him, I am objectifying him in a degrading sense. I am ignoring his character as a free, self-conscious, intelligent subject and treating him like a thing. What is involved here is an attempt by one person to harm, dominate, control, or manipulate the other. In a broader sense, alienation is any kind of inappropriate objectification that estranges me from myself, other people, or being. For instance, if I think of myself simply as a physical object, then I am excluding those realms of feeling, thinking, and freedom that cannot be described in physical terms. If I think of being simply as the sum total of mathematical objects or as simply comprehensible, then I am overlooking all aspects of being that cannot be mathematicized or comprehended.

Normative objectivity is still a sixth kind of objectivity—the fidelity to the dictates of inquiring intelligence and reasonableness.[9] When I tell a person to "be objective," I am asking him or her to give the voice of reason priority over other voices, to be attentive to evidence, and to ignore irrational bias. I am asking him or her to be faithful to the standards of evidence as they pertain to a particular field of inquiry. The explicitly and methodically rational disciplines such as science, logic, and philosophy are the best examples of such normative objectivity; but this fidelity to standards is present in other areas as well.

If a film critic insisted on applying the standards of stage drama to film, he would not be objective in the normative sense. In criticizing a film stressing the visual possibilities of the medium for having little or no dialogue, he would be imposing on one sphere standards appropriate for another, the stage. In reading such a critic, we would find his observations arbitrary and unfounded.

Finally the seventh kind of objectivity is experiential—the given data crucial for reaching truth in any inquiry.[10] These data are basically two kinds, data of sense and data of consciousness. Data of sense are the realm of perceived objects, the first kind of objectivity mentioned above. Data of consciousness are the human subject's experience of himself or herself in relation to the world. Data of sense, not to be understood as isolated atoms but as gestalts, are crucial for verifying the propositions of the physical and social sciences. Data of consciousness are essential for verifying propositions in philosophy. For instance, in trying to distinguish seven different kinds of objectivity, the philosopher must reflect on his own experience of these types of objectivity.

Interrelationships

The relationships between and among the kinds of objectivity are two sorts, negative and positive. Negative relationships are present simply because there are seven distinct types of objectivity, none of which is simply identified with the others. However, this nonidentity has a strong and a weak sense. The strong sense is that A is not and can never be B. For instance, perceptual objectivity is not universal objectivity, nor is factual objectivity experiential objectivity. The weak sense of nonidentity is inexhaustibility. For instance, perceptual objectivity is a type of thematic objectivity, but cannot be simply identified with such objectivity because universal and factual objectivity are also thematic. All perception is thematization, but not all thematization is perception. There are important implications, to be explored in the next section, flowing from these negative relationships.

Positive relationships are also of three kinds: class inclusion, eidetic unity, and foundation. One example of class inclusion has already been mentioned: perception, as well as universal, factual, degrading, and experiential objectification, is a type of thematization. Indeed thematization seems to be the most universal kind of objectification, present on all levels of conscious experience. All consciousness is consciousness of an object or theme explicitly present to consciousness. Whether one is looking at a table, imagining a pleasant trip to Canada, thinking about a mathematical proof, or choosing a life's vocation, he or she is considering a thematic object.

Eidetic unity between and among types justifies us in calling them *objectivities.* What are the common threads that run through all the types of objectivity? One such thread is the structure of thematization, in which a theme is present to consciousness but not reducible to it. Thematization can be seen not merely as a kind of objectivity existing alongside other kinds but as a structure permeating all other kinds. One aspect of this structure is consciousness-independence or consciousness-transcendence. Thus, the meaning of a perceptual thing or a mathematical proposition such as $2 + 2 = 4$ is present to consciousness but at the same time transcends consciousness because of the experienced difference between the multiplicity of conscious acts and the one public meaning. The act of perceiving is experienced as private, proceeding from me as the perceiving agent, in contrast to the one public, perceivable thing accessible to many knowers. The mathematical proposition $2 + 2 = 4$ is one in contrast to the many acts of one knower and to many individual knowers.[11]

Independence is also present in the different kinds of objectivity insofar as they are different and specific. Any objectivity is essentially related to a subjectivity engaged in transcending itself. Indeed there are two relationships to subjectivity here, two types of transcendence: negative and positive. The negative is the factual as opposed to merely wishful thinking, the universal as opposed to the merely individual, the normative as opposed to mere subjective, irrational bias. The positive relationship is present insofar as the act of judging is related to the noematic fact, the act of conceiving to the content thought, the act of fidelity to the norms of a particular discipline or level of consciousness.

Objectivity as foundation is present when A cannot be itself without B; B is the foundation of A. For instance, perception can exist without the universalization of science, but science presupposes perception. As I have already indicated, science has to verify its hypotheses through perception. Again, insofar as perceptual, universal, and factual objectivity are affairs of truth, they are founded on normative objectivity, a fidelity to the rules for correct perceiving, and so on. A third example of foundation is that factual objectivity presupposes experiential objectivity insofar as the claims of science, psychoanalysis, and philosophy are founded on the evidence that is given.

Consequences

The first consequence that emerges from this analysis is the possibility and necessity of objectifying the subject. Much ink has been spilt over this issue in phenomenology and existentialism because insufficient attention has been paid to the kinds of objectivity, their distinctions, and their interrelationships. One cannot objectify the subject, so the argument goes, because in trying to do so one turns the subject into an object. Subjectivity is lost in the process of conceptualizing it, and one thus becomes alienated from oneself.[12]

In two ways there is some truth to the argument. First of all, any reflection on human experience is necessarily on past experience. For example, to reflect on the experience of perceiving is to reflect on this experience as having lapsed. I cannot reflect on the experience of reflection as present. If I try to do so, then that experience slips into the past and becomes the object or theme of a second reflection taking place in the present. Second, in no reflection does the original experience in its immediacy survive on the level of reflection. What does emerge is the meaning of that experience, universal and thematic. Just as the original experience of green does not survive in the scientific account of green in terms of wave length, so also the original experience of perception does not survive in the reflective account of perception.

Do the preceding concessions to the arguments against objectifying the subject imply that there is no valid sense in which it can be objectified? As the reader must suspect, the answer has to be a resounding no. To say that the subject cannot in any way be objectified because of the reasons mentioned above is to confuse experiential with thematic objectivity. To say that objectification of the subject cannot occur because such objectification turns the subject into a thing is mistakenly to identify thematic with perceptual or scientific objectivity. What is thematized in a philosophical account of subjectivity is its meaning as no-thing, as conscious, free, and intentional.[13]

Such accounts are not just pale reflections of the original, rich experience. This empiricist claim does not recognize that reflective thematization and insight *enriches* our experience—we know more about ourselves afterwards than we did before. What is merely confused and vague on an immediate, experimental level becomes clear and explicit on a reflective level. For example, on a prereflective level our awareness of the kinds of objectivity, their rules, and interrelationships is at best implicit and unclear. When we philosophically distinguish and define the seven kinds of objectivity, not only our reflection but our common sense and scientific practice are illuminated and clarified.

What gives the argument against objectifying the subject plausibility is the lumping together of various kinds of objectivity, perceptual, scientific, thematic, and experiential. Once these senses are clearly distinguished, then the paradox disappears. Not only *can* the human subject be objectified, but at times, if self-knowledge is to occur, he or she *should* be objectified.

Second, objectification of the other person can occur without degradation or alienation because thematization and degradation are two distinct senses of objectification. If I say to another person, You are very wise, such a statement certainly is a thematizing; but it is not intended to degrade or hurt the other person, nor does he or she experience it as such. Rather what can and does happen is that such a statement builds up the relationship and contributes to the other person's sense of worth and dignity. He or she experiences him- or herself as exalted, liberated, and enlightened by my expressed esteem.

There are, of course, forms of behavior that do objectify in a degrading sense. If with insufficient provocation, I call another person an idiot or a scoundrel or a charlatan, then clearly I am using language to humiliate him or her. What I am denying here is that such degradation is an inevitable result of my thematizing the other person and my relationship with him or her. Sartre gets mileage out of his argument for such a claim by uncritically lumping together the three distinct senses of perceptual, thematic, and alienated objectivity.[14] However, not all "looks" are alienating because some only thematize whereas others degrade and humiliate. Looking at another person with reverence and esteem is essentially, logically different from staring a person down, judging him or her, shaming him or her.

There are times when objectification of my own body can be experienced as liberating. For instance, when I have a broken leg, I want the doctor to objectify me, to use his knowledge of science to help me get well. The doctor's objectification of my body is liberating because he is helping me to do what I want to do, get back on my feet. This kind of objectification is a different sort of thing from that experienced by a beautiful woman leered at or whistled at as she walks down the street. The first is positive and enhancing, the second is degrading and disconcerting.

Finally, a third consequence of my analysis is that a conceptual knowledge of being can reveal and enlighten. Conceptual, representational thinking is not necessarily a thinking that distorts and covers up being, as Heidegger claims.[15] Only if one identifies the thematization proper to philosophy with that of perceptual, scientific, alienating, or experimental objectification can such a claim be true.

Philosophy as practiced in this paper is phenomenology, the universal, reflective, conceptual thematization of human subjectivity in relation to being. Thinking is conceptual because it is universal and expressive, a working out into language of notions initially vague and incomplete. What the thinker experiences is a movement from an initially indeterminate, vague, incomplete notion to one that is determinate, explicit, and complete. Thinking has a preconceptual moment, but this is experienced as incomplete until it is expressed and conceptualized. Just as the painter does not fully know what he wants to say until he has added the final brush stroke, so also the philosopher reflecting on subjectivity or being does not know what he wants to say until he has said it.[16]

Such a claim has to be true because any attempt to deny it refutes itself. Any attempt to deny the conceptual and universal ends up implicitly asserting them. Thus, Heidegger's attempt to arrive at a postconceptual, postmetaphysical, postrepresentational thinking actually uses such concepts as "presence," the "fourfold," "involvement," and "releasement."[17]

Is *being* an object? Clearly Heidegger has a point in denying that being is an object in the sense of perceived thing, scientifically known thing, or dominated, reified person or thing.[18] Experience of being is not of an object but of an implicit context or ground within which objects appear. Reflection on such experience, however, thematizes being as "horizon" or "that which regions."[19] In this sense being is an object. In describing being this way, Heidegger is articulating a definite, universal, thematized notion of being. Otherwise his very illuminating discussion would mean nothing to us.

In making such a claim for conceptual knowledge, however, I am not arguing for a total comprehension of being.[20] Such a claim would be alienating in the broader sense of that word—an inappropriate objectification. Because of our finitude and our immersion in a necessarily implicit context of language and being, Heidegger is surely correct in denying the possibility of such comprehension. The language that I use in talking about anything is always composed of sedimented meanings that cannot be totally thematized at the time I use them.[21] For instance, if I am discussing music with a person, there is always a taken-for-granted set of meanings and words that are utilized but not explicitly reflected upon or justified. The world is always present to me as more than I can thematize or conceptualize at any one time. There is always an implicit background from which the explicit meaning emerges, always unanswered questions enveloping those which I do answer. If I have answered the question about the seven kinds of objectivity, their interrelationships, and their consequences, there are always further questions. Does my analysis reopen the possibility of metaphysics? What are the implications for ethics, political philosophy, aesthetics?

I am arguing for a middle ground between saying that objective, conceptual thought can tell us nothing about being and saying that it can tell us everything. Although there is not space to develop the point adequately in this paper, I would suggest that Heidegger's practice, in contrast to his explicit conception of what he is doing, is on such middle ground. To think being in a nonalienated fashion is to think it conceptually as mystery, as gift, as beyond total comprehension.[22] Philosophical knowledge is not total enlightenment about ourselves in the world but light emerging from darkness, unconcealment arising from concealment. The task of philosophy is to articulate conceptually, as much as possible, this necessary concealment, not to remain silent about it or to overlook it.

Conclusion

Objectivity turns out to be many splendored. Because of this fact, objectivity can have a role to play that is authentic and liberating. One question that might arise is whether my description of the seven types of objectivity is exhaustive. A claim of exhaustibility goes beyond the evidence presented in the paper and is not essential to the argument of the paper. Such a claim goes beyond the evidence because I have given no argument against the possibility that there may be other kinds. Exhaustibility is not essential to the argument because I have shown that there are *at least* these seven kinds and that these have important implications for certain issues in phenomenology and existentialism. A possible eighth or ninth kind of objectivity would not affect the argument here.

What has to happen is a restoration of objectivity to its proper place in relation to subjectivity. Only with such a restoration can existentialism and phenomenology avoid replacing a one-sided objectivism with an equally one-sided subjectivism. The conceptual knowledge that is restored is chastened and humble, aware of its own limits but also capable of illuminating our quest for truth.

Contributors

John M. Anderson (Distinguished Professor of Philosophy, Pennsylvania State University) is author of *The Individual and the New World*, *The Realm of Art*, and *The Truth of Freedom*. He is coeditor of the international philosophical quarterly, *Man and World*. He has written and lectured widely on topics in mathematics, logic, metaphysics, and philosophy of culture.

Mildred Bakan (Associate Professor of Philosophy and Social Science, York University) has published numerous papers in journals and anthologies on the mind-body problem and on topics in philosophical anthropology and social thought.

Linda A. Bell (Associate Professor of Philosophy, Georgia State University) has edited an anthology, *Visions of Women: A Philosophical Chronicle*; has published articles on Sartre; and has completed a manuscript on Sartrean authenticity and traditional ethics.

Ronald Bruzina (Professor of Philosophy, University of Kentucky) is the author of *Logos and Eidos: The Concept of Phenomenology*. He is the translator of Kostas Axelos' *Alienation, Praxis, and Technē in the Thought of Karl Marx* and he has written various articles on Merleau-Ponty, Husserl, and Heidegger.

David Carr (Professor of Philosophy, The University of Ottawa) is the coeditor of a previous volume in this series, *Explorations in Phenomenology*, the translator of Husserl's *The Crisis of European Sciences and Transcendental Phenomenology*, and the author of *Phenomenology and the Problem of History*, among other writings.

Arleen B. Dallery (Associate Professor of Philosophy, La Salle College) has coedited an anthology, *Death and Society*; has published articles on Continental thinkers and on social philosophy and the philosophy of medicine; and is currently writing a manual on the philosophy of work.

Bernard P. Dauenhauer (Professor of Philosophy, University of Georgia) is the author of *Silence: The Phenomenon and its Ontological Significance*. He is currently preparing a longer work on issues in social and political philosophy, a field in which he has published a number of shorter articles in the past.

Cyril W. Dwiggins (Associate Professor and Chair of Philosophy, Dickinson College) has written articles and presented papers on topics in phenomenology and aesthetics. His book, *Experiencing Metaphor*, is forthcoming.

283

Contributors

Thomas R. Flynn (Associate Professor of Philosophy, Emory University) has published numerous articles on Sartre, Marx, and Heidegger and has completed a manuscript on collective responsibility.

Richard F. Grabau (Professor of Philosophy, Purdue University, until the time of his death in 1980) had authored articles on the philosophy of Karl Jaspers and had translated Jaspers' *Existenzphilosophie*.

William S. Hamrick (Associate Professor of Philosophy, Southern Illinois University at Edwardsville) has published articles on phenomenology and social philosophy and has presented numerous papers at professional meetings in both the United States and Europe. He is an assistant editor of the *Journal of the British Society for Phenomenology*.

David Levin (Associate Professor of Philosophy, Northwestern University) is the author of *Reason and Evidence in Husserl's Phenomenology*. He has made numerous contributions to professional journals, dealing with a wide range of topics in phenomenology. He is currently completing a book on Heidegger.

James L. Marsh (Professor of Philosophy, St. Louis University) has published in the areas of existentialism, phenomenology, Hegel's thought, and critical social theory. He has a book in progress, to be entitled *Post-Cartesian Meditations*.

J. N. Mohanty (Research Professor of Philosophy, University of Oklahoma) is the author of *Edmund Husserl's Theory of Meaning*, *Phenomenology and Ontology*, and *The Concept of Intentionality*. He has published numerous articles and has lectured widely throughout the world.

Mary C. Rawlinson (Assistant Professor of Philosophy, State University of New York at Stony Brook) is the author of *Psychiatric Discourse in the Feminine Voice* and of articles in the philosophy of medicine and of literature.

Tom Rockmore (Associate Professor of Philosophy, Fordham University) is the author of *Fichte, Marx, and German Philosophy*, of two forthcoming books on Marxism, and of numerous articles in both English and French on topics in contemporary Continental philosophy.

George A. Schrader, Jr. (Professor of Philosophy, Yale University) has authored numerous articles, published both in the United States and abroad, on the philosophy of Kant, ethics, and existential philosophy. He is the editor of *Existential Philosophers: Kierkegaard to Merleau-Ponty*.

Reiner Schürmann (Associate Professor and Chair of Philosophy, The New School for Social Research) has published three books—*Le Principe d' anarchie: Heidegger et la question de l' agir*, *Meister Eckhart, Mystic and Philosopher*, and *Les Origines*—and many articles on modern and contemporary philosophy.

Hans Seigfried (Professor of Philosophy, Loyola University of Chicago) is the author of *Wahrheit und Metaphysik bei Suarez* and has written numerous articles on Kant, Heidegger, and the philosophy of science.

Robert R. Williams (Associate Professor of Religion, Hiram College) is the author of *Schleiermacher the Theologian* and has written articles in phenomenology and philosophy of religion.

Richard Zaner (Ann Geddes Stahlman Professor of Medical Ethics, Vanderbilt University Medical School) is author of *The Problem of Embodiment*, *The Ways of Phenomenology*, and *The Context of Self*. He is also the author of numerous articles on the phenomenology of medicine and lectures widely on the topic.

Notes

Notes to Chapter 1

1. *Being and Nothingness*, trans. Hazel E. Barnes (New York: Philosophical Library, 1956), p. 581.
2. Ibid., p. 70n.
3. Ibid., p. 412n.
4. Ibid., p. 615.
5. Ibid., p. 627.
6. Ibid.
7. *Critique of Dialectical Reason*, trans. Alan Sheridan-Smith (Atlantic Highlands: Humanities Press, 1976), p. 678.
8. Ibid., p. 668.
9. Ibid., pp. 538–39.
10. Ibid., p. 540.
11. "The Wall," in *Existentialism from Dostoevsky to Sartre*, ed. Walter Kaufmann (New York: The World Publishing Company, 1963), p. 239.
12. *The Devil and the Good Lord*, trans. Kitty Black (New York: Vintage Books, 1960), p. 143.
13. Ibid., p. 145.
14. Ibid., p. 149.
15. Ibid.
16. Simone de Beauvoir, *Force of Circumstance*, vol. 1, trans. Richard Howard (New York: Harper and Row, 1977), p. 243.
17. *In the Mesh*, trans. Mervyn Savill (London: Andrew Dakers Limited, 1954), pp. 124–25.
18. *Dirty Hands*, trans. Lionel Abel, *No Exit and Three Other Plays by Jean-Paul Sartre* (New York: Vintage Books, 1955), pp. 223–25.
19. Ibid., p. 225.
20. Ibid., p. 246.
21. "Jean-Paul Sartre: Man, Freedom, and *Praxis*," in *Existential Philosophers: Kierkegaard to Merleau-Ponty*, ed. George Alfred Schrader (New York: McGraw-Hill Book Company, 1967), p. 286.
22. *The Schizoid World of Jean-Paul Sartre* (Atlantic Highlands: Humanities Press, 1977), p. 22.

Notes

23. *Being and Nothingness*, p. 580.
24. Ibid.
25. Ibid., pp. 580–81.
26. *Critique of Practical Reason*, trans. Lewis White Beck (New York: Bobbs-Merrill, 1956), p. 127.
27. *Being and Nothingness*, p. 580.
28. *Kierkegaard's Concluding Unscientific Postscript*, trans. David F. Swenson (Princeton: Princeton University Press, 1941), p. 421.
29. Søren Kierkegaard, *Either/Or*, vol. 2, trans. Walter Lowrie (Garden City, New York: Doubleday, 1959), p. 352.
30. *Concluding Unscientific Postscript*, p. 466.
31. Ibid.
32. *Being and Nothingness*, p. 59.
33. *The Emotions*, trans. Bernard Frechtman (New York: Philosophical Library, 1948), pp. 62–63.
34. See Sartre's analysis of the group in fusion in the *Critique of Dialectical Reason.*

Notes to Chapter 2

1. M. Merleau-Ponty, *Signs*, trans. Richard C. McCleary (Evanston: Northwestern University Press, 1964), p. 20. My modification of McCleary's translation. Hereafter *S*.
2. Other special cases are specific religions, specific arts, and specific educational enterprises.
3. Ferdinand de Saussure, *Course in General Linguistics*, trans. Wade Baskin (New York: McGraw-Hill, 1966), pp. 7–10, 71–78, and 90–100. Hereafter CGL.
4. M. Merleau-Ponty, *Adventures of the Dialectic*, trans. by Joseph Bien (Evanston: Northwestern University Press, 1973), p. 103. Hereafter *AD*.
5. *S*, pp. 218–219. For another version of this relation with a notably different emphasis, see Bertrand de Jouvenel, *Sovereignty*, trans. J. F. Huntington (Chicago: The University of Chicago Press, 1957), pp. 137–138. Hereafter *Sov.*
6. *S*, pp. 274–275. See also M. Merleau-Ponty, *Humanism and Terror*, trans. John O'Neill, (Boston: Beacon Press, 1969), pp. xxxii–xxxiii. Hereafter *HT*. It is no surprise that Themistocles, Aristides, Pericles, and Thucydides could not teach their sons to be statesmen. See Plato, *Meno*, trans. G.M.A. Grube (Indianapolis: Hackett, 1976), pp. 26–27.
7. *S*, p. 276.
8. M. Merleau-Ponty, *Sense and Non-Sense*, trans. Hubert L. Dreyfus and Patricia Allen Dreyfus (Evanston: Northwestern University Press, 1964), p. 143. Hereafter *SNS*.
9. *S*, pp. 302–303. As de Saussure says, "In language there are only differences." *CGL*, p. 120.
10. According to de Saussure, the synchronic laws of language report states of affairs but are not imperative. Thus, the state of affairs is precarious. *CGL*, p. 92.
11. *S*, p. 336. See also *S*, p. 35, where Merleau-Ponty says, "History never confesses, not even her lost illusions, but neither does she dream of them again."
12. *S*, pp. 323–324.

13. *AD*, p. 23. See the useful, related remarks by de Jouvenel, *Sov*, pp. 105–107.

14. M. Merleau-Ponty, *Signes* (Paris: Gallimard, 1960) p. 47.

15. *S*, pp. 328, 335. See also Merleau-Ponty, "Pour La Vérité," *Les Temps Modernes*, 1945, p. 600.

16. *AD*, p. 124. See also James Miller, *History and Human Existence* (Berkeley: University of California Press, 1979), pp. 209–212.

17. *AD*, p. 143.

18. M. Merleau-Ponty, *Themes from the Lectures at Collège de France, 1952–1960*, trans. by John O'Neill (Evanston: Northwestern University Press, 1970), pp. 40–41.

19. *S*, pp. 289 and 349. See also *SNS*, p. 152 for an earlier version of this insight of Merleau-Ponty's. In another related context, Merleau-Ponty has said: "The presence of the individual in the institution and of the institution in the individual is evident in the case of linguistic change. It is often the wearing down of a form which suggests to us a new way of using the means of discrimination which are present in the language at a given time. . . . The contingent fact, taken over by the will to expression, becomes a new means of expression which takes its place, and has a lasting sense in the history of this language" (M. Merleau-Ponty, *In Praise of Philosophy*, trans. by John Wild and James Edie [Evanston: Northwestern University Press, 1963], p. 55. Hereafter *IPP*.

20. *CGL*, pp. 77–78.

21. See M. Merleau-Ponty, *Phenomenology of Perception*, trans. Colin Smith (London: Routledge and Kegan Paul, 1962), pp. 183–184 and M. Merleau-Ponty, *The Primacy of Perception*, trans. James Edie (Northwestern University Press, 1964), p. 134.

22. *SNS*, p. 143 and *AD*, pp. 120 and 150–151.

23. *AD*, pp. 53 and 206.

24. *AD*, p. 22.

25. *AD*, pp. 225ff. It may be noteworthy that the politics of present-day Western Europe is attempting to act as a third force between the United States and the Soviet Union. But regrettably, from Merleau-Ponty's standpoint, it is hardly a "left" force. See William Pfaff, "Reflections: Finlandization," *The New Yorker*, September 1, 1980, pp. 30–34.

26. *HT*, pp. xxiv–xxv.

27. *AD*, p. 198.

28. *AD*, p. 207.

29. *AD*, p. 226.

30. *SNS*, p. 148 and *S*, pp. 348–349.

31. *HT*, pp. xxiv–xxxv. See also de Jouvenel, *Sov*, pp. 18–25 and 31–33.

32. *S*, p. 336.

33. See Willy Brandt et al., *North-South: A Programme for Survival* (Cambridge, Mass.: MIT Press, 1980). "It is now widely recognized that development involves a profound transformation of the entire economic and social structure. This embraces changes in production and demand as well as improvements in income distribution and employment. It means creating a more diversified economy, whose main sectors become more interdependent for supplying inputs and for expanding markets for output.

"The actual patterns of structural transformation will tend to vary from one country to another depending on a number of factors—including resources, geography, and the skills of the population. There are therefore no golden rules capable of universal application for economic development. Each country has to exploit the opportunities open to it for strengthening its economy. Structural transformation need not imply autarky. Some countries might find it feasible to pursue inward-looking strategies that rely, at least in the early stages, on using their domestic markets. Others may diversify and expand their exports. Exports can become more fully integrated with the rest of the economy, as the domestic market comes to provide a larger base, or as export industries secure more of their inputs from local sources. Yet others will concentrate initially on distributing income more evenly in order to widen the domestic market for locally produced goods and to lay the foundations for a better balance between the rural and urban sectors. But all countries need an international environment that will be responsive to their development efforts. Herein lies part of the rationale for a new international economic order" (pp. 48–49; See also pp. 127–128.)

34. *S*, p. 4.

35. *S*, p. 35. My modification of McCleary's translation.

36. *AD*, p. 155.

37. *AD*, pp. 144 and 194.

38. *S*, pp. 324 and 328.

39. Machiavelli's weakness was that he did not have such a guideline. See *S*, pp. 221–223.

40. *S*, p. 307.

41. *IPP*, p. 32.

42. Gabriel Marcel, *Homo Viator*, trans. by D. S. Fraser (New York: Harper Torchbooks, 1962), pp. 29–67. Hereafter *HV*. My conception of Merleau-Ponty's politics of hope is at variance with that of Barry Cooper. See his *Merleau-Ponty and Marxism: From Terror to Reform* (Toronto: University of Toronto Press, 1979), pp. 53–55.

43. *HV*, p. 60.

44. *HV*, p. 67.

45. I do not, of course, want to suggest that Merleau-Ponty's politics rests upon anything like the absolute Thou which Marcel says is the "very cement which binds the whole into one" (*HV*, pp. 60–61). On the nonterminal character of political conduct, see de Jouvenel, *Sov.*, pp. 129–130.

46. *HT*, p. xxxv.

47. *S*, pp. 314–318.

48. Perhaps the stringency of this guideline could be attenuated without loss of fidelity to Merleau-Ponty's intentions, in the following way: A policy or deed is justified if it is recognizable to everyone, *at least mediately*, as something that each man or state could rationally endorse being carried out by someone, even if not by oneself. Thus *A*, who cannot immediately approve of *B*'s policy or deed, can approve of *C*'s policies and deeds even when these latter involve an endorsement of that performance of *B*, that *A* cannot directly accept. Through and only through the acceptability to *A* of *C*'s policies and deeds is *B*'s policy or deed made acceptable to *A*. Such an attenuation would forestall the fault of legitimating too little.

49. *HT*, pp. xxxiv–xxxv and *SNS*, p. 152.

50. *AD*, p. 196.

51. *AD*, p. 29.

Notes to Chapter 3

1. Sheldon Wolin, *Politics and Vision* (Boston: Little, Brown, 1960), p. 25.
2. See my *"L'Imagination au Pouvoir: The Evolution of Sartre's Political and Social Thought,"* *Political Theory* 7 no. 2 (May 1979):176, n. 22.
3. Leszek Kolakowski and Stuart Hampshire, eds., *The Socialist Idea* (New York: Basic Books, 1974), p. 9.
4. Jean-Paul Sartre, *The Communists and Peace*, cited by Maurice Merleau-Ponty in *Les Aventures de la Dialectique* (Paris: Gallimard, 1955), p. 197.
5. Jean-Paul Sartre, *Literary and Philosophical Essays*, trans. Annette Michelson (New York: Collier Books, 1962), p. 253.
6. Jean-Paul Sartre, *Anti-Semite and Jew*, trans. George J. Becker (New York: Schocken Books, 1956), pp. 148–149.
7. Jean-Paul Sartre, *Saint Genet, Actor and Martyr*, trans. Bernard Frechtman (New York: Mentor Books, 1964), p. 590.
8. Merleau-Ponty, *Les Aventures*, p. 209.
9. Jean-Paul Sartre, *The Communists and Peace*, with *A Reply to Claude Lefort*, trans. Martha H. Fletcher and Philip R. Berk (New York: George Braziller, 1968), p. 252.
10. See Jean-Paul Sartre, *Critique of Dialectical Reason*, trans. Alan Sheridan-Smith (London: New Left Books, 1976), pp. 113, 374–76, 735.
11. Jean-Paul Sartre, *Situations*, 10 vols. to date (Paris: Gallimard, 1947–), 3:192.
12. *Situations*, 3:218.
13. Jean-Paul Sartre, *L'Idiot de la famille: Gustave Flaubert de 1821 a 1859*, 3 vols (Paris: Gallimard, 1971–1972), 3:189. He thus shares with Michael Harrington the view that "material abundance is a precondition for socialist development" and that "we should measure progress by the reduction of necessary work and by the growth of leisure" (cited by Kolakowski and Hampshire, *Socialist Idea*, p. 9).
14. See Raymond Aron, *Marxism and the Existentialists* (New York: Harper and Row, 1969), pp. 30ff. This seems to underlie the recent controversy between Peter Singer and Robert Heilbroner over the compatibility of socialism and liberal political ideals. See "Letters," *The New York Review of Books* 27, no. 20 (December 18, 1980):66.
15. Gajo Petrović, "Socialism, Revolution and Violence," in Kolakowski and Hampshire, *Socialist Idea*, p. 100.
16. First enunciated in an interview with *Comoedia* in 1943, it was given a kind of theoretical justification in *Existentialism is a Humanism* (1946) and guided Sartre's political and social commitment thereafter. See Michel Contat and Michel Rybalka, eds, *The Writings of Jean-Paul Sartre*, 2 vols., *A Bibliographical Life*, trans. Richard C. McCleary (Evanston: Northwestern University Press, 1974), 1:87.
17. See my "Praxis and Vision: Elements of a Sartrean Epistemology," *Philosophical Forum* 8 (1976):21–43.
18. Jean-Paul Sartre, *Being and Nothingness*, trans. Hazel E. Barnes (New York: Philosophical Library, 1956), p. 440.
19. "The Responsibility of the Writer," *Reflections on Our Age* (New York: Columbia University Press, 1949), p. 83.
20. See Philippe Gavi, Jean-Paul Sartre, and Pierre Victor, *On a raison de se révolter* (Paris: Gallimard, 1974), pp. 78–79; hereafter *ORR*.

21. *Sartre, un film*, ed. Alexandre Astruc and Michel Contat (Paris: Gallimard, 1977), p. 100.

22. Simone de Beauvoir, *The Ethics of Ambiguity*, trans. Bernard Frechtman (Secaucus, N.J.: The Citadel Press, 1948), pp. 133, 148.

23. *Situations*, 4:127.

24. See his interview "A Long, Bitter, Sweet Madness," *Encounter* 22 (June, 1964):62.

25. *L'Idiot*, 3:48.

26. *ORR*, p. 288.

27. See *ORR*, p. 345.

28. See my "An End to Authority: Epistemology and Politics in the Later Sartre," *Man and World* 10, no. 4 (1977):448–465.

29. See *ORR*, pp. 284–89 and 345.

30. *Critique*, p. 662.

31. See his essay by that title in Jean-Paul Sartre, *Life/Situations*, trans. Paul Auster and Lydia Davis (New York: Pantheon Books, 1977), p. 198. For Sartre's second thoughts on elections in Western democracies, see his interview with Benny Lévy, *Le Nouvel Observateur*, no. 801 (17–23 March, 1980), especially p. 56.

32. See *ORR*, pp. 75–77.

33. Lucien Goldmann, *Marxisme et sciences humaines* (Paris: Gallimard, 1970), pp. 358–359.

34. Jean-Paul Sartre, *Between Existentialism and Marxism*, trans. John Matthews (New York: Morrow Paperbacks, 1974), p. 24. For his final remarks on violence, including the hope that a nonviolent society might someday be achieved, see the Lévy interview, *Le Nouvel Observateur*, 52–58.

35. Frantz Fanon, *The Wretched of the Earth* with Preface by Jean-Paul Sartre, trans. Constance Ferrington (New York: Grove Press, 1968), p. 24.

36. *Critique*, p. 736.

37. Simone de Beauvoir, *Ethics*, p. 133.

38. See Simone de Beauvoir, *Prime of Life*, trans. Peter Green (New York: Lancer Books, 1966), pp. 46, 88.

39. Cited by Lucien Rioux and René Backmann, *L'Explosion de mai* (Paris: Robert Laffont, 1968), p. 14. This book offers one of the most complete summaries of these events available.

40. See Epistémon [Didier Anzieu], *Ces idées qui ont ébranlé la France* (Paris: Feyard, 1968), pp. 78–87.

41. *Critique*, p. 401.

42. Rioux and Backmann, *L'Explosion*, p. 347.

43. See his interview with Michel Sicard in the special "Sartre" issue of *Obliques*, nos. 18–19 (1979), p. 15.

44. Lévy interview, *Le Nouvel Observateur*, no. 802 (24–30 March, 1980), p. 60.

Notes to Chapter 4

1. Maurice Merleau-Ponty, *Sens et non-sens*, 6th ed. (Paris: Nagel, 1966), pp. 208–209 (my own translation).

2. (Paris: Gallimard, 1945), p. 202 (my own translation).

3. *Die protestantische Ethik und der Geist des Kapitalismus*, p. 83, cited in Merleau-Ponty, *Les aventures de la dialectique* (Paris: Gallimard, 1955), p. 27 (my own translation). (This text will be referred to hereafter as *AD*.)

4. Merleau-Ponty, *Résumés de cours* (Paris: Gallimard, 1968), p. 50 (my own translation).

5. "Freie Rechtsfindung und freie Rechtswissenshaft," 9 *Modern Legal Philosophy Series* 65, cited in Benjamin N. Cardozo, *The Nature of the Judicial Process* (New Haven: Yale University Press, 1974), pp. 16–17.

6. "Positivism and Fidelity to Law—A Reply to Professor Hart," *Harvard Law Review* 71 (1958), p. 613.

7. Maurice Merleau-Ponty, *Humanisme et terreur* (Paris: Gallimard, 1947), p. 9 (my own translation). Referred to hereafter as *HT*.

8. *Signes* (Paris: Gallimard, 1960), p. 31.

9. *Law, Liberty and Morality* (Oxford: Oxford University Press, 1963), p. 71.

10. *Law, Liberty and Morality*, p. 71.

11. See my paper "Towards a Phenomenology of Toleration," *Journal of the British Society for Phenomenology* (forthcoming).

12. "Limits to the Free Expression of Opinion," in Joel Feinberg and Hyman Gross, eds., *Philosophy of Law* (Encino, CA: Dickenson, 1975), pp. 148–149.

13. Feinberg, *Philosophy of Law*, p. 149.

14. Feinberg, *Philosophy of Law*, p. 149.

15. *U.S. v. Schenck*, 249 U.S. 47 (1919), cited at 52. In the same vein, Holmes also said, and Merleau-Ponty would surely agree, that a "word is not a crystal, transparent and unchanged, it is the skin of a living thought and may vary greatly in color and content according to the circumstances and the time in which it is used" (*Towne v. Eisner*, 245 U.S. 418 (1918), cited at 425).

16. "Poem, Or Beauty Hurts Mr. Vinal," in *100 Selected Poems* (New York: Grove Press, 1954), p. 19.

17. *Social Philosophy* (Englewood Cliffs: Prentice-Hall, 1973), pp. 2–3.

18. Feinberg, "Limits to the Free Expression of Opinion," p. 149.

Notes to Chapter 5

1. Martin Heidegger, *Wegmarken* (Frankfurt: 1967), p. 191. Trans. D. Krell; *Basic Writings* (1977), p. 238f; although for all quotes I refer in these notes to the published English translations, all translations are mine.

2. See below, n. 43.

3. Friedrich Nietzsche, *Götzen-Dämmerung*, in vol. 2 of *Werke in drei Bänden*, ed. Karl Schlechta, (Munich: 1955), p. 963. Trans. Walter Kaufmann, *The Portable Nietzsche* (New York: 1968), pp. 485f.

4. Martin Heidegger, *Sein und Zeit* (Halle a.d. Saale: 1941), p. 39. Trans. John Macquarrie and Edward Robinson, *Being and Time* (New York: 1962), p. 63.

5. Heidegger, *Zur Seinsfrage*, Frankfurt 1959, p. 36, trans. Jean Wilde and William Kluback, *The Question of Being*, New Haven: 1958, p. 93. Heidegger spoke of "*Abbau*" already in the lecture course of 1927, "Die Grundprobleme der Phänomenologie", *Gesamtausgabe*, vol. 24, Frankfurt 1975, p. 31.

6. Heidegger, *Zur Seinsfrage*, p. 43, trans. p. 107.

Notes

7. Heidegger, *Holzwege*, Frankfurt: 1950, p. 204, trans. William Lovitt, *The Question Concerning Technology*, New York: 1977, p. 65. See the very similar list in his *Nietzsche*, Pfullingen: 1961, vol. 2, p. 273. Heidegger's technical term for these configurations is *Prägung* (stamp). "There is being only in this or that particular historical stamp: *Physis, Logos, Hen, Idea, Energeia*, Substantiality, Objectivity, Subjectivity, the Will, the Will to Power, the Will to Will"; in *Identität und Differenz* (Pfullingen: 1957), p. 64. Trans. Joan Stambaugh, *Identity and Difference* (New York: 1969), p. 66. The point is that with "the end of metaphysics," these epochal "stamps" disappear altogether: "The event of appropriation is not a new historical stamp of being" (*Zur Sache des Denkens* [Tübingen: 1969], p. 44. Trans. Joan Stambaugh, *On Time and Being* (New York: 1972), p. 40f.
8. *Zur Seinsfrage*, pp. 7f., trans. p. 35f.
9. Martin Heidegger, *Was ist Metaphysik?*, Einleitung, (Frankfurt: 1960), p. 9.
10. Martin Heidegger, *Der Satz vom Grund* (Pfullingen: 1957), pp. 40 and 42.
11. Karl Marx, *Das Elend der Philosophie, Frühe Schriften*, ed. H.J. Lieber and P. Furth, vol. 2 (Darmstadt: 1975), p. 750. *The Poverty of Philosophy* (New York: 1963), p. 115.
12. Martin Heidegger, "Etwas Durchgängiges", *Der Satz vom Grund*, pp. 153f. and *Identität und Differenz*, pp. 65f. Trans. pp. 67f.
13. Jacques Derrida, *De la grammatologie* (Paris: 1967), particularly pp. 21, 55. Trans. G. C. Spivak, *Of Grammatology* (Baltimore: 1976), pp. 10, 37.
14. "Perhaps patient meditation and painstaking investigation . . . are the wanderings of a way of thinking that is faithful and attentive to the world that is ineluctably to come and that proclaims itself to the present, beyond the closure of knowing" (ibid., p. 14; trans. p. 4).
15. Ibid., pp. 21–39, 142, 206. Trans. pp. 10–24, 93, 143.
16. "Wo aber Gefahr ist, wächst / Das Rettende auch," quoted, for instance, in Heidegger, *Vorträge und Aufsätze* (Pfullingen: 1954), p. 36. Trans. *The Question Concerning Technology*, p. 28.
17. Heidegger, *Der Satz vom Grund*, pp. 123f.
18. Heidegger, *Vorträge und Aufsätze*, p. 25. Trans. *The Question Concerning Technology*, p. 18.
19. Heidegger, *Nietzsche*, vol. 2, p. 428. Trans. Joan Stambaugh, *The End of Philosophy* (New York: 1973), p. 25.
20. Martin Heidegger, *Kant und das Problem der Metaphysik* (1973), p. 195. Trans. James Churchill, *Kant and the Problem of Metaphysics* (Bloomington:1962), p. 206.
21. Ibid., pp. 237f. trans. p. 253. The most explicit "confession of ignorance" in Heidegger concerns the question of politics: "It is a decisive question for me today how a political system, and of what kind, can at all be coordinated with the technological age. I do not know the answer to this question. I am not convinced that it is democracy" ("Nur noch ein Gott kann uns retten", *Der Spiegel*, May 31, 1976, p. 206; Trans. David Schendler, "Only a God Can Save Us Now", *Graduate Faculty Philosophy Journal* 6 no. [1977], p. 16).
22. "Das Wesen des Gestells ist die Gefahr . . . Martin Heidegger, *Die Technik und die Kehre* (Pfullingen:1962), p. 40. Trans. *The Question Concerning Technology*, p. 41.
23. René Char, *La parole en archipel* (Paris:1962), the title and p. 73.

24. Heidegger, *Vorträge und Aufsätze*, pp. 133f.. Trans. F. D. Wieck and J. G. Gray in David F. Krell, ed., Martin Heidegger, *Basic Writings* (New York:1977), p. 349.

25. See above, note 5.

26. Heidegger, *Der Satz vom Grund*, pp. 72f.

27. Martin Heidegger, *Wegmarken* (Frankfurt:1967), p. 153. Trans. F. A. Capuzzi and J. G. Gray, *Basic Writings*, p. 202.

28. Martin Heidegger, *Gesamtaugsgabe*, vol. 55, p. 132. This thesis has been popularized by Michel Foucault, *Les mots et les choses* (Paris:1966), pp. 15, 319–323, 396–398. *The Order of Things* (New York:1973), pp. xxiii, 308–311, 385–387.

29. Martin Heidegger, *Vorwort* to William Richardson, *Heidegger: Through Phenomenology to Thought* (The Hague:1963), p. xxiii, trans. ibid., p. xxii.

30. Heidegger, *Zur Seinsfrage*, p. 42; trans. p. 105.

31. The reference to the Freudian *durcharbeiten* seems to be implied when Heidegger writes that the surmounting (*Verwinden*) of metaphysics "is similar to what happens when, in the human realm, one gets over grief" (*Die Technik und die Kehre*, p. 38; trans. p. 39).

32. Martin Heidegger, *Zur Sache des Denkens* (Tübingen:1969), p. 25. Trans. Joan Stambaugh, *On Time and Being* (New York:1972), p. 24.

33. Martin Heidegger, *Unterwegs zur Sprache* (Pfullingen:1959), p. 267. Trans. P.D. Hertz, *On the Way to Language* (New York:1971), pp. 135f.

34. Heidegger, *Identität und Differenz*, p. 72; trans. p. 73.

35. *Nicomachean Ethics*, I, 1, 1094 a 1, trans. Richard McKeon, *The Basic Works of Aristotle* (New York:1941), p. 935.

36. Martin Heidegger, *Holzwege*, p. 3; trans. D. F. Krell, *Early Greek Thinking* (New York:1975), p. 3. Hannah Arendt, in "Martin Heidegger at Eighty", *The New York Review of Books* (October 21, 1971), wrote of "thinking," that according to Heidegger, "one cannot say that it has a goal . . . The metaphor of 'wood-paths' hits upon something essential," p. 51. Elsewhere she developed more in detail the idea that "all questions concerning the aim or purpose of thinking are as unanswerable as questions about the aim or purpose of life" (*The Life of the Mind* [New York:1977], vol. 1, p. 197). In formulations like this, at least as far as Heidegger is concerned, "thinking" does not designate the activity of the mind but stands for what he earlier called *Dasein*.

37. Heidegger, *Gesamtausgabe*, vol. 55, p. 367.

38. Friedrich Nietzsche, *The Will to Power*, sect. 25, *Werke*, vol. 3, p. 530. Quoted in Heidegger, *Nietzsche*, vol. 2, p. 283. On the absence of end (*Ziellosigkeit*) in Nietzsche, cf. *Human, All Too Human*, I, 33 and 638, *Werke*, vol. 1, pp. 472 and 730.

39. Heidegger, *Wegmarken*, p. 312. Trans. T. Sheehan, "On the Being and Conception of *Physis* in Aristotle's *Physics* B, 1," in *Man and World* (1976), p. 224. Cf. *Der Satz vom Grund*, p. 111.

40. Hannah Arendt, *The Life of the Mind*, vol. 1, pp. 179f. Arendt describes the absence of any striking characteristic in the personality of Adolf Eichmann, whose trial in Jerusalem she attended, except one: "It was not stupidity but *thoughtlessness*" (ibid., p. 4).

41. Heidegger, *Gelassenheit* (Pfullingen:1959), p. 13. Trans. J. M. Anderson and E. H. Freund, *Discourse on Thinking* (New York:1966), p. 45.

42. Heidegger, *Holzwege*; pp. 328, Trans. *Early Greek Thinking*, p. 42. In the "fourfold", on the contrary, "None of the four insists on its own separate

particularity" (*Vorträge und Aufsätze*, p. 178; trans. A. Hofstadter, *Poetry, Language, Thought* [New York 1971], p. 179). See also Hannah Arendt, op. cit., vol. 2, p. 193f.

43. It has been clear from the start that the question "When are you going to write an ethics?" (*Wegmarken*, p. 183; trans. *Basic Writings*, p. 231), posed to Heidegger after the publication of his major work, arose from a misunderstanding. But it is only in his last writings that the issue of action finds its adequate context: the genealogy of a finite line of epochal principles and the "retrieval" of presencing as "an-archic" as well as of action according to presence so understood.

44. *Le nu perdu* (Paris: 1962), p. 48.

45. *Commune présence*, (Paris: 1964), p. 255.

Notes to Chapter 6

1. J. Habermas, *Knowledge and Human Interests*, trans. J. J. Shapiro (Boston: Beacon Press, 1968), p. 302.

2. Ibid., p. 317.

3. Cf. M. Heidegger, *Being and Time*, trans. J. Macquarrie & E. Robinson (New York: Harper & Row, 1962) p. 437 (marginal pagination of the seventh German edition). Abbreviated in the text as *SZ*.

4. "Only a God can Save us: *Der Spiegel's* Interview With Martin Heidegger," trans. M. P. Alter & J. D. Caputo in *Philosophy Today* 20 (1976):279f.

5. M. Heidegger, *Platons Lehre von der Wahrheit. Mit einem Brief über den Humanismus*, 2nd ed. (Bern: Francke, 1954), pp. 104f/295. Abbreviated in the text as *BH*. The second number refers to the English translation by E. Lohner in vol. 2 of *Philosophy in the Twentieth Century*, ed. W. Barrett & H. D. Aiken (New York: Random House, 1962). See also Heidegger, "Only a God can Save us," pp. 280f. In this paper I presume that there is a genuine need for theoretical and conceptual transparency and for the explicit planning of human action. (See my paper "Heidegger's Longest Day: *Being and Time* and the Sciences," in *Philosophy Today* 22 [1978]:326.) What I try to demonstrate is that sufficient theoretical transparency of human action *can* be achieved within the framework of Heidegger's writings, both earlier and later.

6. Others have already argued in this direction, e.g., F. A. Olafson in his *Principles and Persons: An Ethical Interpretation of Existentialism* (Baltimore: Johns Hopkins Press 1967) and G. Prauss in his *Erkennen und Handeln in Heideggers "Sein und Zeit"* (Freiburg: Karl Alber, 1977). See also the critical discussion of Olafson's book by B. Sitter, "'Sein und Zeit' als Theorie der Ethik," in *Philosophische Rundschau* 16 (1969):273–282.

7. R. Schürmann in his paper, "Heidegger's Deconstruction of Action," read at the Thirteenth Heidegger Conference, 1979 (and, somewhat less thematically, in several published papers: "Questioning the Foundation of Practical Philosphy," *Human Studies*, 1 [1978]:357–368; "Political Thinking in Heidegger," *Social Research* 45 [1978]:191–221; "The Ontological Difference and Political Philosophy," *Philosophy and Phenomenological Research* 40 [1979]:9–122), and G. Prauss, *op. cit.*, especially pp. 102ff., have recently argued in support of this allegation, although Prauss takes exception to what he calls the "*Praktizismus*" of *Being and Time*. The later Heidegger, after the "*Kehre(turn),*" Prauss contends, denounced the promising insights for a theory of action in *Being and*

Time and went "back" to a utopian contemplative thinking of being that provides no help for a theory of action.

8. The remarks about the higher rigor of the thinking of being are made in the discussion of the relationship between ontology and ethics, or the question whether it is possible to derive from the thinking of being directives for action (*BH*, pp. 110f./297f.).

9. M. Heidegger, "Zeit und Sein," *Zur Sache des Denkens* (Tuebingen: Niemeyer, 1969), p. 88. Abbreviated in the text as *ZS*. The second number refers to the English translation by J. Stambaugh in *On Time and Being* (New York: Harper & Row, 1972).

10. See also M. Heidegger, *On the Way to Language*, trans. P. D. Hertz (New York: Harper & Row, 1971), p. 128.

11. This "deduction" is the reason for introducing the notion of *Ereignis* into the discussion of the law of being, in the first place. Being is not to be understood *as Ereignis* but as originating *from* it, that is, the reflection on *Ereignis* is supposed to make conceptually transparent *how* being and its law originate. See *On the Way to Language*, p. 129, note.

12. For this whole paragraph see M. Heidegger, "Moira (Paramenides 8, 34–41)" and "Aletheia (Heraclitus, Fragment 16)," in *Vorträge und Aufsätze* (Pfullingen: G. Neske, 1954), pp. 231–282/79–123, especially pp. 238f/85f. and 260f/105f. The second set of numbers refers to the English translation by D. F. Krell & F. A. Capuzzi in *Early Greek Thinking* (New York: Harper & Row, 1975).

13. Ibid., p. 238/85. See also *ZS*, 10/10.

14. Ibid., p. 239/86. "That is why the essential thinkers always say the same thing," after all (*BH*, p. 118/301).

15. Heidegger himself claims in his *Nietzsche*, vol. 2 (Pfullingen: G. Neske, 1961) p. 415/14f.—the second number refers to the English translation by J. Stambaugh in *The End of Philosophy* (New York: Harper & Row, 1973)—that the destruction was not yet conceived in terms of the history of being. Referring to "Time and Being" (especially *ZS*, pp. 18–20/17–20), one might want to support such a claim by saying that the destruction tried to demonstrate only one thing, against a tradition which covers it up, namely, the *Temporalität* of being, that is, that being as such has always been conceived in terms of time. It did not yet try to show, as does the thinking in terms of the history of being, that the ways in which being and time take place are always determined by the fateful interplay, described above. But this reasoning won't do because the destruction was meant to be carried out with the historicalness and *Zeitlichkeit* of man's being as its all-decisive clues. And *Being and Time* leaves no doubt that both are essentially factical and fatefully finite. More about this below.

16. Cf. M. Heidegger, *Der Satz vom Grund* (Pfullingen: G. Neske, 1957). The *Vortrag*, pp. 191–211, has been translated by K. Hoeller, "The Principle of Ground," in *Man and World*, 7 (1974):207–222.

17. Cf. M. Heidegger, "The Question Concerning Technology," in *The Question Concerning Technology and Other Essays*, trans. W. Lovitt (New York: Harper & Row, 1977), pp. 3–35. For a partial list of such epochal determinations, see *Nietzsche*, vol. 2, p. 470/65f.; also *ZS*, p. 7/7.

18. Cf. M. Heidegger, *Nietzsche*, vol. 2, p. 485/78.

19. See also M. Heidegger, *On the Way to Language*, p. 127.

20. Cf. *ZS*, p. 24/24: "*Nur dies: Das Ereignis ereignet.*"

21. M. Heidegger, *Nietzsche* vol. 2, p. 485/78.

22. Cf. M. Heidegger, *Der Satz vom Grund*, pp. 186–188; also, "The Thing," in *Poetry, Language, Thought*, trans. A. Hofstadter (New York: Harper & Row, 1971), pp. 180–182.

23. Cf. M. Heidegger, *Nietzsche*, vol. 2, p. 489/82: Being, in establishing its truth *"im Seienden,"* calls on man. See also "The Anaximander Fragment," in *Early Greek Thinking*, p. 58, and "The Turning," in *The Question Concerning Technology and Other Essays*, p. 38f.

24. For *Fügung* see M. Heidegger, *Nietzsche*, vol. 2, p. 485/78f, and *BH*, p. 111/298. For *Entsprechung* see M. Heidegger, *Der Satz vom Grund*, p. 185; also the letter to Buchner, in *Poetry, Language, Thought*, pp. 183–186.

25. R. M. Rilke, *Duino Elegies*, German text with English translation by J. B. Leishman & S. Spender (New York: Norton, 1963), pp. 43–45 (4th elegy).

26. Emphasis added.

27. *BH*, p. 115/300: "It is superior to all contemplation" and theoretical seeing.

28. See note 7.

29. Heidegger himself raises this question in *BH*, p. 115/300.

30. I. Kant, *Critique of Practical Reason*, trans. L. W. Beck (New York: Bobbs-Merrill, 1956), pp. 167f.

31. See his letter to Buchner in *Poetry, Language, Thought*, pp. 183–186.

32. See his letter to Richardson, used as Preface in W. J. Richardson, *Heidegger: Through Phenomenology to Thought*, 2nd ed. (The Hague: M. Nijhoff, 1973), p. xxii.

33. See *Being and Time*, section 13, and the remarks on the ontical foundation of ontology (*SZ*, p. 436).

34. See Rilke's letter to Ficker on Trakl's "Helian": " . . . ein paar Einfriedungen um das grenzenlos Wortlose: so stehen die Zeilen da. Wie Zäune in einem flachen Land, über die hin das Eingezäunte fortwährend zu einer unbesitzbaren grossen Ebene zusammenschlägt" (I. Zangerle, ed., *Erinnerungen an Georg Trakl: Zeugnisse und Briefe*, 2nd ed., [Salzburg: O. Mueller, 1959], p. 10). See also Heidegger's remarks about thinking as "the topology of being," in *Poetry, Language, Thought*, p. 12.

35. Cf. *BH*, p. 115/300 to find "the abode in the truth of being."

36. These original conditions must be distinguished from the derivative conditions that arise from subsequent modifications, namely, (1) from the conditions under which it is possible to experience the kind of things that we find in bare perceptual cognition when we *hold back* "from any kind of producing, manipulating, and the like" (*SZ*, p. 61) and (2) from the conditions under which it is possible to objectify things as in scientific observation and explanation when we "thematize" and "enframe" things in specific ways. For a discussion of this difference, see my paper "Scientific Realism and Phenomenology," *Zeitschrift fuer philosophische Forschung* 34 (1980), pp. 395–404.

37. *SZ*, p. 383: "One's anticipatory projection of oneself on that possibility of existence which is not to be outstripped—on death—guarantees only the totality and authenticity of one's resoluteness. But those possibilities of existence which have been factically disclosed are not to be gathered from death."

38. Recall the claim that authentic existence is a mere modification of inauthentic existence (*SZ*, p. 130; see also p. 179).

39. I will show below that this impression is not fully justified by the analyses of *Being and Time*, although they seem to invite the kind of excessive con-

servatism Heidegger himself displays in the 1966 *Spiegel* interview (see n. 4, above) in his remarks on the historical roots of greatness, particularly in art, and in his hostility to contemporary literature and modern art in general (somewhat of a surprise, especially in view of his essay "The Origin of the Work of Art," in *Poetry, Language, Thought*, pp. 15–78). Cf. M. Heidegger, "Only a God can Save us," pp. 277, 283.

Notes to Chapter 7

1. Jan M. Broekman, *Structuralism*, trans. Jan F. Beekman and Brunhilde Helm, (Boston: Reidel, 1974).
2. Karel Kosik, *Dialectics of the Concrete*, trans. Karel Kovanda (Boston: Reidel, 1976), p. 1.
3. Ibid., p. 122.
4. Ibid., p. 147.

Notes to Chapter 9

1. E. Husserl, *Crisis of European Sciences and Transcendental Phenomenology* (Evanston: Northwestern University Press, 1970) pp. 103, 155.
2. I. Kant, *Critique of Pure Reason* (hereafter *KdrV,*) Norman Kemp-Smith's translation altered slightly, Bxvii.
3. Robert Paul Wolff, *Kant's Theory of Mental Activity* (Cambridge: Harvard University Press, 1963) p. 42.
4. *KdrV*, A90, B123.
5. *KdrV*, A111; cf. A120.
6. *KdrV*, A112.
7. *KdrV*, B153.
8. *KdrV*, A19, B34.
9. Ibid.
10. *KdrV*, A239, B298.
11. Ibid.
12. *KdrV*, A240, B299.
13. *KdrV*, A245.
14. *KdrV*, A696, B724.
15. M. Heidegger, *Kant and the Problem of Metaphysics* (Bloomington: Indiana University Press, 1962) esp. 27–42 and *What is a Thing?* (Chicago: Henry Regnery, 1967) esp. 134ff.
16. *Kant and the Problem of Metaphysics*, p. 28.
17. Ibid.
18. "But a concept is always, as regards its form, something universal that serves as a rule" (*KdrV*, A106).
19. *What is a Thing?*, p. 144ff.
20. *KdrV*, B141.
21. *What is a Thing?*, p. 150.
22. *KdrV*, A11f, B25.
23. *KdrV*, A237, B296.
24. *KdrV*, A126, 127.
25. *KdrV*, B165.

26. *KdrV*, A255, B310f.
27. *KdrV*, A626, B654.
28. *KdrV*, A633, 3661; A548, B576ff.
29. *KdrV*, A548, B576.

Notes to Chapter 10

1. Both common sense and science extrapolate from that which is given in conceptualizing objects. That much, at least, they have in common. Thus, to bracket theorizing is to set aside both common sense and science. Extrapolation is fundamental to both modes of experience.

2. Curiously enough, this would require a bracketing of the "phenomenological standpoint."

3. This reading of Kant is by no means restricted to phenomenologists.

4. Cf. A 363: "The identity of the consciousness of myself at different times is therefore only a formal coherence, and in no way proves the numerical identity of the subject." As Kant states elsewhere, neither does it entail the *substantial* identity of the subject.

5. *Logik*, I, sec. 4; Cassirer ed., vol. 8.

6. Cf. A 113: "All possible appearances as representations belong to the totality of a *possible* self-consciousness." A 118: "Whether this representation [I] actually *occurs*—does not concern us." (my emphasis)

7. Cf. B 157: ". . . I am conscious of myself, not as I appear to myself, but only that I am. This representation is a thought, not an intuition."

8. Cf. Lefebvre, *Everyday Life in the Modern World*, 1971.

9. Cf. Preface to part 1, p. 5, Liberal Arts Edition: "It sounds arrogant, egotistical, and to those who have not yet renounced their old system, disparaging, to assert that before the critical philosophy arose there was no philosophy at all." Yet Kant proceeds to assert that that is the case.

References for Chapter 11

Committee for Economic Development. *Building a National Health Care System*. Washington, D. C.: Government Printing Office, 1973.

H. Tristram Engelhardt, Jr. "The Philosophy of Medicine: A New Endeavor." *Texas Reports on Biology and Medicine*, 31, no. 3 (Fall, 1973): 443–452.

Samuel Gorovitz and Alasdair MacIntyre. "Toward a Theory of Medical Fallibility." *Journal of Medicine and Philosophy* 1 no. 1 (March 1976): 51–71.

André Hellegers. "The Beginnings of Personhood: Medical Considerations." *Perkins Journal* 27, no. 1 (Fall 1973): 16–19.

Hans Jonas. "The Concept of Responsibility: An Inquiry into the Foundations of an Ethics for Our Age." In *Knowledge, Value and Belief*, edited by H. T. Engelhardt, Jr., and D. Callahan. Hastings-on-Hudson, New York: The Institute of Society, Ethics and Life Sciences, 1977, pp. 169–198.

Hans Jonas. *The Phenomenon of Life: Toward a Philosophical Biology*. New York: Harper and Row, 1966; Dell, 1968.

Hans Jonas, *Philosophical Essays: From Ancient Creed to Technological Man*. Englewood Cliffs, N.J.: Prentice-Hall, 1974.

Leon Kass. "Regarding the End of Medicine and the Pursuit of Health." *The Public Interest*, no. 40 (Summer, 1975), pp. 11–42.

Eike-Henner Kluge. *The Practice of Death*. New Haven: Yale University Press, 1975.

Edmund D. Pellegrino. "The Most Humane Science: Some Notes on Liberal Education in Medicine and the University." Sixth Sanger Lecture. *Bulletin of the Medical College of Virginia, Virginia Commonwealth University*, 67 no. 4 (Summer, 1970).

Edmund D. Pellegrino. "Medicine and Philosophy: Some Notes on the Flirtations of Minerva and Aesculapius." Philadelphia, Pa.: Society for Health and Human Values, 1974.

Paul Ramsey. "The Indignity of 'Death With Dignity' ". *The Hastings Center Report* 2, no. 2 (May 1974): 47–62.

Guenter B. Risse. "The Quest for Certainty in Medicine: John Brown's System of Medicine in France." *Bulletin of the History of Medicine* 45, no. 1 (January/February 1971), pp. 1–12.

Guenter B. Risse. "Kant, Schelling, and the Early Search for a Philosophical 'Science' of Medicine in Germany." *Journal of the History of Medicine and Allied Sciences* 27, no. 2 (April 1972): 145–158.

Max Scheler. *Man's Place in Nature*, trans. Hans Meyerhoff. Boston: Beacon Press, 1961.

Peter H. Schuck. "A Consumer's View of the Health Care System." In *Ethics of Health Care*. Washington, D.C.: Institute of Medicine, National Academy of Sciences, 1974, pp. 95–118.

Oswei Temkin. *Galenism: Rise and Decline of a Medical Philosophy*. Ithaca and London: Cornell University Press, 1973.

J. H. van den Berg. "A Metabletic-Philosophical Evaluation of Mental Health." In *Mental Health: Philosophical Perspectives*, edited by S. F. Spicker and H. T. Engelhardt, Jr. Dordrecht, Holland: 1977.

Notes to Chapter 12

1. Susan Sontag, *Illness as Metaphor* (New York: Farrar, Straus, and Giroux, 1978).

2. Richard M. Zaner, "Context and Reflexivity: The Genealogy of The Self," in *Evaluation and Explanation in The Biomedical Sciences*, Engelhardt and Spicker, eds. (Dordrecht-Holand: D. Reidel, 1975), p. 159.

3. See, for example, H. Tristram Engelhardt, Jr., "Ideology and Etiology," *Journal of Medicine and Philosophy* 1, no. 3 (1976): 256–268; Marx Wartofsky, "Editorial," *Journal of Medicine and Philosophy* 1, no. 4 (1976): 289–300; and Richard M. Zaner, "The Unanchored Leaf: Humanities and the Discipline of Care," *Texas Reports on Biology and Medicine* 32, no. 1 (Spring, 1974).

4. H. Tristram Engelhardt, Jr., "The Concepts of Health and Disease," in *Evaluation and Explanation in the Biomedical Sciences*, p. 135.

5. Marx Wartofsky, "Organs, Organisms, and Disease," in *Evaluation and Explanation in The Biomedical Sciences*, p. 73.

6. Ibid., p. 81.

7. H. Tristram Engelhardt, Jr., "The Disease of Masturbation: Values and the Concept of Disease." *Contemporary Issues in Bioethics*, Beauchamp and Walters, eds. (Encino, California: Dickenson, 1978), p. 112

8. Cf. Martin Heidegger, *Being and Time*, trans. Macquarrie and Robinson (New York: Harper and Row, 1962); p. H.73ff.

9. Ibid., p. H.56.

10. Ibid., p. H.135.

11. See, for example, Sigmund Freud, "Anxiety and Instinctual Life," in *New Introductory Lectures*, trans. and ed. James Strachey, (New York: Norton, p. 96).

12. Herman Feifel et al., "Physicians Consider Death," reprinted from the *Proceedings, 75th Annual Convention, American Phychological Association*, 1967 by the Hastings Center, Hastings-on-Hudson, New York.

13. Bernard Bressler, "Suicide and Drug Abuse in the Medical Community," in *Suicide and Life-Threatening Behavior*, 6, no. 3 (fall, 1976): 169.

14. Ibid., p. 176.

15. Richard I. Shader, *Manual of Psychiatric Therapeutics* (Boston: Little, Brown, 1975), p. 171.

16. Freedman, Kaplan, and Sadok, eds., *Modern Synopsis of Comprehensive Textbook of Psychiatry* (Baltimore: Williams and Wilkins, 1972), p. 701.

17. Engelhardt, "The Disease of Masturbation," p. 112.

Notes to Chapter 13

1. My colleague Stuart Spicker has pointed out that medically speaking we do not know the positive possibilities of the mentation of the elderly because we presuppose that aging is a disintegration of adult processes. We judge the mental functions of the elderly with norms of adult rationality and find them dysfunctional or deficient. But are there not "natural" norms of mentation in the elderly to be discovered without imposing adult standards, which are quite specific to scientific rationality? Or will we only discover some form of thought disorder as a counterpart to the denial of the limitation of aging? Stuart Spicker, "Gerontogenetic Mentation: Memory, Dementia, and Medicine in the Penultimate Years," (Case Western Reserve University, 1976).

2. Caroline Whitbeck, "Health: The Transition From Patient to Agent", unpublished paper.

3. I would suggest that the limitation that is denied by medical practitioners is the limitation of medical knowledge. What Gorovitz and MacIntyre have defined as the necessary fallibility of medical knowledge, a science dealing with particulars, has its correlation in a doctor's own experience of the limitedness of medical knowledge, the lack of certainty of diagnosis—despite the fact that physicians are constituted with the meaning of Asclepian authority, especially by the ill person. The isolation that doctors feel contributes to this denial. For the acceptance of the limitedness of one's knowledge would require those sorts of reciprocal relationships where one's experience is validated by others. Such reciprocal relationships, as Rawlinson points out, are rare, owing to the early socialization of doctors into the professional roles of *dominance, authority, and autonomy*. Cf. Samuel Gorovitz and Alisdair MacIntyre, "Toward a Theory of Medical Fallibility." *Journal of Medicine and Philosophy* 1, no. 1 (1976): 51–71.

4. Tristram Engelhardt, Jr., "Ideology and Etiology," *Journal of Medicine and Philosophy* 1, no. 3 (1976): 267.

5. For a sociological account of the history and functions of these groups, see *Journal of Applied Behavioral Science* 12, no. 3 (1976). This is a special issue on self-help groups.

6. Christopher Boorse, in his treatment of the concepts of health and disease, has claimed that such lay initiatives in health care only change the methods, while still maintaining the traditional goals of health as absence of disease. This view seems shortsighted particularly in the case of chronic disease in which health, as absence of disease, is unachievable. But health in another sense is achievable—partially. Christopher Boorse, "Health as a Theoretical Concept," *Philosophy of Science* 44 (1977): 568.

7. One commentator on self-help groups has stated that "to date not a single adequate study of the effectiveness of self-help groups exists." If the "effectiveness" is measured by medical criteria, then it is no wonder that such a study does not and *cannot* exist (Morton A. Leiberman and Leonard D. Botman, "Self-Help and Social Research," *Journal of Applied Behavioral Science* 12, no. 3 (1976): 459).

Notes to Chapter 14

1. A version of this essay was presented in 1976 at a bicentennial celebration dedicated to American art at Kalamazoo College (Michigan). A later version was presented to the Society for Phenomenology and Existential Philosophy at its meeting at Purdue University in 1979. In the broader context of the history of Western thought the occasion of this essay began with Kant's Third Critique which gives back to art the important place it had for philosophy in Classical Greece. In Plato's *Symposium* art stands as *the* competitor of philosophy; and philosophy as the epitomization of art. In Kant art provides the first intimation of that harmony of man and the given which Hegel later called the truth of spirit. But although building on Kant's thought, Hegel takes this harmony to mean that while art is necessary for the appearance of truth it is only this appearance, and must be transcended by thought to achieve the truth of spirit. Thus Hegel sees art as having made its most significant contribution to truth in Classical Greece, a contribution accepted and developed since then first by religion and next by philosophy. However Kierkegaard and Heidegger have understood art to be essential to the truth of spirit at all times. My essay makes this claim again by taking it as a necessary and necessarily repeated beginning.

2. For another version of this story see my book *The Individual and the New World*, The Dialogue Press, University Park, PA., 1983.

3. Christopher Columbus: *The Northmen, Columbus and Cabot*, Julius Olson and Edward Bourne, ed., New York, 1906, p. 125.

4. Thomas Wolfe: *The Story of a Novel*, Scribner's Sons, New York, 1936, pp. 31–35.

5. Gerard Manley Hopkins: *Poems and Prose of Gerard Manley Hopkins*, W. H. Gardner, ed., Baltimore, 1953, p. 125.

6. Martha Smith: *Going to God's Country*, Boston, 1941, pp. 11, 12, 13, 41, 56, 57, 60, 173, 185, 186.

7. I am indebted to an unpublished manuscript by Professor Robert Goff for the suggestion of this example.

8. Herman Melville: *Moby Dick*, Heritage Press, New York, 1943, pp. 3–5.

Notes

9. Ibid., p. 614.
10. Ibid., p. 615.
11. Ibid., pp. 445–446.
12. Ibid., p. 615.
13. Ibid., p. 446.

Notes to Chapter 15

1. James Jarrett, *The Quest for Beauty* (Englewood Cliffs, N.J.: Prentice-Hall, 1956), p. 36.
2. This is true even in the case of the verbal arts. A poem or a novel is a concrete utterance, not a conceptual structure as such.
3. Jarrett, *Quest for Beauty*, p. 35.
4. *The Dehumanization of Art*, trans. W. Trask (Garden City, N.Y.: Doubleday, 1956), p. 23.
5. See Samuel J. Todes, "Sensuous Abstraction and the Abstract Sense of Reality," in *New Essays in Phenomenology*, ed. James M. Edie (Chicago: Quadrangle Books, 1969), pp. 15–23.
6. This is Richard Wollheim's point in *Art and Its Objects*.
7. Todes, "Sensuous Abstraction," pp. 19–21.
8. Calvin Schrag, *Experience and Being: Prolegomena to a Future Ontology* (Evanston: Northwestern University Press, 1969), pp. 18, 38, 40.
9. Maurice Merleau-Ponty, *Phenomenology of Perception*, trans. C. Smith (London: Routledge and Kegan Paul, 1962), pp. 144–146.
10. Schrag, p. 90.
11. "Die Stimmung hat je schon das In-der-Welt-sein als Ganzes erschlossen und macht ein Sichrichten auf . . . allererst möglich" (*Sein und Zeit*, 10th ed. [Tübingen: Max Niemeyer, 1963], p. 137).
12. "In der Befindlichkeit liegt existenzial eine erschlieszende Angewiesenheit auf Welt, aus der her Angehendes begegnen kann" (*Sein und Zeit*, pp. 137–138). Heidegger explicitly discusses fearfulness and, of course, anxiety in *Being and Time* and in "What is Metaphysics?" gives a similar treatment to boredom and elation.
13. "Wir müssen in der Tat *ontologisch* grundsätzlich die primare Entdeckung der Welt der 'bloszen Stimmung' überlassen" (*Sein und Zeit*, p. 138).
14. "Ontologically, therefore, our moods and dispositions must be considered as being the basic condition of the possibility of discovering the world, for they alone render us open to what comes from the world" (J. L. Mehta, *Martin Heidegger: The Way and the Vision*, rev. ed. [Honolulu: University Press of Hawaii, 1976], p. 156). See also Wolfgang Blankenburg, "The Cognitive Aspects of Love," in F. J. Smith and Erling Eng, eds., *Facets of Eros: Phenomenological Essays* (The Hague: Martinus Nijhoff, 1972), pp. 23–29.
15. Jean-Paul Sartre, *The Psychology of Imagination*, trans. Bernard Frechtman (New York: Philosophical Library, 1948), p. 88.
16. Sartre, *The Emotions: Outline of a Theory*, trans. Bernard Frechtman (New York: Philosophical Library, 1948), pp. 87–89.
17. *The Emotions*, p. 89. *The Emotions* first appeared in 1939. The next year saw the publication of *The Psychology of Imagination*, in which Sartre was speaking of *affectivité* rather than *émotion*. *Affectivité* seemed to have to do with objects rather than with worlds. On the other hand, *émotion* was

described in terms of extreme situations (the horrifying face at the window), whereas *affectivité* was placed in relatively calmer contexts (the delicate white hands that I love). I think it not unreasonable to read the later essay as concerned more with modulations of an existing world-sense than with radical transformations of it into some other sense. In this way *émotion* and *affectivité* might be seen as two major groupings of feelings along an affective continuum. See *The Psychology of Imagination*, pp. 87–94; and for an interpretation of Sartre's views along the lines I suggest here, Joseph P. Fell, III, *Emotion in the Thought of Sartre* (New York and London: Columbia University Press, 1965), esp. pp. 137–138.

18.   See Ricoeur's *Fallible Man*, trans. Charles Kelbley (Chicago: Henry Regnery, 1965), pp. 121–202; "Le Sentiment," in *Edmund Husserl 1859–1959* (The Hague: Martinus Nijhoff, 1959), pp. 260–274, an earlier and often more detailed discussion of the *Fallible Man* material; and "Philosophie, sentiment, et poésie: la notion d'*a priori* selon Mikel Dufrenne," *Esprit* 29 (March 1961): 504–512, an English version of which appears as the Preface to Mikel Dufrenne's *The Notion of the A Priori*, trans. Edward S. Casey (Evanston: Northwestern University Press, 1966), pp. ix–ixvii.

19. *Fallible Man*, p. 129.

20. I am speaking here of what Sartre calls "consciousness in the first degree, or *unreflected* consciousness," whose awareness of itself is not positional, that is, it is "not for itself its own object." See *The Transcendence of the Ego*, trans. Forrest Williams and Robert Kirkpatrick (New York: Noonday Press, 1957), pp. 40–41.

21. *The Phenomenology of Aesthetic Experience*, trans. Edward S. Casey (Evanston: Northwestern University Press, 1973), p. 452.

22. *Phenomenology of Aesthetic Experience*, p. 460.

23. *Phenomenology of Aesthetic Experience*, p. 461, n. 35.

24. The aesthetic datum is not alien in its physical presence but in its affective essence. The sonata and the pleasing landscape have their obvious physical reality; but to perceive *only* that (or exclusively in terms of that) is not to experience them aesthetically, at least not in the usual sense whereby *aesthetic* and *ordinary* perception are distinguished from each other.

25. This is not mysterious or extraordinary. We always dwell in *the* world by living in several subworlds, some simultaneously (I am a member of my profession and a citizen of my country) but some only consecutively, because their grounding commitments cancel or contradict each other (I alternate the worlds of work and of play). Usually I can move at will from one subworld to another (by changing the subject of a conversation or by turning from activity in one subworld to activity in another, as I do when I leave off working at my manuscript to visit my friend in the hospital). I am usually aware in such transition only of turning my attention to a different set of objects that in fact happen to be grounded in a different subworld; usually I do not notice that the objects are different for me chiefly because they *are* so grounded. The child turns toward his toy, and he has entered his play world; we turn to a different topic of conversation and have entered the world that grounds it. In aesthetic experience I dwell for the moment in two worlds that can neither be reduced one to the other nor coordinated one under the other but that are experienced as equal possibilities of *the* world. The move into this ambiguous situation is just as easy as the move from one subworld to another. The aesthetic datum presents itself as belonging to this sort of world (or subworld). It is not that

I need to choose *whether* to generate the mood which is the sense of such a world. To the extent that I am perceiving aesthetically, I *have* generated an affective sense of the world in which the datum and I can be present to each other.

26. See John Anderson, *The Realm of Art* (University Park and London: Pennsylvania State University Press, 1967).

27. The aesthetic datum may even *be* a gesture, even my own gesture, as it is for the dancer. But again, the datum is the vehicle, the stimulus, of my sense of being-placed. My gesture stimulates in me, or demands that I have, the same sort of resonances any other aesthetic datum would stimulate or demand.

28. Maurice Merleau-Ponty, "Indirect Language and the Voices of Silence," in *Signs*, trans. R. McCleary (Evanston: Northwestern University Press, 1964), p. 77.

Notes to Chapter 16

1. "Maintenant, si le langage humain a toujours comporté cette possibilité de 'parler sur parler', de parler sur le langage et sur ses propres institutions, de les réfléchir, . . . autrement dit la réflexivité, on peut imaginer que des gens, des civilisations, n'en aient pas usé; mais, une fois que nous avons commencé d'en user, nous sommes en face, en quelque sorte, d'un 'ingénérable', au sens où Spinoza dit, à propos du troisième genre de connaissance: Une fois qu'il est né, qu'il est apparu, il est éternel, il ne peut pas ne pas avoir été, bien que ce soit contingent qu'une conscience y accède; mais, une fois cette contingence survenue, cela apparaît comme inéluctable . . . et inépuisable" (Paul Ricoeur, *La philosophie: Sens et limites*, Week-end de philosophie, 13–14 février, 1965, Cahiers "Paraboles," p. 18).

2. *Logical Investigations*, vol. 2 Introduction, no. 3, and also no. 6, note 2. The latter is, of course, the first mention of the famous "zigzag" of terminological and conceptual clarification.

3. Some examples: *Ideen I*, nos. 66 and 84; *Krisis*, no. 91; *Erste Philosophie II*, pp. 477–478.

4. The general critical point raised here is much the same as that discussed by Eugen Fink in his essay, "Operative Begriffe in Husserls Phänomenologie," in Fink, *Nähe und Distanz: Phänomenologische Vorträge und Aufsätze*, ed. Franz-Anton Schwarz (Munich: Alber, 1976), pp. 198–202. (This essay also appears in French in the proceedings of the 1957 Royaumont conference: *Husserl* (Paris:Minuit, 1959), pp. 214–230; the pages here referred to are 227–229.)

5. Iso Kern traces the history of Husserl's project of revising the *Cartesian Meditations* in his "Einleitung" to *Husserliana* vol. 15 (*Zur Phänomenologie der Intersubjektivität*, pt. 3:1929–1935), pp. xxxiv–lxvi. His hesitations about Fink's work are spoken of on pp. lxii–lxiii. In great part the difficulties are apparently not with particulars of basic phenomenological points but with the overall thrust, which is Kantian in format and Hegelian in its speculative inclination. On this difference between Husserl and Fink, see Fink's "Die intentionale Analyse und das Problem des spekulatives Denken," in *Nähe und Distanz*, pp. 139–157. (This same essay appeared earlier in French in *Problèmes actuels de la phénoménologie* (Paris:Desclée de Brouwer, 1952).

6. "Wird bei immer weiterschreitender phänomenologischer Erkenntnis die Naivität der prädikativen Explikation überwunden, die mundanen Begriffe immer mehr von den anhaftenden natürlichen Assoziationen befreit, so kann es doch nie gelingen, die Divergenz des [aquivoken] Bedeutens, die in jedem transzendentalen Satze vorhanden ist zwischen dem natürlichen Wortsinn und dem damit indizierten transzendentalen Sinn, *aufzuheben*. Viehmehr wird immer ein immanenter Widerstreit und Widerspruch in jeder transzendentalen Prädikation bleiben. Ja es ist nicht enimal ein *Desiderat*, dass diese Divergenz überhaupt jemals verschwindet. Die Idee einer transzendentalen Sprache, die nicht einmal der Vermittlung der natürlichen Sprache bedürfte, ist in sich widersinning" (*Cartesianische* Meditationen) pp. 118–119. (The word in brackets was added by Husserl; italics are Fink's own.)

7. "Auch wenn der Phänomenologe eine neue Sprache erfinden wollte, bedürfte er dazu der näturlich-äquivoken Sprache als ersten Ausdrucks seiner phänomenologischen Feststellungen, als ihren direktesten. Und die indirekte neue Sprache wäre eben dadurch selbst wieder äquivok definiert" (*CM VI*, p. 119/7–14).

8. "Bleibt zwar die Sprache als Habitualität durch die Epoché hindurch erhalten, so verliert sie aber nicht den einzig *auf Seiendes bezogenen Ausdruckscharakter*" (*CM VI*, p. 107; Fink's underlining.)

9. "Die menschliche Habitualität (das Seiende in der Welt) wandelt ihren Seinsinn zur Habitualität des transzendentalen Ego—das sage ich, der Zuschauer, aus und werde in eins selbst als dieser thematisch, so sage ich wieder aus und immer spreche ich die natürliche Sprache, aber in transzendental geändertem Sinn" (*CM VI*, p. 107/8–18).

10. "Eine phänomenologische Sprache hat prinzipiell nur Sinn, nur Möglichkeit als verwandelte natürliche Sprache, so wie das transzendentale Phänomen Welt nur Sinn hat als verwandelter Seinsinn Welt" (*CM VI*, p. 107).

11. "Die natürliche Gewohnheit ist in ständiger 'Rebellion' gegen das Phänomenologisieren, so sehr auch das Gewohnheit stiftet und gewohnheitsmässig dann verläuft, auch die Gewohnheit des Phänomenologen, sein allgemeiner Lebensmodus ist in beständiger Spannung gegen die natürliche Gewohnheit. Letztlich ist das auch für die transzendentale Sprache enscheidend" (Husserl's comment, lower side margin on p. 109, referring to Fink's point in using the expression "*Rebellion*" on this same page).

12. These expressions are all drawn from both main text (Fink) and annotations and comments by Husserl on pp. 108–109, 112.

13. This whole problem is also raised in the closing pages of Fink's 1933 authoritative essay, "The Phenomenological Philosophy of Edmund Husserl and Contemporary Criticism," in R. O. Elveton, ed., *The Phenomenology of Husserl:Selected Critical Essays* (Chicago:Quadrangle, 1970), pp. 73–147. Very much related to that problem is the issue of how a philosophic position that challenges existing conceptions would even *begin* (also discussed by Fink in the 1933 essay, pp. 104ff.). Husserl sketches out this question in *CM VI* on p. 108, comment in the whole lower side and bottom margins, and on p. 112, comment by lines 1–12. See also *Erste Philosophie I*, pp. 313–314 (Beilage IV).

14. "Indem sich die lebendig aktuelle theoretische Erfahrung des Phänomenologisierenden, die in unmittelbar einsichtiger Evidenz verläuft, nun umsetzt in die prädikative Fassung, verwahrt wird in Begriffen und Sätzen im Medium einer Sprache, die keine eigentlich angemessenen Ausdrücke, sondern nur analogisierende bereit stellt, erwächst die Gefahr, dass der natürliche ursprüngliche

Sinn der Worte über den analogisch damit indizierten 'transzendentalen' Sinn Herr wird, ihn überwuchert und verdeckt, so dass ein zurückkommendes Verstehenwollen, das nur auf den Wortlaut eingeht, notwendig in die Irre gehen muss" (*CM VI*, p. 112). The continuation of this passage, making a most important point for understanding the Husserlian position, is given below on p. 14, note 23.

15. See the most interesting and pertinent discussion in *Erste Philosophie II*, no. 39, for a discussion of a parallel to this point but regarding not simply words but a variety of psychological performances.

16. The German text is quoted in note 10 above. In section 11 of Fink's *CM VI*, further elaboration of the transformation process is provided by his discussion of the relationship between transcendental truths (for the "phenomenologizing" transcendental I) and natural attitude (naive) truths, as for example in the following lines: "Vielmehr lässt die transzendentale Selbstinterpretation des Phänomenologisierens die naiven Wahrheiten bestehen, aber sie interpretiert diese, indem sie die *Beschränktheit* ("Abstraktheit") derselben in ihrer Bezogenheit auf eine *konstituierte* Geltungssituation nachweist und sie nun als '*befangene*' *und einseitige* Wahrheit einbaut in die—durch die phänomenologische Analytik zu Tage tretende—"Konkrete" konstitutive Wahrheit. Die Überlegenheit der transzendentalen Wahrheit ist also kein komparativisches Wahrersein (kein grösserer Wahrheitsgrad), sondern besteht darin, dass die mundane Wahrheit selbst von der transzendentalen *umgriffen* wird und in ihr ihre eigene letzte lucide Verständlichkeit gewinnt" (p. 143/3–15). Harry Reeder, in a recently published essay, "Language and the Phenomenological Reduction:A Reply to a Wittgensteinian Objection," *Man and World* 12 (1979):35–46, argues for an understanding of Husserl's treatment of language in very much the same direction as that given here.

17. This seems to me to be the sense of things that weaves through Husserl's reflections in Beilage XXIX in *Erste Philosophie II*, especially pp. 475–478. This seems also to be the implication of Fink's words in the following passage: "Denn keineswegs sind alle mundanen Bedeutungen *im selben Masse* falsch, wenn es gilt, transzendentale Sachverhalte auszudrücken. Sonst wäre ja eine transzendentale Explikation absolut unmöglich. Viehmehr bestehen ganz bestimmte *Affinitätsrelationen* zwischen den transzendentalen Sachverhalten und den jeweils mit dem naiven (d.i. dem durch Absehen von der Analogiefunktion gewonnenen) Wortsinn der natürlichen Ausdrücke bezeichneten Sachverhalten. Erst diese Affinitäten ermöglichen es, dass das phänomenologisierende Ich— scheinbar die Sprache der Natürlichen Einstellung sprechend—in eben natürlichen Begriffen und Vorstellungsweisen seine auf die transzendentale Weltkonsitution bezogene theoretischen Erfahrungen prädikativ zu explizieren vermag. In ihnen verdichtet sich die Problematik der transzendentalen Explikation" (*CM VI*), p. 116/15–30. Husserl's only comment to these lines is to say that this is a matter for higher order phenomenological reflection and that it is not necessary to be dealt with by the beginning phenomenologist.

Finally, some support for the interpretation I am making here is found in the way Husserl objects to Fink's phrasing of the mode of usage the transcendental subject makes of language as a "taking possession" of it (*Übernahme*), as if from some external position. Husserl remarks on one page (*CM VI*, p. 107/24–25) that the expression *Übernahme* is misleading and in another passage rephrases Fink's wording, as follows: "Der Notstand nun, dass das phänomenologisierende Ich die Sprache als die sedimentierte Disposition des konstitutierenden Ich übernehmen muss [Husserl: in verwandeltem Sinn gebrauchen muss und keine andere als diese intentional verwandelte Sprache haben kann], . . ." (*CM VI*, p. 112/5–7).

On the other hand, the phenomenological reduction does not result from a natural human questioning process in a smooth continuity. Fink points out the *qualitative gap* between the two (*CM VI* 41ff.) and Husserl confirms this in a marginal note: ". . . Man gewinnt es [reduction-level reflection] erst in einen Sprung des sein natürliches sich selbst, sein Menschsein Übersteigens" (*CM VI*, p. 41). In the end, subjectivity, even though it begins "in der Selbstobjektivation als Mensch" (ibid., Fink), in the disguising appearance of humanity ("in der Selbstverhüllung als Mensch"—ibid., Husserl), transcends that human situation, undoing itself in order to direct its concern to that which ultimately grounds it, namely, the fundamental structure of the constituting process.

18. See the passage from *CM VI*, p. 116 quoted in note 17 above. Here mention should be made of the Fink introduced the notion of a "*transzendentale Apophansis*," that is, a *process* of articulation in language wherein conflict and insufficiencies are asserted, wherein *indication* is made through those deficiencies to the needed transformed order of significance, wherein *negation* is a way to discovery. The idea seems to be that the difficulty of the problem is diminished when one recognizes the *whole train* of thinking, "intuiting," and saying as the articulation of transcendental phenomenological insight, rather than simply concentrate on certain sets of words as isolable, presumed quintessential characterizers. See *CM VI*, pp. 108–109, and 113/22.

19. Words as the articulative trace of specifically formed meaning can be meaning-directions for the guidance of intentional activation: thus the listener. Or they can suggest new lines along which original intentional search can proceed: thus words as leading to new insights.

20. The overall point here is very much meant to be congruent with the position Paul Ricoeur has developed, for example, in Ch. 1, "Language as Discourse" in *Interpretation Theory:Discourse and the Surplus of Meaning* (Texas Christian University Press, 1970), pp. 1–23.

21. Section 11:*Das Phänomenologisieren als "Verwissenschaftlichen."* One should note also the set of Husserl's own MSS from 1933 and 1934 (B IV 5 - *Zur "VI" Meditation*) which are explicitly addressed mostly to one or another page of this section. See also Husserl's statements in the *Krisis*, nos. 29, 53–54, 73; also *Erste Philosophie II*, pp. 505–506.

22. On a page where Fink discusses a "reduction of language" (p. 114), Husserl writes:"Est ist auch nicht angängig von einer Reduktion der Sprache zu sprechen. Der natürliche Sprachsinn ist nicht durch eine daran zu übende Reduktion ins Transzendentale überzuleiten."

23. "Phänomenologische Sätze können demnach nur [wirklich] verstanden werden, wenn die Situation der Sinngebung des transzendentalen Satzes immer wiederholt wird dh. wenn [wenn die Epoche als andere Haltung der gewohnten Wirklichkeit lebendig aktiv gehalten und] die prädikative Explicate immer wieder an der [wirklich transzendental] phänomenologisierenden Anschaung verifiziert werden" (*CM VI*, p. 112).

24. "Die benutzten Worte mögen aus der allgemeinen Sprache stammen, vieldeutig, ihrem wechselnden Sinn nach vage sein. Sowie sie sich in der Weise aktuellen Ausdrucks mit dem intuitiv Gegebenen 'decken', nehmen sie einen

bestimmten, als ihren hic et nunc aktuellen und klaren Sinn an; und von hier aus können sie wissenschaftlich fixiert werden" (Husserl, *Ideen* I, no. 66).

25. See, for example, *Ideen* I, no. 124, and of course the first *Logical Investigation.*

26. As Mohanty points out, for Husserl meaning (*Bedeutung*) "is the meaning of expressive *acts* (*ausdrückende Akte*), of speech acts, and not of words or sentences taken as such. . . . [Husserl's] concept of meaning is related to his concept of intentionality. His interest in the First Logical Investigation is not in words or sentences, but in the acts constituting them into meaningful expressions." "On Husserl's Theory of Meaning," *Southwestern Journal of Philosophy* 6 (1974): 233.

27. Cf. Ludwig Langrebe, "Phenomenology as Transcendental Theory of History," in Frederick Elliston and Peter McCormick, eds., *Husserl: Expositions and Appraisals* (Notre Dame:University of Notre Dame Press, 1977), pp. 101–113, and "A Meditation on Husserl's Statement:History is the grand fact of absolute Being," *Southwestern Journal of Philosophy* 4 (1974):111–125.

28. For example, Fink can speak of natural language as "mere means' (*CM VI* 14/24) for transcendental explication; and Husserl in another research MS (BI5I) speaks explicitly of the uninhibited freedom of the transcendental I to endow available language with the meaning intended, making of them "sheer egological symbols."

Notes to Chapter 17

1. Maurice Merleau-Ponty, *Phenomenology of Perception* (New York: Humanities, 1962), p. 320.

2. Merleau-Ponty, "The Interwining—The Chiasm," *The Visible and the Invisible* (Evanston: Northwestern University Press, 1968), p. 155.

3. Merleau-Ponty, "Eye and Mind," *The Primacy of Perception* (Evanston: Northwestern University Press, 1964), p. 186.

4. Merleau-Ponty, *Phenomenology of Perception*, p. 288.

5. Martin Heidegger, "The Nature of Language," in *On the Way to Language* (New York: Harper and Row, 1971), p. 98.

6. Heidegger, "The Anaximander Fragment," *Early Greek Thinking* (New York: Harper and Row, 1975), p. 55.

7. Heidegger, "Andenken," *Erläuterungen zu Hölderlins Dichtung* (Frankfurt a. M.: Vittorio Klostermann, 1971), p. 96.

8. Edmund Husserl, *The Crisis of European Sciences and Transcendental Phenomenology* (Evanston: Northwestern University Press, 1970), p. 341.

9. Merleau-Ponty, *Phenomenology of Perception*, p. 62.

10. Ibid., p. 63.

11. Preface, ibid., p. xx. Also see pp. viii, x.

12. The method of focusing, the relationship between experience and the languaging which expresses it, the concept of a "bodily felt sense," and the concept of an experiential "shift," are rigorously defined in Eugen Gendlin, "Experiential Phenomenology," in Maurice Natanson, ed., *Phenomenology and the Social Sciences* (Evanston: Northwestern University Press, 1973), pp. 281–319, and "Experiential Psychotherapy," in Raymond Corsini, ed., *Current Psychotherapies* (Itasca, Illinois: F. H. Peacock, 1973), pp. 317–352.

13. Merleau-Ponty, *The Visible and the Invisible*, p. 102.

14. Ibid; italics added.
15. Merleau-Ponty, *Phenomenology of Perception*, p. 194.
16. Merleau-Ponty, *Phenomenology of Perception*, pp. 388–392.
17. Ibid.
18. Ibid., p. 179. Italics added.
19. Ibid., p. 187.
20. Heidegger, "The Nature of Language," op. cit., p. 100.
21. Heidegger, *Being and Time* (New York: Harper and Row, 1962), p. 205.
22. Heidegger, *What Is Called Thinking?* (New York: Harper and Row, 1972), p. 37.
23. Heidegger, "The Nature of Language," op. cit., p. 59.
24. Heidegger, op. cit., p. 98.
25. Heidegger, "The Nature of Language," op. cit., p. 126.
26. Heidegger, "The Anaximander Fragment," op. cit., p. 19.
27. Heidegger, *What Is Called Thinking?* p. 144.
28. Merleau-Ponty, *Phenomenology of Perception*, p. 197.
29. Heidegger, *What Is Called Thinking?* p. 10.
30. Heidegger, "Words," in *Poetry, Language, Thought* (New York: Harper and Row, 1975), p. 155.

Notes to Chapter 19

1. Eugen Fink, "The Phenomenological Philosophy of Edmund Husserl and Contemporary Criticism," in *The Phenomenology of Husserl*, R. O. Elventon, ed. (Chicago: Quadrangle Books, 1970).
2. Paul Ricoeur, "Introduction to Ideas I," in *Husserl: An Analysis of His Phenomenology*, (Northwestern University Press: Evanston, 1967) p. 29.
3. Jean-Paul Sartre, "Existentialism is a Humanism," in *Essays in Existentialism*, W. Baskin, ed. (New York: Citadel Press 1967) p. 62.
4. Jean-Paul Sartre, *Being and Nothingness: An Essay on Phenomenological Ontology*, trans. Hazel Barnes (New York: Philosophical Library, 1956) p. 90. Hereafter cited as *BN*.
5. *BN*, p. 566.
6. *BN*, p. 90.
7. *BN*, p. 623.
8. *BN*, p. 89.
9. Jean-Paul Sartre, *Transcendence of the Ego*, trans. Forrest Williams and Robert Kirkpatrick, (New York: Noonday Press, 1957), pp. 100–103. Hereafter cited as *TE*.
10. *BN*, p. 553.
11. *BN*, p. 217.
12. See Michel Haar, "Sartre and Heidegger," in *Jean-Paul Sartre: Contemporary Approaches to His Philosophy*, H. Silverman and F. Elliston, eds. (Pittsburgh: Duquesne University Press, 1980).
13. *BN*, p. 38.
14. *BN*, p. 615.
15. *TE*, p. 98.
16. *BN*, pp. 440–441, 94.
17. *BN*, p. 485.

18. See Iso Kern, "The Three Ways to the Transcendental Phenomenological Reduction in the Philosophy of Edmund Husserl," in *Husserl: Expositions and Appraisals*, F. Elliston and P. McCormick, eds. (Notre Dame: University of Notre Dame Press, 1977).

19. Ibid.; *see also* L. Landgrebe "Husserl's Departure from Cartesianism" in *The Philosophy of Edmund Husserl*, R.O. Elveton, ed.

20. *BN*, pp. 200–202; *see also* Thomas W. Busch, "Sartre's Use of the Reduction: Being and Nothingness Reconsidered," *Jean Paul Sartre*, op. cit.

21. *BN*, p. 200.

22. Michel Haar, op. cit. p. 172.

23. *BN*, pp. 627–628.

24. See Richard J. Bernstein, *Praxis and Action* (Philadelphia: University of Pennsylvania Press, 1971), pp. 153–155; Thomas Anderson, *The Foundation and Structure of Sartrean Ethics* (Regents Press of Kansas, 1979).

25. *BN*, p. lxi.

26. *BN*, p. 566.

27. *BN*, p. lxii.

28. *BN*, p. lxvi.

29. See Hans Jonas, *The Gnostic Religion: The Message of the Alien God and the Beginnings of Christianity* (Boston: Beacon Press, 1963). Cf. the Epilogue on the affinity between Sartre and Heidegger and the gnostic religion.

30. Maurice Merleau-Ponty, *The Visible and the Invisible*, trans. Alphonso Lingis, (Evanston: Northwestern University Press, 1968), p. 85.

31. Edmund Husserl, *Cartesian Meditations*, trans. D. Cairns, (The Hague: Martinus Nijhoff, 1960); *see also* Richard M. Zaner, "Reflection on Evidence and Criticism in the Theory of Consciousness," in *Life World and Consciousness: Essays for Aron Gurwitsch*, ed. L. E. Embree, (Evanston: Northwestern University Press, 1972), pp. 209–30.

32. Friedrich Schleiermacher, *Der christliche Glaube*, 7th ed., Martin Redeker, ed. (Berlin: Walter de Gruyter, 1960); English translation: *The Christian Faith* (ed. and trans. H. R. MacIntosh, (Philadelphia: Fortress Press, 1976), paragraph 4. Hereafter cited as "*GL*."

33. *GL*., paragraph 33.

34. *GL*., paragraph 16 Postscript: "A proposition which had originally proceeded from the speculative activity, however akin it might be to our propositions in content, would not be a dogmatic proposition." See also Schleiermacher's important distinction between the three forms of theological propositions and three degrees of objectification, *GL*., paragraph 30. For Schleiermacher's anticipation of phenomenology as well as his divergence from classical theism and Hegel's theism, see my *Schleiermacher the Theologian* (Philadelphia: Fortress Press, 1978).

Notes to Chapter 20

1. Edmund Husserl, *Cartesian Meditations*, trans. D. Cairns (The Hague: M. Nijhoff, 1960), pp. 128f.

2. Ibid., p. 132.

3. *The Crisis of European Sciences and Transcendental Phenomenology*, trans. D. Carr (Evanston: Northwestern University Press, 1970), p. 188.

4. *Husserliana*, vol. 14, *Zur Phänomenologie der Intersubjektivität: Zweiter Teil*, I. Kern ed. (The Hague: M. Nijhoff, 1973).

5. Alfred Schutz, *The Phenomenology of the Social World*, trans. G. Walsh and F. Lehnert (Evanston: Northwestern University Press, 1967), p. 199.

6. See Wilhelm Dilthey, *Der Aufbau der geschichtlichen Welt in den Geisteswissenschaften*, ed. M. Riedel (Frankfurt: Suhrkamp, 1970), pp. 351–355.

7. The importance of the common world in this analysis reveals the limits and ultimately the inappropriateness, in my view, of the Leibnizian concept of monadology, which Husserl invokes in the Fifth Meditation and elsewhere.

8. Cf. *Cartesian Meditations*, pp. 115–116, 126ff.; *Crisis*, p. 185; and *Husserliana*, vol. 14 pp. 199–200.

9. *The Phenomenology of the Social World*, p. 165.

10. Ibid. p. 164.

11. See *Being and Time*, trans. J. Macquarrie and E. Robinson (New York: Harper and Row, 1962), pp. 153ff.

12. G.W.F. Hegel, *Phenomenology of Spirit*, trans. A.V. Miller (Oxford: Clarendon Press, 1977), p. 113.

13. *Husserliana*, vol. 14, p. 169.

14. Ibid. p. 403.

15. Ibid. p. 169.

16. Ibid.

17. *Phenomenology of Spirit*, pp. 116ff.

18. *Husserliana*, vol. 14, p. 193.

19. *Phenomenology of Spirit*, p. 110.

20. Though not, of course, a necessary condition: there can be common projects without a common language.

Notes to Chapter 21

1. Søren Kierkegaard, *Concluding Unscientific Postscript*, trans. David Swenson (Princeton: Princeton University Press, 1941), pp. 25–55, *Samlede Vaerker*, ed. A. B. Drachmann, J. L. Heibeg and H. O. Lange, vol. 9: *Afsluttende Uvidenskabelig Efterskrift, Første Halvbind*, ed. A. B. Drachmann (Copenhagen: Gyldendal, 1963), pp. 24–52. Friedrich Nietzsche, *On the Genealogy of Morals*, from *On the Genealogy of Morals and Ecce Homo*, trans. Walter Kaufmann and R. J. Hollingdale (New York: Vintage Books, 1967), pp. 148–56; *Werke*, vol. 7: *Jenseits Von Gute und Böse. Zur Genealogie der Moral* (Leipzig, C. G. Naumann, 1905), pp. 467–76. Jean-Paul Sartre, *Being and Nothingness*, trans. Hazel Barnes (New York: Citadel Press, 1964), pp. 235–50; *L'être et le néant* (Paris: Gallimard, 1943), pp. 317–34. Martin Heidegger, *What Is Called Thinking?* trans. Fred J. Wieck and J. Glenn Gray (New York: Harper and Row, 1968); *Was heisst Denken?* (Tubingen: Max Niemeyer, 1954).

2. Husserl, Merleau-Ponty, and Ricoeur have always aimed at scientific, universal, conceptual, eidetic truth in phenomenology. See Edmund Husserl, *Cartesian Meditations*, trans. Dorion Cairns (The Hague: Martinus Nijhoff, 1960), pp. 7–16, 69–72; *Gesammelte Werke*, general ed. H. L. Van Breda, vol. 1, *Cartesianische Meditationen und Pariser Vortrage*, ed. S. Strasser (The Hague: Martinus Nijhoff, 1950) pp. 48–57, 103–106. Maurice Merleau-Ponty, *Phenomenology of Perception*, trans. Colin Smith (New York: Routledge and Kegan Paul, 1962), p. vii, xiv–xvii; *Phénoménologie de la Perception* (Paris: Librarie

Gallimard, 1945), pp. i–ii, ix–xii. Paul Ricoeur, *The Philosophy of the Will*, vol. 1: *Freedom and Nature: The Voluntary and the Involuntary*, trans. Erazim V. Kohak (Evanston, Illinois: Northwestern University Press, 1966), pp. 13–17. *Philosophie de la volonté*, vol. 1: *Le volontaire et l'involontaire* (Aubier: Editions Montaigne, 1963), pp. 7–8, 17–20.

3. Sartre, *Being and Nothingness*, pp. 235–50. *L'être et le néant*, pp. 317–34.

4. Nietzsche, *On the Genealogy of Morals*, pp. 148–56; *Werke*, vol. 1, pp. 467–76.

5. Martin Heidegger, *The Question Concerning Technology and Other Essays*, trans. William Lovitt (New York: Harper and Row, 1977), pp. 107–109; *Holzwege* (Frankfort: Vittorio Klostermann, 1963), pp. 241–43.

6. James L. Marsh, "Lonergan's Mediation of Subjectivity and Objectivity," *Modern Schoolman* 53 (March 1975):249–61. "The Two Kierkegaards," *Philosophy Today* 16 (Winter 1972):313–22. "Concluding Scientific Postscript," *The Southwestern Journal of Philosophy* 6 (Fall 1975):159–70. "The Triumph of Ambiguity: Merleau-Ponty and Wittgenstein," *Philosophy Today* 19 (Fall 1975):243–55. One more original effort is my "The Paradox of Perception," *Modern Schoolman* 54 (May 1977):379–84.

7. See James L. Marsh, "The Paradox of Perception," for a fuller discussion of perceptual objectivity.

8. Bernard Lonergan, *Insight: A Study of Human Understanding* (New York: Longman's Green, 1957), pp. 377–80. My "factual objectivity" is "absolute objectivity" for Lonergan.

9. Ibid., pp. 380–81.

10. Ibid., pp. 381–83.

11. Edmund Husserl, *Formal and Transcendental Logic*, trans. Dorion Cairns (The Hague: Martinus Nijhoff, 1969), pp. 162–66; *Formale und Transzendentale Logik* (Halle: Max Niemeyer, 1929), pp. 145–50.

12. Karl Jaspers, *Philosophy*, vol. 1, trans. E. B. Ashton (Chicago: University of Chicago Press, 1969), pp. 56–58, 65–68; *Philosophie*, vol. 1. (Berlin: Springer, 1956), pp. 15–17, 24–28.

13. Sartre, *Being and Nothingness*; pp. 3–45, *L'être et le néant*, pp. 37–84.

14. Ibid., pp. 235–50; *L'être et le néant*, pp. 317–34.

15. For Heidegger's argument that thinking is not conceptual, see *What Is Called Thinking?* pp. 211–13; *Was heisst Denken?* pp. 127–29. For his argument that genuine thinking of being is not objectifying in any sense, see *The Piety of Thinking*, trans. James G. Hart and John C. Maraldo (Bloomington, Indiana: Indiana University Press, 1976), pp. 22–31; *Phänomenologie und Theologie* (Frankfurt: Vittorio Klostermann, 1970), pp. 37–46. For a description of representational thinking, see *The Question Concerning Technology*, p. 127, 130–31; *Holzwege*, pp. 80–81, 83–84; *On the Way to Language*, trans. Peter Hertz (New York: Harper and Row, 1971), p. 74; *Unterwegs zur Sprache* (Pfullingen: Neske, 1959), pp. 178–79; *Discourse on Thinking*, trans. John Anderson and E. Hans Freund (New York: Harper and Row, 1966), p. 67, 69; *Gelassenheit* (Pfullingen: Neske, 1959, 1959), p. 43–46.

16. See James L. Marsh, "Consciousness and Expression," *The Southwestern Journal of Philosophy* 9 (Spring 1978):105–109, for a fuller discussion of expression and its relation to thought.

17. Heidegger, *What Is Called Thinking?* pp. 235–39; *Was heisst Denken?* pp. 142–45; *Poetry, Language, Thought*, trans. Albert Hofstadter (New York:

Harper and Row 1971), pp. 149–51; *Vorträge und Aufsätze* (Pfullingen: Neske, 1954), pp. 149–52; *Discourse on Thinking*, pp. 67, 74; *Gelassenheit*, pp. 43, 52.

18. Heidegger, *Discourse on Thinking*, p. 67; *Gelassenheit*, p. 43.

19. Ibid., pp. 67–73; *Gelassenheit*, pp. 43–51.

20. See James Marsh, "The Triumph of Ambiguity: Merleau-Ponty and Wittgenstein" for a discussion of the limits of objective knowledge.

Index

Index

RELATED TITLES FROM SUNY PRESS

PHENOMENOLOGY: DIALOGUES & BRIDGES. William L. McBride
and Calvin O. Schrag, editors.

HUSSERL AND HEIDEGGER: The Question of a Phenomenological
Beginning. Timothy J. Stapleton.

RECONSTRUCTION OF THINKING. Robert C. Neville.

THE SLAYERS OF MOSES: The Emergence of Rabbinic Interpretation in Modern Literary Theory. Susan A. Handelman.

EROS AND IRONY: A Prelude to Philosophical Anarchism. David
L. Hall.

THE QUEST FOR WHOLENESS. Carl G. Vaught.

EXISTENTIAL TECHNICS. Don Ihde.

WITTGENSTEIN AND PHENOMENOLOGY: A Comparative Study
of the Later Wittgenstein, Husserl, Heidegger, and Merleau-
Ponty. Nicholas F. Gier.